The Last Liberal
Republican

THE LAST LIBERAL REPUBLICAN

An Insider's Perspective on Nixon's Surprising Social Policy

John Roy Price

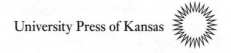

University Press of Kansas

Published by the University Press of Kansas (Lawrence, Kansas 66045), which
was organized by the Kansas Board of Regents and is operated and funded by
Emporia State University, Fort Hays State University, Kansas State University,
Pittsburg State University, the University of Kansas, and Wichita State University

Library of Congress Cataloging-in-Publication Data

Names: Price, John Roy, Jr., author.
Title: The last liberal Republican : an insider's perspective on Nixon's surprising
social policy / John Roy Price.
Other titles: An insider's perspective on Nixon's surprising social policy
Description: [Lawrence, Kansas] : University Press of Kansas, [2021] | Includes
bibliographical references and index.
Identifiers: LCCN 2020042496
  ISBN 9780700632053 (cloth)
  ISBN 9780700632060 (epub)
Subjects: LCSH: United States—Politics and government—1969–1974. | Nixon,
Richard M. (Richard Milhous), 1913–1994—Friends and associates. | Price, John
Roy. | Presidents—United States—Staff—Biography, | Moynihan, Daniel P.
(Daniel Patrick), 1927–2003. | United States—Social conditions—20th century. |
Republican Party (U.S. : 1854–)—History—20th century. | Political culture—
United States—History—20th century.
Classification: LCC E855 .P74 2021 | DDC 973.924092—dc23
LC record available at https://lccn.loc.gov/2020042496.

British Library Cataloguing-in-Publication Data is available.

Printed in the United States of America

10 9 8 7 6 5 4 3 2 1

The paper used in this publication is acid free and meets the minimum
requirements of the American National Standard for Permanence of Paper for
Printed Library Materials Z39.48-1992.

To My Family

My wife, Svetlana, my children, Matthew and his wife, Veerle,
John Mason, Alexandra, Philippe
My sister, Ellen

And in loving memory of Peter and Nelrose Maravell

Contents

Over the decades, I have been a diarist. Not every day, not every week, but when an event or a mood moved me, I wrote. A brief note sometimes, a long reflection at others, and with attempts to capture details in conversations always.

Once spurred into this project, I located my diaries, which I called *Diary* or *Daybook* or *Daily Notes* at different times, but I also found detailed minutes I kept of meetings of the Council for Urban Affairs, the cabinet body Richard Nixon created and chaired for the first eighteen months of his administration. The diaries are a most important supplement to the minutes, which themselves can be quite revealing and frank. The diaries include comments made to me by many of the figures in the White House and in the decade of my political involvement with the Ripon Society and with Nelson Rockefeller through the 1960s that led to my White House job.

I have also invoked the records others kept of discussions, most notably John Ehrlichman's "Notes of Meetings with the President," and materials by other White House Staff personnel, such as Kenneth Cole, Ehrlichman's deputy. I have given dates of the notes Ehrlichman or others made. They are contained in Nixon Library, White House Central Files (WHCF), Staff Member Office File (SMOF), in various boxes of Ehrlichman's or other's. A couple of my own memoranda are included in the WHCF, SMOF under my name. Ehrlichman's notes, interestingly, are duplicated in the "Hoover Institution, John D. Ehrlichman Papers, White House Special Files, 01/20/1969–04/30/1973." In Palo Alto, they are to be found in Boxes 1 and 2 of the Ehrlichman files.

For me, my diaries, minutes, and memories, and those of others, made this era alive again.

Acknowledgments

This adventure began with an invitation from Dr. Nigel Bowles, director of the Rothermere American Institute (RAI) at the University of Oxford, to give a talk there in the spring of 2011, on Richard Nixon. I had just finished my five-year tour as CEO of a bank in Pittsburgh during the financial crisis. My wife, Svetlana, then pregnant with our youngest, Philippe, and son John Mason and daughter Alexandra made the trip with me. Nigel's interest, his continued encouragement, reading my typescript, and his comments and guidance deserve my deepest appreciation. All his successors at RAI have cheered me on. Dr. Gareth Davies, of St. Anne's College, and expert in Great Society programs, helped me. So, too, did Dr. Daniel Sledge of the University of Texas, whom I met in the Nixon Library as both of us were reading from my files on health. Two others are from far earlier in my life. Reading my work from the beginning, they have given me caring and enthusiastic support, criticism and strategy: Dr. Reed St. Clair Browning, my friend from kindergarten, and through his fine career in history and as provost and acting president at Kenyon College; and Dr. Bruce F. Pauley, my Grinnell College roommate and Hapsburg and Austrian historian at the University of Central Florida. I thank former president of Grinnell and historian George Drake, retired literature professor James Kissane, professors Barb Trish, Bill Ferguson, and Sarah Purcell, all at that nurturing place, and Dr. Phil Thomas, one of my favorite teachers there long ago. I am beholden to my Grinnell thesis advisor, the late Dr. Joseph F. Wall, a Bancroft Prize winner, on my paper on the 1928 presidential election. Timothy Dickenson, part of our family's life since he miraculously materialized on these shores in early 1965, has been of inestimable help, with his phenomenal grasp of history, his ability to crystallize thinking, and his enthusiasm in discussing Nixon and American politics with me over the decades. I thank Dr. Luke Nichter of Texas A&M University–Central Texas, as his knowledge of both the Nixon era and the academic and publishing world has been materially helpful. Sharpening my thinking about Nixon (and, hopefully, occasionally sharpening my prose) has been David Shribman, the former executive editor of the *Pittsburgh Post-Gazette* and Pulitzer Prize–winning journalist. Martin

Schram, the White House correspondent and later Washington bureau chief for *Newsday* in those times, was of great help.

To reorient me from a banking career to writing and publishing, another boyhood friend, gifted and dedicated banker Ronald M. Freeman, egged me on. Gritty help and strategic advice came from Art Klebanoff, of Rosetta Books. Derek Leebaert, businessman turned author, shepherded me through the author submission process, as did Dr. Jay Geller of Case Western Reserve and John Delaney of ICM. Chris DeMuth of the Hudson Institute was helpful in many ways, not just in recalling with me the thrilling days of yesteryear. I am grateful to Mark Steinmeyer of the Smith Richardson Foundation and to Joel Scanlon of Hudson, for their assistance during much of the project. Theodore Eugene Charles-Jean Barreaux was encouraging.

Where I have relied on archives and not my diaries, memoranda, or memory, I have the greatest gratitude for those at the Nixon, Reagan, and Hoover presidential libraries, the Hoover Institution, and the Library of Congress for their steady support. While he was at the Nixon Library, Ira Pemstein was the archivist who opened and organized my voluminous files. Ira went on to the Reagan Presidential Library, where he is the supervisory archivist, and I thank him and his colleague there, Jennifer Mandel. Besides Meghan Lee Parker, the domestic policy guru at the Nixon Library, I appreciate the help from Greg Cumming, Dorissa Martinez, and Carla Braswell and the constant willingness to find something from Ryan Pettigrew, the A/V expert there, and his former colleague, Pam Eisenberg. The director of the Library, Michael Ellzey, has been encouraging, as have the staff at the Richard Nixon Foundation. There, Jonathan Movroydis gave me solid support before heading off to the Hoover Institution at Stanford, and his colleagues, Jim Byron, Jason Schwartz, Joe Lopez, and Chris Nordyke, have my thanks. At the Hoover Presidential Library, Craig Wright, its supervisory archivist, Spencer Howard, and Matt Schaefer were all welcoming. Valoise Armstrong at the Eisenhower Presidential Library was helpful. Thanks to Emily Gibson, archivist at the Hoover Institution, who is processing the papers of Martin Anderson. I owe particular debts to Geoffrey Kabaservice, interpreter of moderate Republicans and their fall, for his counsel, and his unpublished history of the Ripon Society and memoir of Robert Price; and to John R. Hauge for access to the unpublished memoir of his father, Dr. Gabriel Hauge. Archibald L. Gillies's 1966 congressional campaign in my home district was where I first cut my teeth in elective politics, writing policy statements for him. I have Arch to thank for recollections of Nelson Rockefeller and of John Hay Whitney.

My special thanks go to Elizabeth Brennan Moynihan and Maura Moynihan, the widow and daughter of Daniel Patrick Moynihan. From welcoming my family with cassoulet dinners in Cambridge and country fare at Pindars Corners, New York, at the Moynihan farm, Liz has been generous also in her recollections and reactions to my probing. Maura, who would every morning take coffee to her father while he wrote in the old schoolhouse on the farm, has made properly preserving the memory of her father a major goal of her life. Liz granted me access to the Daniel P. Moynihan papers at the Library of Congress. Casper Weinberger Jr. did the same for me with his father's papers there.

For photo permission tracing efforts, I thank Amy Fitch at the Rockefeller Archive Center, Jim Conzelman at the Ripon Society, Javon at Time Syndication, Bill Landis at Yale University Library, Nicole Ward at the Greentree Foundation, Erik Huber at the Queen's Library in New York, and Craig Wright at the Hoover Presidential Library.

Lee W. Huebner and I talked constantly over the years of his course on Nixon at Northwestern University and his understanding of the man. Bill Ruckleshaus was a wonderful raconteur when I last spent time with him in Seattle. I relived the 1968 campaign with former Governor Daniel J. Evans, as I did with my friend Robert M. Pennoyer and my campaign colleague Tanya Melich Silverman. Walter DeVries, a key George Romney advisor in that campaign, was most helpful to me. I relived the 1960s with grad school friend Dennis Shaul. Paul O'Neill and Richard Nathan spun their recollections for me over many Ritter's Diner breakfasts with Paul in Pittsburgh and times at his home with Dick Nathan in Florida. Secretary George P. Shultz was welcoming at the Hoover Institution in Palo Alto. Don Rumsfeld spent time with me. Bill Kilberg recalled working with George Shultz. Steve Kurzman and William Howard Taft IV, Dr. James Cavanaugh and Dr. Stuart Altman were helpful as I tried to piece together Nixon's health initiatives. William Hoagland and Tyler Barton of the Bipartisan Policy Center were interpreters of Food Stamp issues. Dwight Chapin, Tod Hullin, Sandy Quinn, and Frank Gannon were of great assistance as they knew Nixon longer, deeper and in different contexts than I. Sam Tanenhaus, at work on a biography of William F. Buckley Jr., was helpful and encouraging as we swapped stories. Allan Ryskind was generous in supplying me with back issues of *Human Events* and fun to spend time with, despite our having been at war fifty years ago. It was frequent adversary Patrick J. Buchanan who wrote me years ago that he and I "were on opposite sides of the barricades," but time mellows, and through many conversations in the last half dozen years, Pat has helped me and concurs in my premise that Nixon was the end of the line for Eisenhower moderate Republicanism.

My newer friends from our years in Pittsburgh have been supportive, though enduring much from me, about my project. Thanks to Andres Carde-

nas, Terrence Murphy, Boyd Murray, and Marty Powell. To these boon com-
panions and to Montana friends Bob "Fitz" Fitzgerald, Tom Bray, Rusty
Harper, Jay and Mary Bentley, political junkies all, I raise a glass.

I thank those Ripon Republicans with whom I worked through the 1960s:
Tim Petri, Emil Frankel, Lee Huebner, Lee Auspitz, Chris Bayley, Bob Pa-
tricelli, Peter Wallison, Howard Gillette, John Topping, Frederic "Frits"
Dulles, Bob Davidson, Marty Linsky, Mike Brewer, Don Bliss, Robert
Behn. We remember those who are gone: John S. "Jack" Saloma, J. Eugene
Marans, Frank E. Samuel Jr., Roger P. Craig, and Edward S. "Ned" Cabot.

I express my deep gratitude to my editor, Dr. David Congdon, for his help
and encouragement to me, and to him, the readers of my manuscript, and the
Editorial Committee of the University Press of Kansas, my thanks for their
willingness to publish this book.

Abbreviations

ACU	American Conservative Union
AFDC	Aid to Families with Dependent Children
AHIP	Affordable Health Insurance Plan
BOB	Bureau of the Budget
CEA	Council of Economic Advisors
CED	Committee for Economic Development
CEQ	Council on Environmental Quality
CHIP	Comprehensive Health Insurance Program
CORE	Congress on Racial Equality
CUA	Council for Urban Affairs
DOL	Department of Labor
EITC	Earned Income Tax Credit
EOB	Executive Office Building
EOC	Economic Opportunity Council
EPA	Environmental Protection Agency
FAP	Family Assistance Plan
FHIP	Family Health Insurance Plan
FSS	Family Security System
HEW	Department of Health, Education and Welfare
HUD	Department of Housing and Urban Development
NGA	National Governors Association
NIT	Negative Income Tax
NSA	National Student Association
NWRO	National Welfare Rights Organization
OEO	Office of Economic Opportunity
OMB	Office of Management and Budget
PRWORA	Personal Responsibility and Work Opportunity Reconciliation Act
RGA	Republican Governors Association
RNC	Republican National Committee
SNAP	Supplemental Nutritional Assistance Program
SSI	Supplemental Security Income
UBI	Universal Basic Income

UP	Unemployed Parent
USDA	United States Department of Agriculture
YAF	Young Americans for Freedom
YRs	Young Republicans

Introduction

This is a memoir of the most politically active decade of my life. It is a recollection of a period in American politics when I joined good friends to try to restore, or even keep alive, a centrist—it would be called "liberal" today—Republican Party. We were too young to be a part of Eisenhower's Era of Good Feelings. We were just the right age to watch and work against the 1960s takeover of the party by the conservative movement. We hoped for a restoration of the Eisenhower model of moderate or "modern" Republicanism, as he called it. After the Goldwater defeat in 1964, we looked to those governors and legislators who supported a role for government in reaching those who needed its help.

The Republican nominee in 1968 was Richard Nixon. The fourth time he ran on a national ticket, he won, in his own right. Nixon in his dogged pursuit of that goal embodied a hundred years later the energy that Billy Herndon attributed to his law partner Abraham Lincoln: "His ambition was a little engine that knew no rest."

I was not an obvious person to become part of Richard Nixon's senior White House staff when he finally triumphed and took the ultimate office. My family were Republican, but without the constant, strident partisanship that many believed defined Richard Nixon. Mother and dad automatically pulled the Republican lever in the voting booth every two or four years. In this my mother, Pauline, took after her father, dairy farmer Earl Beswick Milnes. Grandpa Earl would go to the Lucas County, Iowa, courthouse to cast his straight Republican Party ballot every election. After the Nineteenth Amendment to the Constitution was ratified, in August 1920, giving her the right to vote, my grandmother, Nellie Snow Wiltsey Milnes, would accompany Earl to the courthouse, where she would vote the straight Democratic ticket, nullifying Earl's vote. They would then head home for a nice midday meal, "dinner" as it was called on farms and in towns in Iowa and most of rural America in those times. Good-humored after that visit to the booth with the dueling votes, they went back to milking cows and gathering eggs. The mood of those Election Days in the farmhouse was as in Dylan Thomas's "A Child's Christmas in Wales," where "I made a snowman and my brother knocked it down and I knocked my brother down and then we had tea."

Energized by some of the same curiosity about American politics as I later would be, my father, J. Roy Price, as a twenty-three-year-old, made the trip from his home in West Virginia to Washington, DC, where he watched and photographed the funeral procession of Republican president Warren G. Harding in August 1923. His father, John Milton Price, was a coal miner who was killed in a mining accident. My father began working in the West Virginia coal mines at age twelve himself, only later to finish high school and talk his way into West Virginia Wesleyan College.

West Virginia was a Union State, carved out of Virginia, the capital of the Confederacy. Its birth was due to the Civil War and was almost simultaneous with the birth of the Republican Party. It had almost no slaves because it did not have a slave crop economy, like tobacco to the east or cotton to the south. To be Republican in West Virginia in the 1920s was to identify with the dominant party both nationally and statewide.

My father's family, having moved multiple times a year from coal camp to coal camp, treasured stability almost above all else. Disorder in the coal fields accompanied the organizational efforts by the United Mine Workers (UMW), led by the fiery and effective Welshman, John L. Lewis. Lewis was tough and determined. His distinguishing physical feature was his black eyebrows. They were as high and as dense as hedgerows along a Welsh country lane. Despite obvious sympathies with their fellow coal miners, violence was deeply unsettling to the Prices. Republicans nationally seemed to embody order. The 1920 presidential campaign slogan of Warren Harding was a return to normalcy.

In the early 1920s, my father was teaching school in Red Jacket, West Virginia, to send money home to his widowed mother and eight siblings. Red Jacket was just one "holler" over from Matewan, where brutality occurred in UMW organizing and in management response. In a remarkable and serendipitous connection in my mother's, father's, and Lewis's lives, Lewis himself was born and raised in Lucas, Iowa, a Welsh-populated mining town only seven or eight miles away from my grandfather's farm. He likely worked the seams of soft coal under it as a young miner. In a heartwarming moment for them, my mother, father, and John L. Lewis met at a Washington dinner decades later and discussed these interconnections in their lives. My mother said that Lewis was charming.

When Franklin Delano Roosevelt died, in April 1945, there was no beating of breasts or rending of garments in our home. Nor was there exuberant partisan celebration, driven by bitter opposition to the New Deal, for my parents knew Great Depression privation and frugality and were personally aware of the lives lived at the edge by many in their extended families. My grandfather's farm was foreclosed on by the bank. My father, having a job, was able to buy it back for him. They went about their business of work and of raising my sister, Ellen, and me. I frankly cannot recall the death of FDR nearly as vividly as I do V-J Day, just months later, on August 15, 1945, when World War II came to its end.

I grew up during World War II increasingly aware of Roosevelt, Winston Churchill, Charles de Gaulle, and Joseph Stalin, figures larger than life to a boy who was growing curious about the world. Thomas E. Dewey, the Republican governor of New York, cast a shorter shadow into my consciousness, but it lengthened when, as a nine-year-old, I put up Dewey for President posters on phone poles on my street in 1948. That first campaign venture of mine ended with the stunning defeat of Dewey by the Missourian, Harry S. Truman. By 1952, I was aware enough about home-grown politics to grasp Dewey's role in helping nominate Dwight Eisenhower over the strenuous opposition of the conservative forces in the Republican Party, led by Senator Robert A. Taft of Ohio. My father and I witnessed the Eisenhower campaign motorcade through our North Shore, Long Island, New York, town of Manhasset in autumn of 1952, and I began to take closer notice.

It was another election year, 1956, when I arrived at Grinnell College in the town of that name in Iowa. Standing for reelection that fall was the Republican governor of Iowa, Leo A. Hoegh, who was from my mother's small town of Chariton and whom my parents knew well and respected. Hoegh lost, and the mood at Thanksgiving weekend, which Leo and Mary Louise asked that I share with them in the governor's mansion in Des Moines, was lugubrious.

Hoegh had served under General Eisenhower during the war, and he was asked by the president to take a seat on the National Security Council as head of the Office of Civil and Defense Mobilization. He turned to my father to come to Washington and run the defense mobilization part of the job, since Dad was a chemist who had done the original research on Vinyl plastics in 1930–1931 for his employer, Union Carbide, and then followed product development for Carbide. He worked on wartime applications of plastics and chemicals with the government during World War II. Dad joined Gov. Hoegh in the Old Executive Office Building in 1958.

Consequently, my father was on a perch from which he saw Nixon at close quarters, because Dad made occasional presentations to the president and cabinet. My father told me at the time that he was uncertain about Nixon. He was not at odds with him. He did not distrust him. He was just unsure. In his view, Nixon was too intensely political, something my father—and apparently often President Eisenhower—could not fully relate to.

From a greater distance, I, too, saw Nixon in 1958. I watched Eisenhower's vice president emerge from a lunch he'd given at the F Street Club with his guest, Arturo Frondizi, the president of Argentina. I stood across the street in a crowd and gaped. I was standing on F Street NW because I had come for a semester in Washington from Grinnell, along with juniors from colleges across the country. A Grinnell classmate was with me in the program and we spent much time in each other's company. He was Jerry Voorhis Jr.

Jerry was the son of Congressman Jerry Voorhis of California, a New Dealer. Voorhis was the congressman whom Richard Nixon defeated in the Republican sweep election of 1946. It had become known as a rough campaign that Nixon ran, rife with suggestions of Voorhis being softheaded about communism. Like so many American Left liberals of the time, Voorhis was attracted by the Soviet model of socialism, long before the United States and the USSR became allies in World War II. Voorhis did not take Nixon seriously and only started campaigning at the end of September, and Nixon had a runaway victory, after which Nixon and Voorhis actually met. Upon his 1946 victory, Nixon took a seat on the House Un-American Activities Committee, and that platform took Nixon to national prominence. Nixon won both the Republican and the Democratic nominations for Congress in 1948, running uncontested. Then in another controversial campaign, he beat California Democratic US senator Helen Gahagan Douglas in 1950 and moved across the Capitol to the Senate. Only two years later, he was selected by Eisenhower as his running mate in 1952.

Jerry Voorhis Jr. in 1958 was still full of bitter family memories of Nixon, and he was most keen to share them with me and any others willing to listen. Decades later, at a class reunion at Grinnell, he told me of the euphoric atmosphere on election night in November 1960, in Chicago, when Nixon and John F. Kennedy were competing to succeed Eisenhower. His father had rented a suite at the Blackstone Hotel, the regular Democratic Election Night spot. He filled the bathtub with ice, beer, and wine and had handy every possible kind of liquor and mix. As the results came in, former congressman Voorhis would invite all comers in for a drink, or two, or three, to share his exuberance when Nixon went down to defeat by Jack Kennedy. By the time of that reunion, Jerry of course knew that I had worked in the Nixon White House. He learned there was a twisting tale to that unlikely outcome.

One reason had to do with 1958 and the national and state elections that we students were observing up close. The new comet in the political sky that night was Nelson Rockefeller, who was elected governor of New York. His victory immediately catapulted him into national prominence. Beyond Rockefeller's name and wealth, the governorship of New York sixty years ago still afforded a commanding position in American party politics. I was powerfully attracted to him and to his brand of liberal but Republican politics. Nelson had a glow.

Conservative and individualist Barry Goldwater of Arizona was reelected to the US Senate that same day. The two of them—Goldwater and Rockefeller—were to become the main rivals for setting the direction of the party. Conquest of the party organization and nominating conventions was crucial, as it rightly presumed the subsequent loyalty of the foot soldier—the ordinary Republican voter. My mother sighed with exasperation when Goldwater won the 1964 nomination struggle, since she and an overwhelming majority of Republicans polled nationally before the convention opposed him. But following the convention in San Francisco, she said, simply, "I guess I will have to vote for him now." The struggle leading up to the Goldwater convention, and the contest afterward to try to point the party back toward the center, played out over the years of my twenties.

As the 1960 election drew close, I helped organize a "mock" convention on campus. I pulled together the Rockefeller for President students and served as the platform chair for the event. My early interest in issues presaged the work I would take up as a group of us formed the Ripon Society, a Republican research and policy organization, where I served as research director—its first paid employee—while finishing law school. I was on my odyssey through the 1960s, and Nixon was proceeding on his. Our paths converged only in 1968.

Nixon appeared to me and to many others as an intensely political, staunchly anti-communist, dogged Republican. He was obviously intelligent. He was clearly diligent. Yet he was awkward. He bristled with resentments. As I later found, he was also very solicitous and kind to individuals. Yet he with febrile intensity developed "enemies lists." Few likely thought he was creative, though he proved astonishingly so, and many concluded the opposite: that he was a destroyer.

This was a complicated, contradictory man. When Eisenhower felt the need for a sharp-edged partisan rejoinder to something, he enlisted his vice president. Yet he had come recommended to Eisenhower by Thomas E. Dewey, from the Eastern and liberal reaches of the party. Out of ignorance of Republican history, I did not see the place within the Republican Party that Nixon held. Since I was only ten years old in the late 1940s, I did not spot the signals of the liberal impulses in policy he displayed for anyone interested to discern them.

There was a partition that emerged in the post–Herbert Hoover Republican Party. There were those who felt the entirety of the New Deal was an enemy to liberty, a fettering of the unbridled nature that must be given back to capitalism to give it the horsepower that would lead the country back to economic greatness. For them, the goal was to repeal the New Deal. They saw no need to replace the safety net they would repeal, but simply to return the social order to the status quo ante, which they confidently felt would unleash powerful and positive economic forces.

The others—the moderates and liberals within the Republican Party— saw much in the New Deal that was overreaching or unnecessary; much that was bureaucratic and stifling of initiative; much that needed to be pruned, eliminated, reformed. However, these other Republicans remembered Theodore Roosevelt's drive for governmental regulation of markets first in New York, then in the nation, where untrammeled economic forces might otherwise tolerate exploitative child labor, allow unsafe foods or drugs, or turn a blind eye to industrial combinations that would marshal overwhelming force against workers' concerns or would drive up costs of goods and their transport through collusion. They were the wing of the Republican Party that did not want to overturn protections for the economic security of the retiree, the disabled, the jobless or the dependent, or relax regulation in ways to put the public at risk.

The liberal wing of the Republican Party had been led by Thomas E. Dewey in his three terms as Republican governor of New York and in his 1944 and 1948 presidential bids. On domestic issues, he had throughout his political career consistently been a liberal reformer. He was a believer in civil rights and in the rights of labor. He showed deep concern for the powerless and low-income Americans, all the while appreciating the central role of business and corporate productivity in America. He believed in fiscal prudence.

Dewey's organizational skills and his allies and their national network made the Eisenhower nomination possible, and Dewey's interest in Nixon was of the greatest importance in Nixon making the leap onto the 1952 ticket. Nixon was a willing beneficiary.

So many of Richard Nixon's generation had fought a world war, and they were not willing upon return home to fight a domestic war against those parts of the New Deal that were the front line in the protection of the basic economic security of American individuals and families. General Eisenhower was to marshal the forces to challenge those who would repeal the New Deal. As Dewey had attempted, Eisenhower defended crucial parts of the New Deal not just to safeguard family and economic security but also to expand them, in the areas of both social welfare and health. At the end of eight years, Nixon set out on his own path. After his cliff-hanging defeat in 1960 by John F. Kennedy, Nixon went on to another wounding defeat in 1962 for the governorship of California. He attributed being beaten to efforts by the Far Right, the growing "John Bircher" wing within the California Republican Party, which fought him in the Republican primary and then sat on their hands in the autumn election. Patrick J. Buchanan, his conservative consigliere during the 1960s in his "wilderness" years and during the White

House years, attests to Nixon's distance from the Right. Buchanan notes in *Nixon's White House Wars* that Nixon could never speak of the conservatives as "we." Rather, it was always "they."[1]

After the successive defeats, Nixon's trajectory stalled. He retreated into New York corporate law practice. He watched and waited. The conservative movement was capturing the party. When the 1964 San Francisco convention nominated Barry Goldwater, Nixon sought to be a bridge to the moderates over which they could walk, but Goldwater torched it with an inflammatory speech. Nevertheless, Nixon campaigned for Goldwater. After the calamitous results, Nixon began to pick up the pieces. The sleepless ambition was at work. In winter of 1965, Senator Hugh Scott of Pennsylvania was with a handful of us in Cambridge, Massachusetts. Scott had been Governor Dewey's chair of the Republican National Committee in 1948 and, after Everett McKinley Dirksen, Senate Republican leader, died in the summer of 1969, Scott succeeded him as leader. Scott told us, "Richard Nixon is the man with the portable middle."

The early 1960s saw Eisenhower moderate alumni pushed aside within the party by a newer breed of "fundamentalist" or archconservative Republican. There was a clash in the younger generation of this new wave and of those who were instinctively more in line with the Eisenhower centrist or moderate approach, as my Ripon friends and I were. These years saw the emergence on the Right of publications, pressure groups, and mass membership organizations. On the more progressive side was the Ripon Society, which became the principal liberal voice within the Republican Party. It profited from the quest on the part of some of the key Eisenhower backers to find the next generation of leadership of their ilk. For Ripon, most importantly these included John Hay Whitney, Eisenhower's finance chief in his presidential campaigns and owner of the *New York Herald Tribune*. Walter N. Thayer, his colleague and president of the "*Trib*," was a major factor on the more liberal side of the party during these years. I used to call Walter the "Secretary General of the Eastern Republican Establishment." The ever-stronger support of Whitney and Thayer in financial help, in exposing Ripon to other moderate Republican organizations, and especially in giving the Society a "megaphone" in the higher reaches of the American media world meant that the research Ripon was doing would have wide exposure and could become a part of the program for a new Republican administration.

For me through the 1960s, it was Rockefeller, always Rockefeller. In 1963, I did some of the original "opposition research" for "NAR," as we called him, when he was running against Barry Goldwater. When the trumpet sounded again in 1968, I worked for John Deardourff in the Rockefeller campaign as the director of delegate intelligence. We lost to Nixon in Miami. Then Nixon gave a moving, inclusive acceptance speech, with great lift and hope for the troubled times of 1968.

After the 1968 Miami convention, Walter Thayer called and asked that I work for Nixon. I was most hesitant. John Deardourff and Doug Bailey, with whom Deardourff formed one of the first campaign management organizations, were also approached and turned Nixon down. Years later, Bailey told me they had said no because they had reservations about Nixon's character. After Thayer's call, I phoned my boss at the Bedford-Stuyvesant (Brooklyn) community development corporation from which I had been on leave for the Rockefeller campaign. At Junior's Restaurant, on Flatbush Avenue in Brooklyn, we sat down to breakfast. I poured out my hesitations, my uncertainties about Nixon. He asked me, "You're a Republican, aren't you?" I replied I was. He said, "Don't be squeamish about it. Look at the other side [the Democrats]. You have John Connally [governor of Texas], Dave Dubinsky [head of the International Ladies Garment Workers Union], and Dick Daley [the mayor of Chicago who had just presided over the wild Democratic National Convention weeks earlier]." He added, "Of COURSE you work for Richard Nixon!"

He was persuasive. I joined the Nixon campaign. The man who persuaded me to work for Nixon was formerly a practicing attorney and Republican in New Richmond, Wisconsin. He had come to Washington to join the brand-new Civil Rights Division within the Justice Department when it was created by Eisenhower after the 1957 Civil Rights Act. He was asked to stay on when Kennedy won and his brother Robert F. Kennedy took over the Justice Department. He became Bobby Kennedy's assistant attorney general for civil rights. He was John Doar. He later became the lead special counsel for the House Judiciary Committee's impeachment proceedings against Richard Nixon.

The 1968 election was a narrow thing won only with a plurality. 1968 was a year of fraught politics, grave tensions, and a feeling of lack of compass and failing confidence in institutions. A racist Southern governor, George Wallace of Alabama, ran a segregationist and grievance campaign attracting millions, many of whom were appalled by the protests against the Vietnam War, and many were working-class and middle-class voters, overwhelmed by economic insecurity and feeling disdained by elites. They cheered when Wallace thumbed his nose at them, and more than ten million voted for him. Nixon was himself no son of privilege.

He was the first president in more than a century who at the beginning of his first term lacked majorities of his party in either house of Congress. His relationship to his own party quickly changed. He almost immediately kicked over the traces of party regularity. He had tried to overcome the old stereotypes during the campaign, with a push for "The New Nixon." More important, in tone, in his acceptance speech, in his victory remarks, and pointedly in his inaugural address in January 1969, he made a turn away from partisanship. But nothing prepared the "old bulls" in party leadership for what he did in policy initiatives. He broke away from the pack and the pack was stunned. He was trying to climb out of Republican orthodoxy. He was to go beyond Dewey, beyond Eisenhower in his belief in and use of government. He was not going to be able to pull his party along with him. The Republican Party by the end of the 1960s was going in another direction. Nixon would prove to be the "end of the line" or the "last liberal Republican."

In early 1969, instead of denouncing the "Democrat" Party, he was outthinking it. He disconnected from the Republican Party as we had known it and from its permanent officials. He wanted to be a national president and to transcend the base that had elected him. A nation dreams and hopes. Presidents—most of them—feel the pressure of the expectation.

Nixon was such a mixture of intense qualities—work, resentments, guile, brilliance, courage. What ultimately enabled him to be bigger was that he was a man who felt so many anxieties himself and could feel those of the ones less well off and of those who felt condescended to or disdained. He was a man of a most rigid self-presentation, and with his obvious energy for political success, people thought that was all there was to him. To get behind that iron curtain is hard.

From the vantage point of fifty years, I see qualities I believe were at work. I see a Quaker determination. Tenacity, not just ambition. The Quakers were accustomed to antipathy, in fact persecution for their pacifism but also for being "different." The quiet yet determined picking oneself up and persisting after setbacks and ostracism was ingrained. It was an almost reflexive Samurai or Juncker dismissal of misfortune. Eighty years ago, there was a far more widespread awareness of Quakers and stereotypes about them than there is today. In the hit Hollywood comedy of 1940, *The Philadelphia Story*, Cary Grant is trying to woo back the mainline Philadelphia woman to whom he had been married, then divorced. Pennsylvania, especially its eastern half, was the heart of the Quaker colony in the settlement of America. Many memories and views remained of the Quiet People. At one point, Grant says to his once before and yet again to be mother-in-law, Mrs. Lord, "That's the old Quaker spirit, Mother Lord. Keep swinging!" Audiences understood the connection between Quakerism and determination to overcome resistance and adversity. To keep swinging.

There are those who think that Nixon's references to his mother, Hannah, such as in his acceptance speeches, or his 1974 resignation speech, were maudlin or only politically motivated. They should think again. He imbibed from her, and her grit and purpose, a foundational conviction that we cannot pass through the world without consciously and continuously working for the general good. What made Nixon a liberal is not quite secular.

As much as it struggles with our view of Nixon, which, alas, he gave us many reasons to hold, I think that he entered the presidency hoping in areas of human need to hitch power to decency. Early in his presidency, there was an explosion of ideas to provide help to those in need: his April 1969 relief of millions of Americans with incomes under the official government poverty line from federal income tax liability; his May 1969 message on hunger, outlining the radical expansion of food stamps and nutrition help to the poor that was soon implemented; and his August 1969 proposal for what we today would call a Universal Basic Income, his Family Assistance Plan that aimed to put a federal floor under the incomes of all American families with children.

In February 1971, he hearkened back to his dramatic health care and insurance proposals of the late 1940s. These were for universal private insurance coverage, with subsidies for those who could not afford premiums. He renewed this in the 1970s, including mandating employers to cover employees and with generous benefits, including covering preexisting conditions and prescription drugs as needed for everyone.

These social policy proposals took the breath away from his regular Republican colleagues. He faced not just shock but active resistance on the part of many. He faced stony reluctance of liberal Democrats to credit him with good will or good policy. So many initiatives failed. But many made it onto the books: occupational safety, pension reform, the creation of the Environmental Protection Agency, education policy, the abolition of the draft, the lowering of the voting age to eighteen, enabling the District of Columbia to govern itself and not be run by Congress, and helpful and inclusive policies about Native Americans. It is the social policies with which I am familiar that I focus on. For these alone, Nixon can be seen as the last liberal Republican, or even as a new kind of liberal Republican.

I was a participant in the White House in the first three years of Nixon's presidency and was involved in much of the domestic policy development and the attendant battles. I am helped by my diaries, my memories, my official notes of meetings, my conversations of the time and since, and those many volumes already written by players in the drama. The historians of his presidency already are legion. Still, I believe this effort of mine will provide a fresh look at Nixon, and that my accounts of the Nixon White House will force some searching rethinking. This account underlines his being the last gasp of Eisenhower/Dewey moderate Republicanism but also makes clear he was a hinge figure. I concede that all the time he was proposing remarkably progressive policies, he was enabling or at least accompanying the party's evolution toward a very different, no longer liberal party. The politics was often different from the policy.

Nixon was an intriguing man, even a man of mystery. In 1969, we had no idea of what would unfold three years later, vitiating a historic presidential reelection victory with the turmoil and the retreat into a chaotic White House that would finally collapse. Those first three years were exhilarating. The subsequent Shakespearian tragedy was as yet casting no shadow over these active and hopeful moments. As my colleague Richard P. Nathan recalls of those first years, "We were doing serious things. It was our Camelot."

CHAPTER 1

The Path to Eisenhower and Nixon
The Struggle for the Soul of the Republican Party

Dwight Eisenhower's supporters had a steep challenge in securing the general's nomination in 1952. Chicago's GOP convention that year was not a coronation but a pitched battle between long-established factional contestants and their prescriptions for the direction of the Republican Party. Eisenhower, the novice party politician, owed his nomination to the leader of the progressive faction in the party, New York governor Thomas E. Dewey, and others in that camp such as Henry Cabot Lodge Jr. So too did Richard Nixon, a young and astute politician, owe his selection as Eisenhower's vice president to Governor Dewey. Nixon would himself finally grasp the presidency in 1968, having been initially unsuccessful in 1960, as Tom Dewey had twice been before.

Clinching the nomination and winning the election was followed by the necessary lancing of the Joseph McCarthy carbuncle in the body of the Republican Party. McCarthy's behavior led his fellow senators to formally condemn him. McCarthy's diatribes even then did not quickly cease, but the post-censure draining of McCarthy's political support relieved the pressure on Ike. Without McCarthy's collapse as a political force, Eisenhower could not have created the unifying image of the party and the direction of policy that characterized his administrations. Even in this moment, Dewey's hand could be discerned.

In a review of *Ike and McCarthy*, Thomas Mallon noted that the televising of the Army–McCarthy hearings featured a grand confrontation between Senator McCarthy and outside Army Counsel Joseph Nye Welsh, who offered "the extravaganza's most quotable utterance—'Have you no sense of decency, sir, at long last?'" Welsh was a lawyer who had imbibed some of his values at Grinnell College, the Iowa school from which I also graduated. Mallon notes that "Welsh had been cast in his role by Thomas E. Dewey after Eisenhower approved having the New York governor search for just the right lawyer to oppose McCarthy."[1] The death from cancer in 1953 of Senate Republican leader Robert A. Taft, his opponent for the nomination in Chicago, gave Ike still more freedom of action, because the power of the regulars or conservatives in the party was subdued.

Eisenhower's election after twenty years of Democratic administrations and his presidency itself provided the excitement and the glue of purpose and patronage that holds politicians in current—even if temporary—common interest. It quiets, though never entirely eliminates, the more common factional rancor and internecine warfare of being the "outs." It helps when the party's leader and president is a magnetic and charming human being and one who can relate comfortably to ordinary people. Eisenhower was such a leader, someone who appeared disarmingly apolitical.

Eisenhower had extraordinary experience in dealing with difficult, tetchy, or grand personalities. As an aide to General Douglas MacArthur in the interwar US Army, Ike says, "I studied dramatics under him for five years in Washington and four years in the Philippines."[2] He worked with Winston Churchill, Franklin Roosevelt, Generals Montgomery and Patton, the demanding De Gaulle, Harold Macmillan, Harry Truman, and many others during his time in the European theater of World War II, and his leadership in the formation later of the North Atlantic Treaty Organization. Consequently, he was able to deal effectively with the powers in the House and Senate of an opposite party, which characterized three-quarters of his eight years as president. He had the great good luck and consummate skill to preside over an era of contentment for most Americans and public confidence that the country was in competent if unglamorous hands.

Still, divisions within political parties can lie somnolent during periods of having the responsibility of governing and enjoying the fruits of electoral victory. When an Era of Good Feelings, like the Eisenhower presidency, draws toward a close, the dormant beasts of faction or ideology once again begin to stir.

Faction was nothing new to the Republican Party. At its very founding in the mid-1850s, disparate groups coalesced in the new party, which was born in Ripon, Wisconsin, in the heart of the Midwest, indeed on the frontier. The Republican Party started by picking up shards of the broken Whig Party, including Whig advocates of national infrastructure or "Internal Improvements." Lincoln started the first transcontinental railway, and Eisenhower himself, with his decision to create the Interstate Highway system, can be seen as a lineal descendant of this Whig/Republican tradition.

The dynamism—indeed, zealotry—of the abolitionists was another element in the infant party's DNA. Congregational ministers such as Henry Ward Beecher of the Plymouth Church in Brooklyn Heights, New York (whose daughter Harriet Beecher Stowe wrote *Uncle Tom's Cabin*) were of this strand. Zealous also was "The Iowa Band" of ministers who formed Grinnell College in 1846. The Grinnellians were friends and hosts of John Brown, of Harper's Ferry fame. In his intensity about slavery, "even William Lloyd Garrison's [editor, *The Liberator*] teachings were not radical enough for the fiery young Grinnell."[3]

There was a similarly strong strain in the new party of social reformers and crusading journalists, such as Carl Schurz, the civil service reformer and journalist who had fled Prussia after Europe's failed 1848 liberalizing revolutions, and Horace Greeley, editor of the *New York Tribune*, which for a century was the pinnacle of Whig, then Republican thought and influence.

Another powerful faction was the many Northern industrialists and financiers whose consequential role for the North in the American Civil War only enhanced their influence in postwar society. The industrial potency of the North had been crucial for Union victory, and the sinews of manufacturing, transportation, and finance grew tighter as the industrial revolution gathered momentum. New York began its long, influential ascent. Industrialists of other regions, like the Henry Clay Fricks and Andrew Carnegies of Pittsburgh, with their Croesus-like fortunes built from coking coal and Bessemer steel processes, moved to New York. The oil industry, begun also in Western Pennsylvania, by John D. Rockefeller, largely consolidated into Standard Oil (Exxon today). Rockefeller took Standard Oil headquarters to 26 Broadway, at Bowling Green in lower Manhattan, the very office where I began my career in law practice. He built his spectacular mansion, Kykuit, in Pocantico Hills, overlooking the Hudson River, and the family owned a consequential part of the Chase Manhattan Bank.

By the time of the William Jennings Bryan Democratic presidential campaign of 1896, a perception of the East, and particularly of New York, pitted much of the rest of the country against the financial and industrial establishment centered there. The "Cross of Gold" acceptance speech by the "Silver Tongued Orator of the Platte" at his party's nominating convention in Chicago railed against the concentration of financial power in the hands of gold standard bankers, bond dealers, and New York.

The unexpected ascent of Theodore Roosevelt to the presidency after McKinley's death less than a year after his 1900 reelection was a disruption in the prevailing order within the Republican Party. Mark Hanna, the Karl Rove of his day, warned the Republicans not to nominate Roosevelt for the vice presidency with McKinley that year, calling the governor of New York "that damned cowboy."[4] His forebodings were justified.

Roosevelt's support for breaking the concentrated power of the various trusts that controlled major industries and his concern for the environment and the pristine parts of American nature were a strong counterweight to the views of the industrial and financial figures who had become so dominant in Republican politics. Roosevelt became the "Pole Star" for an element in the Grand Old Party (GOP), which was to be in contention with the "Regulars" for decades. "TR" was a personal idol for me, as I lived only fifteen miles from the Roosevelt family home near Oyster Bay. When I was a Boy

Scout, our troop would make "pilgrimages" to the Sagamore Hill shrine. Years later, Ethel Derby, TR's daughter, treated me and a friend, Christopher Bayley, to a weekend with her at her home in Oyster Bay, and we followed Sunday church in the Roosevelt family pew with a visit to the Sagamore Hill manse before hordes of tourists arrived. There, Mrs. Derby lifted the ropes that were to keep tourists on their restricted path, pulled us into the living room, sat down at her father's desk, and yanked open drawers to show us family photos, including ones of TR on horseback with Kaiser Wilhelm of Germany before the Great War.

Theodore Roosevelt was a polestar for Richard Nixon. He placed an oil painting of TR in the Cabinet Room when he became president. Poignantly, he made reference to Roosevelt in his "abdication" address to his staff on August 9, 1974, citing Roosevelt's urging that one be "always in the 'arena,'" in the battle.

Roosevelt's presidency, before the full effect of his "trust-busting" initiatives was felt, coincided with a high-water mark of tightly held private financial and economic power that remains unmatched. At the end of his presidency, in the winter of 1907–1908, there was a dramatic financial panic that quickly spilled over into the "real economy," as we would call it today, with catastrophic results. Its impact was profound. On October 23, 1907, the Pittsburgh Stock Exchange closed for three months. The year 1907 saw events that could have led to the total collapse of the American economy. There was no "safety net": no unemployment insurance, no social security, no government-supported medical care, no government source of liquidity as "lender of last resort" for the financial or corporate sectors. While banks collapsed and companies faltered or failed, the human misery was immense. My own father, seven years old at the time and one of nine children of a coal miner and his wife in West Virginia, told me that his family subsisted throughout that entire winter on a diet solely of sorghum and black strap molasses.

J. P. (Pierpont) Morgan was head of the House of Morgan. His financing and ownership connections reached throughout the economy, and for that he was targeted by critics as having dangerous control over economic affairs. He had an uneasy relationship with the progressive Republican Roosevelt. Now, at the eye of the storm, Morgan convened his coterie of friends, cajoled and pressured others, and put his own money with theirs into the critical joints and arteries of the economy to avert collapse.

Jean Strouse, in her introduction to *Morgan: American Financier*, writes, "At the end of the twentieth century, responsibility for sorting out answers to [economic and financial questions] rests with the Treasury and Justice Departments, the Federal Reserve, the SEC, the FTC, the Group of Seven, the IMF and the World Bank. At the end of the nineteenth, with predictably mixed and controversial results, Morgan acted largely on his own."[5] This near disaster in 1907–1908 was followed by the Great War and then a giddy period of the 1920s, with Republicans in the White House for a dozen years. The prevailing mood was one of "animal spirits." It was called "normalcy" by the Republicans.

One illuminating insight into the regular Republican ethos at this time comes in diary entries by one Republican cabinet member of that era about another. The diarist was Andrew Mellon. Mellon was one of the wealthiest men in America, founder of the Mellon Bank in Pittsburgh, and a key investor in many of the companies that grew to dominance in the industrial era, from US Steel and Koppers Coke to Alcoa.

Mellon was named secretary of the treasury by Warren Harding, after Harding's 1920 election, and remained in that position through all three Republican administrations of the 1920s until the Franklin Roosevelt election twelve years later. He was the longest-serving treasury secretary in American history but one.[6] Mellon was not only an industrialist and financier. He was a tightly connected and powerful Republican Party leader, who, with allies, firmly controlled Pennsylvania politics and cut a swath through the national party as well. At the point when the Sphinx-like Calvin Coolidge (president after Harding died in office in 1923) was interpreted to have said he would not seek reelection, Mellon had a brief flirtation with a presidential run.

His cabinet colleague, and the man who made that presidential run in 1928, was Herbert Clark Hoover. Hoover was the man the history books paint as the embodiment of conservatism and the man whose policies and values the New Deal was destined to overturn. Yet there was a different perception of Hoover prevalent in the 1920s, before his presidency and the Great Depression.

Hoover became a public hero in the chaotic aftermath of World War I when he organized the relief effort in Belgium, Germany, Russia, and other war-torn European countries to bring food, medicine, and supplies to the many starving and homeless people. One of his junior assistants in that effort was a young Ohioan named Robert A. Taft—the Taft who was later to do battle for the direction of the Republican Party with New York governor Tom Dewey and then with General Eisenhower. Taft took away from his experience with that work on relief with Hoover little sympathy or concern for Europe, its peoples, or its struggles.[7]

Hoover always had a muscular side when there was desperate public and human need. Mellon accurately recognized this, but he was antagonistic to it. It flew in the face of Mellon's and other Regular Republicans' staunch view that the economy should not be tampered with by any government action. Theirs was a profound conviction that economic laws would and should always be uppermost and that human misery should be addressed through charity. In deprecating and irritated entries, he speaks in his diary of Hoover, whom he saw as an activist and as "frequently unsound." The two were then "in constant competition for dominance in both the Harding and Coolidge cabinets."[8] Hoover was elected president in 1928 against the Irish Tammany Democrat New York governor, Alfred E. Smith. Throughout the post-1929 crash remainder of his presidency, Hoover experimented, initiated, and implored, as Mellon had anticipated he would.[9]

For all of Hoover's exhortation and hopes, energy and exploration, he became the very symbol of Depression suffering: "Hoovervilles," shacks of the hungry and homeless. It is an ironic twist that Hoover, the activist, and in many ways Mellon's nemesis, later became the icon for the conservatives in a Republican Party entrenched in its hostility toward the Roosevelt New Deal.

Arthur Larson, in *A Republican Looks at His Party*, published in 1956, at the midpoint of the Eisenhower presidency, asserts that attitudes in US politics crystallized and hardened around two moments in time in the prior sixty years. The first moment came in 1896 and spurred an ideology with adherents in both parties, namely, that business should have completely free rein, that when working people got together to improve their lot by collective means it was apt to be either a conspiracy or a riot, that the federal government should confine itself to waging an occasional war, delivering the mail, and enforcing the tariff, and that individual suffering unrelated to military or public service was not a proper concern of the general government.[10]

The second benchmark came in 1936. By then, the New Deal was firmly established. Business was suspect, individual capitalists were called out as "economic royalists," and it was an article of faith that the national government would create a new "economic order" with power centralized at the federal level. As in the Great Recession of our own time, there was a deep division of opinion in American politics. Many felt that the excess and irresponsibility that preceded economic collapse were attributable to the private sector, to cupidity, and even to criminal conduct and had gone largely unpunished. Others, the avatars of the economic system that had performed fine—until it didn't—were convinced that the spasm of reaction and outrage and resultant heavy regulation would strangle and subvert the possibility of the private sector once again leading the country to prosperity and opportunity.

The 1952 contest was an intra-party clash with echoes of each view. Robert A. Taft was not a proponent of the 1896 ideology holding a senate seat in the mid-twentieth century. However, he was the Not New Deal Republican. The Taft-Hartley labor law revisions of the late 1940s, for example, were a rollback of some of the organizational power that New Deal labor laws had accorded trade unions. Yet, Taft was not averse to the federal government having a role where he felt it was essential. His support for a federal role in education, for example, is widely recognized. He also, remarkably, supported a minimum income for individuals and families, as he recognized that there are dislocations or differences in economic opportunities, often owing to a lack of relevant training, and that a sense of basic economic security was a critical component of the social contract. On most issues, Taft was "Mr. Conservative." Dewey was not.

The Dewey Ascent to Party Leadership

While it was Eisenhower and Taft who tangled in state conventions and primaries leading up to Chicago's national nominating convention in 1952, an antagonism of much longer duration was that between Thomas E. Dewey, governor of New York, and Taft. Dewey and Taft had been factional enemies in the party for almost fifteen years. Dewey was an inheritor of the strand of Republican politics that had seen Theodore Roosevelt and Charles Evans Hughes (himself a progressive Republican standard-bearer for president in 1916) in the vanguard on social legislation, in New York and then the nation, from building codes to child labor laws, civil rights, and beyond. Dewey was convinced that no party could survive if it tried to uproot the measures that had been taken during the Depression to assure economic security for the average family. He added to this an assiduous, dogged organizational skill that emphasized superb political management and not policy alone.

As was true in national Republican politics in the 1920s, such a clear pivot also occurred within the New York party, with increased Republican opposition to progressive measures. Democratic New York governors such as Al Smith, Franklin Roosevelt, and Herbert Lehman adopted reforms that had once been promoted by the Teddy Roosevelt progressive wing of the GOP. Old Guard Republicans in the New York state legislature fought vigorously against these Democratic efforts.

In New York City's Young Republican Club in the late 1920s, a number of young men came together with a shared penchant for what they called "scientific humanism," which picked up both the TR heritage in the party and reflected Herbert Hoover's then pragmatic and humane image.[11] Two new members in 1928 were Tom Dewey and Herbert Brownell. Dewey was a trained classical singer with an ambition to perform grand opera. He was to perform on a different stage. The two of them had come to New York City from the Midwest, Dewey to go to law school and practice law "and, on the side, to continue his voice training lessons."[12] Decades later, Brownell notes, long after their involvements at the pinnacle of American politics, at lunches at the Recess Club in Manhattan, "in summer season we reverted to our midwestern upbringing and ordered a large slice of watermelon."[13] Analyzing Dewey, Brownell notes his faults: that he could be prosecutorial, that he was smarter than most of the people around him and did not suffer fools gladly, that he was not a "seasoned backroom politician such as Al Smith," and that he was impatient. But for all of these, Brownell admired Dewey "because he got things done. . . . He was a true reformer and not a self-interested politician."[14]

The focus for Brownell and Dewey was working for the election of Herbert Hoover, "the hero of Republican liberals, the Great Engineer who mingled the humane and scientific impulse that powered the Young Republican Club."[15] By the early 1930s, however, Herbert Hoover incorporated the National Young Republican Federation, and it, like Hoover himself, came to embody a conservative anti–New Deal ethos. In a major change of heart, the young Manhattan activists fought to wrest control locally from the Hoover conservatives and to run campaigns of progressives of their own bent. An early and important electoral victory was that of Herbert Brownell for the New York State Assembly or lower house. Brownell writes, "In 1931, a group of Young Republicans, rebelling against the moribund city Republican organization, decided to support the Seabury investigation by selecting one of their members to run for the New York State Assembly in order to sponsor legislation needed by the investigating committee. I was chosen to be the candidate, and Thomas E. Dewey, the future governor of New York, was named as my campaign manager."[16] Brownell came to know the powerful labor leaders in Albany, including George Meany, later national head of the AFL-CIO ("he regarded me as just another hopeless Republican"), and Brownell helped manage a bill that got eight-hour days for the transit workers,[17] endearing himself to their union head, Mike Quill, who later warmly endorsed Dewey's gubernatorial bid. It would not be too many years before the roles of manager and candidate would be reversed, when Brownell ran Dewey's presidential campaign.

Many of these young men wound up as lawyers working for Dewey when he was appointed by Governor Herbert Lehman, a Democrat, as a special prosecutor. Dewey launched a blistering campaign against political corruption and organized crime. In 1937, this led to the nomination and election for district attorney of New York County (Manhattan) of the once aspiring young opera singer.

Dewey and his most important partners in the building of the new Republican Party were not Eastern Establishment figures. Dewey was originally from Owosso, Michigan, a town of moderate size, and went to the University of Michigan. Brownell was born in a rural part of Nemaha County, Nebraska, where he grew up, and graduated from the University of Nebraska in Lincoln. His parents had been rural upstate New Yorkers before moving to Nebraska. The non–New York City background and understanding were useful to Brownell in his Albany legislative life and also later nationally, as he was entirely conversant and comfortable with the ways of rural and midwestern life.

Another figure in the Dewey organization was Gabriel Hauge, son of a first-generation Norwegian Lutheran pastor who would preach Sunday mornings at five different churches in the area of Hawley, Minnesota, where Hauge was born, raised, and then attended a Lutheran College, Concordia. Hauge worked for Governor Dewey as an economist in the state's Banking Department, gaining the attention of Elliott Bell, Dewey's formidable advisor and banking superintendent. In Dewey's 1948 presidential campaign, Hauge served as the economic issues and policy director. For the 1952 presidential campaign, Hauge was the research director of Citizens for Eisenhower, on Dewey's recommendation. In turn, Eisenhower brought him into the White House, where he was the special assistant to the president for economic affairs and a frequent speech writer and spokesman. Along with Arthur Larson, Hauge became an articulate exponent in the Eisenhower years of a credo of moderate Republicanism. Larson himself was born in Sioux Falls, South Dakota, and went to the local Lutheran College, Augustana. These men were midwestern, and like so many others of their generation, including my own father and most of his friends, they were promoted to, or drawn to, opportunities in New York.

Dewey had a rustic twist. He bought a five-hundred-acre working dairy farm. Not unlike Ronald Reagan and his Rancho del Cielo near Santa Barbara, California, Dewey pined for the weekends at his farm, Dapplemere, sixty-five miles north of New York City. Off would come the homburg hat, suit, tie, and wingtip shoes and on would go working clothes and boots.

The mortgage was paid off in no small part by the dairy cows, whose milk was sold to a nearby "co-op," Sheffield Farms, and on to consumers in New York City. An early memory of mine was occasional family trips in the Chevy "coupe" to Pawling to glimpse the governor's farm. For a family descended from generations of Yorkshire dairy farmers transplanted to Holstein cow farms in Illinois, then Iowa, this was a natural pilgrimage, a milkman's "hadj."

Dewey and his allies began forcefully challenging those leading the party. They combined into an organization and a drive, at the front of which was Dewey, to build and fashion the Republican Party that culminated in the elections of Eisenhower and Nixon. Robert Moses was the Republican candidate in 1934 for governor of New York. He lost handily, by a massive 800,000 votes, and with him sank much of the Empire State's then Republican establishment, which were from the Hoover, not the Theodore Roosevelt, wing of the party.

The 1934 defeat of Moses and leading regular Republicans left a vacuum in New York that was filled by a group of Young Turks, who successfully took over the Speaker's and Senate Majority Leader's spots from the conservatives. There were victories around the state that laid the foundation for a resurgence of a state party in the mold of TR. It was the beginning of deep organizational efforts, with fundraising and dispensing and patronage utilization. Russell Sprague from Nassau County, Long Island, built the Republican machine there that renewed the influence it had once enjoyed under its Oyster Bay resident, Theodore Roosevelt.

Sprague was a supremely capable political boss. He did proscribe the usual form of corruption, "no fingers in the cookie-jar" as Norton Smith terms it.[18] Sprague gathered solid financial backing and insisted that no candidate could contribute to his own campaign: the money had to come from the organization, which meant the organization had control of the campaigns. Sprague, state party chairman Ed Jaeckle of Buffalo, and others were now looking for new faces, for winners, for a "contender who could lend popular appeal to [Sprague's] . . . efforts to retake the GOP[,] for a kind of progressive conservatism that had been all but surrendered in the hysteria following Democratic blitzkriegs of 1932 and 1934."[19] Sprague talked with Dewey about the district attorney race in Manhattan in 1937 and even the governorship in 1938.

Dewey was a press-worthy, focused, and tough-minded young man. He had quickly become famous as special prosecutor, successfully hitting organized crime and corruption in the New York Tammany Democratic machine. Dewey was attracted by the district attorney race in Manhattan and jumped in with intensity. Organized labor backed him strongly. Dewey had helped smash racketeers' penetration of the labor unions in New York. Sidney Hillman, the Lithuanian-born founder of the Congress of Industrial Organizations, later to join the American Federation of Labor to form the AFL-CIO, was grateful. Michael Quill, the young head of the Transport Workers Union (TWU), said that Dewey "had dared more gunmen and done more to end rackets in labor unions" than anyone else. The American Labor Party endorsed him. The International Ladies Garment Workers Union (ILGWU), then a powerful New York force, gave him one of his two largest campaign contributions, the other coming from the Rockefeller family. Dewey started to meet also with the "kaleidoscope" of voters, including Russians, Czechs, Poles, Syrians, Scandinavians. Smith writes, "It was the start of a lifelong ethnic fascination for Dewey, more typical of the average Democratic precinct captain than any Republican outside Union Square."[20]

Pressure quickly mounted for Dewey to run for governor the next year, 1938. It was awkward, opposing Governor Herbert Lehman, the very man who had appointed him special prosecutor and launched him on his way. Dewey ran and Lehman defeated him. Dewey's running mate, in a metaphor that would have been widely understood in those days of rail transportation, said, "The GOP had to get out of the Pullman cars [sleepers] and into the day coaches." In the campaign, Dewey championed the rights of labor and farmers.

Dewey displayed a mentality and drive that Theodore Roosevelt would have understood. Dewey "associated the virtues of private compassion and public competence."[21] One of Dewey's Young Turks paraphrased Theodore Roosevelt, emphasizing Dewey's competence and tough-mindedness in support of a progressive agenda: "It is all very well to mean well, but not to mean well weakly. You must mean well strongly, and you will get something done. Mr. Dewey means well strongly."[22]

Dewey embraced New Deal, social-safety-net measures and added some of his own. Dewey announced that the elderly, blind, and infirm were entitled to "shelter from the winds of chance."[23] Dewey swept upstate New York by margins better than those of Hoover himself in his landslide 1928 victory. Dewey was rebuilding an anemic party and making "New Yorkers extend their memories back to a time when Republicans had worn the badge of liberals, and earned their dominance by anticipating, not resisting, the momentum of reform."[24]

The Dewey-Taft Rivalry

While Dewey lost statewide in 1938, Republicans in the United States Senate and House of Representatives were successful in a resurgence from the calamity of the early FDR years. Among those elected was freshman Ohio senator Robert A. Taft, the oldest son of former president William Howard Taft. Young Taft was an erudite, formal, and somewhat forbidding Yale and Harvard Law School graduate (first in his class at both institutions), who after his election in 1938 soon became the paragon of conservatism in the Senate.

The rivalry between Dewey and Taft emerged as the 1940 presidential election loomed. It may have smacked of hubris that Dewey, elected to office in only a single county, New York County (Manhattan), entertained the idea of a presidential nomination. Yet his run at the governorship, New York's concentration of media power in radio networks and magazine publications from which most Americans got their news, and the celebrity that his crusading gave him brought name recognition throughout the country with a reputation for racket-busting and probity.

Dewey started with some wind at his back as polls after the 1936 election had shown that more than half of Republicans considered themselves liberals. He was cautious, however, about policy on international relations. There was no widespread support for US involvement in the emerging and dark European situation. Taft went further. As British forces were evacuating at Dunkirk, Taft told a St. Louis audience in May 1940 that a German victory would be preferable to American participation in the war.[25]

Dewey did well in some of the early primaries, but into this confusion swept a new face. He was Wendell Willkie, originally from Indiana, an animated lawyer turned utilities executive. Completely unlike Dewey—or Taft—who thought through positions meticulously both from fact-based and political points of view, Willkie seemed to make up his mind as he went along. Willkie and his supporters stampeded the convention and won the Republican nomination. Dewey did support Willkie and dedicated some of his close allies to the Willkie campaign. Among them were John A. Wells, an attorney, and Elliott Bell, who had been a *New York Times* and *New York Herald Tribune* financial writer and was now economic advisor to Dewey. Dewey used the 1940 election mainly to solidify his control of the party in New York, looking to 1942 and the governorship.

Dewey continued to craft a Republican approach to social welfare. At a Lincoln Day dinner in 1941, "he spoke of a need for medical insurance for the poor within a private enterprise framework."[26] When Dewey did win the governorship in 1942, he put in place a strongly managed, highly progressive administration. It had the very first Fair Employment Practices Commission, wrote very sympathetic labor and labor organization laws and the strongest civil rights laws yet, and appointed female and Black citizens to his cabinet. He enhanced corporate law so that New York had some of the most effective, accommodating bodies of corporate law in the country.

With consistent fiscal discipline while maintaining a balanced budget, Dewey managed to enhance the state university system and build the New York State Thruway. Taken together, the progressive program, the concern for the social and economic security of families, and the fiscal discipline were the model Dewey sought to transform into a national mandate and winning program through his two candidacies as the Republican presidential nominee. The congressional wing of the party—with Taft and others such as Congressmen Dewey Short of Missouri and Congressman Hamilton Fish of New York, outliers and strong isolationists—were the antiphonal voice to Dewey's determined direction in New York.

1944: A Liberal Republican Party Platform and the Governors

Dewey's firm grip on the New York and then the national party meant that the 1944 platform was his to write. There were some rhetorical points assailing the excesses of the New Deal, but these were consistent with Dewey's distrust of the overreaching of the FDR Democrats and were not intended merely to please the leaders of the congressional wing, Senators Taft and Bricker of Ohio and Congressman Joe Martin of Massachusetts. Dewey, like Eisenhower later, was a firm believer in the private sector as the crucial engine of the American economy, but like Ike, he was alert to its temptation to ignore human need. The 1944 platform contained the strongest civil rights plank yet to appear in a major party platform. It called for a national Fair Employment Practices Commission modeled after New York's, anti-lynching laws, a federal constitutional amendment barring poll taxes, and an investigation into racial discrimination within the armed forces.[27]

He turned for support to the twenty-six Republican governors. They were nearly all more supportive of social programs like those the New Deal had put in place than were the Republicans in Congress. This split paralleled the later division of the Republican Party in the 1960s, where the moderates were dominant among the Republican governors and the congressional Republicans were largely economic conservatives, although they did provide crucial support for the civil rights legislation Eisenhower pushed in the 1950s and again when they gave the 1960s civil rights acts their crucial margin of victory.

After the Convention, Dewey convened a meeting of the Republican governors in St. Louis and pounded away, clarifying some program areas that had been left vague in the platform adopted at the recent convention. Keeping them up until 2:30 in the morning, Dewey slogged, getting unanimous agreement with them on such issues as consolidating federal welfare programs, better coordinating federal and state efforts, developing a policy on water power, and reducing and simplifying taxes.

Looking back to 1952 at the Dewey-Taft cleavage, their differences also forestalled the development of a coherent and widely accepted Republican alternative to the FDR New Deal and the Fair Deal program of Harry Truman in domestic affairs. It would take the force of Eisenhower's personality, and the death of Taft in 1953, for the Republicans to achieve the kind of political unity that was needed to make them a viable governing alternative to the Democrats.

The Dewey Group

As the team prepared for the 1948 nomination and campaign against Harry Truman, Gabriel Hauge was brought into the Dewey inner circle and helped Elliott Bell in domestic and international economic and financial policies. Hauge wrote an unpublished memoir.

Dr. Hauge was, when I met him, the chairman of the Board of the Manufacturers Hanover Trust Company, a major New York bank. One of my most touching and intimate memories of Gabe Hauge is from at the end of his life and reaches back to his Norwegian ancestry. He had retired a year earlier and had an office on the top floor of the Bank's building on Park Avenue. He was to die of cancer in not more than a year. We often had enjoyed lunch together; on this occasion he invited me to his aerie. He was dressed in a blue cardigan sweater. He had ordered sandwiches for us. As we sat down together, he asked me, "Would you be alright if I ask the blessing in the original Norse, the same Grace my father used to say at our table?" By the time I knew him, Gabe had lost an eye to the malignancy that returned at his retirement. He wore a black, glass eye covering held in place by plastic frames. He was utterly unself-conscious about this burden. At lunch some years before, after he had returned from Manila in the Philippines, where our bank was "agent bank" for the Philippines sovereign debt, he spoke of the Marcos husband and wife. Of the famous Imelda, he offered, "She is a woman of blinding beauty."

Hauge painted pictures of Dewey's entourage, who worked well together and helped secure the nomination and election of Eisenhower and Nixon in 1952. Of Bell himself Hauge says, "I was completely captivated by Elliott Bell. . . . Bell struck me at once as a man of the highest intelligence, with a sparkling wit."[28] Hauge discovered him to be a "gifted writer as well as a scintillating conversationalist."[29] Hauge came into contact with the governor himself as Dewey was starting to gear up to run in 1948, writing, "The relationship between Bell and Dewey was one of complete mutual respect. . . . There was no deferential relationship there. Each man was an achiever in his own right, and each respected the other for it."[30] Hauge's take on Brownell was a very positive one. He saw Brownell as

a warmhearted man with an easy style that was most helpful in calming ruffled tempers when disputes arose. Brownell . . . possessed a remarkably good political personality, with a ready smile and no sharp edges, and with a reputation as being a man of his word. He represented the political, the managerial element in the group. . . . There was no second-tier mind among them because Dewey himself set the level and his was a first-class mind.[31]

As to Hauge's impressions of Dewey himself, Hauge says,

I never reached the point where I called him "Tom." I don't think I ever saw him without a collar and tie, and am not even sure that I ever saw him with his jacket off. There was never a loose hair on his head, or a tie that was askew, or a shirt that wasn't perfect. That was simply the way he was. He did not engender any ease of association. He tended to be all business, and when he did relax, it sometimes appeared to be an obvious effort. But for all that, I did not find him stuffy; I appreciated his hearty laugh, and I found him easy to work with. In my dealings with him I found him to be fair, reasonable, and willing to bat ideas back and forth.[32]

Hauge was impressed that Dewey could manage as a Republican in New York and saw a responsiveness to the "needs of New York's multifarious society," which Hauge thinks was the reason Dewey was governor for three terms. "His manner was always very much that of the efficient, logical administrator and student of government, and he was regarded as being all machine and no heart—a public perception that later cost him the presidency." (Hauge mentions the quote attributed variously to Dorothy Parker and to Alice Roosevelt Longworth, characterizing Dewey as "the little man on the Wedding Cake."[33] Claire Booth Luce often is named as the author of the phrase as well.)

Dewey's 1948 bid against Truman failed owing to overconfidence and, more importantly, the congressional wing of the party. Congressional Republicans were carping and critical in a special session in 1948. Nothing constructive was put forward. Their unwillingness to accommodate their presidential candidate was damaging. Brownell writes, "The conservative Republicans in Congress had for too long been accustomed to attacking Roosevelt and his New Deal programs, taking essentially a negative stance. Now with Truman at the helm and the nation yearning for new policies that would move the country forward in peacetime, a more affirmative program by the Republican party was needed. Dewey attempted to develop this approach into a winning strategy but was thwarted by the Republican conservatives on the Hill."[34]

An interesting exception was Senator Everett McKinley Dirksen of Illinois, who served as Midwest coordinator for Dewey in 1948. Hauge says, "Dirksen's support of Dewey for President in 1948 was quite a brave thing for him to do because he came from a part of the country that backed Governor John Bricker of Ohio, Dewey's chief rival for the nomination."[35] Dirksen, like most of the Dewey insiders, counselled a "Don't rock the boat" strategy. It failed. Dirksen's support in 1948 had turned to vinegar by the 1952 Chicago hotly contested Taft-Eisenhower battle. Witness to one of the most memorable of convention vignettes through all of American political history, Dirksen's 1952 excoriation of Dewey, was my friend J. Robert Barr. Then a young summer intern for Dirksen and later for many years the Republican county chair for Cook County, Illinois (Chicago), Barr snuck in to the convention floor and stood near his boss, imprinting in his memory that unforgettable moment. In one of the debates that wrested control away from Taft forces, Dirksen, now a leading Taft spokesman, stood defiantly in opposition. "We followed you before, Tom Dewey, and you took us down the road to defeat. Don't do this to us!," thundered the Illinois senator, pointing at the governor. The convention erupted in seething anger as Dewey sat calmly at his seat in the New York delegation.[36]

Despite two national defeats, despite the public image of a formal and forbidding man, Dewey did make his way into pop culture. A friend from my school days, Reed St. Clair Browning, recalled for me a jingle that we kids learned in 1948:

> Dewey was an Admiral, at Manila Bay;
> Dewey ran for President, just the other day.
> Dewy were her eyes when she said, "I do."
> Do we love each other? I should say we do.

My former White House secretary, Susan Lee Johnson, recalled another bit of doggerel, perhaps more on the lips of 1948 children at a kindergarten playground:

> Truman's in the White House, waiting to be elected;
> Dewey's in the garbage can, waiting to be collected.

The Eisenhower Candidacy

Twice a loser, Dewey had no appetite to be a Republican William Jennings Bryan and seek a third nomination. He focused on becoming the kingmaker in 1952. Dewey was cautious and tried to be invisible and offstage, as he understood he carried a lot of baggage from past intraparty battles. Herb Brownell, along with Dewey, Henry Cabot Lodge of Massachusetts, and General Lucius Clay, who was very close personally to Eisenhower, encouraged Ike to run. Brownell was asked to come secretly to Paris. There, he spent ten hours closeted with General Eisenhower. Eisenhower probed Brownell about the split between the Dewey wing of the party and the congressional conservatives, especially the isolationist tendencies of the latter. He confided to Brownell that he and Taft had a secret meeting before Eisenhower went to the NATO command in 1951. He said he told Taft he would announce that he would not be a candidate for President if Taft would announce his support for NATO and the internationalist role for the United States. Taft told Eisenhower he could not in good conscience do so. This strengthened Eisenhower's interest in the presidency.

Brownell, for his part, wanted to assure himself that Eisenhower would be supportive of those progressive policies that were most important to Dewey and himself, including civil rights. Brownell, during this secret meeting, told Ike that the core of Ike's support in the party would be from the Dewey wing, to which these progressive positions were important. Eisenhower responded that he had been approached also about running by a number of Southern Democratic conservatives, who opposed civil rights. "I felt that Eisenhower's heart was in the right place on civil rights, but his statement signaled to me that he would not lead the charge to change race relations fundamentally in the United States."[37] Brownell mentioned that there was discussion during that ten-hour marathon meeting of Governor Earl Warren of California. Warren had been Dewey's running mate in 1948. It was clear that Warren was a liberal, and on civil rights, notably so. Brownell concluded that Eisenhower therefore knew what he was getting when he named Earl Warren to head the United States Supreme Court.

Henry Cabot Lodge was officially the campaign manager, but there were many holes in his knowledge of the national Republican organization and he was facing an increasingly difficult campaign for reelection (against John F. Kennedy) for his Massachusetts seat in the United States Senate. In an echo of his 1944 mobilization of the Republican governors to embrace detailed progressive proposals, Dewey in 1952 played a crucial behind-the-scenes role just before the convention at a meeting with the governors. Dewey persuaded them nearly unanimously, despite many being Taft supporters, to back the so-called Fair Play amendment, which went to the seating of delegates and which was a crucial Eisenhower forces move.[38]

Before the convention, Dewey had developed an interest in freshman senator Richard M. Nixon of California becoming Eisenhower's running mate. The cause of his initial interest is not clear. Most likely, it was Dewey watching Nixon in the Hiss case confrontation in the later 1940s. This August 28, 1948 confrontation between Alger Hiss and his accuser, Whitaker Chambers, was the first ever televised Congressional hearing. Nixon's careful preparation of his case against Hiss as a Soviet agent impressed Dewey. Both Thomas Dewey and President Eisenhower were later to tell Nixon that Hiss made the difference.

The Republican Party all drank from the same cup when the draught was that of anti-communism. Dewey would appreciate Nixon's careful crafting of his case. It was not demagogic in style, as Senator Joseph McCarthy's was to become. Rather, it showed relentless investigation and it brooked no nonsense. Years later, Dewey made a comment to Tanya Melich Silverman, a friend of mine, who was helping him edit for publication some lectures he had delivered. They were speaking in 1967 of Arlen Specter of Philadelphia.

He was a district attorney seeking higher office as the Republican candidate for mayor of Philadelphia. Dewey commented about Specter, in a quite positive tone, as they watched a news segment. In a telephone conversation with me on October 25, 2016, Silverman told me Dewey said to her, "He reminds me of a younger Richard Nixon."

By contrast, Dewey was appalled by the reckless manner of Wisconsin Republican senator Joseph McCarthy. McCarthy's exaggerated tales of his World War II exploits as "Tail-Gunner Joe" were as nothing to the allegations he made against the State Department and then the Defense Department, the various services, and, most cruelly, the wartime chief of staff, secretary of state, and conceiver of the Marshall Plan, then Defense Secretary George Catlett Marshall. In an overwhelming vote of the Republican-controlled Senate of 67 to 22, in December 1954, McCarthy was censured.

Not all who were part of the McCarthy fan club were archconservative Republicans. Robert F. Kennedy, a Democrat, was counsel to the Senate Permanent Subcommittee on Investigations. My friend, luncheon companion, and sharer of reading suggestions for more than fifty-five years, Robert M. Pennoyer, experienced McCarthy's and Kennedy's slings and arrows firsthand. Pennoyer was a special counsel in Eisenhower's Defense Department, assisting witnesses at a Senate hearing before that committee. Bobby Kennedy was working both with the committee chair and with Senator McCarthy, who was the senior Republican. Kennedy, his father, and his sisters were friends with McCarthy. The hearings were rancorous, and with Kennedy feeding him prompts, McCarthy tore into Pennoyer repeatedly. A mutual and close friend of the Kennedys and of the Pennoyers was Charles Bartlett, a man extremely close to President John F. Kennedy. Seeking to smooth over the testy feelings from the hearing, the Bartletts invited the Pennoyers and Ethel and Bobby Kennedy for a dinner for six. At the dinner table, Bobby turned to Pennoyer and said, "The trouble with you Republicans is that you have done away with the best man your party has!" Pennoyer asked, "Who is that?" Kennedy answered, "Senator McCarthy," to which Pennoyer said, "You can't mean that!" Kennedy said, "Of course I mean it. I think so well of the man I made him a godfather of one of my children."[39]

Clarity in his conviction about Nixon came to Dewey when he heard Nixon give a talk in New York City in May 1952. This followed by only three weeks the governor's rout of the Taft forces within the New York delegation bound for the presidential nominating convention. Dewey would have weight there. Richard Nixon was the main speaker that night, and he spoke well and—as we after all these decades of Nixon on the world stage became accustomed to—without notes. He argued the need for a Republican who could attract millions of Democratic and independent votes. When Nixon finished,

Dewey stubbed out his cigarette and took Nixon's hand. "That was a terrific speech. Make me a promise; don't get fat, don't lose your zeal, and you can be President someday." He invited the senator up to his suite, where Nixon learned of Dewey's interest in him as a possible vice president. According to Dewey, Nixon said he would be "greatly honored." The governor then called in both Russell Sprague and Herbert Brownell, to make sure his key people were aware of his desire to help Nixon. Of his choice he later explained, "He had a very fine voting record in both the House and the Senate, good, intelligent and middle of the road, and at this time it was important to get a Senator who knew the world was round. . . . His age was a useful factor. He had a fine record in the war. Most of all, however, he was an extraordinarily intelligent man, fine balance and character."[40]

Just weeks later at the Gridiron Dinner in Washington, Herbert Brownell noted strong interest in Nixon.

> Dewey had told Nixon that he was Dewey's candidate for the position. I had met Nixon on these occasions, and Dewey had told me of his decision to secure a place for Nixon on the ticket and for several months pledged me to keep it a secret, which I had done. Thus . . . I knew that Nixon was the candidate of the Dewey forces in the party. I had even told Eisenhower beforehand what the outcome would be unless he personally offered another choice.[41]

Brownell had dinner alone with Eisenhower the night Ike was nominated and explained the procedure for nominating a vice president. Ike wrote out a list of six or seven names without prompting from Brownell. It included Richard Nixon. Ike had met Nixon twice, once during the Hiss-Chambers confrontation in 1949 and once in 1951 in Europe. Ike then asked Brownell to call a meeting of his convention leaders the next morning to recommend the vice presidential nominee. In that meeting, several names were mentioned, "but Governor Dewey carried the day when he presented Nixon's name."[42]

The Eisenhower Presidency

The eight years of the Eisenhower presidency were seen by some as years of consolidation, peace, and essential economic stability; by others, they were seen as somnolent. Eisenhower himself was viewed (accurately) as not interested in partisan politics. He was viewed (inaccurately) as someone above the fray, not knowing where to place and spend his political capital. Anyone who had watched him function during the war would have quickly dismissed this mistaken notion.

Arthur Larson said that Eisenhower discovered and established the authentic American center in politics.[43] The consensus itself came about partly because there was a common social and historical background, not "trailing centuries of class consciousness and class warfare." He advanced a common ideology but also, just as important, a "gradual maturing and moving-together of the interests that have provided our principal conflicts. Responsible labor and business leaders are proclaiming the doctrine that labor and management have far-reaching fundamental interests in common. These are 'long term' factors which made the Consensus possible."

Republicanism as defined by the Eisenhower administration admitted it is "true that some of the component parts have been adapted from the New Deal, as in the case of some social and labor legislation."[44] Dewey would agree.

Larson doubted the Democrats could hold the middle ground politically, as its two largest blocks were "the most conservative element in the country—the Southern Democrats—and the most radical—the ultra–Fair Dealers. Within the Democratic Party, the cleavage is abrupt and extreme, and the two segments are ideologically almost not on speaking terms."[45]

Herbert Brownell, who had been in the eye of the storm with both Thomas Dewey and Dwight Eisenhower as had no other, makes the point.

Perhaps Dewey's greatest achievement, even in defeat, was to pave the way for the kind of moderate Republican philosophy that Eisenhower was to follow. Dewey's efforts in the 1940s were instrumental in turning the Republican party from the essentially isolationist views of Taft and the Old Guard toward internationalism, which it has since represented even more strongly than has the Democratic party. Dewey also encouraged acceptance of most parts of the New Deal among most Republicans; the Republican party retained its concern for fiscal responsibility during the Eisenhower years, but there were no serious efforts to dismantle Roosevelt's popular domestic programs.[46]

Eisenhower embraced this moderation in a revealing, long letter of November 8, 1954, to his brother Edgar. Edgar had written criticizing many of the policies Ike embraced. Eisenhower found the concerns superficially thought through and ill founded. He responded at length and in tart fashion. Eisenhower warned of too much centralization of government. He then cautioned that "should any political party attempt to abolish social security, unemployment insurance, and eliminate labor laws and farm programs, you would not hear of that party again in our political history."

Thomas Dewey had said as much while drinking the bitter cup of his 1948 defeat. In a Washington, DC, speech on February 8, 1949, he spoke with great candor. After noting that the party had been split wide open for years, he said, "We have in our party some fine, high-minded patriotic people who honestly oppose . . . unemployment insurance, old age benefits . . . and other social programs. These people believe in a laissez-faire society and look back wistfully to the miscalled 'good old days' of the nineteenth century." He urged the Republicans to "stop bellyaching about the past" and work for the overwhelming majority who felt government must be more than "a cold and impartial umpire."

Eisenhower did not attempt to turn back the clock. On Social Security, he resisted efforts to trim or crimp it and instead expanded it. On this, he enjoyed the categorical support of his vice president, Richard Nixon.

On civil rights, his decisions often cut against the grain of the background of his youth in Kansas and Texas. Eisenhower was not in the vanguard for desegregation. Yet the general had a sense of duty about enforcement of the law. He spent most of his military career in a "Jim Crow" Army, but he had been appalled and embarrassed in London during the war as Black officers and enlisted men were treated to abuse by many of the white American soldiers, to the shock of the British.

When the Eisenhower court unanimously decided the landmark *Brown v. Board of Education of Topeka* case, it had to decide about implementation. Eisenhower and his attorney general, Herbert Brownell, sent an amicus curiae brief to the Court as it considered the follow-on decision to *Brown*, in 1955. The brief urged the Court to require plans to be submitted within ninety days for the school district. They wanted immediate compliance with the Court's order. To Eisenhower's disappointment—and spurring great concern on Brownell's part—the Court directed that desegregation should proceed instead with "all deliberate speed."

The Court's reluctance to require immediate enforcement led to fifteen years of mounting resistance. Richard Nixon was to be handed the hot potato when, in *Alexander v. Holmes*, the Court directed in 1969 that compliance must occur "at once." Here, too, as Eisenhower did, Nixon enforced the Court's order, in Nixon's case by creating and working with multiracial committees in states all over the South to bring about a peaceful compliance with the Court's decree. He did this despite the transitions the Republican Party had begun in the 1960s and its struggles over its path on civil rights, including forceful resistance from some in his own White House.

Eisenhower enforced the *Brown* decision with the unprecedented use of federal troops to assure the safety of the children. He also intervened in Little Rock, Arkansas, in 1957. Following passage of the 1957 act, he created the Civil Rights Division in the Department of Justice.

Ike as president enforced the desegregation of the armed forces after

Harry Truman's order to do so had been largely ignored by the military, especially in the South. Likewise, Ike desegregated the District of Columbia. Democratic president Woodrow Wilson had resegregated it when he took office some forty years earlier. Wilson had also resegregated all federal employment, which the Republicans had desegregated decades before. In his final State of the Union message, just days before leaving office, Eisenhower for the first time characterized civil rights as a moral issue.[47]

On the safety net issues, Ike did not simply block a rollback. In 1954, Eisenhower greatly expanded Social Security in the first major change since its creation in the New Deal, extending its benefits to ten million additional American workers. Among the most durable results in health care of the Eisenhower presidency were laws centered on employer-provided health insurance for employees. The Eisenhower reforms became the central bulwark of health protection.

Two authors described Eisenhower's accomplishments—and failures—on the health-care front. David Blumenthal and James A. Marone sympathize that Eisenhower was always trying to square moderate or liberal notions of health-care coverage, which he emotionally supported, with a pervasive fiscal prudence and budget mindedness.[48]

> On the upside, Eisenhower worked assiduously at health care, took risks (repeatedly crossing the American Medical Association, for example), and, in the end, crafted a moderate Republican position that shifted the American health care debate. . . . Eisenhower successfully bolstered the private health insurance system for workers and their dependents. The tax exemption for workplace health insurance spurred the rapid growth of private plans—a distinctive American institution that now covers 160 million people. In the 1950s the United States chose its unique social insurance route.[49]

Eisenhower sought to move into the area Dewey had mapped out in 1944 of coverage for the elderly, the disabled, or otherwise indigent. The president tried to induce private sector insurers to find a way to underwrite these higher risk persons—"more difficult terrain," as Blumenthal and Marone put it.

Eisenhower in his last year again supported broad health-care efforts and backed an expansion of the Kerr-Mills legislation, which was about both hospital construction and services to those in need of health care. He had the solid support of Nixon on this. The support he did not have was Barry Goldwater. Only two votes in the United States Senate were opposed: Barry Goldwater and South Carolina's Strom Thurmond. This pair was the same one who would defy the vast majority of Republicans in the civil rights battles that were to become central in 1964.

Dewey, Eisenhower himself, and Arthur Larson all pointed to the political imperative of a progressive Republican Party. Gabriel Hauge gave a speech on October 14, 1955, in San Francisco to the Commonwealth Club of California, in which he proposed the "Economics of Eisenhower Conservatism," which promised growth and opportunity.[50] In an indication of how close the president and his special assistant were, Hauge put a handwritten note on the copy he sent to Ike. He told the president that this was an early birthday present, and inscribed it: "With Affectionate Regards."

But it was in his resignation letter of July 7, 1958, in a very concentrated, brief, and powerful line, that Hauge sets out the assimilation by the Eisenhower party and Republicans of so much of what Tom Dewey had striven to have them embrace. It succinctly summarizes the core sense of Eisenhower Republicanism. It is my view that Richard Nixon carried this impulse forward into the White House.

Hauge's summary is eloquent, vivid, and simple. It is almost pastoral in its imagery.

Hauge wrote to the president, "You have put a platform over the pit of despair, without sacrificing the principle of self-reliance."

CHAPTER 2

The Disruptive Decade
The 1960s and the Formation of the Ripon Society

The Eisenhower years for most Americans were ones of steady economic improvement. There were major increases in homeownership, in college entrance for children of a growing middle class, and in travel. The country was not smug, but it was satisfied. TV shows of the era, pop music, and most films reflected back to the society its relative contentment. The country, after the end to the Korean War, returned to its post–World War II glow of national pride: invasions of Suez by allies; overthrows of regimes in Iran and Guatemala; an almost Gilbert and Sullivan American intervention in Lebanon, in which Marines landed on beaches where young Lebanese women were sunbathing in bikinis. All seemed distant, unthreatening. Americans were detached, even though they now knew the United States exercised global leadership. These events were happening on Eisenhower's watch. They had an easy trust that he would manage the interests of the United States well. There would not be reckless adventures. The anti-communist rhetoric about rolling back the Iron Curtain advanced by his secretary of state, John Foster Dulles, had messianic, or, at least, Presbyterian, zeal to it. When the Hungarian uprising of autumn 1956 occurred, that rhetoric plumbed a lower decibel level. We became a destination and home for the refugees from the Soviet crushing of the Hungarians, but we did not send US tanks across the Fulda Gap into East Germany toward Budapest.

Yet the seams of the tight-fitting suit of conformity and moderation were stretching. Elvis Presley appeared. Important changes in the nation's attention were imminent. Two issues in particular would dominate the decade of disruption of the 1960s.

One issue that moved to the center in the 1950s and would be a crucible for societal and political realignment in the 1960s was that of race. It of course had never gone away. Not since the Constitutional Convention, not since the Missouri Compromise, not since *Dred Scott*, not since the Civil War, and not since *Plessy v. Ferguson* at the end of the nineteenth century. *Plessy* was a Supreme Court decision that, in its "separate but equal" decision about school facilities for white and Black Americans, countenanced a two-track system, the reality of which made a mockery of the language of the Court.

For decades, the seamiest and most brutal features of race relations—

lynchings, the denial of voting rights, and the lack of basic justice for African Americans—had not prompted national action. This was true despite Governor Dewey's strong support for civil rights in the 1944 Republican Party platform and despite efforts by liberals like Hubert Humphrey in the Farmer/Labor Party of Minnesota.

Two events in the mid-1950s sped the country's engagement with civil rights issues. The first was the *Brown v. Board of Education of Topeka* Supreme Court decision. In 1954, the Warren Court, so named for Eisenhower's appointee Earl Warren as chief justice, overturned *Plessy v. Ferguson*. Eisenhower, despite hardly being in the vanguard of advocating civil rights, was determined to enforce the law and did. He and his attorney general, Herbert Brownell, feared that the language of "deliberate speed" the Court employed would encourage resistance to the Court's order. That is exactly what occurred, and White Citizens' Councils formed all over the South to stall desegregation. It was not until the *Alexander v. Holmes* decision, in Richard Nixon's first year as president, that the Court mandated what Eisenhower and Brownell had implored it to do at the time of the *Brown* decisions.

The other event with powerful national impact was the death in 1955 of young Emmett Till, a Chicago boy who had gone to visit relatives in Mississippi. He was brutally murdered and disfigured by whites for allegedly making improper advances to an older white woman. His funeral, at his church in Chicago with an open casket displaying what had been done to him, drew thousands of mourners, and it brought visually and powerfully home the violence that all too often befell African Americans and went unnoticed. It deeply shocked Attorney General Brownell. With President Eisenhower's approval, he prepared and sent to the Congress the most sweeping and powerful civil rights bill ever submitted. The Democratic chair of the House Judiciary Committee, Emmanuel Cellar of Brooklyn, New York, who had a pending bill of his own, agreed to substitute the Eisenhower/Brownell bill for his legislation. Lyndon Johnson, the Democratic majority leader in the Senate, was still the darling of the Southern Bourbons who dominated the Committee structures of both houses of Congress but especially the Senate. Lyndon's position on civil rights was complex. He had innate sympathy with the underprivileged and had taught Mexican American kids in school. His political base was Texas. It was not as segregationist as Mississippi or Alabama, but its politics would not allow the election statewide of a progressive on race during the 1930s, 1940s, and 1950s. At the same time, Lyndon's dreams extended far beyond Texas. He was ambitious to become the Democrats' presidential nominee in 1956 and feared that if the Eisenhower bill passed the House and came to the Senate, the weeks of unsightly wrangling and the bitterness of division in the Democratic Party would be so highlighted that his chances would be doomed. He called on his fellow Texan, Speaker Sam Rayburn, to slow down the progress of the House bill until it would be too late in the session for it to come to the Senate for full consideration and debate. Rayburn obliged his protégé and fellow Southern Democrat.

The huge and wrenching impact on both parties of the civil rights movement and the realignment of sectional party interests would await the convergence of Lyndon Johnson's public conversion and commitment—soon after he became president—to the cause of civil rights with the strong and deep support by almost all Republicans for that same cause. Republican support was the sine qua non for the passage of the landmark civil rights legislation of the mid-1960s. The glaring exception to that Republican support was Senator Barry M. Goldwater and that proved no small exception, as the Arizona senator became the party's presidential nominee in 1964.

A second upheaval during the 1950s that had profound implications was that of Soviet technological breakthroughs in space. The suppression of the Hungarian uprising in 1956, and of others in Poland and East Germany earlier, had left no doubt about the power of Soviet land forces in Europe, nor its willingness to assert that power. The delivery of H-bomb secrets to Russia by the Soviet spy, Klaus Fuchs, had likewise been cause for alarm about the speed of weapons development by the Soviets. Yet there was a relative sense of security that the Soviets were not on a par with the Americans in space technology.

That sense of security was shattered in autumn 1957, when the Soviets were the first to launch an orbiting satellite, called Sputnik, which sped around the globe, visible at night to the naked eye. A chemistry major at Grinnell College, Roger Soderberg, corralled me one evening that October, a couple of nights after Sputnik started circling the sky, and we went out to the north of the small Iowa town, where the darkness of the sky permitted easy sighting and following of the moving man-made object. I watched and marveled. I phoned my grandmother, Nellie Milnes, the next day, the farm wife who annually went to the ballot box and voted the straight Democratic ticket, nullifying my Republican grandfather's party-line Republican vote. I told her of what I had observed. "It cannot be up there. God would not permit it." But permit it He had.

Eisenhower pushed a massive federal effort to support education in the sciences that would start to close the perceived gap. The US support for space programs went on steroids, and the National Aeronautics and Space Administration (NASA), the civilian space agency, was formalized and strengthened. The new perception was of a vastly greater Soviet threat, prowess we had not credited them with, and it colored the 1960 presidential election. Nixon (and Eisenhower) came under attack from Democratic candidate John F. Kennedy, who charged that we had condoned the Soviets achieving technological superiority and were insufficiently willing to resist Soviet aggression and the Chinese threat. His inaugural address spoke of taking up the burden around the globe for the defense of democracy. His Roman Catholic background suggested an ingrained anti-communist view, possible clues to understanding Kennedy doing what Ike did not, namely, get deep into Vietnam. Ike, like Republican presidents Herbert Hoover before him and Richard Nixon after him, was a member as a child of a "Peace" church. Hoover and Nixon were raised Quakers. Eisenhower was raised in the "River Brethren" church, originally a Pennsylvania Mennonite sect of German origin, which opposed war. Pacifism was in the air in the childhood homes of all three. For Eisenhower, though, reluctance to enter Vietnam was certainly also the consequence of a hard-eyed understanding of the French failure there.

The Vietnam War and the protest movements that followed, on the one hand, and the growing civil rights movement, on the other, were the two forces that more than any others shaped the moral and political landscape of the coming decade. The decade began with a presidential campaign that saw Richard Nixon easily capturing the Republican nomination to succeed Eisenhower. His steps to consolidate the nomination demonstrated where Nixon thought the center of gravity of the electorate lay. In 1958, Nelson Rockefeller erupted on the scene with a victory in his first try for office, becoming governor of New York. When Rockefeller first sought the governorship in 1957–1958, he invited former governor Dewey to lunch at the executive dining room at Radio City Music Hall. When hardly in his thirties, Nelson had been the family's overseer of the construction of the massive urban redevelopment at Rockefeller Center, employing thousands in the depth of the Great Depression and erecting a monument to the depth and reach of Rockefeller power. It housed the National Broadcasting Company (NBC) and its studios, from which newscasters broadcast even today, looking out at the public skating rink and the seasonal towering Christmas tree.

If Rockefeller intended his invitation to lunch on his ground at Rockefeller Center to be intimidating to Dewey, it was not the case. Dewey's signal accomplishment within the Republican Party had been the creation in New York of a strong organizational structure, for which my county, Nassau County, was the paradigm of people waiting their turn and moving up with the organization's blessing. The other key lever of control was that the party, not the candidate, finance the campaign, thus giving the party more control over candidates and content. Dewey was nonplussed that Rockefeller wanted to go immediately for the governorship. He no doubt feared that Nelson's and his family's financing of his effort would undercut the party's role—and control. When Rockefeller told Dewey of his intention, Dewey said he was not well known enough, and then, "after a frowning pause . . . 'You know, I think I could arrange to have you appointed postmaster of New York City!'"[1] This was not what Rockefeller wanted to hear. He went on his quest without Dewey's blessing and won Dewey's old job running the Empire State. Unlike the scene with Claude Rains and Humphrey Bogart at the end of *Casablanca* as they strolled off together into the night, with Dewey and Rockefeller it was not "the beginning of a beautiful friendship."

Rockefeller, by virtue of vast wealth, charm, his victory, and his outsized personality, became an instant contestant for the presidential nomination in 1960. To see him off, Nixon worked the grassroots in a way Rockefeller never did in his three quests of the Republican presidential nomination. Rockefeller did not seem temperamentally fashioned to do so. He dropped quickly from contention. To seal "Rocky's" exit, and secure the governor's support, Nixon went to Rockefeller.

James Reichley, once legislative secretary to Governor William Scranton of Pennsylvania, later at the Brookings Institution, said Nixon felt at the end of the Eisenhower administration that the center of gravity of the Republican Party had begun to shift back toward what Reichley calls the "Stalwarts": on the one hand, the old Taft wing and, on the other, the pushy newcomers, the "Fundamentalists," represented by Goldwater. However, Nixon believed that the center of American politics, not the rightward-shifting center of the Republican Party, was where the election would be won. Therefore, he courted the progressive wing of the party with the general election in mind. Nixon's meeting with Rockefeller was only three days before the convention.[2]

Nixon acceded to a host of Rockefeller's policy positions, whose embrace by Nixon the governor insisted on. Nixon felt it worth risking upset on the Right. Nixon further appealed to the liberal wing of the party with his selection of Henry Cabot Lodge, Jr., of Massachusetts, as his running mate. The concordat with Rockefeller was substantively no detour from the platform the party was set to embrace only days later, nor from the Eisenhower administration's policies. Yet, this visible issue by issue discussion with the New York governor came to be seen as a Munich moment of surrender by the growing and mobilizing movement conservatives. Called the Fifth Avenue Compact for the opulent, art-filled apartment on Fifth Avenue where Rockefeller lived, it symbolized, to the conservatives' displeasure, Nixon's willingness to stretch to the Left. Following his defeat in the 1960 race, and then the gubernatorial race in California in 1962, Nixon joined a New York law firm, and he and his family moved into the same Fifth Avenue apartment building as his once and future rival, though with a separate entrance on the south, or Sixty-Second Street, side facing the Knickerbocker Club, not the Fifth Avenue and

Central Park side. Nor was his apartment a sprawling duplex that displayed on the mantel and throughout its rooms, and even bathrooms, the work of Fernand Leger, Picasso, and Miro, among other priceless original paintings.

The highwater mark of modern Republicanism may have been, as Ike exulted in it, his moment of triumph in 1956. That election night, Ike appeared at the Sheraton-Park hotel in DC and told exuberant supporters, "I think Modern Republicanism has now proved itself. And America has approved of Modern Republicanism."[3] Nixon demurred when Arthur Larson asked him to write an introduction to a new edition of *A Republican Looks at His Party*, planned for 1960, Nixon's election year. David Stebenne, Larson's biographer, asserts that Nixon was "unwilling to antagonize New Rightists such as Buckley and Goldwater . . . [and] studiously avoided any action that might identify him as a firmly committed member of the GOP's Modern Republican wing,"[4] even though his deal with Rockefeller was far more of an irritant than an introduction to a book would have been.

The Compact may have formally brought around his only real competitor and paved the way toward the general election campaign, but it occurred only because Rockefeller had been outmaneuvered in the arena of presidential nominating politics that counts: the delegate hunt and harvest. Nixon demonstrated his enormous tactical skill in 1960 and saw the fruit born of the endless attention he paid to the political network that was so essential to corralling delegates in those days. Nixon understood the functioning of politics at the local level, always retaining, as an astute baseball fan might, a deep understanding of the "stats" or election data and what they meant in electoral politics down to the precinct level. Even in his presidency, with so many matters of policy demanding his attention, he never lost that instinct, nor his detailed awareness of what was going on in all 435 congressional districts. He embodied the very thing that Ike had not. Nixon was a political animal.

He wooed the Republican delegates who were members of Congress. He stroked the members of the Republican National Committee. He courted the three thousand–plus county chairs and their local leaders, many of whom he knew by name. The difference between Nixon and Rockefeller was night and day in this essential element of building that vital majority at the quadrennial family conclaves of delegates and alternates. Rockefeller was episodic in his attention to the grit and grassroots of party politics. Nixon was relentless—completely tenacious—in his attention to it. Nixon thus was wholly attuned to the nomination process as it existed at the time. This was before the increase—in both parties—in the numbers and importance of primary contests, as opposed to state-nominating conventions.

Rockefeller's approach was more a direct appeal to the public with ideas. He was of course by now accustomed as governor to the give-and-take and deal making with the legislature and several very powerful county leaders in New York State. Yet somehow he believed that in the presidential race, the voting public would be positively swayed by detailed policies and well-researched positions. His assumption was that the pressure of public opinion would be felt by the party leaders, who would bow to the public's embrace of the policy positions the governor spoke out on. These he had staff people working on constantly. He also commissioned frequent and expensive outside advisory groups. His policy papers were legion. Nixon was himself one of the most intellectual and probing of presidents on issues both foreign and domestic. With Nixon, though, this strong intellectual grasp of policy was always leavened or informed by a cold-eyed and often prescient sense of the politics of an issue. As to being chosen by the party, Nixon innately understood, as Rockefeller failed to, that the first order of business was to nourish relations with the local party roots, from which would ultimately grow the nomination. One of the governor's longtime associates, Joseph Persico, sums up Nelson at the end his book *The Imperial Rockefeller*: "He was . . . always a better government man than a political man. . . . It does credit to his seriousness of purpose that he long resisted, even disbelieved, the idea that a President was born of a thousand chicken dinners and a hundred thousand small-town handshakes. But it suggests a naivete that it took him so long to learn this lesson."[5]

The convention duly chose Nixon. But Barry Goldwater, the Republican senator from Arizona, had picked up the mantle from Robert Taft for the conservatives. Goldwater was young, and his Arizona Senate seat was a harbinger of the increasing influence of the Sun Belt within the Republican Party and within American politics. At Nixon's convention, Goldwater threw down the gauntlet. He announced his support for Nixon but then exhorted conservatives to "take back this party." That they set about to do.

The 1960 campaign was bitterly disappointing for Nixon. He was in most every respect the moderate in the race. He drew a very strong percentage of the African American vote, even with the decades-long slow desertion of that voting group from the Republicans to the New Deal, then Truman and his "Fair Deal."

Perhaps the proximate cause for Nixon's loss to Kennedy was voting fraud in Cook County, Illinois, and parts of Lyndon Johnson's Texas, which put up numbers causing Kennedy to carry those two states. When Nixon returned to DC after the vote, party leaders insisted he at least probe Cook County's returns. He asked a close friend, lawyer "Jack" Wells (John A. Wells, a veteran of the Willkie and Dewey campaigns), to go to Chicago and report back to him and the Republican National Committee on the results there. Wells found palpable evidence of large-scale voter fraud, enough, he told Nixon, to support lodging a legal case to overturn the results. Wells told me years later that Nixon struggled about it, as it would mean a chance the election results could be reversed and he, Nixon, might become president. Nixon finally told Wells that he "could not put the country through another Tilden-Hayes" and told the National Committee not to pursue it. Nixon was not willing to subject the country to the emotions and uncertainty of a challenge. 1876 saw a cliffhanger in the presidential race between Samuel Tilden and Rutherford Hayes, whose outcome was not settled for months.

Another loss for Nixon followed. He returned home to California. There, in 1962, he sought the gubernatorial nomination and had to fight a primary against an archconservative opponent. Joseph Shell, a former football hero and Republican Assembly leader in Sacramento, was a figure closely in tune with an emerging right-wing group called the John Birch Society, a resurgence of the McCarthy element of the party. This group painted Eisenhower as a weak leader, outmanned by, if not sympathetic to, the communists worldwide and even in America. While Nixon saw off Shell in the primary, Shell's candidacy drew a substantial number of southern Californian hard conservatives who then refused to vote in the general election and delivered the election to Pat Brown, the Democrat and father of the once, and yet again, California governor, Democrat Jerry Brown. This ultraconservatism or radicalism, not really aligned with the Republican Party but happy to try to conquer it and bend it to its own uses, was to harness the Goldwater movement. It caused Richard Nixon ever after to be wary of the arch conservatives, Nixon's long-time associate and later my colleague, John C. Whitaker, told me.[6]

With Nixon suffering two defeats in two years and declaring himself out of politics in a peevish press conference in November 1962, the insurgents gained traction. At this stage, both national parties had geographic and ideologically mixed characteristics. Both the Republican and the Democratic Parties had liberal and conservative elements. Each party internally was accustomed to compromise, despite often harsh rhetoric. Republicans in most states were approachable by labor and were sensitive to the needs of working people and families. Both national parties supported the social safety net that the New Deal had put in place.

On civil rights, the Republican administration had been forcefully in the fray. This was especially so at Eisenhower's Justice Department. Arthur Larson had aptly characterized the Democratic conundrum: it had both the most liberal or extreme progressive element and the most conservative and outright segregationist element. As he noted, it is hard to call yourselves the party of the center if you have a dumbbell distribution of power with such differences on issues of importance to supporters. Yet, this tension within the party had not disabled it. The balance between the national Democratic

Party and its congressional wing was precarious but mutually advantageous. It won and held the presidency for all but eight years in seven election cycles. Likewise, it held the Congress for most of the years since 1932.

The Republican Party had its more conservative congressional caucus, some of whom made common cause—especially on defense and economic issues—with conservative southern Democrats. Yet, even within the Republican caucus in Congress, the moderates, liberals, and conservatives coexisted, united on many points—not the least of which was the desire to be the majority party. The liberals included Senators Jacob K. Javits of New York City and Kenneth B. Keating of upstate New York, Clifford Case of New Jersey, Thomas Kuchel of California, and Hugh Scott of Pennsylvania. Moderates were many, including senators from Kentucky and Maryland. Conservatives included William Knowland of California, Karl Mundt of South Dakota, Carl Curtis of Nebraska, and John Tower, elected from Texas in 1961 in a special election to fill the seat that Lyndon Johnson vacated after he became vice president.

The Republicans also had progressive governors and state legislatures. Eisenhower's election victories had pushed the frontiers of the party back into states that had not been Republican since Reconstruction, including Virginia, Tennessee, Florida, and Texas. Ike's two terms saw a movement of many young professionals in the Deep South to the party. Furthermore, he—and Nixon, as noted—held the African American vote at very high levels despite the secular decline in that vote for Republican candidates since FDR.

In 1960, as Eisenhower's two terms drew to a close, the historic Republican divisions again pulled in different directions. Conservatives cried that Republican liberals were "Me, too" Republicans, those anxious to embrace the New Deal but to spend a little less money doing so. The charge was a precursor to the catchy acronym used by conservatives in current days to apostatize those only slightly less conservative Republicans: RINO, or Republican in name only.

Geoffrey Kabaservice, in his exhaustive examination of post-1960 Republican politics, acts for us as a skilled lepidopterist. He sorts and displays by subspecies the wings of the party in the post-Ike era. He spreads and pins the occasionally beautiful, now often extinct, creatures into his written display case, *Rule and Ruin: The Downfall of Moderation and the Destruction of the Republican Party, from Eisenhower to the Tea Party*.[7]

Social Institutions in Change
It was not the Republican Party alone that was to undergo pains of transition. The 1960s saw radical changes within organizations as diverse as the Na-

tional Student Association (NSA) and the Roman Catholic Church (through the Second Vatican Council). The NSA consisted of hundreds of colleges and universities, represented by their student body presidents. The issues with which NSA was concerned included the degree to which a university should act "in loco parentis" (i.e., in place of the student's parent) or how a university could most successfully apply for grants to support research. As W. Dennis Shaul recalled, student government in the 1950s was fraternities and sororities "right out of mainstream middle America." As far as any political position was concerned, NSA was "primarily dedicated to containing the far left within the United States."[8] "But," he added, "there was tension with the outer world which was changing around them." Only in the very early 1960s did such subjects as supporting the opportunity for speakers to talk at universities about unpopular or controversial topics become part of NSA's efforts. That was an early indication of its moves to embrace more diverse student populations and interests. As Shaul observed, "The big transition was in 1960 or 62. . . . Civil rights became for NSA its real calling card."

More broadly, Shaul observes that the growing activism was a natural reaction by many younger students to what they saw as the passivity of the Eisenhower administration and the complacency of American society in general. "It was like a 'stoppered bottle.'" He characterized this in a very positive fashion: using civil rights as an example, he said students did feel they could make a difference. There was "enough feeling of accomplishment and that the country could be turned around—there was an optimism and absence of cynicism."

I and my friends in the early 1960s were of this view; we felt a bond in our yearning to be of some use in our lives. I had read an early biography of Benjamin Disraeli, the British Conservative nineteenth-century prime minister, by Monypenny and Buckle. In it was a letter Disraeli wrote to his sister while on a trip up the Rhine, escaping his law practice briefly. He told her of his intent to flee from law and his quest for something more meaningful. I also was touched by a quote at the ending of his novel, *Sybil*,[9] which I had been spurred to read by reading Monypenny and Buckle: "We live in an age when to be young and to be indifferent can be no longer synonymous. The claims of the Future are represented by suffering Millions; and the Youth of a Nation are the trustees of Posterity."[10]

As Disraeli spoke to me, so did he come to influence Richard Nixon. In their first months together, Daniel P. Moynihan brought Disraeli to Nixon's attention and gave him the then recent Robert Blake biography, which Nixon devoured. Blake, the provost of Queen's College at Oxford, had published his wildly acclaimed one-volume treatment of Disraeli in 1966, shortly before Nixon and Moynihan were to come together in partnership on framing an entirely new governing strategy for Nixon's policies in social welfare and economic security. Moynihan made much to Nixon of Disraeli as the Tory or conservative reformer. Blake made much of Disraeli discerning the unmet needs of vast swaths of the British population in the mid-nineteenth century and of Disraeli's finding social reform not only essential but also fruitful politics for the Tories as well. These were liberal and necessary reforms from a conservative party leader. Nixon was much influenced by it.

The highly traditionalist Roman Catholic Church itself was subjected to the winds of change in the early 1960s. Pope John XXIII convened the Second Vatican Council, to last from 1962 through 1965. In the words of Notre Dame alumnus Dennis Shaul, "The Church had missed out on the Enlightenment." He says, "It had been at war with science . . . and to some extent with history and did not understand the extent to which they had become authoritarian. . . . It fought many of the most important minds." The pope's entreaty to the Church was to "open a window." It was to become open as well to the communities in which the church served.

The years following *Brown v. Board of Education* and the murder of Emmett Till witnessed the inception and growth of organizations specifically organized around the issue of civil rights. As early as 1957 the Southern Christian Leadership Conference (SCLC) had come together, led by clerics like Martin Luther King, Jr. As was the Congress on Racial Equality (CORE), founded fifteen years earlier by James Farmer and others, SCLC was dedicated to a nonviolent approach to broadening rights. New groups were launched, fueled by the growing resistance in the South with the proliferation of the White Citizens' Councils. The Student Non-Violent Coordinating Committee (SNCC) was born in 1960 with John Lewis among its early leaders. It became a leader of the efforts to register Black voters in the South, especially in Mississippi, in the Freedom Summer project, pulling together the long-established civil rights groups and masses of volunteers and financing, especially after the murder of three Northern volunteer students in Mississippi. For a long while, it was in the vanguard.

That same year, 1960, the Students for a Democratic Society (SDS) was formed in Ann Arbor, Michigan, initially motivated by civil rights issues. It did have a more Left-leaning bias and, along with civil rights, was concerned with corporate power and income inequality. Its formal credo was issued a couple of years later, in 1962, and was called the Port Huron Statement.

The Vietnam War grew ever more divisive as the 1960s progressed. SDS shifted focus from civil rights, radicalized by the escalation of the war. Some of its adherents spun off to form a terrorist organization, the Weathermen, whose militants manufactured bombs. In a dramatic incident, they lost many of their own when one of their bombs accidentally went off in a town house in Greenwich Village, New York, that they were using to manufacture the weapons.

The sexual revolution, the women's movement, and bra burning as a protest (followed by draft-card burning as war protests intensified), the widespread use of drugs, and the vigorous and hostile reaction provoked by all of these among Americans who were offended or appalled by them were still somnolent in 1960. Yet in everything from music and media to theater, the emergence of the new generation that was on the road to Woodstock, Haight-Ashbury, or Canada to escape the draft could begin to be discerned.

Nixon and Kennedy

The Kennedy election moved to front stage a representative of a new generation, in contrast to Eisenhower (seventy in his last year in office), whom he succeeded. Kennedy's government, but even more its Camelot social style and sense of purpose or destiny and the ability to move the world, which swept into town in January 1961, was a departure from the Eisenhower decade. Kennedy seemed to have captured the future from other politicians.

Governmentally, it was not a turn in a radical direction. Indeed, his national security advisor, secretary of defense, and secretary of state and of the treasury were moderate Republicans in background and party registration. The difference was that much of his generation and younger were drawn to him for reasons of style and youth. Nixon and Kennedy were contemporaries, only four years separating them, fellow veterans, fellow freshmen in the 1946 congressional election, having adjoining office space in the House, and, actually, friends. Kennedy had about him an ease, fashion, and comfort that the striving Richard Nixon could never inhabit. Despite his phenomenal success, Nixon was lacking self-confidence and harboring deep resentments, even though he was self-controlled. Nixon could not disguise his sleepless ambition. Eisenhower by contrast could conceal his ambition, or at least plant pleasant gardens around it.

Kennedy's charm, his wit in press conferences, and his coterie of glamorous friends masked the fact that he did not have the kind of hand-on-the-throat ability, combined with inducement and persuasion, of a Lyndon Johnson, or a Speaker Sam Rayburn, to move the government where he wanted to go. Kennedy never managed to grasp full control of his divergent party. It was a struggle for him to have Congress enact his proposals, despite the Democrats' control of both houses.

Yeast and Ferment in the Republican Camp

Despite the glamor of the Kennedy administration, much of the yeast and ferment of the early 1960s occurred within the Republican Party—in both its liberal and its conservative camps. Part of the "snap-back" of the conservatives after the centrist and inclusive politics of Eisenhower was an intellectual exploration of liberty, economic freedom, and a caging of government. Its largest fermentation cask had been Yale University, which graduated William F. Buckley, Jr. Buckley found and fostered young conservatives, many of them recent Yale alumni. In 1955, Buckley and his brother-in-law, Brent Bozell, launched the magazine *National Review*, a communion table for the new believers. Young people were flocking into the Republican Party, but as cause conservatives. In September 1960, a seminal event was held at Buckley's weekend estate in Sharon, Connecticut. A manifesto was issued, called the "Sharon Statement." It was the founding document of the Young Americans for Freedom (YAF). YAF's first chairman was a young man named Robert M. Schuchman, whose databank mind held troves of election results, likely a near match for Richard Nixon in his encyclopedic historic knowledge of election results and their interpretation. Schuchman's heart held a fervent commitment to conservative principles, accompanied by a wonderful sense of humor. At a dinner I had in Seattle in April 2017, with Bruce K. Chapman, a fierce warrior for the Republican liberals in the early 1960s, Chapman recalled that Schuchman had a winning sense of humor.

YAF grew into a membership organization, with its apogee a rally of thousands held in New York at Madison Square Garden. The Garden had a history of hosting the late, lamented Ringling Brothers, Barnum & Bailey circus, the Gene Autry Rodeo, or the Billy Graham Christian Crusades. At the Garden in early 1952, my close friend Robert Pennoyer with other New York City Young Republicans (YRs) put together a rally to persuade Dwight Eisenhower to run for president. Thousands attended. Pennoyer says that when Eisenhower was shown the films of the rally, it brought tears to his eyes and helped convince him to challenge Taft.

A decade later, in March 1962, the Garden hosted the YAF rally. It was to turn the party away from the Eisenhower legacy and back toward old guard Republicanism—or rather to the new more radical right-wing brand. The rally theme was "Victory Over Communism." It turned into a massive demonstration for the Arizona senator, Barry Goldwater, who was on his way to the 1964 Republican nomination. The evening featured Katanga (a province of the Congo) president Moise Tshombe (in absentia)—a Christian anti-communist who opposed the Moscow-supported Patrice Lumumba when the Congo gained independence from Belgium—and Senator Strom Thurmond, the energetically anti-communist Democratic US senator from South Carolina. He and Goldwater also shared resistance to civil rights legislation Kennedy was beginning, unsuccessfully, to push. The freshman Texas Republican senator John Tower appeared, as did former president Herbert Hoover.

By the early 1960s, the conservatives had recovered their balance and their voice and had emerged from their suppression during the Eisenhower era. They had a membership organization in YAF. Soon, they also had potent lobbying from the American Conservative Union (ACU), a conservative pressure group. *Human Events* was purchased by Allan Ryskind and Tom Winter and reenergized. Against this dynamic, there seemed to be almost no Republican moderate presence among young people. The party's moderates or Eisenhower Republicans were older. They had fought their battles and, for the most part, had put the sword and buckler into the attic.

Kennedy had a magnetic pull for many younger people, with his emphasis on idealism and public service, to say nothing of his humor and intelligence. Those of us young people who had an attachment to moderate Republican politics were confused, conflicted. We instinctively embraced the Eisenhower centrist way of thinking, felt we were Republican, but were slightly embarrassed to be attached to something that was now seen as dated, musty, out of focus. There were some impressive new Republican faces, often in statehouses around the country, yet their reach and the enthusiasm they generated was limited. There was no single candidate among the moderates who was drawing all the others to him or to whom they were willing to yield precedence (and there was no "her" in this era, other than Maine senator Margaret Chase Smith).

Meanwhile, the conservatives were unifying behind Goldwater as their candidate for the 1964 election. They were also grasping for the real levers of power in the party. Two notable things about this early conservative revival were lack of interest in the civil rights movement, in fact opposition to it, and an initial tolerance of fringe right-wing groups and nostrums. William F. Buckley, Jr.'s family roots were deeply Southern and he was not at all initially sympathetic to the increasingly urgent demands for racial equality. Not as dramatically as Lyndon Johnson turned to support civil rights once he was president, Buckley turned, too. Buckley finally both understood and sympathized with the aims of civil rights campaigners. And he proscribed and excommunicated the John Birchers.

At least as consequential as the formation of the conservative groups like YAF or ACU was the deliberate and successful takeover by conservatives of the main arms of the Republican Party. By 1963, the conservatives controlled the leadership and the staff of the Republican National Committee. Bruce Chapman and George Gilder, in *The Party That Lost Its Head*, took note of this: "The breakdown of the Eisenhower compromise and the rout of its advocates in official party positions was a quiet, stealthy affair. It left the old leadership and, indeed, Republican progressives of all sorts unaware of their loss until it was beyond rescue."[11] A powerful indication of a new direction charted by those now in charge of the RNC was that they dropped the National Committee's Operation Dixie, an Eisenhower initiative to reach Black voters in the South and recruit them for the Republicans.

Conservatives made a pitched effort to grasp leadership of the National Young Republicans. This afforded them the grassroots organization experience at selecting delegates and managing convention tactics. Combined with the zeal of the convinced, this training was of inestimable use in the steady effort to take over the party from the ground up and assure that a conservative would be the next Republican nominee. Control of the Young Republicans was a way station to replacing the established luminaries in the states (state chairs and National Committee members). In early 2014, Bill Timmons, a key player in the YR fights and later Richard Nixon's assistant for congressional relations, and I met for lunch at DeCarlo's Restaurant, at Yuma Street and Massachusetts Avenue, in Washington. Timmons told me that the struggle for dominance of the youth group was intense. His conservative faction, which its members called the "Saints," used as an emblem the stick-figured, halo-crowned logo of the then popular television series, starring Roger Moore (later an elegant, slightly bemused James Bond). They were termed the "Syndicate" by the more moderate Young Republicans. In turn, Timmons and his friends called the moderate opposition the "Bad Guys." The Bad Guys included people like Charlie McWhorter, a former president of the YR (and legislative assistant to Nixon when he was vice president) and Jean McKee, the New York State YR leader and a Rockefeller and Senator Jacob K. Javits loyalist.[12]

Fifty years before that lunch with a leader of the "Saints," in spring 1964, I attended the Massachusetts YR convention. Here I had my first real exposure to the energy and cultural revolution intensity of many young activists—the movement. Theirs was a messianic call. They waved aloft their Maoist "Little Red Book," in this case titled *Conscience of a Conservative*, by Barry Morris Goldwater. Just as Goldwater was drafted, or appropriated, by the conservative movement to run, so, too, this book was mostly written by others but published under Goldwater's name.[13] The evangelical zeal of movement members forced me to question the hopes for ultimate victory of those of us who identified as moderate.

Mostly these were politically adept and smart conservatives. Some of the fringe, however, were extreme such as the New Jersey Young Republicans' "Rat Finks," who actually sang National Socialist (Nazi) songs and were racist and anti-Semitic. The John Birch Society, whose leader insisted that the United States was 60 to 80 percent communist, was particularly strong in southern California. The resistance to the *Brown* decision had spurred a renewed awakening of anti-civil rights politics in the South, which was still a

Democratic fiefdom, though some Republicans had begun to ride that resistance.

What of the Moderates? Formation of the Ripon Society

The same year as the YAF Madison Square Garden rally, there were stirrings among some younger people in the moderate wing of the Republican Party. A small group formed the Ripon Society, which was to become a powerful symbol of a lively progressive Republicanism. Ripon's policy papers were to have a measurable impact on the Nixon administration's embrace of ideas like welfare reform, revenue sharing, a volunteer military, and the opening to China.

In autumn 1962, I was a first-year student at the Harvard Law School. In a civil procedure class sitting a row behind me was Emil Frankel, who had just returned from England, where he had a Fulbright Scholarship in Manchester. There he had studied the Bow Group, an outgrowth of the Conservative or Tory Party. It was made up of the Young Turks of the Tories, whose motivation was to try to bring new policy ideas into the established party. They respected academia. They were increasingly successful at making their voices heard. Harold Macmillan, the prime minister of the moment, although of an older generation, was influenced by them, as he and his restless friends in the late 1930s and early 1940s had themselves influenced and changed the Tory Party of their time.

Emil returned home and to law school with a conviction that the Bow Group could serve as a model for an entity within the Republican Party. Two of our other classmates, to whom I was not yet close, had gone to Harvard College. There they had been a part of Republican Advance, an undergraduate effort spearheaded by George Gilder and Bruce Chapman that published a periodical called *Advance*. They were Eugene Marans and "Tim" (Thomas E.) Petri, both now in law school, and they proved crucial to the group.

Emil connected with an assistant professor at MIT, John S. (Jack) Saloma, who was deeply committed to the liberal wing of the Republican Party and himself close to Gilder and Chapman. Saloma also had taken a Fulbright in England and was well informed on the Bow Group. Saloma cut his teeth in politics working for Congressman Tom Curtis of Missouri, a reform-minded and energetic House Member, and for Leverett Saltonstall, a US senator from Massachusetts. Frankel and Saloma became the magnet around whom we began to coalesce. By the fall of 1962, the numbers included some Tufts, MIT, and Harvard University graduate students and teaching assistants. Among them were Douglas L. Bailey, working with Henry Kissinger at the Center for International Studies, and Lee W. Huebner, a PhD candidate in history at Harvard.

Kissinger, after the publication in 1957 of his *Nuclear Weapons and Foreign Policy*,[14] had begun to work with Nelson Rockefeller in 1959 during the creation and publication of a series of papers that Rockefeller promoted as part of his effort to secure the presidential nomination the following year. Kissinger was to become one of the most dominant figures in foreign policy of anyone in American history, serving as Richard Nixon's national security advisor, then as his secretary of state.

On February 27, 1963, I had my first exposure to Henry Kissinger. I moonlighted from my studies at the law school and went to a defense policy seminar of his. That evening, I told my diary, "He is a moon-faced, pudgy man, given to compulsive quipping, to interrupting even the most eminent speakers." I was to have many interactions through the decades with Dr. Kissinger and many conflicting impressions. Doug Bailey at one point observed to me that Kissinger was among the most idealistic of the strategic thinkers. Walter Isaacson's biography of Kissinger, as well as my own observations, suggested that idealism was not the central feature of Kissinger's makeup. However, I remained and do remain in awe of his articulation of policy. While in the White House, even though I was working on the domestic policy side, I would ravenously consume transcripts of his "anonymous" background briefings, admiring their tidy and tight structure and their persuasive power, even though they were extempore.

Our campus-based group in Cambridge was nameless, although due to Emil's work in England, he suggested the American Bow Group for an initial moniker. This persisted for a time, but in late fall 1962, Tim Petri suggested to Lee Huebner that the group should have a more American-based name. Petri and Huebner were both from Wisconsin. Petri suggested that Ripon, where they had first met five years before, at a "Boy's State" conclave, was ideal. Ripon was the site of a meeting with national pretensions to create a new party and where a definitive set of principles was laid out. The Republicans were born in Ripon, progressive, partisan, and a frequently unwieldy coalition of interests.

The name of the group became the Ripon Society.

Mort Halperin, a young teacher in the Harvard Government Department, organized a dinner on December 12, 1962, at the Harvard Faculty Club to which seventeen young men came. Most, like myself, were vaguely or constitutionally disposed toward Eisenhower Republicanism. MIT assistant professor Saloma urged that the group identify virgin issues around which we could coalesce, preempting both the Republican Old Guard and liberal Democrats. The interest in ideas was central, as was a hope to recruit young professionals to the Republican Party. Over the next two and a half years, we pitched ourselves increasingly into the most important issues of

Ripon Society Executive Committee, early 1965. *Front to back*: John Roy Price,
Christopher T. Bayley, Jonathan Bulkley, George Nolfi, John S. Saloma, J. Eugene
Marans, Emil H. Frankel, Lee W. Huebner, and Thomas E. Petri. John Roy Price
personal collection.

our generation: racial justice and the struggle for equal rights. We also built
bridges with the older generation of Eisenhower Republicans, who sought
us out and supported us. We connected with the Republican Governors Association (RGA), whose numbers included many distinguished and active
moderate political leaders, such as George Romney and later Bill Milliken of

Michigan, Bob Ray of Iowa, Dan Evans of Washington State, and John Volpe of Massachusetts.

Eugene Marans of Ripon (originally of Butte, Montana), along with Saloma and Lee Huebner, were the principal Ripon intermediaries with the governors. Lee Huebner worked on a joint publication with the Republican Governors' Association on Revenue Sharing that resonated. It was a proposal to have the efficient federal tax gathering apparatus employed to share, on a formula basis, federal tax revenues with the states on a nonrestricted or "non-categorical" basis.

Eugene Marans was present at a January 1965 meeting of the Republican governors at which civil rights was sharply in focus. Marans had become the point person in the group on this issue and authored most of the drafts of statements under the Ripon name, often working with a team of five or six Ripon lawyers supporting him from Cambridge. I remember the sights and smells of reproducing copies of manifestoes or drafts of bills on "mimeograph machines" with blue or purple ink (a technology now found only in the Smithsonian Institution's basement somewhere, perhaps near Indiana Jones's Ark of the Covenant).

President Kennedy made a significant speech on race in June 1963, and the civil rights movement was invigorated. Sadly, the movement was also propelled by the murder of Medgar Evers in Mississippi the same month. Ripon reached out to many of the civil rights advocates and organizers and to Republican members of Congress whose support would prove absolutely crucial for the legislative victories of 1964 and 1965 on public accommodations and on voting rights.

Early in winter 1963, we met on a snowy night with John Chafee. He had, in November 1962, been elected governor of neighboring Rhode Island. He was young, intelligent, and thoughtful and in such an overwhelmingly Democratic state that he needed to appeal beyond a narrow Republican base, and he did so.

The single most important connection made in these early days was with a prior generation's leaders on the financial side of the Republican Party. John Hay Whitney was the grandson, born in 1904, of John Milton Hay, who had been Lincoln's private secretary and then secretary of state under McKinley and Theodore Roosevelt. Hay lived long enough to see his grandson and namesake. On his paternal side, Whitney was the grandson of William Collins Whitney, who served President Grover Cleveland as secretary of war. An outsized creature of his class and his time, William Collins Whitney and his wife, Flora, were fixtures in the highest reaches of conspicuous consumers. While he was secretary of war, his wife entertained more than sixty thousand guests in four years, with such flows of champagne that a branch of

Ripon Society members with Governor John Chafee, summer 1967. *Front row, left to right*: Josiah Lee Auspitz, Thomas E. Petri, Governor Chafee, John Roy Price, Robert Behn. *Back row, left to right*: Bruce K. Chapman, Michael Chabot Smith, George D. Brown, Steven Minikes, David R. Young. John Roy Price personal collection.

the Women's Christian Temperance Union passed a resolution condemning her.[15] John Hay, or "Jock," Whitney was a more modest and circumspect figure, enjoying his extraordinary affluence and its accompanying influence. Whitney was a man of serious intent, fully conscious of the achievements of his ancestors and anxious to have an impact on his time.

He was not an especially partisan figure, or at least not one imprisoned in a set of dogmatic beliefs. On September 19, 1936, just before the election, in a famous *New Yorker* cartoon that caricatured the super wealthy, one group of tiara and fur-clad women and their formally dressed husbands urge others, standing above them on a balcony of a palatial home, to "Come along. We're going to the Trans-Lux to hiss Roosevelt!" Whitney was comfortable with Roosevelt. He was later to marry Betsey Cushing Roosevelt, who had been the wife of James, the eldest of FDR's sons. His biographer says, "Whitney then seemed to many of his friends to be politically ambivalent. One said of him that he would regularly go to bed a Democrat—indeed, after a few drinks and some debate, almost a socialist—but would always wake up a Republican."[16]

Starting in the 1952 Eisenhower campaign, Whitney became a singularly important figure for the Republican Party. Helped by William A. M. Burden, a balding, Cuban cigar–smoking tycoon who was one of the Vanderbilt heirs, Whitney served as chair of the Finance Committee for Ike's campaign. They were rewarded, respectively, with the ambassadorships to the Court of St. James (always most coveted of the patronage ambassadorships) and to Belgium. Walter N. Thayer first appeared on the scene with them in 1952, as counsel to the Citizens for Eisenhower effort that Whitney was steering. Thayer deeply impressed Whitney with his intelligence, focus, and organizational skill. Consequently, Thayer joined the Whitney publishing empire in 1955, coming to work at 630 Fifth Avenue, where both William Burden's office and the Whitcom, or Whitney Communications, offices were housed.

With those skills, Whitney asked Thayer to be part of both of Whitney's worlds: publishing and politics. They were mutually reinforcing, and Thayer's role running the *New York Herald Tribune* for Whitney extended his reach in Republican circles and well beyond. With Whitney's connections, money, and interest, Thayer became a figure of great importance. I characterized Thayer as the secretary general of the Eastern Republican Establishment. William O'Shaughnessy, CEO of Whitney Global Media, describes Thayer as "a mandarin of the Liberal Republican–Rockefeller Eastern Establishment." But Thayer's clout was recognized by other party activists beyond Eastern Establishmentarians: "Richard Nixon called Walter 'the toughest SOB in this country . . . and one of the brightest.'"[17]

Whitney had inherited and expanded a vast fortune, left to him by his father, Payne Whitney, one of the wealthiest men in America. His estate when probated in 1924 was the largest yet in American history. He was not to be outdone until the death over a decade later of John D. Rockefeller. Through the 1930s, Jock had been visible in the horseracing world, and the Whitney Stables' green and white colors were well known and their horses often champions. On the business side, he put energy and leadership into what is now called "venture capital." The venture capital concept initially was limited to a small handful of families—the Rockefellers, the Whitneys, the Rosenwalds, and few others—taking a model from a nineteenth-century figure, Spencer Trask. As Whitney was to buy the *New York Herald Tribune*, generations earlier, Trask bought the *New York Times*. Whitney and Trask were investors in the initial launch of business ideas. They invested in entrepreneurs. Spencer Trask financed Thomas Edison as a "start-up" with dazzling results.

With his investments in Edison's electric light company, Trask lit up America's homes and streets. For his part, Whitney lit up the silver screens

Walter N. Thayer and John Hay Whitney. Courtesy Yale University.

all over America. Whitney became a film producer, serving as chairman of Darryl F. Zanuck's mighty Hollywood production machine. Whitney most notably succeeded with *Gone with the Wind*, as executive producer, certainly one of the films of paramount importance from the 1930s, if not of all time. Other less glamourous but profitable investments of Whitney's included the frozen foods brands, Minute Man and Birds' Eye.

By the time we became close to him, Whitney's enterprises had bifurcated. J. H. Whitney & Co. was the investment holdings entity, whose chief executive was Benno Schmidt, later on the board of the Bedford-Stuyvesant Development Corporation, where I went upon abandoning the practice of law. The other was Whitney Communications, or Whitcom, which included the *Herald Tribune*, *Retirement Living*, *Oil Daily*, the *Booth Newspapers* in Michigan, and a string of "Delmarva" (Delaware, Maryland, Virginia) area weeklies. It was in 1958, subsequent to his ambassadorship in London, that Whitney bought the *New York Herald Tribune* from the very Republican family of Whitelaw Reid. Thayer and Whitney were joined at the hip in this venture, as Thayer became the *Trib*'s president. Thayer was a central figure, not just as president of the *Herald Tribune* but also as Whitney's key companion in dealing with Republican Party and political issues.

Whitney was of particular interest to me, since for us youngsters (and our parents) growing up in Manhasset, he was the "Lord of the Manor." One of his homes, on a magnificent 435-acre estate bordering Northern Boulevard (NY Route 25A) and Shelter Rock Road, was the grandest of the Manhasset estates. Greentree, as it was called, was bordered to the south by the estate of Whitney's sister, Joan Payson, later the owner of the New York Mets. Abutting them was the spread of William S. Paley, the redoubtable head of Columbia Broadcasting System (CBS) and brother-in-law of Whitney, having married Barbara "Babe" Cushing, sister of Jock's wife, Betsey Cushing Roosevelt.

When I got to know him, Whitney was deeply interested in public policy. He was modest but understood well the range of his influence. He wore glasses with clear plastic frames. His complexion was not rubicund but suggested it; he had a slightly pinkish and youthful coloring. He had a mild speech impediment. According to Archibald L. Gillies, former president of the Whitney Foundation, this led him to decide against a career in politics, since he was worried it would impede his path. His efforts lay instead through his impressive influence on players and policy.

Through persistent efforts of Jack Saloma and some of the Republican Advance alumni, Thayer's and Whitney's attention by 1963 fell on our new group of young moderates. Thayer and Whitney always were looking for young, competent people for their many interests. When it came to politics, they were interested in perpetuating the type of Republican Party that had begun to revive since the end of the 1930s, trying to abandon visceral antipathy to every aspect of the New Deal and turning the party away from isolationism. They sought the restoration of the progressive wing that Theodore Roosevelt's ego and energy had largely drained from the party in the Bull Moose defection of 1912, leaving the GOP to the regular Republicans, who were dominant for several decades thereafter. Whitney's vision was of a party that nominated Governor Thomas E. Dewey of New York in 1944 and 1948 and, most importantly, Eisenhower in 1952 and 1956. E. J. Kahn said that he was looking for spokesmen for the Republican Party who were not "close-minded" and who could make their party "fit to rule," a term he favored because John Hay had once used it as the title for a speech he gave. Kahn described the connection between Ripon and Whitney: "Hoping to accelerate the discovery of new blood, Whitney was an early, vigorous, and enduring supporter of the Ripon Society—a group of liberal young Republicans whose aspiration was to have much the same ameliorating influence in Republican circles that the Americans for Democratic Action had among Democrats. From the time the Ripon Society was founded, in 1962, Whitney alone furnished close to half of all its operating funds."[18]

Whitney became comfortable with us after several meetings and after reading some of our early efforts at policy development. He determined to support us as he would one of his businesses in which he had faith. In the same manner that he would broaden the investor group in a fledgling company, he invited close friends to join in his new venture: the Ripon Society.

There ensued evenings at Whitney's town house on East Sixty-Third Street in Manhattan. A handful of us would meet with him on the second floor before the dinner, mounting a spiral staircase on whose winding walls were Matisse and Van Gogh originals. On the fireplace opposite the head of the stairs was Picasso's magnificent "Blue Boy." After strategizing, and as the guests appeared, we would move downstairs to the ground-floor dining room. The guests on these occasions were few but notable: Sidney Weinberg, the senior partner of Goldman, Sachs (when Goldman was still a partnership); Gus Levy, who would succeed Weinberg; John Loeb, Sr., of Loeb, Rhodes; Benno Schmidt of Whitney's venture capital arm, and Walter N. Thayer, of course; William Burden; David Rockefeller, and a small number of others, including William S. Paley, the chairman of CBS. Certainly to provide appropriately excellent food and drink to his peers, and not to please us (although I was rapturous at what was put in front of me), he served splendid courses, accompanied by Bernkasteler Doctor Graben Kabinett, followed by vintage Lafite Rothschild, and in turn, at dessert, Château D'Yquem. After the guests had departed, Whitney would take us back upstairs to collapse into easy chairs while he sipped his scotch and we did a postprandial analysis of whether we might be successful at broadening our support. Raising and then lowering his thumb back and forth, he would ask us, "Bull or Bear?" His arm-twisting was highly effective, and the financial base for Ripon was put in place.

The connections and basic cohesion of the leaders of the business, financial, and media communities in New York at this time were strong. This meant that they were at ease with one another; their views were not widely at variance. In turn, exercising power came naturally to them. At the time, there was no other place in the country in which the power to influence public opinion was so concentrated. Paley's presence at the Whitney dinners was not only because of his brother-in-law link to Jock. Whitney's world was in media, too, broadcasting and print. The leaders of the television and the newspaper and newsmagazine worlds were well acquainted, competing directly for readership and viewership. As Richard Nixon had analyzed things in 1960 and concluded that the election was to be won in the center, the media focus of these days was at the center and the broadest point of reach in demographics. While they were fighting for the same audiences (and advertisers), a social bond existed among these often pioneering and influential figures. These ties went beyond the fact of geographic concentration of power in Manhattan. They knew that they were opinion leaders and prized that. First radio and now television had emerged as a formidable influence in the public forum. Its leaders were visible and important.

Paley was nearly a generation younger than David Sarnoff, the intense and intelligent figure who had created the National Broadcasting Company. Paley outdid him. Paley became by instinct, drive, and luck the person who put together a strategy of advertising sales and programming that made CBS the most potent force in the television world. Its news bureaus attracted star broadcasters, and Paley backed them, viewing CBS News as his crown jewel. He aspired to a high level of cultural programming but also was quick to find and recruit shows for mass audiences, which held up his ratings and advertising revenues.

Jock Whitney made an interesting assessment one night of the influence of television on opinion. We were in William Paley's opulent and sprawling Manhattan apartment. Whitney, Thayer, Paley, Lee Huebner, and I were watching the Wisconsin primary returns of winter 1968 on Paley's large living room television screen. As the obvious impact of Vietnam dissent spoke through the returns, Whitney turned to us and noted that television had been singlehandedly responsible for the breadth and intensity of the protest. Never before in an American war, he said, had the reality and the horror of war intruded so into American consciousness. Print media and correspondents' filings were often probing, but the camera's eye, in real time, capturing often horrific ongoing events, brought war home intensely. In Whitney's view, American politics would be changed forever.

On February 25, just weeks earlier, I had spent an hour and a half with Whitney at Greentree. He had expressed to me on that visit his depression about the Vietnam War and said, "No public has ever been asked to look at the sort of thing we must every evening." Ordinarily not a television viewer, while in Georgia the week before, in the absence of good newspaper coverage, he watched frequently and was appalled.[19]

Paley understood this. He knew the effect of his medium was extraordinary. His level of personal attention to the stations was legendary, not only in advertising statistics but also in the carriage and presentation of the news. As he was forceful in road testing and eliminating possible successors to himself over the years, so, too, would he be merciless about cutting someone out who was underperforming on the air. Tim Petri recalls watching one of his CBS news broadcasts with Paley when Paley mused that the anchorperson was not performing as he formerly had. Within days he was gone.

John Hay Whitney and Walter N. Thayer with new Sunday Edition of *New York Herald Tribune*. Ike on cover. Courtesy Yale University.

Petri also told of an event that demonstrates the close links between the figures of this world, despite competition between their organizations. He was watching an evening news show, "Huntley-Brinkley," on NBC television. The outspoken and right-wing California state superintendent of public instruction, Max Rafferty, made a comment that was carried on the newscast that the Ripon Society was a "Communist Front Organization." While charges like this were common coming from John Birchers about people like Dwight Eisenhower, this was from a statewide Republican official, and Tim took it personally. He called Walter Thayer immediately, noting that Huntley-Brinkley had not challenged the statement about Ripon. Petri said that he thought Thayer should know that he was raising money for a communist front organization. Thayer said he knew the head of NBC News and would call him. At the end of the next three- or four-minute commercial break, Huntley came on the air and opened with a statement that NBC did not in any way countenance the charge made moments earlier by Rafferty about Ripon and that it was insupportable.

I had breakfast with Lee Huebner in spring 2017, when he headed the George Washington University School of Media and Public Affairs. On that sun-filled Washington morning as Lee looked over my shoulder from our table at the Hay Adams to Lafayette Square and the White House beyond, he reflected on the media world in the 1960s. It was, he said, in terms of the more common rivalries and conflicts of journalists and their outlets, a "golden age." There were just the three networks and the dominant print media. The splintering and isolating of views and, more crucially, of news carriage itself had not yet begun (although even the *National Review* and the *Ripon Forum* certainly were, in their way, publications and news sources with particular viewpoints). In the same vein, earlier, Tim Petri noted that the three networks were all headquartered in and around Rockefeller Center and that there were just about eleven or twelve key people in the news world at those networks, in management positions, all of whom knew one another well, as illustrated by his anecdote about Huntley and the Rafferty charge.

The importance to Ripon of support from Whitney and Paley cannot be overemphasized. We were provided megaphones in the television world and reach in the print media, through the *Tribune*, its syndicated columnists and, indeed, its competitors taking note of stories about us. On our own merits and because what we were saying was important—newsworthy—but also with the enormous lift from these sympathetic sponsors, Ripon began more and more to be in the media, with consequent, occasionally disproportionate, influence.

CHAPTER 3

Partisan Strife, San Francisco's 1964
Convention, and Electoral Calamity

In 1963, Nixon moved to New York and became name partner in the law firm of Nixon, Mudge, Rose, Guthrie, and Alexander. Tim Petri sent a letter to the former vice president. He spoke of the newly formed Ripon Society and emphasized its roots in the academic community, reasoning that Nixon would be lacking in resources for his continued policy interests.

Petri asked for an appointment, thinking the former vice president might be receptive to Ripon doing some research for him. His instinct was sound. This was not just because Nixon had no staff at the moment but also because of Nixon's interest in hearing from all points of the compass. Patrick Buchanan, who soon was to join Nixon as his only policy and political aide at the law firm, rather reluctantly writes in *The Greatest Comeback* that Nixon "ideologically . . . was . . . an eclectic."[1] Nixon acceded and Tim Petri and Lee Huebner met with the former vice president.

Nixon and the Ripon Society were both now dealing with a party in flux. By 1963, Barry Goldwater had become a visible and charming conservative counterpoint to New York's Governor Nelson Rockefeller. The Arizona senator was well into his drive to control the Republican Party. After his speech to the 1960 Convention urging conservatives to "take back" their party, Goldwater was their chosen instrument to do so. After four years, the convention goers bore no resemblance to the delegates who had nominated Eisenhower for two campaigns and had chosen Nixon in 1960. Jock Whitney, who knew thousands throughout the party, remarked to me after the 1964 convention that he would step into the elevators in the convention hotels and recognize—no one.

True, there were a number of moderate Republican officeholders, senators among them. Senators do not have patronage that can be used to dominate or lubricate politics, but that was not holding back Barry Goldwater, who used his national platform on the floor of the Senate to build backing. Some of the governors—Nelson Rockefeller of New York, William Warren Scranton of Pennsylvania, and George Romney of Michigan—who held more raw political power than any senator, attracted supporters. However, they did not have national followings. Among the tools in the moderates' kit was no mass membership organization. None of them had the cohesion the conservative movement was achieving. Even in New York State, the Republican Party, despite Rockefeller's financial largesse, was not monolithic, nor could it project its power nationally as it had for Tom Dewey.

On the policy front, there was a slightly different picture. A handful of individuals from the Eisenhower wing of the party attempted to keep it focused on trade, strong defense, education, and civil rights. The former president's brother, Milton Stover Eisenhower, president of Johns Hopkins University, was a leading intellectual figure in the party. Dr. Eisenhower chaired a series of study papers, both during and after Ike's presidency, via the Critical Issues Committee. Its efforts were supported on a part-time basis by Jim Clark, who worked for Walter Thayer, who functioned as a nerve center for the moderate wing of the party. It was related to a big tent group that former president Dwight Eisenhower convened in 1963. Through it, he hoped to perpetuate the party in a moderate vein. Called the Republican Coordinating Committee, it included former presidents Hoover and himself, past nominees for the presidency Dewey and Nixon, a number of members of Congress, and half a dozen governors. This effort was quietly undercut by Congressman William Miller of New York, who was then the Republican National Committee chair. Miller was clandestinely helping Goldwater and later was made the vice presidential nominee on the 1964 Goldwater ticket.

Thayer and Whitney put us in touch with Dr. Eisenhower, to see how we could assist on future publications by his group and reach a new and younger audience. Policy development found footing not only in Buckley's *National Review* and in a Ripon/Milton Eisenhower effort among the moderates but also in the "Republican Papers," a series of essays by different authors on various issues organized by Congressman Melvin Laird, of Wisconsin, a conservative member of the House Republican Caucus.

Meanwhile, the battle for control of the party was shaping up as a struggle between Rockefeller and Goldwater. After two successive defeats, Nixon was not convinced that 1964 was the right time for him to try again, so he hung back and kept in close contact with all factions. As spring 1963 moved into summer, I sought a position in the Rockefeller organization. On his staff that summer, I did some of the original "opposition research" on Senator Goldwater, and Graham Molitor picked it up when I returned to law school. I worked for a young John Deardourff, who was in the midst of moving from issues research into the political side of the governor's staff. That autumn, as I headed back to Cambridge, I was asked by Rockefeller's political chief, George Hinman, Republican National Committeeman from New York, to work on delegate hunting for Rockefeller in southern New Hampshire. As often as I could, I traveled there, meeting with local party leaders and seeking their support for a Rockefeller 1964 effort in their primary. I found that many of them had lingering irritation about having gone out on a limb for Rockefeller in 1960, only to have his effort abruptly shut down. Even the former governor, Hugh Gregg, to whom Hinman first directed me, was cool, but he tried to cooperate while sharing his misgivings with me.

On November 8, 1963, I spent the day campaigning for Rockefeller in the small town of Tilton, New Hampshire, along with Ripon friend Ned Cabot (who would be among the first Ripon Society members to change parties). Returning to Cambridge after a long day, I was soon next to "a weather-beaten old pianist in a bar on Kirkland St., with truckdrivers and myself standing around singing 'Redwing' tonight."[2] In this way, the autumn proceeded, with politics giving me more pleasure than the classroom.

And then Kennedy went to Dallas.

Kennedy Assassination: Ripon Takes a Name

Exactly two weeks later, I was in the parking lot outside of Harkness dining hall at the Harvard Law School with a couple of my canvassing colleagues, loading large photos of Nelson Rockefeller mounted on sticks into the back of a station wagon, to take up to New Hampshire for rallies. Suddenly, Ned Cabot, who walked with crutches, having suffered a childhood onslaught of infantile paralysis, or poliomyelitis, burst out of the dining hall door toward us, moving as fast as he could. He breathlessly announced to us that Kennedy had been shot. Our world turned upside down as we learned it was mortal, and we followed events as Lyndon Johnson was sworn in and returned to Washington with a blood-spattered Jaqueline Kennedy on Air Force One.

For several hours, I strolled with my classmate and friend, John H. Shenefield, all over the Harvard campus, trying to make sense of this senseless moment. Only a year earlier, he and I had walked out of the law library as the Cuban Missile Crisis broke. We then had wondered if our world was going to come to an end. The importance of exams and study for them diminished in urgency. Larger questions about life intruded.

Later that afternoon of Kennedy's assassination, I was in Shenefield's married student apartment, with John and his wife, Anna. Anna's mother, Florence (Mrs. Arthur) Larson, was there for a visit. Florence was a glamorous, animated, rather theatrical woman. She and I were sitting next to each other on a small sofa, and all of a sudden, she threw herself across my lap and began beating her fists on a pillow. "NO! NOT THAT MAN PRESIDENT!" She and her husband Arthur were Washington insiders, given Mr. Larson's service for President Eisenhower. It was he who had authored the book *A Republican Looks at His Party*, which Eisenhower said most reflected his own views, especially the critical need to capture the center of American politics. According to Larson's biographer, David Stebenne, Lyndon Johnson had been

Larson's "chief tormentor" when he was head of the United States Informa-tion Agency.[3] Yet Florence's anger at Johnson tapped into a far more wide-spread apprehension about his ascension.

For the first time, I began to think through the implications of the change from the Kennedy presidency to a Johnson presidency. This was true of all of us who had begun to cohere and work together in the unnamed small Republican policy group. November 22 was followed by a flurry of meet-ings, deliberations, and the drafts of a credo for our group. The discussions endlessly circled back to how we could have a moderate political creed and appeal to the younger age cohort, whom Kennedy seemed effortlessly to have attracted.

We decided to proclaim that there was deep need for policy informed by research and influenced by facts, not simply by ideology. It was this convic-tion that gave me common ground with my later boss and mentor in the White House, Daniel Patrick Moynihan. Moynihan's love of data and its use to underpin policy development or criticism was central to his persona. It was to be on full display in his White House days as Nixon's urban affairs advisor.

In January, we issued the first paper under the Ripon Society name: *A Call to Excellence in Leadership*. After the Kennedy assassination, there was great interest in where the Republican Party might position itself, and the press's attention to the *Call to Excellence* was great and due in no small part to the fact that Whitney and Thayer were increasingly aware of and comfort-able with the group. Whitney's *New York Herald Tribune* was still the voice or house organ of the Eastern Establishment part of the Republican universe. The *Tribune* trumpeted the new Ripon Society, and there followed a whirl-wind of press attention picking up on this new moderate Republican group.

On the politics front, our efforts in New Hampshire redoubled. In addition to operating canvassing teams for Rockefeller, I organized "Truth Squads." These were dispatched, frankly, to hector and badger Senator Goldwater, confronting him with some of the positions he had taken in the past few years, all certain to meet with hostility in the town halls of New Hampshire. In a burst of anger in one town hall meeting, he yelled out at us, "That's the same question you asked me yesterday!" In the event, on Primary Day, Rock-efeller was the victim of a lack of enthusiasm, and Goldwater was hobbled by his positions that were unpopular there. Henry Cabot Lodge triumphed. Lodge was the Massachusetts patrician running mate of Nixon in the 1960 campaign. He was a geographic favorite; a known name and pedigree. He conducted the campaign, such as it was, from Saigon, where he was the US ambassador. No state other than New Hampshire went to Lodge.

Rockefeller's people might have been well advised to respond to an offer for help early in the New Hampshire primary struggle. On April 14, 1964, just a month after Lodge's victory, George Cabot Lodge, the son of Ambassador Lodge and then a teacher at the Harvard Business School, told me that he had offered his help for the governor's campaign in December 1963 to Rod Perkins, who was overseeing domestic policy for Rockefeller, but that there had been no follow up. "Think of the trouble I could have saved them!" In San Francisco, following a drink with Milton Eisenhower, Doug Bailey and I rode the bus together to the Cow Palace. Doug said that George Lodge had no political future because he was too soft and friendly. George had sat in on encounters that Henry Cabot Lodge had had with vacillating Massachusetts delegates at an earlier convention. George told Bailey that his father was "a very tough man." George later was a sacrificial lamb for the United States Senate against Edward M. "Ted" Kennedy, youngest brother of the sitting president. At the time of his election, November 1962, Ted Kennedy was not yet of age to take his seat in the Senate under the Constitution, but he had the halo's light of the Kennedy name. As his brother Jack had beaten Henry Cabot Lodge for the Senate in 1952, so did the kid brother Edward defeat Lodge's son for the Senate a decade later. Lodge was thoughtful, provocative, gentlemanly, and idealistic. I wrote that night that I wished that "the Republican Party could be molded more in his image. Perhaps he was a metaphor for the unlikelihood of success of Ripon's ideals and hopes about the center and the moderates." Certainly this was true in 1964, but, sadly, it remained true over the coming decades.

As the 1964 primary and state convention season was drawing to a close, there was intense national focus on the issue of civil rights. The Republican Party in the Senate and the House of Representatives in the 1960s was still dominated by midwestern and Northern members. They were the inheritors of a tradition reflecting the alignments in the American Civil War, the abolition movement and Reconstruction. The Republican Party had for decades held the allegiance of African Americans. Of central importance was an Ohioan who was the Ranking Member of the House Judiciary Committee, Republican William M. McCullough. He epitomized the constructive— indeed crucial—role of the Republican Party as the civil rights movement came to national attention. Lyndon Johnson, once he became president, emerged as a leader in the battle. One often mentioned story is of Johnson discussing with his staff his desire to push for the civil rights bill that Kennedy had been unable to get through Congress. Johnson's staff urged caution, citing the resistance. Johnson retorted, "What's the presidency for?"

This was a parallel in some ways to how Richard Nixon was to break free of the programmatic and ideological constraints of his party on many issues when he finally held the presidency. Johnson moved away from his decades-long cultivation and enjoyment of support from the Southern and segregationist Senate and House Democratic leadership. Nixon was even more of a coiled spring, as we shall see.

LBJ directed his vice president, Hubert Humphrey, to work on the Republican Senate leader, Senator Everett McKinley Dirksen of Illinois, to help bring cloture against what became the longest filibuster in Senate history. Johnson knew the cloture attempt and civil rights bill passage would not succeed without the Republicans. The Republican Whip, Senator Thomas Kuchel of California, met daily with Humphrey, religious and civil rights leaders, and staff of Robert F. Kennedy, the holdover attorney general, to work on votes against the filibuster led by Richard Russell, a Democrat of Georgia. Russell was the preeminent leader of Southern resistance and Lyndon Johnson's greatest earlier patron and booster in his Senate career.

Johnson was right. Republicans were the critical factor in the bill being passed. Cloture broke Russell's resistance on June 10. Only forty Democratic senators voted for cloture and twenty-eight Democrats voted to kill it. On the Republican side, Dirksen delivered twenty-seven Republican senators. With the Republicans, there were exactly enough votes for cloture. Senator Goldwater was joined by only five other Republicans in opposing cloture. Republicans voted by 5 to 1 in the Senate for civil rights while Democrats voted less than 2 to 1 for it. The House vote showed equally strong Republican support for the civil rights legislation. Republican Senate leader Dirksen could anticipate what was going to happen in the 1964 election. Southern and segregationist Sen. Eugene Talmadge, with a sinking feeling, concluded Dirksen wasn't about to let the Republicans be on the wrong side of history. The man from the "Land of Lincoln" delivered. On the wrong side of history was Barry Goldwater, standing side by side with Strom Thurmond, the Democratic South Carolina senator and segregationist presidential candidate in 1948. Johnson signed the bill on July 2, just eight days before the Republican convention.

For us in Ripon, the Republican Party was now being pulled in precisely the wrong direction, entirely at war with its historical alignment with the rights and protections for which the Civil War was fought, and subsequent constitutional amendments were enacted to ensure. Goldwater's embrace of Strom Thurmond was a bone in our throat. We issued a "Declaration of Conscience" on our national holiday, the Fourth of July, excoriating Senator Goldwater for turning his back on the core founding principle of his party and calling on the party to turn elsewhere for its nominee. We issued it on the steps of the Little White Schoolhouse in Ripon, Wisconsin. In 1854, this very schoolhouse was the scene of the first efforts to form a party opposed to any further extension of slavery—the Republican Party.

The putative Republican presidential nominee, Senator Goldwater, had just voted against the 1964 Civil Rights Act. After Dirksen delivered his twenty-seven Republicans to hit the necessary vote for cloture, he literally thumbed his nose at Goldwater on the floor of the Senate, underlining how out of step with his party's principles and his Senate and House colleagues Goldwater was. The Ripon statement on Independence Day made that point but also cried alarm about the effect on the party that a Goldwater nomination would have in the fall: a presidential defeat of potentially historic proportions whose carnage would cascade down ballot, from Congress, to the Senate, and through statehouses to the local level.

A stunning victory had been won by Nelson Rockefeller in the Oregon primary just weeks before, engineered by John Deardourff and Bob Price, a brilliant operative who was working at the time for Congressman John V. Lindsay of Manhattan in New York. In March 1964, Lindsay had reluctantly loaned Price, who had masterminded all Lindsay's congressional campaigns in New York's "Silk Stocking" district on the East Side of Manhattan, to Governor Rockefeller after Rockefeller's embarrassing third-place finish in the New Hampshire primary. Geoffrey Kabaservice, who worked on a never-published memoir with Price, told me, "Lindsay refused to allow Price to go on to manage Rockefeller's California primary in June. . . . Rockefeller blamed Price and Lindsay for his loss, shouting at Price in San Francisco, 'If you had listened to me, we would have won California and I would be the nominee. This disaster is all your fault!' This was the beginning of the Rockefeller-Lindsay feud that intensified when Lindsay became New York mayor the following year."[4]

San Francisco in July 1964 played host to the Republican National Convention. The California primary election in early June saw the Goldwater victory over Nelson Rockefeller. This winner-take-all triumph at the end of the primary season provided near assurance that the Arizona senator would be the party's nominee. The governor campaigned as an electable Republican who in his statewide runs had handily persuaded independents and, as he repeatedly put it, "discerning Democrats" to vote for him. His strategy was to convince party voters that a centrist, inclusive approach was the only winning one.

The party was having none of it that year. The type of Democrat to which an appeal was now being made was the Southerner who was trying to cling to a social and political order that was under assault. Rockefeller in 1964 was pitted as a Northeastern liberal against a Southwesterner who had begun his career in politics without much of a worldview. Goldwater and his brother, both in the family retailing business in Arizona, had years earlier decided that it would be sensible for business if each of them belonged to a different political party. Accordingly, a coin was flipped, and Barry Morris Goldwater became a Republican and his brother a Democrat. The legend does not record who had won the toss.

Once in the Senate, Goldwater began to stand out. This was partly owing to his undeniable personal warmth but also because the conservative wing of the party was lacking younger leadership after Taft's death in 1953. Goldwater's geography was also a plus. Population had begun to shift toward the Sun Belt, with a steady increase in congressional seats after each decennial census apportioned to the South and Southwest. After the 1930 census, for example, Arizona had one congressional seat, and after the 1960 census, it had three. In Florida, the count went from six to twelve, and in Texas, from twenty-one to twenty-four. This shift of course affected Electoral College votes as well.

"John, They've Got the Place Locked Up"

Leaving the schoolhouse in Ripon, Wisconsin, after Ripon's broadside for civil rights and against Goldwater, I arrived in San Francisco the week of the meetings of the Convention's Platform committee, Credentials committee, and others. I rode in from the airport with a fellow attorney from the law firm where I was then a summer intern. Jack McGrath had often taken leave from his law firm—as John Ehrlichman did for Nixon's campaigns—to "advance" Rockefeller's campaigns. This was the task of locating venues for events, promoting them, turning out partisan crowds for their candidate, putting some color and animation into the surroundings, finding good visual backdrops for photos or interviews, and the like. In Rockefeller's case, the advance man's task included ensuring that a glass of Dubonnet and a cigar would be on the governor's night table beside his hotel room bed in whatever town, large or small, the governor wound up at day's end.

As we came off the freeway ramp into downtown San Francisco, the hardened and experienced McGrath expressed admiration at the degree to which the Goldwater forces had covered the city with billboards, posters, parades, mini rallies, attractive young people—"Goldwater Girls" on every street corner with Goldwater paraphernalia—and other ways to show momentum and excitement. He marveled at the organizational strength that effort demonstrated. He said, shaking his head with wonder, "John, they've got the place locked up."

The smoothly functioning Goldwater effort dominated not just the advance work. Their delegate operation had been deeply successful, despite polls of the broader public showing that Goldwater was not favored, even among Republicans. A nationwide poll of Republican voters two weeks before the convention showed Governor William Scranton of Pennsylvania leading Goldwater with 54 percent of the vote.

Coming out of a surprise victory just weeks earlier in Oregon, Governor

Rockefeller showed a thirteen-point lead over Goldwater in the polls in California. Rockefeller had mounted an aggressive negative advertising campaign about Goldwater's danger to the country. "Who do you want in the room thinking about the use of an H Bomb?" Rockefeller asked rhetorically. But Goldwater not only had an organizational grip on the delegate population but also luck.

Only three days before the California polling on June 3, Happy Rockefeller gave birth to their child. Nelson flew home to New York, and Goldwater immediately unleashed a tough—indeed, lethal—campaign impugning Rockefeller's morals and family life and contrasting them with his own. The birth of Nelson Jr. and the caustic Goldwater ads brought the senator from behind to a three-point margin of victory in California. The memories of the scandal of Nelson and Happy breaking up two families in order to marry each other were revived, and Rockefeller's chances collapsed.

The prolonged delegate selection process had already resulted in a preponderance of Goldwater supporters, some early and fervent, others party regulars who saw him as the imminent nominee and were falling in line. These delegates had been selected from across the country, some in primaries but more often at state party conventions that were worked well, often using very hard-ball tactics.

In spring 1964, Richard Nixon came to Johns Hopkins University to give a speech and met before that with Dr. Milton Eisenhower at Eisenhower's home. Nixon said the Goldwaterites had been working diligently to build a wave of support from the ground up. In Nixon's view, Goldwater "would not be a good President. He has to be stopped."[5] Nixon went on to say that "whoever tries [to stop Goldwater] may himself be committing political suicide." Nixon throughout the rest of the spring was doubtless torn between these two convictions. He wanted Goldwater barred from the party's nomination but was not ready to commit intraparty hara-kiri. His reactions at succeeding events showed his frustration and his ambivalence.

The Scranton Effort

After the Rockefeller defeat in California, things moved quickly but disjointedly. Governor William Warren Scranton of Pennsylvania was from the eponymous town in northeastern Pennsylvania that Joe Biden has recently again made famous, had served in the US House of Representatives, and had been elected governor in 1962. He came from a long line of establishment Republicans. His mother had served as national committeewoman from Pennsylvania for twenty years. He was a steady, moderate governor who had a completely nonpatronizing manner; indeed, he was self-deprecating. He had considerable natural warmth. He was thoughtful and had surrounded himself with good staff, such as James Reichley, a policy and political aide who served as his legislative secretary.

Scranton had from his first moments in the Congress after his 1960 election found himself aligned with the Republican reformers, and he joined many of their causes. One of the most significant was the expansion of the membership of the House Rules Committee over the vehement opposition of its Southern and segregationist Democratic chair, Virginian Howard "Judge" Smith. Smith, while aligned with other Southerners favoring New Deal programs such as Social Security and the Agricultural Adjustment Act, was the leader of a conservative coalition in the House that often aligned with Republican opponents of many other aspects of the New Deal. These entanglements of Southern Democrats and Republican revanchists continued the alliance that many Republican congressional conservatives enjoyed in the 1940s and into the 1950s. After successful efforts to outnumber Smith on the Rules Committee by adding new members, moderates and liberals of both parties secured the ability to bring crucial civil rights legislation to the House floor. Around the Pennsylvania governor, the remnants of the Goldwater resistors rallied—albeit at the last minute, with no organizational ground laid. After Rockefeller struck his tent, Goldwater looked to be unopposed. Scranton considered it but realized it was a virtual impossibility and announced that he would not be a candidate.

Yet, between the California primary and the convention, the civil rights bill had been passed. Goldwater's challenge to Republican Senate leader Everett Dirksen on the civil rights cloture vote had a galvanizing effect on Scranton. He phoned Dr. Eisenhower, with whom he was close owing to shared moderate politics and the Gettysburg, Pennsylvania, connection with General Eisenhower, who had retired to his farm adjoining the historic battlefield. Scranton told him he was going to run. In the same conversation, he told Dr. Eisenhower that Nixon had phoned Maryland US senator "Mac" Mathias from London to ask him to set up a breakfast meeting in Washington the next week. "I think he is going to announce his candidacy for the nomination," Scranton said.

Only two days after the Senate civil rights vote, Scranton declared his candidacy as he appeared at the Maryland State Republican convention. Scranton feared the effect on the party at the state and local levels and was concerned with the recklessness of Goldwater's thinking about the conduct of foreign affairs. In those days of slower communications, Nixon, returning that day from the United Kingdom, was unaware of Scranton's turnaround. When the press queried Nixon as he stepped off his plane, he replied with pique. He said that a man who could not make up his mind whether to run would not make a very decisive president.

But Nixon was not finished. Late at night, he phoned Milton Eisenhower. Nixon said he was going the next morning to Gettysburg to discuss the problem with the former president, as he thought a public statement from the general was a recourse that might change things. Adding to that, Nixon speculated to Milton Eisenhower that if George Romney were to declare as a candidate, then the three—Romney, Rockefeller, and Scranton—might gain enough votes to deadlock the convention. "I felt he had in mind the probability that in the event of a deadlock the convention might again turn to him," Eisenhower recalled.[6]

In the meantime, Scranton plunged in and tried to make the most of an almost impossible task. Jim Reichley thinks there was a deeper motivation for Scranton than prospective party losses or unease about Goldwater's potential management of foreign affairs. Scranton ran "in part because he thought there was still some chance of shaking loose Midwestern stalwarts like Dirksen and Rhodes [governor of Ohio]. But also because, as one whose family had been active in the Republican party since the Civil War and who regarded maintaining the traditional values of the party as a kind of trust, he believed it was important that some other banner beside that of the hard right be raised at the San Francisco convention."[7]

Some Ripon Society members, among them cofounder John S. Saloma, went in those waning June weeks to Harrisburg to help on issues and speech-writing. More important, former governor Dewey tried to motivate some of his old organization around the country at the last minute on Scranton's behalf. Dewey had hung back from supporting Rockefeller. After that bizarre lunch at Rockefeller Center with the aspiring Nelson, which ended in Dewey's musing about the New York postmaster job for Rockefeller rather than the gubernatorial nomination, he had no appetite for advancing Rockefeller. Now he threw himself into the fray for Scranton.

But, as Reichley observed, "the structure of the Republican party, and indeed the financial structure of the United States, had changed since the New York establishment had played a major role in bringing off Eisenhower's nomination in 1952. Banks and law firms in the South and West were no longer so responsive to calls from Wall Street, and most of the state and local politicians who at earlier critical moments had aligned themselves with the establishment were retired or dead."[8] This was a shrewd perception of what had become of the once storied ability of the tight-knit, Eastern-dominated Republican apparatus to affect politicians and races across the country.

After a few hours on the phone in his New York law firm office, Dewey rolled his sleeves back down, put on his jacket, and headed for the door, telling his colleagues, "Boys, it's not going to work. I'm going home." "Dewey was right," says Reichley. In June, there were few levers left for the moderates to pull, as the delegate selection process was complete. The Rockefeller and Scranton forces decided there was the lingering possibility that nominally pro-Goldwater delegates might be swung to Scranton if a fight on the platform could demonstrate to the waverers or soft supporters the intransigence and frightful zeal that characterized the core of the Goldwater movement. With the tide-turning Eisenhower Fair Play amendment fight of the 1952 convention in mind, the hope was to show that Goldwater's views would repel voters in the middle of American politics and thereby to pull the party back from the precipice.

The Platform "Steering Committee"

Accordingly, a small working group was set up to mount a platform fight, chaired by Pennsylvania senator Hugh Scott. Scott had come to prominence early in his career as a hinge figure, at a young age, in Governor Thomas E. Dewey's clinching the 1948 nomination for the presidency on the third ballot. Requiring three ballots was an almost unheard-of cliffhanger in modern Republican conventions, whose outcomes have typically been decided on the first ballot. Dewey, in recognition of Scott's help, made Scott the chair of the Republican National Committee. Scott energetically maintained over the years many key contacts he had made in that national campaign.

Scott had been quick to sound the alarm about the Far Right takeover of the party in the early 1960s. George Gilder and Bruce Chapman noted that "more than anyone else Scott grasped the realities of intraparty politics and was willing to risk his prestige to advance the progressive cause. . . . [He] was willing to go to the ends of the continent to raise money for moderate projects and candidates."[9] In 1962, he focused on electing Scranton governor of Pennsylvania and immediately began an unsuccessful effort to persuade Scranton to pursue the 1964 presidential nomination.

In San Francisco, Scott convened a small group of moderates that included Congressman Silvio Conte, of Western Massachusetts; Bayard Ewing, the National Committeeman from Rhode Island; Ted Stevens of Alaska, later an influential and less moderate US senator; Congressman Peter Frelinghuysen, of New Jersey, whose ancestry had included four New Jersey US senators; and others. The group was called the "Steering Committee."

Rockefeller dispatched to the group his former counsel, and now an outside policy advisor, Roswell ("Rod") Perkins. Rockefeller had met Perkins when Rockefeller served as the undersecretary of the then newly combined Department of Health, Education and Welfare, created by Eisenhower, and where Perkins was a very young and highly competent assistant secretary. Perkins asked me to come to San Francisco to help him.

I was not the only young lawyer coming to the convention from my small

New York law firm of Casey, Lane and Mittendorf. Richard Nixon may have been eclectic, but so was my law firm. There was Rockefeller's long-standing advance man Jack McGrath. And there was Bob Schuchman, an associate at the firm and key to the creation of Young Americans for Freedom. Schuchman would be a Goldwater operative in San Francisco, along with Clifton White, Dean Burch of Arizona, who was made Republican National Committee Chair by Goldwater, and William Rusher.

The Scott group met daily—and into the evening, if the Platform Committee was in drafting mode. With the anticipated calamitous effect of a Goldwater candidacy on Republican chances at the state and local levels, our group hoped to peel away some of his more hesitant, and practical, supporters. We decided that three battles enacted on platform planks held the most promise for this strategy.

The first was a plank condemning extremism. What made this an issue with which the convention must be confronted were Goldwater's often incendiary, if offhand, remarks; the long drumbeat and accusation by the John Birch Society that Eisenhower was a willing communist tool; and the conduct of the California primary just weeks earlier.

Second was a plank meant to illustrate Goldwater's recklessness. This addressed the issue of nuclear weapons and war with which Lyndon Johnson that fall mercilessly destroyed the Goldwater bid. Goldwater advocated that local field commanders be given authority to decide about the use of these weapons. This seemed extreme, despite the fact the rules of delegation under Eisenhower were much looser than officially acknowledged. Combined with his quips about turning the water off to Cuba from the US Guantanamo base on the island, the tactical nuclear control issue made Goldwater vulnerable to charges of shooting from the hip. The proposed plank would underline the need to have a disciplined, steady hand on American foreign policy—and on the bomb.

The third plank was a very forceful pro–civil rights statement. Like the Ripon Society statement in Ripon, Wisconsin, days earlier, it was explicit in saying that the party could not go down a path so contrary to its origins, long-agreed principles, and commitments.

The Steering Committee, once the issue had been selected for its political effect on the convention floor through the rallying of any waverers, settled on language to be offered in the Platform Committee. A member of the Steering Committee who was also on the Platform Committee would carry the fight there.

As our work began, I would trot behind Rod Perkins. He was taller by several inches than I, so I could not see from that angle the thinning hair on top of his head as we jogged from breakfast at our lodgings in the Palace to the St. Francis Hotel, where the Scott Committee met and that served as the convention headquarters hotel. Our group convened in a hotel room a couple of floors from where Richard Nixon and his assortment of aides were ensconced. Perkins loped those blocks every time we went back and forth. In fit condition with a steel trap mind, he was a strong Rockefeller presence in the often frustrated and discouraged Scott group. He consulted with Rockefeller, who agreed to seek time to address the convention on the extremism plank, since the governor was still feeling the sting of the California defeat and was incensed at the tactics the opposition had employed.

Scott's attention then turned to the nuclear weapons plank. Congressman Peter Frelinghuysen was the only member of our small group who both had a seat on the Platform Committee and served on the Armed Services Committee in the House. So, he carried the spear on this issue. As debate in the Platform Committee dragged on, Frelinghuysen would send out increasingly desperate, small handwritten notes to us, asking for more arguments to make or testimonials to adduce. Perkins turned to Henry Kissinger, who was at the convention with us on the Rockefeller staff. Henry drafted points favoring the plank, and they were given to the congressman. Then Kissinger lit on the idea of reaching out to a couple of Eisenhower's Secretaries of Defense, Thomas Gates and Neil McElroy, in hopes of getting their support for our position. He got Gates quickly to agree to language, and we fed it to Frelinghuysen. Not long after, the congressman plaintively asked for more ammunition, saying his quotation of the Gates testimonial had grown threadbare with repetition.

The predictable outcome occurred. The three moderate proposed planks were crushed. The only true test vote of the three was the extremism plank offered by Senator Scott to the full convention and supported in his convention appearance by Nelson Rockefeller. It went down to defeat by a vote of 874 to 409, thus demonstrating convincingly Jack McGrath's chastened comment to me, "They have the place locked up."

During a quiet moment in the convention, I had occasion to phone Governor Rockefeller about a logistical detail. He was at this point out of the fray. He was in his room and in a reflective mood and in no hurry to hang up. To me, our conversation felt poignant. He told me, "John, the best people I have ever met in my life I have met through politics. And the worst people I have met in my life, I also met through politics."

Eisenhower Deployed, Rockefeller Entreaty

Despite being outgunned, there was one more cannon of large caliber that the moderates sought to fire: former president Dwight D. Eisenhower. Just as Nixon had thought to enlist Ike to oppose Goldwater in the final days, so, too, did the Scranton forces and the people close to the general from involvement in his 1952 and 1956 campaigns. Eisenhower and Walter Thayer spoke by phone on June 4, the day after the California primary. Eisenhower was irate that Goldwater had not criticized some of his partisans, who were attacking Eisenhower. "He burns me up," the general told Thayer and suggested that they concentrate efforts on electing Republican governors and members of Congress. Thayer disagreed and said to Eisenhower that the presidential nomination was the most immediate problem.[10] Scranton, Rockefeller, Thayer, and Whitney prevailed on the former president to speak to the convention. They hoped he would take a firm stand in public against the more zealous Goldwater supporters and turn the Goldwater tide. Their hopes were disappointed.

On the day the platform—and amendments—were being considered, Eisenhower spoke to the convention, calling on it to reject any form of extremism, either from the Left or from the Right. However, diluting the effect of that call to arms, he seemed then to vacillate and straddle. The Ripon account in *From Disaster to Distinction* captures the moment:

> His commendation of Republican senators and congressmen who had worked hard to pass the civil rights bill was greeted with an embarrassing silence that only a few delegations tried vainly to fill with applause. But when he attacked "sensation-seeking columnists and commentators" a bored convention roared to life and the General looked like a lion-tamer who had lost his chair and whip. Delegates stood, shook their fists at the press booths, and cursed reporters or cameramen on the floor.[11]

His lack of a clarion call against these elements of the Goldwater movement was a definitive setback for his fellow Pennsylvanian, Governor Scranton, whose quest now was quixotic. Already the Scranton forces had been defeated on a credentials battle when they sought unsuccessfully to seat an African American delegate from Tennessee.

Only two hours after Eisenhower, Governor Rockefeller took the podium as the proponent of the resolution from Senator Hugh Scott condemning extremism—the one that had not cleared the hurdle into the platform. Rockefeller was at first welcomed with sustained cheering only from the New York, New Jersey, Pennsylvania, and several New England delegations. The cheering soon became drowned in jeers and catcalls, a crescendo of animus and hatred, as he launched into his statement.

I was standing directly below the governor at the base of the podium, which towered over the convention floor. Immediately in front of me was the front row of the California delegation, just won by Goldwaterites and led by William F. Knowland, a former US senator and briefly majority leader as Taft's successor during the two years after Ike's 1952 victory when the Republicans held the Senate. That legacy fit him like a glove. He thought Eisenhower was far too moderate. Rockefeller was beyond the pale.

Knowland and his fellow delegates were dressed Western: cowboy hats, gold-colored vests, and boots. Fresh from their victory over Rockefeller, and right below him, they started to give full-throated cries of anger as he began to condemn extremism. Rockefeller said that there was no place in the Republican Party, long a liberal home for rights and opportunity, for extremists. He called on the platform to repudiate communists, the Ku Klux Klan, and the "Birchers," commingling the three. He said that exactly a year earlier, on July 14, 1963, he had warned of the risk of subversion by well-financed minorities, wholly alien to the middle course that accommodates the mainstream of this nation. As he was saying these words, there were derisive shouts and Bronx cheers. He continued, "The methods of these extremist elements I have experienced first-hand," from being barred from speaking at a university "to outright threats to my person" and bomb threats to some of his California campaign headquarters.

At this point, the Cow Palace echoed with roars of hatred. The governor told the delegates that ours was "still a free country," and then yelled over the succeeding din, "You may not like to hear it, Ladies and Gentlemen, but it's the truth!" At this statement, the entire first row of the California delegation, not fifteen feet in front of me, stood on their chairs and spat at the governor, though I was more directly in their line of fire. Amid the tumult, the chair of the convention, Senator Thruston Morton, and Congressman Mel Laird, the platform chairman who had introduced Rockefeller, tried to move the governor away from the mikes. The governor refused and was heard to say, "I have five minutes more and I am taking them," planting his compact body in such a way that said to them, "Don't mess with me." He finally vacated the rostrum as the spiteful roars continued.

At that moment, John D. Ehrlichman, later Nixon's counsel and then assistant for domestic affairs in the White House, and Leonard Garment, Nixon's New York law partner and confidant, were sitting in the Nixon box at the Cow Palace as Rockefeller was booed. In his memoir, Ehrlichman described the scene: "[A] huge, fist-shaking William F. Knowland [who was] a U.S. Senator and that night he was the leader of the cowboy suited California delegation. Knowland was down in the front row leading the charge against Nelson Rockefeller as Rockefeller tried to speak to the Convention. Garment and I were deeply troubled when Rockefeller was booed off the platform by Knowland and the Goldwaterites."[12] Ehrlichman notes, "As the 1964 election campaign began to warm up, I watched with detached interest. My sympathies lay with Nelson Rockefeller, William Scranton, and the other Republican moderates who were ineptly trying to derail Barry Goldwater, but I did nothing to try to get involved."[13] This may have been a bit disingenuous. With Nixon still speculating on a deadlock at the convention, as he acknowledged in his phone call to Milton Eisenhower, he had his most trusted campaign colleagues there with him at the Cow Palace.

Nixon may have sidelined himself for the moment. But the hope burned eternal for a man who was incapable of not seeking the presidency. At the convention, Nixon's mode meant that there was no work for the moment for the Ehrlichmans, Haldemans, or Whitakers of the Nixon circle, but they could be immediately mobilized if events took a turn toward a Nixon opportunity. They all were at the 1964 Convention on the lookout for such an opportunity.

The opportunity to grasp a nomination in a deadlocked convention was not on offer to Nixon. Goldwater walked away with the nomination. But Nixon then saw a chance to look past the outcome his instincts must have foreseen for the November results and to emerge on the other side with a greatly enhanced position.

As Ehrlichman observed, in San Francisco, Nixon was the titular leader of the party. As such, he "persuaded Goldwater, William Knowland, and the other convention planners that they should give him a chance to try to heal the divisions in the Republican Party."[14] He was given the chance and he seized it. He introduced Barry Goldwater effusively, as Mr. Republican, and predicted a strong victory in the fall.

Goldwater Acceptance Speech: Olive Branch to Me

Goldwater then proceeded, in his acceptance speech, to jolt the Convention hall to rapture and in the same breath to lose the election. I was standing immediately by Mrs. Peggy Goldwater, wife of the senator, who was listening to her husband from their box at the edge of the floor of the Cow Palace. Goldwater reached the peroration of his acceptance speech. With all the tensions in the air from the platform debate on Birchers, the Klan, and others, Goldwater announced that "extremism in the pursuit of liberty is no vice." It won throaty approval from the bulk of the delegates. Pat Buchanan's father was watching the event on television with Pat at their home a coast apart from San Francisco. When Goldwater spoke this line, Pat's father said, "He's finished!"[15]

It sealed his defeat in the fall. Buchanan was to become Nixon's outreach, his "Tribune" or ambassador to the conservatives and the right wing in the party. He saw Nixon in his address to the convention as positioning himself to soothe its divisions. He understood Nixon was "trying to build a bridge for moderates to cross over and come home." Buchanan, with a sinking feeling about Goldwater's focus on his narrow base for his inflammatory speech, "knew the cause in which I [Buchanan] believed and the movement to which I belonged were headed for a crushing defeat."[16]

Soon after the fateful phrase, Goldwater's speech closed and the rafters of the Cow Palace opened. Thousands of balloons dropped onto ecstatic delegates on the convention floor. The movement had nominated its own. It had thwarted, perhaps slain for good, the liberal establishment, which was in profound apprehension and deep discouragement. Horns brayed, bands played, and people were dancing, hopping, and crying for joy in the aisles.

Not all people. I was exhausted, having been working for two weeks with almost no sleep. I was aghast at what I had seen. Henry Kissinger, a native of the German city of Fürth, in Bavaria in the south of Germany, was deadened with shock, worrying about its echoes of what had driven his family from Germany in 1938. He later came to have warm feelings about Goldwater the man, as did so many, and a friendship with him, but at this convention in 1964, the 1930s Nuremberg rallies were more on his mind, and he told that to us Rockefeller colleagues of his.

As I was slumping near the Goldwater box, an ebullient Bob Schuchman came up to me, glowing with happiness at the outcome and, at the same time, proffering the olive branch to me. He commiserated briefly with me and then said that he and a few of the Goldwater organizers had rented a large cabin up at Lake Tahoe for a few days. He asked if I would like to come and join them to recuperate from the convention stress. All of my exhaustion and my emotions at having observed the Goldwater juggernaut operate over the past year in many settings, with hot-eyed, zealous, and humorless young men and women pushing aside the moderates, welled up and boiled over. The Goldwater acceptance speech had been the last straw. With an uncontrolled reflex I said to him, almost stammering, "Bob, all your right-wing friends suffer from either a physical deformity or an emotional abnormality!" Bob blinked. Then, breaking into a broad ear-to-ear grin, he said, "Yeah, I know exactly what you mean. The Acne and the Ecstasy."[17]

I wilted with laughter in relief and fatigue. I thanked him and begged off because exhaustion. Also, while Bob had reached out to me, I did not know how other senior Goldwater operatives might feel about my inclusion. Sadly, this man of political skill, humanity, and humor was lost to American politics only two years later, when, at age twenty-seven, he suffered a fatal cerebral hemorrhage.

Richard Nixon seized the moment with a sure grasp. He went on from that Cow Palace introduction of Goldwater to campaign tirelessly across the country for Goldwater. He thereby burnished his reputation as a consummate party man. Senator Hugh Scott may well have been right when he told us a few months later that "Richard Nixon is the man with the portable middle." Here, it served him well. The conservative Leviathan overpowered the party. Rockefeller, Romney, Scranton, and others knew what the nomination portended: a rout. They were right. Their reaction was either to refuse to support the ticket or to give it the most tepid acceptance. This hostility, even flight from the ticket, was remembered by the core conservatives.

The liberal Republicans, of whom New York's US senator Kenneth B. Keating was one, faced a Hobson's choice. Either they would endorse the party's presidential nominee, and, in geographies like New York, greatly increase the risk of their defeat, or they would, as Keating did, go further and stride out of the convention in protest.

Nixon of course knew the end of the play in 1964 as well, but he chose to campaign for Goldwater until the final curtain came down. Ronald Reagan, the rising movement star, in the January following the general election debacle, accused those who did not support Goldwater of treachery and unpardonable betrayal. Goldwater was forever after grateful to Nixon for his efforts and angry at the moderate governors and others who had run from him. Nixon, after the Cow Palace, was on the comeback trail for certain.

Dewey's Last Clarion Call

The New York State Republican convention fell just weeks after the national party convention. The inevitable devastating effect Goldwater would have on Republicans in the Northeast was obvious. That state convention was the only time I heard former governor Thomas E. Dewey speak in person. This was the same Governor Dewey for whose 1948 presidential campaign I, at age nine, dutifully covered telephone and power poles in Munsey Park with posters urging his election. This was the same Governor Dewey who was castigated at the 1952 national party convention.

Besides Goldwater himself, there was another very visible casualty in New York in 1964. New York's Roosevelt hotel at Forty-Fifth Street and Madison Avenue had been Republican Party state headquarters from time immemorial, or at least from the Dewey governorship in the 1940s, when he kept a suite there when in New York City and not in Albany. The Republican Party held its state nominating convention there. This was after Robert F. Kennedy, President Johnson's holdover attorney general and keeper of the Kennedy flame, decided to seek the US senate seat held by upstate Republican Kenneth B. Keating. Keating went further than Rockefeller or his fellow senator, Jacob Javits, in distancing himself from the nominee and disavowed Goldwater. Keating's position held some irony: the Rochester, New York, congressional seat that Keating had vacated to become a US senator had been taken over by William Miller, now Goldwater's running mate.

In the small Roosevelt ballroom, former governor and presidential aspirant Thomas E. Dewey entered the hall. Dewey strode to the podium to put Kenneth B. Keating's name forward, unopposed, for the Republican renomination for his Senate seat. The New York GOP, the diminutive and dapper former governor said, as he slowly turned his head from side to side, was warmly embracing its own Senator Keating to continue his job for New York. This was a relationship between a party and its candidate that was cordial, even affectionate. It was filled with respect, Dewey observed.

Dewey then tilted his head upward and jabbed with his hand while his eyes flashed. His baritone voice was operatically trained. While a young lawyer, he had paid for voice lessons and honed his singing as a cantor in New York synagogues. On this occasion, in that full, rising, sonorous voice, he declaimed, "We nominate here today a fine statesman who has long and deep relations with the party and New York State. Compare this to that SHOTGUN WEDDING down the street, of Robert Kennedy and the New York Democratic Party!" The small crowd in the Roosevelt Ballroom erupted in a hopeful if uncertain note of defiance.

Keating himself did not show much confidence. He understood what would befall him after the Goldwater nomination and after the Democrats' nomination in early September of the brother of the fallen president as his opponent. Keating was nervous and sallow. He had all the sangfroid of a rabbit in front of a rattlesnake.

At the request of Walter Thayer, three of us went down at the very end of October to New York and closeted ourselves in a suite in the Roosevelt. We drafted a speech for the Keating campaign, to be given either by Thomas Dewey or Nelson Rockefeller. Thayer edited it slightly for us. On October 29, I took the speech to Herbert Brownell. This was the only meeting with Dewey's and Eisenhower's campaign czar I ever had. We went over it together. I found Brownell very impressive but could not escape the conviction that in these circumstances Bob Kennedy would best even him. Keating's candidacy never ignited; he was fighting the anti-Goldwater tide in New York. He lost handily. These Republican disasters and shifts in control were repeated in state after state.

The Election Tsunami

Only a couple of weeks before the election, a number of startling events portended upheaval across the globe. First, in the Soviet Union, Nikita S. Krushchev was deposed on October 15. His denunciation of Stalin had become public and gave fodder to his unreconstructed enemies. On the same day, the Tories lost to Labor in Great Britain. Less than a week later, on October 21, Herbert Clark Hoover, the icon of conservative Republicans, died.

Days later, in the American general election, there unfolded an unmitigated catastrophe for the Republican Party. The immediate results for the party in 1964 showed grievous bodily harm had been done to it outside the South, and, in 1964, the Republican Party still had its home outside the South. Goldwater carried only Arizona and six southern states, four of which his newly Republican friend, Strom Thurmond, had carried in his 1948 Dixiecrat and segregationist campaign against Thomas Dewey, Harry Truman, and Henry Wallace. The African American vote was turned decidedly into the Democratic column enabling Lyndon Johnson to carry states such as Florida and Arkansas and North Carolina, with heavy Black voter participation. The final Electoral College tally was 486 votes for Johnson versus 52 for Goldwater. Johnson's forty-three million votes to Goldwater's twenty-seven million meant LBJ's percentage was 61.1 percent of the popular vote, or one of the greatest landslides in American presidential history. It was almost equaled eight years later by Richard Nixon's victory over George McGovern of 60.7 percent. The trumpeting by the Goldwater partisans that "27 million Americans can't be wrong!" seemed to be whistling past the graveyard.

My home state of New York was bloodied, as were other Northern states. Four Republican members of the New York congressional delegation who had supported Goldwater, including my local Long Island member of Congress, Steven Derounian, sank in the general election. A notable political drowning occurred on the Atlantic Ocean shore of Long Island. In a heavily Democratic district (six to one Democratic to Republican registration), an impressive and accomplished Italian American Republican, Joseph F. Carlino, had defied for years the party registration odds and repeatedly won a state legislative seat, rising to the position of Speaker of the assembly in Albany. Carlino was a first-class legislator. He was highly effective in working across the aisle with Democrats in his speakership from 1959 to 1964. In part because of Carlino's skilled bipartisanship and in part because the State Senate was securely in upstate Republican hands, Carlino and the governor were able to realize many goals, including the creation of the New York State University system. Carlino also shepherded through the assembly some of Rockefeller's progressive and controversial open housing and civil rights measures.

Yet by 1964, Carlino had allowed his ambition to overcome his judgment. After Rockefeller had won his second term in 1962, and even more after Rockefeller had been beaten at the San Francisco convention, Carlino saw a chance for realizing his own ambitions for the executive chamber. He understandably thought Rockefeller might not seek a third term. Carlino was attractive, smooth, and smart. He was now alert to the growth in power of conservatives and to the zeal of their supporters.

The Conservative Party was formed in 1962, posing problems for Republican officeholders as they sought to win renomination from the party or in a general election. This fissure weakened the New York party, even in its strongest redoubts. Given that the Republican Party regularly nominated liberal-leaning candidates for statewide office, such as US senator Jacob K. Javits, Attorney General Louis Lefkowitz, and of course Nelson Rockefeller as governor, an aggrieved group of conservatives organized in 1962. The new Conservative Party was headed by two Manhattan Irishmen in quick succession, brothers-in-law, in fact, Kieran O'Doherty and Daniel Mahoney. They were in their way a conservative answer to the brothers-in-law liberal pair of Jock Whitney and Bill Paley. It did not matter that liberal Republicans kept being reelected in New York with regularity. The conservatives felt no great loyalty to the Republican Party.

Dyspepsia or ideology aside, there was a logical tactical reason for forming the Conservative Party. In New York election law, multiple parties were able to aggregate votes for a candidate. For example, the Liberal Party vote (largely older, former Central and Eastern European anti-communist trade unionist and social democratic voters) could be added either to the Republican nominee's vote numbers if that candidate ran on both lines or, likewise, to the Democratic candidate's numbers. The Liberal Party's longtime leader, Alex Rose, had perfected to a fault the game of choosing a dance partner in every election. Rose had been chair of the American Labor Party until communists became powerful in it. He and David Dubinsky of the International Ladies Garment Workers Union then broke with the American Labor Party and formed the Liberal Party in 1944. Mayoral candidates, and statewide aspirants in New York began to seek and enjoy the marginal help of a Liberal Party line. The Conservative Party looked to imitate the Rose/Dubinsky tactics.

The conservatives typically would not prevail in a Republican state convention where the old Dewey, Brownell, and more recently Javits and Rockefeller forces held a commanding position. Likewise, the conservatives were not apt to win in a statewide primary campaign. Most registered Republicans were Manhattan liberals and suburban or upstate moderates or traditional conservatives, not movement conservative types.

Consequently, the conservatives determined to exercise their influence on the party from outside it. By having a candidate run in general elections, their voice, which was muted within the Republican Party, would be heard. Those conservatives who felt disfranchised could vote Conservative and, by withholding votes from the Republican in the general election, start to influence the selection of the Republican candidates themselves, pulling them more in the conservative direction as opposed to the center-Left, where party nominees tended to concentrate their campaigning.

All of this Speaker Carlino understood. He gave way to temptation and chose to surf the waves of the Goldwater tide, not realizing it was going out rather than coming in. He hoped it would mean conservative support in 1966 for his own candidacy for governor. He and others did not clearly see that the tide brought with it a massive undertow for most candidacies in the North. He was swamped and soundly defeated. Surely the governor felt his loss as both houses of the New York legislature went to the Democrats in the anti-Goldwater vote.

CHAPTER 4

1965–1968
Back to the Center?

·The year 1965 was one of stock-taking by those Republican leaders who were dented or run over in the demolition derby of the 1964 convention and campaign. The Ripon Society had a team of more than thirty working on election night, 1964, in Cambridge, Massachusetts, capturing and analyzing the election results from across the country on a local and statewide basis. In those days of slower communications, Ripon election analysts gleaned and fed the results by fax or phone to news organizations covering the returns or to interested campaign organizations. This became a 140-page, highly detailed published report on the effect on the party of the Goldwater campaign, titled *From Disaster to Distinction*.[1] From the ashes of the election results, Ripon hoped for a Phoenix-like resurrection of moderate Republican policy and officeholders. It was not going to be easy.

The Southern Strategy had its foundation laid in this presidential election, and as a result of the courtship by Goldwater of the South, some notable changes of party affiliation occurred there as the Goldwater nomination wave grew and crested. This pivot to a conservative Republican Party in the South continued while the party collapsed, for the time being, elsewhere. These shifts were underlined by the media's concentration on Strom Thurmond's walk across the aisle in the United States Senate of Strom Thurmond in mid-September 1964. Both Thurmond's short but historic stroll to the Republican desks on the Senate floor and the rebranding of many Southern Democrats were indicative of a strong, broad, and consequential movement. When he embraced the civil rights legislation of the mid-1960s, Lyndon Johnson had forecast that it would cost the Democrats the loss of the South for a generation. It was to be for longer than that.

In 1964, Clarke Reed of Mississippi became a Republican (though he had voted for Dwight Eisenhower in 1952). Reed advanced swiftly from state party finance head to the Mississippi GOP chair in 1966 and remained there for a decade. Reed was important in the South for Nixon's 1968 campaign and a key coordinator in his 1972 reelection. He played a positive role in the Nixon Southern school desegregation drama, following the Supreme Court decision in Nixon's first year, mandating immediate compliance with its direction in the *Brown v. Board of Education of Topeka* case of fifteen years earlier. Reed was important in helping Nixon build community leadership and support committees that crossed party and racial lines. However, Reed fell out of favor with the conservatives when he backed Gerry Ford for renomination in 1976, as the conservative voter was turning to Ronald Reagan.

Numerous other Democrats began to change parties in the mid- and late 1960s, as Reed did. The party in Mississippi did not have great electoral success until later. In 1972, candidates like Trent Lott, who became a Republican that year, and Thad Cochran, who made the shift earlier, in 1967, began their elective careers, with election to the House and culminating in both cases with United States Senate seats.

Lott's case was a metaphor for the increasing influence of the Republican South, and the Deep South, in national politics. During his elective career, the Democratic hold on key positions and committee leadership was wrenched away and converted to Republican control. Some of this turnover was due to Democrats' committee and subcommittee reforms of 1970 to 1975, which reduced incentives for Southern Democrats to stay in the Democratic caucus. A number of Southerners were unceremoniously stripped of their chairmanships. The system changed. Lott held House leadership positions soon after election in 1972. When he moved to the Senate, his climb up the ladder culminated as majority leader. Lott was a man of fastidious attention to detail. This extended to his organization of his sock drawer, with pairs arranged by color or pattern, always in the same place, so he could retrieve a desired pair in perfect darkness while his wife slept.

His own political rise was intertwined with changes in the South about race. He was part of the new Republicanism in the South whose ascent was based no longer on segregation but on other touch points, such as a sense of horror at the anti–Vietnam War protests and the radical cultural clashes of the "disruptive" 1960s. Race never was entirely expunged, in the South or elsewhere. Lott's later fall was due to a tilt back toward more overtly racial politics. He made remarks at an event in 2002 that were interpreted as racist and were called out by his Republican president, George W. Bush, and others in the party. Lott stepped down as Republican leader.

An important player who shifted in 1964 was Georgia's Howard "Bo" Calloway, who ran that year as a Goldwater Republican and was sworn in as the first Republican congressman from Georgia since Reconstruction. Calloway later became the Nixon region-wide coordinator in the South for the 1968 campaign. By early 1965, with the Goldwater loss leaving Northern Republicans reeling and recriminating, Southern Democrats began to turn Republican in ever greater numbers. There came to be a counterpoint in the North to the Southern swing to the Republicans, but it occurred somewhat later, as many moderate or liberal Republicans fled an increasingly Southern and conservative GOP and rebranded themselves as Democrats.

The swing to the GOP saw drama in South Carolina, where Democratic congressman Albert W. Watson, while heading the South Carolina Democrats for Goldwater, was running for reelection. His mentor, Senator Strom Thurmond, backed him against a Republican House candidate, Floyd Spence (even after Thurmond's own party switch in autumn in the midst of the campaign).

Watson, an avowed segregationist, won the House seat narrowly in that turbulent 1964 election, and then in the spring of 1965, he resigned his seat and switched parties, after which he ran for and won election in his new plumage as a Republican, a widely noted bit of theater at the time. Watson, like Calloway in Georgia, became the first Republican member of Congress of his state, South Carolina, since Reconstruction. Other South Carolinians followed his example.

The years 1966, 1967, and 1968 saw the spread into Arkansas and Texas of the conversions. The sawdust trail had been laid and was trod now in many Republican Revival tents throughout Dixie. William Reynolds Archer made his party shift in 1968 and took George Herbert Walker Bush's congressional seat in Houston. Bush himself ran successfully for Congress in the Goldwater year, somewhat uncomfortably supporting Goldwater in opposing the civil rights bill of that year but fitting well into his adopted Texas surroundings. Archer became the chairman of the House Ways and Means Committee at the pinnacle of his thirty-year career in Congress.

Of the party conversions, none was more significant or of longer lasting impact than that of Ronald Wilson Reagan, whose own oath of allegiance to the Republicans was pledged in 1962. Reagan's speech on Goldwater's behalf two weeks before the 1964 election and his stumping for the candidate across the country positioned him as an Elisha picking up the mantle of Elijah after the collapse of the Arizona prophet. Reagan was his natural heir, especially among the Southerners who had been wooed by Goldwater. Yet his appeal was wider than regional. Reagan's midwestern roots, folksiness, and relaxed manner also reassured and charmed many around the country who had been frightened by the tactics and rhetoric of the shrill supporters of the Goldwater campaign, and even of Goldwater himself.

The geological plates of politics in the South had indeed begun their historic shift, which had intriguing consequences for Reagan and for the 1968 and 1972 campaigns. Pat Buchanan notes that he and Nixon had many meetings in the South and about the South between 1965, when Buchanan joined Nixon, and 1968. Their conviction was that the continuance of segregation was an impossibility, both morally and legally. Nixon and Buchanan were saying to the Southerners that they must put paid to support of segregation.[2]

Many of Buchanan's editorials of the time declared this. There was no way defiance could indefinitely continue against the Supreme Court. And Nixon was by conviction opposed to segregation.

But it had been segregation and race that held together the Southern Democratic Party, and it was those Southern Democrats who were now becoming Republicans. Roosevelt had never tinkered with that element of his coalition. The Democrats' Faustian bargain between segregationists and liberals had lasted a long time. For Nixon, a member of the NAACP since 1946 and from a family with abolitionist and Underground Railroad roots, his impulses in the abstract were liberal. He also understood, though, with crystal clarity what Lyndon Johnson told aides when he pushed for the 1964 and 1965 and 1966 civil rights bills: the Democrats have now lost the South for a generation. Nixon and Buchanan believed that an appeal based on a strong national defense agenda and what we would now term "cultural conservatism" would prove very effective in moving Southern states into Republican control over time. Nixon never favored busing or forced integration; indeed, he strongly opposed both. Southerners welcomed that. But forced integration, and busing to accomplish that, had intense and public opposition for liberal Northern Democrats, too. Their own constituencies, such as in Boston, were filled with protest and anxiety about busing. Nixon was in such company as Democratic US senators Abraham Ribicoff of Connecticut and the "liberal lion of the Senate," Edward Kennedy of Massachusetts, whose support for busing for integration now grew quiet. They were among many other liberals of both parties. In his carrying out the decision *Holmes v. Alexander* of 1970, Nixon created biracial local communities that brought the South into compliance with the desegregation decisions of the Supreme Court. He peacefully and successfully saw the implementation of that begun by *Brown v. Board of Education of Topeka*.

Following the publication of the Ripon report on the election, I was on New York television with Kieran O'Doherty, the Conservative Party leader, who chastised me for the Ripon analysis, which I insisted was straightforward: the Goldwater nomination had been an unmitigated disaster for the Republican Party. The Ripon Report merely filled in the details. O'Doherty's own Goldwater-supporting Republicans in New York had been winnowed, cut down as in an autumn wheat harvest. O'Doherty, after the show, grudgingly conceded to me that the results had been painful.

The Restoration? Or More Cromwellism
After its fling with the Puritan-like zealots of the Goldwater movement, the Republican Party seemed to return to the less exhausting church of tradition, organization, and hierarchy. During Eisenhower's first term, in 1954, Ray

Bliss became the chair of the Ohio Republican Party. Bliss was an experienced and reassuring figure. He was a nuts-and-bolts organizer who turned around the fortunes of the Ohio GOP. It was Bliss who was called in by the Republican National Committee at its sepulchral January 1965 meeting to attempt, in a nonideological fashion, to rebuild the national party organization as its chair.

At the same time, in January 1965, Congressman Charles Halleck was stripped by Republicans of his party leadership in the House and replaced by Gerald Ford. Ford was a former male model, easygoing, and middle-of-the-road. He was supported in this leadership fight by the younger and more moderate members of the Republican caucus. Among these at the time was Donald Rumsfeld, who was later to reap the benefit of having supported Ford in this contest, when Ford tapped Rumsfeld to be his chief of staff upon succeeding Nixon to the presidency in 1974.

While the Ripon Society emerged as a leading voice of the moderate Republicans, other groups were part of the post-1964 landscape. The Republican Coordinating Committee, created by former president Dwight Eisenhower, met in the winter of 1965, not long after the annual meeting of the Republican National Committee where the RNC deposed Dean Burch, Goldwater's party chair, and crowned Ray Bliss his successor. Among the attendees were Richard Nixon and Thomas Dewey as former party presidential candidates. Melvin Laird from the House of Representatives offered a ten-page paper that he urged should become the "platform" to emerge from the meeting. It was shapeless, especially on civil rights, the issue that had split the party the previous year.

Some twenty-one years after his 1944 meeting of Republican governors, where Dewey had kept them up most of the night making more concrete the party's platform on which he would run, Dewey once again turned a party group around and won them over to a tough plank on civil rights. This came only months after Goldwater's defeat and his spurning of the party's traditional pro–civil rights posture. In this 1965 meeting, Dewey was still applying his skills to point the party in a direction of reform, and not of reaction, and he was making use of work done by Ripon.

The Ripon Society had prepared a draft platform for the Republican coordinating committee. It urged favorable action on a series of civil rights measures, including abolition of the poll tax, establishment of a powerful federal voting oversight board, federal sanctions against interference with the right to register or vote, and legislation authorizing federal officials to conduct elections when necessary. "Even after the Civil Rights Act of 1964," the Ripon draft platform noted, "many barriers remain that deny minorities equal rights in voting, education, and justice. The elimination of persistent discrimination in jobs, public accommodations, and housing has scarcely begun."

Among the attendees of that 1965 Republican Coordinating Committee was Governor Daniel J. Evans of Washington state. Evans had been the only Republican governor to win an election in the decidedly inhospitable climate of November 1964 against a democratic incumbent.[3] Evans recalled the debate on Laird's proposed civil rights language and confirmed that the effort to liberalize it was spearheaded by Thomas Dewey, who led the drafting. The rest of the Coordinating Committee overturned the Laird proposal and substituted language more along the lines of the Ripon draft—and indeed along the lines of the national platform on which Tom Dewey had run twenty years earlier, in the 1944 election.

Another moderate Republican group, the Council of Republican Organizations, was pleased by the Ripon platform and asked Ripon to serve as the secretariat for the group, led by Congressman Charles Taft of Ohio. This was another step in Ripon's becoming a consequential player in the post-Goldwater party landscape.

Only months later, Ripon issued a joint twenty-one-page paper with the Republican Governors Association on revenue sharing, called "Government for Tomorrow." As Geoffrey Kabaservice describes it, in his unpublished history of the Ripon Society:

> The RGA agreed to give Ripon joint credit for the paper. . . . Lee Huebner and his team emphasized that state and local governments had taken on much greater responsibilities while relying on an outdated and inadequate financial base, and that revenue sharing was a fair and effective approach to solving problems that transcended party politics in areas such as education, fire and police protection, health and sanitation, water resources, welfare, and transportation.[4]

Part of Ripon's effort as Lee Huebner worked with the governors was to think in a context of a political philosophy. Huebner recalled considerable discussion in several Ripon documents and policy proposals of Creative Federalism—as he says, "quite a bit [of discussion]—especially in the Revenue Sharing Document—and, of course, lots of references to the 'New Politics.'"[5]

The *Ripon Forum*, in its issue of November 1966, said these policies should be in the form of a New Federalism.[6] This appears to be the first use of the term "New Federalism" by a political group. It was the very term that Richard Nixon would apply to his seminal array of proposals of August 1969, including welfare reform, federal revenue sharing, and manpower program reforms. The Ripon magazine spoke of how the New Federalism might look. The Great Society vision of centralization was not the way; it was "rich in statistics of progress but devoid of the satisfactions of meaningful public action." With the fountainhead of all political initiatives in Washington, the need to compromise and persuade would atrophy, as people of opposing views abandoned "conversation with each other in favor of shrill, extortionist harangues directed toward the center of national power." The Democrats might build a society that was "merely large, rich and egalitarian," but moderate Republicans could create one that was also "creative, self-respecting and just." The New Federalism would mean

> the involvement of citizens in political activity on a scale never seen before. It means the infusion of social debate into the lowest levels of government, into business corporations, into school systems, mental institutions, mass media, prisons, slums, into problems of housing design, transportation, conservation, and leisure time. It means the development of new techniques for democratic participation, new safeguards for individual rights, and new processes for correcting bureaucratic abuse. It means that politics must become more than a spectator sport.[7]

The *New York Herald Tribune* gave great attention to the revenue sharing paper and Ripon's role. Its syndicated columns were reproduced in papers all over the country. There was a sense of optimism about the party's future. It was the same sense of optimism that Everett Dirksen displayed to the Republican governors gathered in Colorado Springs in December 1966. It was the same optimism about the pickup of Senate and House seats that fall and the prospect of governing.

Another Republican organization was producing research. The Wednesday Group, made up of moderate Republicans from the House of Representatives, produced work on the military draft and foreign aid and spearheaded the Civil Rights Law Enforcement Act of 1966 (with Ripon assistance). Republicans for Progress produced work on topics ranging from water resources to technology growth. Ripon was the most publicly visible. Its conservative counterparts took aim at it. This reinforced Ripon as the group of dominant heft in the center and progressive parts of the Republican Party. The American Conservative Union (ACU) put out a study of the Ripon Society, characterizing the group as "progressive Republicanism's intellectual elite." The *Ripon Forum* commented that the ACU study's information was out-of-date and its view of Ripon's influence "inflated," though its portrait of Ripon's role was "surprising and flattering."

During these post-1964 years, Ripon was striving to lay an intellectual foundation for the next Republican presidency—assuming it would not be a

Ronald Reagan administration. Revenue sharing was a program that would meet with nearly universal embrace by conservative and moderate Republicans, and even Democrats, as the parties' platforms had indicated. Despite the rhetoric that no government was the best government, Reagan and the conservatives would be pleased to receive the federal funds to be used without strings.

Other proposals, like Ripon's support for a fresh look at the policy of isolating communist China, were not going to find support across the internal chasms of the Republican Party. William F. Buckley's *National Review* ignited in April 1966, when the Ripon Society published "Containment and Contact," which proposed a reassessment of US diplomacy toward Taiwan and mainland China. The *National Review* cried that a certain "one-man mimeo shop in Cambridge—purporting to speak for the Republican Party's 'moderate' faction" had joined . . . the 'Peking Lobby.'" *Human Events* announced that leaders of "the ultra-liberal splinter group" were "worming their way into several campaigns throughout the country."

Among the ACU's charges about Ripon was that "these are determined young men who believe that there must be a two-party system divided only on the question of who can manage the Great Society programs more efficiently." This criticism was rebutted by Josiah Lee Auspitz, later Ripon's president: "If you looked at the policies that Ripon advocated, they were not open to the charge of me-tooism. We really did try to locate a third way between conservative Republicans and liberal Democrats. The early policy papers were quite consistently based on a different notion of government than New Deal government."[8] They offered a positive Republican alternative to the Great Society.

Josiah Lee Auspitz (Lee) and Lee W. Huebner were the éminences grises of the early Ripon Society. All others played their hands according to their strengths. Emil Frankel had the vision to create a Republican group with a policy focus, like the Bow Group he had studied. Emil was an energizer, recruiter, and encourager. His good will, upbeat nature, and hopefulness never slackened. Emil went on to a diverse career, including work with Senator Jacob Javits, work during the Nixon Administration at HUD, and then commercial property consulting and workouts. He was commissioner of transportation for Connecticut and US assistant secretary of transportation for President George W. Bush.

Emil and Jack Saloma were complementary, as Saloma also had a vision for where the Ripon Society could place itself in American politics and had practical experience from his work on Capitol Hill. Jack was often as concerned with the machinations of the increasingly powerful right wing as he was with the identification and development of substantive issues for the future. Emil also sought to see where the party could be moved. Gene Marans was a remarkably focused attorney whose clarity and judgment about framing issues was beyond the ability of the rest of us. He got into the weeds, and this ability made Ripon's assistance so welcome to congressional and gubernatorial staffs with whom we often worked. Gene had an illustrious career as an attorney with Cleary, Gottlieb, in their Paris, Hong Kong, and Washington offices. He was outside counsel to the Asian Development Bank and the European Bank for Reconstruction and Development. He also was the default bookkeeper for dinners of many of us, calculating swiftly the allocation of each person's part of the tab, tax, and tip included.

Tim Petri was sui generis. Imaginative, creative, whimsical, often amusing, and always shrewd in his reading of people and situations, Tim was the only one of the early Ripon group to go on to a successful and lengthy career in public office. From the Wisconsin state senate to a kamikaze run at the behest of the state party for the US Senate against incumbent Gaylord Nelson, Tim moved on to the US House of Representatives, serving so many terms representing his Fond du Lac home area that at retirement in January 2015, he was the eighth most senior member of the House.

The two Lees, Auspitz and Huebner, were the members who could most artfully but also most thoughtfully frame the space Ripon sought to occupy. Both were academics. Auspitz's world is philosophy. He became an authority on one of the great philosophers of the twentieth century, Michael Oakeshott. He later was deeply involved in the transition in Eastern Europe, teaching philosophy in Poland after the fall of the Soviet Union. But he was always an astute observer of politics and its movements. He knew how to find and interpret numbers—data. Leonard Garment, at the time of the Voting Rights Act extension, says it was coming to Nixon for signature but contained a provision that would lower the voting age to eighteen, and some Nixon advisors urged a veto. Garment says that Lee Auspitz visited him. Auspitz was "bearing his usual collection of ideas, documents and other scholarly odds and ends. He mentioned a recent study of college-age voting preferences which contradicted the general assumption that eighteen-year-olds would vote Democratic. . . . On request, Auspitz promptly sent me the printouts, which I passed along to Ehrlichman and the president. The bill was signed."[9] Later, Auspitz worked with Patrick Caddell, a former student of his, observing the political moves of the working class and its relation to the Wallace movement and the impulse toward populism. Auspitz shared the findings with the Ford White House.

Lee Huebner did his doctoral work at Harvard on the early twentieth-century evolution of propaganda, represented in his *The Fake News Panic of a Century Ago: Reflections on Globalization, Democracy, and the Media* (2019).

Lee is a wordsmith and an executive as well as an analytical thinker. His work with Richard Nixon while Nixon campaigned for Goldwater in 1964 led to Lee's appointment to Nixon's White House speechwriting staff, ultimately as its deputy head. Lee, like Raymond Price, always felt comfortable writing for Nixon on topics that were uplifting or revealing of Nixon's most humane or empathetic side. Huebner was publisher of *Oil Daily* and *Retirement Living*, then ran the *Paris International Herald Tribune* for fourteen years as publisher and CEO, learning all about the French unions' vexing and constant deployment of "la Grève" or strike and finding necessary workarounds. Later, Lee taught at Northwestern University, including a highly popular course on Richard Nixon, before he took on the management of the George Washington University School of Media and Public Policy.

At the point in 1967 that Huebner identified as a good moment for moderates, there were some issues that offered hope for bringing the party back together. Besides revenue sharing, Ripon and more conservative proponents converged on the abolition of the draft or Selective Service. Bruce Chapman, the cofounder of *Advance Magazine* with George Gilder, took on the issue. In a book published in 1967,[10] Chapman argued forcefully for abolition of the draft and the institution of a volunteer military. Ripon worked later on a more detailed formulation of such a proposal. Conservative Martin Anderson also became an advocate for abolition of the draft. Anderson had come to prominence with his publication of a book condemning the Urban Renewal program. Anderson assisted Nixon in the 1968 campaign on domestic policy, serving subsequently on the staff of Arthur Burns's conservatives in the first Nixon White House. He later played a similar role for Ronald Reagan, with whom he was more in tune than he ever was with Nixon's domestic affairs policies—or its policy-makers. On the draft issue, Anderson and Chapman reached the same conclusion. For reasons of politics as well as policy, Melvin Laird, the defense secretary in Nixon's first term, concluded the same. He understood that elimination of the draft would directly reduce the breadth and intensity of opposition to the Vietnam War. The end of the draft was one of the broadly supported actions of Nixon's presidency.

A proposal for a negative income tax was the main project of the Ripon-related group at Yale, called Republican Advance. As a later Ripon president, Howard Gillette noted, it "was an idea being touted by Yale economists like James Tobin at the time, so it wasn't as though it came out of Ripon as such. But Ripon did a lot of research on it and helped publicize it and move it toward implementation. The idea was to provide the working poor with a minimum income, and then leave it to them to decide whether they wanted to spend their money on housing, education, training, or whatever." Gillette observed that this idea "fit in well with the Ripon and Republican belief in allowing people to decide their own destinies, rather than have the federal government provide for them and in the process give them incentives to destructive behavior, as welfare clearly did. It was a semi-libertarian viewpoint in its skepticism of entitlements, but it also embraced a belief in the importance of government—that's why the Ripon people were moderates." John Topping, the Yale group's chair, in submitting the proposal to the National Governing Board of Ripon said, "I feel strongly that the guaranteed family income is the coming social welfare issue of our generation. . . . I feel it is imperative that we put the Ripon stamp on it. The negative income tax method of implementing this concept is the most viable politically, retains an incentive for work, and can be woven into Republican tradition."[11]

Negative income tax (NIT) sounds more complicated than it is. Income tax brings to mind the Internal Revenue Service and the payment by taxpayers of liabilities they have under the tax code to make tax payments on their income (adjusted in various ways to arrive at "taxable income"). The NIT is a reverse of that. Where people have low incomes, less than the poverty line as prescribed by the government, a NIT would pay them. It is "income tested," meaning the amount paid to the family or individual will be greater as the income goes lower. To the extent that the family through work earns more, it would have its NIT payment reduced on a calculated basis up to the point where the earned income is above a stated amount. That calculation will vary not only according to the amount of income the wage earner makes but according to the size of their family, their dependents, a concept understood for the regular tax code. That family size will reflect the reality of how far those earnings will go. Conceptually, this is quite different from simply granting the same amount of dollars to every man, woman, and child in a family unit, a procedure called a "family allowance." This is a "capitation," or head-count, grant and is the most common approach in many developed countries in the last century. The problem with this approach involves both fiscal impact and equity. It is very costly. It goes to Bill Gates, his wife, and his children as well as to a very poor family. Yes, it may be partially returned in taxes on its receipt from wealthy recipients, but it is a highly inefficient way to combat poverty.

The most important contribution Ripon made to laying a foundation for one of Richard Nixon's central domestic policy initiatives was this work on welfare reform. It was not simply a pastiche or summary of proposals made by others. The initial proposal was crafted by John Topping of the Yale group and Duncan Foley, a young economist at Massachusetts Institute of Technology. Then, a draft bill structuring a negative income tax was prepared and appeared in an edition of the *Yale Law Journal*. It was promoted in Congress by its Ripon authors. It was widely reviewed and commented on. The society's consideration of the proposal highlighted the various arguments and the necessary kinds of inquiry that would be essential for a new president to weigh in his decision-making on the proposal.

The April 1967 *Ripon Forum* carried the original white paper on the negative income tax, which had been refined over the course of seven drafts. Animated debate within the society followed its publication. Peter Wallison, later an American Enterprise Institute voice and *Wall Street Journal* contributor, had reservations about the concept of the negative income tax, but he agreed that it would be "one of the more important subjects of political debate in the next few years; and, consequently, we should have something to say about it right at the start." Wallison accurately anticipated one line of criticism of any cash grant: that the head of household might spend the money on television sets and beer unless strings were attached to the grant. But Wallison felt that "we, as Republicans, have always felt that every man, if given the opportunity, is capable of ordering his life for himself." These very arguments were among those batted back and forth around the cabinet table in 1969 as Nixon listened to endless internal debate on his welfare reform.

Perhaps because of the growing power of conservatives in the party, when more liberal members of the Republican Party advanced proposals and wanted to blunt likely charges that they were little short of socialist, those liberals reached for conservative "authority" in support of such an idea. The Ripon paper on the NIT was no exception. It quoted Robert Taft's belief that American society was producing enough "to give to all a minimum standard of decent living" and concluded, "In five years our economy will be producing a thousand billion dollars' worth of goods each year. We propose to give one percent to those who have so far been left out. The richest nation in history should do no less."[12]

Milton Friedman, the University of Chicago and Nobel Prize–winning economist, was invoked as a totemic figure in the evolution of the negative income tax. In his important *Capitalism and Freedom* (1962), Friedman proposed a negative income tax, and he served as economic advisor to the Goldwater campaign in 1964 and therefore had credentials among conservatives.

While numerous economists had developed academic proposals for a negative income tax (NIT), Ripon was the first partisan political group to embrace the concept. Ripon's negative income tax proposal attracted extensive press. Ohio Congressman Charles Whalen read the paper into the *Congressional Record* and began an effort to write legislation based on the detailed proposal. The paper received further broad exposure when the negative income tax was selected as the National College Debate Topic for 1967–1968. Ripon officer Robert Behn thought the tribute that best fit what Ripon was all about was an April 18 editorial in the *Providence Journal*: "The Ripon Society's action adds powerful political support to the principle that until now has been largely academic."[13] From its earliest days, Ripon's members had conceived of themselves as an effective bridge between the academic community and the political officeholders and policymakers.

Some conservatives fretted about the proposal and its ensuing attention from the press and political office holders. ACU continued to pay backhanded tribute to Ripon, warning that it was part of a liberal drive to take over the GOP and calling it "the 'nerve center' of the Eastern liberal establishment."[14] Much like the joint Federal Revenue Sharing proposal with the Republican Governors Association, the Ripon paper on the negative income tax helped to move NIT onto the front burner. It now found an advocate in a political organization, not a university department.

Politics, during these post-Goldwater years, as much as Ripon or its conservative counterparts might aspire or a Nelson Rockefeller might have dreamed to do, was not moved only by well-researched ideas. Elective politics has a timetable and a dynamic of its own. While many of the proposals that would find acceptance in Nixon's first term were being refined during these years, elections took place with their own rhythms and outcomes.

The 1965 elections resulted in two off-year Democratic gubernatorial victories in New Jersey and Virginia, likely still a reaction against the Goldwater campaign but only in part, as local issues or Republican gaffes played a consequential role. Some Republican first-time local victories in the South, such as mayoral races in Hattiesburg and Greenville, Mississippi (and the Albert Watson special congressional election in South Carolina for his seat formerly held by him as a Democrat), were early indicators of the move in that region toward the GOP. However, the attention of the national Republican leadership, including party officials and governors, was on the Northeast, Midwest, and the West, where statehouse control and congressional seat holdings had been inverted in capitol after capitol and district after district.

Only three months before these 1965 off-year elections, Watts, California, a part of Los Angeles, erupted in a week of rioting, leaving thirty-four dead and several thousand injured. The incident focused that year's campaigns on the tensions and problems in urban areas and the problems of race and poverty. A report on Watts was prepared by a special committee chaired by John A. McCone, the former director of Central Intelligence. The Watts report arrived only in mid-December, following those elections.

Attention was paid to a few mayoral races where there were victories in the North by liberal Republican candidates. These were hoped to be the "first swallows of Spring," harbingers of a comeback after the devastating November of 1964. The remit for Ray Bliss at the National Committee was for broad success in elections all over the country, including in rural, suburban, and urban areas. Still, we thought that in large urban areas there was an additional potential base for the party among urban Black and moderate voters, anxious to release their cities from the grip of politicians working in the Democratic machine. Philadelphia elected a Republican, actually a Democrat, later a Republican, and then later yet a Democrat once more: Arlen Specter. His party shifts had some of the dizzying frequency of those of Winston Churchill.

John V. Lindsay was the victor in New York. Lindsay was glamorous; he was liberal. He sincerely sought to defuse racial tensions, which had become profound. Yet he immediately—indeed, on his first day in office—fell afoul of bargaining with municipal unions and appeared outmatched by them. He also had a constant battle with Albany and the New York governor. Any New York mayor will have their fights with the State Capitol. But the Rockefeller/Lindsay bad blood was constant and beyond any normal institutional rivalry. It helped to spoil Lindsay's chances of further advancement within the Republican Party. It was partly payback by Rockefeller for Lindsay not giving him Bob Price to help in the California primary in 1964.

Specter was a bit of scrambled eggs—a mishmash. His background was very antiestablishment and anti-privilege. He was, always, an acerbic loner. But he was a shrewd vote getter. He was a survivor. And he was one of the most visible victors in the November 1965 elections for Northern urban Republicans. Arlen Specter's election as Philadelphia's district attorney was the first time in twelve years that a municipal candidate there had won on the GOP ticket. Governor William Scranton and Senator Hugh Scott had persuaded Specter to switch parties, lent him their staff, and worked on his behalf.

Two Rockefellers and Reagan at the Broadmoor

In elective politics, Ripon leaders still looked to the Republican governors as the leading hope for a strong moderate presence in the party. The Republican Governors Association met at the Broadmoor Hotel in Colorado Springs in December 1966. The midterm elections had been the GOP's best showing in years, with the number of Republican governors nearly doubling.

Nelson Rockefeller won a third term, which had not been a foregone conclusion. I had taken time off from law practice that summer to help in an upstate campaign swing. Rockefeller even had the help of Richard Nixon, in Rockefeller's moment of need. The Mormon governor of Michigan, George W. Romney, was also reelected, and with Rockefeller's two failures to get the Republican presidential nomination, Romney was hopeful it would be his turn. The spotlight after the November 1966 election was on the new governor of California, Ronald Reagan. This had immediate implications for the balance of power within the Republican Governors Association and for their clout nationally as 1968 approached. The moderates failed to hold on to control of the much enlarged RGA, and Ripon's rivals in the American Conservative Union were encouraged by the results of the RGA conference. The ACU noted that while the number of liberal Republican governors held steady at ten, the number of conservative governors had risen from four to ten. While the RGA had not become a "conservative" group, the association was a weakened vehicle for the moderates or liberals in national and presidential politics. The five-man executive committee, which now included Ronald Reagan, flipped to conservative control.

For me, the Broadmoor conclave had three highlights. The first was seeing Reagan in action in person. Ripon had dispatched Michael Chabot Smith and later Lee Huebner to California on a watching brief in the gubernatorial election of 1966, expecting to encounter a cloven-hoofed candidate. Both were mollified, to their surprise. He was everything he became known for in the coming decades: charming, soft-spoken, amusing, nonthreatening (in manner, although not always in turn of phrase), and attractive.

The second was the opportunity to observe Everett McKinley Dirksen in the full height of his influence. That is saying something, since his Senate career had begun with his dramatic defeat in Illinois of the then Democratic majority leader of the United States Senate. He was also at the height of his oratorical skill. Dirksen gave a florid, rumbling lesson in obscurantist oratory to the Republican governors—and to the small number of other attendees, including gubernatorial staffs and Jack Saloma, Stu Parsons, and myself from Ripon. As he had with his address placing Sen. Robert A. Taft in nomination at the 1952 Chicago convention, Dirksen still spoke with the careful spacing of words; not a cadence nor yet a roll but with a clarity of diction that would bring a broad, proud smile to a high school elocution teacher. By December 1966, he was beginning to rumble in a bit lower voice register. But nothing had changed about the apt biblical allusions or the colorful turn of phrase.

As with today's history books' physical descriptions of Dirksen, my recollection of course includes the descriptor "rumpled," but it also has him with a mane of quite wavy hair, which was a curious amalgam of carrot/orange, straw, and reddish colors. Coming after successful Republican showings in the 1966 off-year congressional elections, Dirksen's enthusiasm for the party's presidential chances the next year was palpable and warmly received by the gubernatorial crowd gathered at the Broadmoor.

Another heartwarming highlight for me of that Colorado Springs conclave was the chance to get acquainted with Winthrop Rockefeller. Winthrop was the youngest, except for David, of the six children of John D. Rockefeller Jr. As a child, he was evidently mercilessly teased by his older brother Nelson for being pudgy. He had a very public and controversial personal life, marrying

"Bobo," a former Miss Lithuania by way of Pittsburgh and Chicago. He had been the nation's most eligible bachelor, and their divorce settlement a couple of years later was record-setting. After that, he had relocated to Arkansas in the 1950s and married a thrice-divorced Seattle woman.

In Arkansas, he became active in a Chicago Cubs version of a Republican Party. Grinding defeat after defeat at the hands of Democratic segregationist Governor Orval Faubus was the story each election morning for Arkansas Republicans. Rockefeller himself had run against Faubus in 1964 and lost. In 1966, as so many other Republicans around the country did, he won. His victory came with heavy support from the African American electorate, which strongly helped his reelection two years later, when he was the only Southern governor to sponsor a day of mourning for the death of Martin Luther King Jr.

He was the first Republican since Reconstruction to be elected governor of Arkansas. As a family "black sheep," this victory must have been of immense pride and emotional balm to Winthrop. George Gilder, who had helped him out with some speechwriting during the campaign, told me of writing Winthrop's inaugural address and being present at its delivery. Nelson came from New York to his brother's inauguration. Gilder said that Winthrop was so deeply moved by his victory and his brother's unwonted pride in him that he broke down in tears during his speech.

I heard the Arkansas governor give a talk at the Colorado Springs RGA meeting. Far more memorable than his speech was the evening I spent with him after it. About half a dozen of us wound up at his hotel suite. There he held most amiable court, lying on his bed with his back on fluffed up pillows against the headboard. On his feet atop the comforter was a pair of handsomely tooled cowboy boots. We talked—he talked—for hours, occasionally interrupted by a visitation to the bar, and then later to a coffee pot that was brought in. We wound up going until dawn and a breakfast. He was warm, uncomplicated, and engaging. Years later, I was delighted to tell this tale to his kid brother, David, who was quite melted by the picture it painted of his often-controversial sibling.

The General James Gavin Boomlet

While the November 1966 elections appeared to cement Romney's position as the leading moderate candidate for 1968, other bookmakers' long shots emerged. Some eighteen months earlier, at the end of 1965, Ripon's Tim Petri mused to us that General James Gavin might be thinking of a run for the presidency. Petri's political antennae, which often seemed to start with whimsy but usually proved astute, did just that here. Gavin was a war hero, having commanded the Eighty-Second Airborne as a young man. He was now the chief executive of a management consulting firm, Arthur D. Little, with broad contacts in the business community and had an excellent reputation. The hardening opposition to the Vietnam War provoked interest in his candidacy.

While Ronald Reagan had a clear "Win it" position on the war, George Romney was still uncommitted, and there were, in early 1967, war opponents other than those who were Far Left or radical. Toward the end of June 1967, an attorney from a New York law firm called to tell me that a representative of SANE (an anti-nuclear war group) had told him they were hoping to run Gavin as a peace candidate in the Republican primaries. SANE had first approached General Matthew B. Ridgway, who had been the commander in chief, United Nations Command, during the war on the Korean peninsula. Ridgway demurred, on grounds of age and poor speaking ability, but suggested his friend Jim Gavin.

The weekend of July 15 and 16, 1967, Jack Saloma, Lee Huebner, Tim Petri, and I went to Wianno on Cape Cod to see the general and continue a conversation we had begun in Westchester County earlier in the week. My diary records, "Gavin is intelligent, and reads widely (he was reading Hugh Thomas's *Suez*, which I had with me in my briefcase) and is very observant about people."

He was strongly opposed to the war and was anxious to run for the presidency although he realized not only that he must appear to be approached but also that in fact he must control those who publicly make the approach to him. He was a little worried about the Westchester group, mostly SANE enthusiasts, and said twice, "I must be hard minded about this."

Saloma later noted that there was an interesting contrast with Kissinger's observation of Nixon (this is 1967, not 1969 or later, and Kissinger had not yet even met Nixon): while in the time we had with him, we were trying to direct Gavin's attention to the political questions, he persisted in talking about issues. Kissenger said Nixon insisted on thinking through the political dimensions of something rather than examining it as a matter of policy. Gavin was good, and his military record was highly impressive. Nonetheless, following a swim, while we made discussion notes, I found myself doubting that a gale force wind such as the one *Time* magazine's Henry Luce created for Wendell Willkie in 1940 to sweep through the Republican convention, could be whipped up for Gavin.

By July 19, the *Boston Globe* called Tim with the rumor that the Ripon Society was about to endorse Gavin; the *New York Times* apparently had a story locked up about the Westchester meeting. Tim let Gavin know of the inquiry. Gavin in mid-August registered as a Republican on the Cape and issued a statement we drafted. The White House was taking notice. General

Westmoreland sent a letter to Gavin suggesting that he and his wife come to Vietnam. While "Westy" and Gavin would tour the battlefield, the wives would go off shopping. It was, as Gavin saw it, a very subtle gesture and had the clear imprint of President Johnson on it. Westmoreland had been Gavin's aide de camp for several years, and Gavin said he would not have written such a letter without being told to do so. "The idea of press on Gavin and his wife, Jean, flying to Asia at government expense then Jean going on a shopping binge in Bangkok, Singapore and Hong Kong, just at the time when a 10% tax increase was being mooted to help pay for the war, and hundreds of GIs being killed every month, was an idea only Johnson could conceive and hope to suck Gavin into doing before he thought."[15] Gavin appeared to have respect for the Ripon group but was bemused by our apparent influence without any obvious power base.

As interesting as getting acquainted with a soldier such as the general, and his wife, Jean, and four daughters was, there was beginning to be a crowd of more realistic possible candidacies as the summer of 1967 moved on, and attention went elsewhere. Eugene Marans was reluctant about Gavin anyway and thought Saloma's enthusiasm for his possible candidacy was "out of desperation." We discussed the possibility of a Lindsay candidacy and agreed to try to see him.[16] I had practiced law with Robert W. Sweet, now Lindsay's deputy mayor, and Gene, Tim, and I were law school classmates of Jay Kriegel, now one of the mayor's senior aides. I was to meet with Sweet the week after Thanksgiving to discuss "the setting up of a clandestine Lindsay organization, looking on a roll of the dice, toward '68, but more realistically, toward the future."[17] This had been first mentioned to me by Robert Pennoyer at one of our periodic lunches six-to-eight weeks earlier.

The tangled relationship of the mayor and the governor kept us—and me—in a cross fire. The Thursday before Thanksgiving, Tim Petri, Gene Marans, and I went to see George Hinman "in his lovely corner room at Room 5600, the Rockefeller family offices on the fifty-sixth floor at 30 Rockefeller Center, with an office for each brother, complete with one of the more beautiful Roualts. Lindsay came up, and as it turned out, Rockefeller must have been holding his 'call off Sid Davidoff' press conference as we were talking. [Davidoff was a senior Lindsay aide and the governor was publicly expressing pique at yet another issue that pitted Albany against Gracie Mansion]."[18] On Hinman's mind was a draft movement for Governor Rockefeller, supposedly started by the New York Young Republicans, and whether Lindsay was behind it. My journal records, "I said that from what I saw, I felt many of the Board of Governors [of the NYYRs] were doing this out of a conviction that NAR was the best man, and out of a frustration at having to accept an almost proxy candidacy by Romney." The Rockefeller forces' uncertainty at this point about what their best strategy would be was compounded by their conspiratorial fears of Lindsay. And Lindsay was attractive. Jock Whitney said to me, at the point even later on, when we were putting together the organized Rockefeller effort, that his preference would have been for Lindsay. He told me "that (though he seems to begrudge it) it simply is too early this time."[19]

Among those also noted briefly as possible Republican candidates was the senator from Illinois, Charles Percy, who had served as platform chair of the 1960 convention. His campaign never achieved first stage ignition, despite his business background and his political geography. Attention focused on governors instead.

Romney—and Always Rockefeller

Reagan was just being sworn in and populating his new administration and not yet attending to an incipient presidential bid, at least not outwardly. It was Romney—and always Nelson Rockefeller—on whom the light now shone. It was indeed the consensus view that Romney was the most likely person around whom moderates would muster. The Mormon governor of Michigan, who had been born of American Latter-Day Saints (LDS) parents in exile in Mexico, had an energy about him that amounted to evangelical zeal. He was self-made. He lacked a completed college education. He was jut-jawed and easily persuaded of his own rectitude. His moral strength, though, was genuine. He wore his convictions on his sleeve. He was not subtle. He had courage, unexpectedly plunging while campaigning, into enemy camps and rallies. At the same time, he was quick to take offense at slights and highly emotional. With all of this, or despite it, he emerged as the front-runner. Rockefeller was at this point out front advancing his—Romney's—cause at every opportunity. And Romney was running with astonishing strength in the polls. "No other Republican candidate in the 1968 election—or for the next four decades, for that matter—could match the Eisenhower-like poll numbers Romney received at his zenith."[20]

On August 17, 1967, Governor William Scranton called me and with some amusement and resignation told me that the New York governor had persuaded Scranton to accept an invitation to what included a "hilarious" game of golf with Romney and Rockefeller in Michigan. Nelson and Happy picked up Scranton and his wife, Mary, in Nelson's plane and then flew him to Michigan. He said Nelson "boxed me in." He would not let up on him until he agreed to endorse Romney. Scranton plaintively said to me, "I had not endorsed George, you know, but what could I do at that point?"[21]

Romney's key strategists, Al Applegate and Walter De Vries, traveled to Cambridge to sound out various Ripon people to work for the Romney campaign. They met with Jack Saloma, who had just returned from meetings in New York with Senator Javits, and Theodore H. White, the author of acclaimed books about the making of presidents. Saloma sensed "a growing coolness toward the governor's possibilities." Despite his pressuring Scranton to support Romney, Rockefeller could not adjust to being entirely out of the race. In a hallway conversation at a Palm Beach Republican governors extravaganza, hosted by the colorful Claude Kirk of Florida, Rockefeller mused that if there were a real draft, he might respond. Applegate and De Vries recorded that "Saloma says Nelson Rockefeller now definitely sees himself as a candidate; has reservations about Romney; and is looking toward a deadlocked convention (just like everybody else). 'Don't underestimate the move in this direction.'"[22]

All the same, Rockefeller continued to help Romney. Walter de Vries told me of Rockefeller turning over to de Vries and Romney the entire corpus of his research papers, a collection that would flatter the Library of Congress. In my phone conversation with him on November 5, 2015, de Vries was still in awe of the resources that Rockefeller poured into issues research:

> NAR opened up all his domestic and foreign policy research to us. It was fabulous and was on about any subject you could mention. It was better than anything you would find in government. He had contracted with experts who had written long reports. I spent four days there in his West Fifty Fifth Street offices going over all of this . . . [and] I moved into a George Romney for President office which we set up in Lansing. I kept up close contact with the Rockefeller forces.[23]

"The Ship of Fools"

In autumn 1967, there was an oceangoing meeting of the National Governors Association, aboard the liner the USS *Independence* sailing to the Bahamas. Wags of the time referred to it as "The Ship of Fools." Rockefeller was along, as were Reagan, Romney, and a huge number of the press corps. DeVries told me, "LBJ at this time was really anxious to get support for his war effort in Vietnam, especially the governors, and the Republican governors. He flew people back and forth on helicopters onto the ship to give briefings."

Romney was still wary of the depth and firmness of Rockefeller's support:

> On the cruise, there was a meeting which I believe has never been reported. There had by now been speculation that Rockefeller would run in '68. Three of us, Romney, Rockefeller and only I in addition, met in Rockefeller's suite on the ship. George Romney said directly to Rockefeller,

"Do you support me for President?" Rockefeller said, "Yes I do." Romney then asked the same question again, and Rockefeller gave the same answer. Then Romney asked, for the third time, "Do you support me for President?" Rockefeller gave the same answer. It made me think of the biblical scene of Christ and Peter.[24]

Rockefeller continued to be helpful to his Michigan counterpart and not just with research. Rockefeller dispatched his advisor Henry A. Kissinger to Mackinac Island in northern Michigan to the governor's home there to brief Romney on foreign policy. He also encouraged George Gilder to help Romney with speechwriting. DeVries said that was the first connection they had with the Gilder/Chapman duo. Romney then reached out to Bruce Chapman, my former New York roommate when he was working on the editorial page of the *NY Herald Tribune* for its editor, Raymond K. Price. The governor commissioned the New York Ripon chapter, which I then headed, to develop a series of proposals for protecting citizens from big, overcentralized government through an ombudsman scheme.

Romney campaigned for governor of Michigan as an activist and liberal figure. The civil rights cause was one in which he deeply, indeed passionately, believed. He was a hard-charging independent type, and the ticket splitting that helped him to victory reached an apogee at this time; it soon after entered a steep decline, with occasional revivals, notably in the 2020 election, where the Republican head of the ticket lost, or had fewer votes than down-ballot races for everything from US Senate and Congress positions to state legislative seats, which were captured or held by Republicans, running ahead of the Republican president.

Romney appeared to be the natural candidate for the remaining moderates in the party to support, given "Rocky's" hesitation. He also enjoyed considerable support from Christian conservatives. While his Mormon background may have held some back, Romney's fervent faith pulled many evangelicals to him—a force that was to grow to ever greater influence within the Republican Party. His polling was far stronger here than Rockefeller's, due likely to the latter's marital mishaps. Rockefeller did labor frequently through what we on his staff called the "BOMFOG" speech. This was the Brotherhood of Man, Fatherhood of God speech. It did not produce the reactions Romney's words and earnestness did among believers.

Romney reached a peak of support early in the cycle and seemed to rely more on conviction than on careful consideration of position. His lead became fragile. The air flowed quickly out of the balloon after an ill-considered remark on return from a Vietnam visit and its usual dose of military and diplomatic briefings. His comment that he had been "brain-washed" went "viral" in the day's context and suggested that he did not have his own clear views on one of the most pressing issues of the time and that he was too easily led.

A further impediment to his campaign was the creation of a duplicative campaign organization, according to De Vries. In later 1967 there was created a Washington Strategy Group, heavily influenced by Leonard Hall, a former RNC chair, "whose only claim to fame was managing Eisenhower's 1956 re-election campaign. ANYBODY could have successfully managed that campaign."[25]

The opening of an office apart from the Lansing group made it more difficult to coordinate the campaign. DeVries finally resigned in December 1967, over a difference in strategy, particularly over New Hampshire. Hall and the "old politics" people on the campaign were pushing for a New Hampshire effort that would be conducted from town to town, meeting locally, basically a few voters at a time. "I disagreed and advised we should skip New Hampshire and concentrate on Wisconsin. American Motors had a major plant there and lots of good will. Also, Romney's polling put him at 50% there, while in New Hampshire he was trailing."

Charlie McWhorter had a drink with me in late autumn 1967. McWhorter, born a West Virginian and a Nixon supporter since his service as legislative assistant to the vice president during the 1950s, was a fixture in the party, ubiquitous and known to all. A piece about him during the 1968 campaign by a journalist told of his sitting on a Nixon campaign plane, playing a small upright piano. It added, "The Republican Party is a loose confederation of individuals, held together only by Charlie McWhorter's Christmas Card list." Charlie was on a very long leash as a government affairs executive for AT&T, the telephone behemoth of the time. He was a bachelor and was devoted to Republican politics. He would crisscross the country constantly. He would arrive in a town with pocketsful of coins and begin at the first available phone booth to reach out to everyone he knew in that city. He spent his day moving between phone calls and a drink or meal with a Republican official or observer. His other outlet was music. He was a founder of the Newport Jazz Festival and a principal organizer of the Interlochen Music Festival in Michigan.

Romney was still leading the polls. McWhorter told me the Romney forces in New Hampshire were ignorant of the fact that most of the New Hampshire Romney delegates in the forthcoming winter 1968 primary were in fact clandestine Reagan supporters, simply trying to use Romney to knock out Nixon.

When DeVries saw the Washington Strategy Group, with Hall calling the shots, he feared nothing would change. "That was old politics," he said, "but ours in Michigan was new politics, with which Rocky agreed." I mentioned that Hall had fought Rocky for the 1958 New York governor's nomination and there might be no love lost between them. He had forgotten that.

Despite the increasing precariousness of the Romney quest, there was some reason for hope for moderate Republicans. By the next spring, in a May piece in the *Ripon Forum*, Lee Huebner was already looking back to the fall of 1967 as the high-water mark for moderate optimism. At that time, Huebner wrote, "the future seemed to belong to the Republican Party. It had the leaders and the momentum." The Democrats had no visible local victories such as Lindsay's in New York City in 1965, no Senate successes to compare to those of Edward Brooke, Charles Percy, Mark Hatfield and Howard Baker in 1966, and no results to compare to "the dynamic corps of GOP governors who were about to revitalize American politics." The party also had powerful ideas.

> Conservative and progressive Republicans alike talked excitedly about tax sharing, ending the draft, a negative income tax, the use of government to structure incentives, greater involvement of the private sector, the renewal of local and even neighborhood political initiative. An unpopular President and his unpopular foreign policy seemed to give Republicans access to the urban voter, the black community, and intellectuals—groups with which it could build a new political coalition which would become the leading force in American politics in the last third of the twentieth century.[26]

On December 11, 1967, there was a festive dinner held by the Ripon Society at the beautifully seasonally decorated Plaza Hotel on Central Park on a cold but clear night. The thronged and cheerfully warmhearted event for Ripon was given in honor of Senator Jacob K. Javits, the venerable liberal Republican warhorse of New York. Javits was less verbose than usual. He was instead heartfelt and almost entirely out of character. Instead of displaying his probing, often steely intellect and serious mien, the short, balding, energetic legislator said that what he felt that evening was love.

Notably, Richard Nixon was present. After his wounding 1962 loss, when Nixon moved to New York, he was treated by the Rockefeller party there as a "leper," as Pat Buchanan put it. Long before the 1960s, Nixon's relation to the Eastern Republican establishment was fraught, complex. The same Governor Thomas Dewey who had sealed Nixon's place on the Eisenhower ticket was within weeks suggesting, before the Checkers speech, that Nixon step off the ticket. Eisenhower's finance chair, John Hay Whitney, was the American Ambassador in London when Nixon, as vice president, made a visit. Nixon had asked Jock to put together a dinner for him. It was on short

December 1967 Ripon Society dinner honoring Senator Jacob K. Javits (*center*).
Richard M. Nixon on left; Governor Nelson A. Rockefeller on right. (Bettman/
CORBIS)

notice, and only twelve to fourteen people were there. Nixon was "furious
with Jock." Perhaps fueled by drink, Nixon complained about the group
Whitney had assembled, including three of the most prominent publishers
in the UK, the prime minister, the chancellor of the Exchequer, and the
Queen Mother.[27]

Despite his intelligence and competence, his position at the pinnacle of
American politics under Eisenhower, his dignified comportment after the
loss to John F. Kennedy, his senior partner status in a distinguished New
York law firm where he was the "name" partner, he felt uncomfortable in
New York's Republican Party circles. While he was often greeted with ap-
plause going out to a restaurant, the political insiders, seeing him as a threat
in 1964 or 1968, treated Nixon as an outsider, someone not quite acceptable.

That snubbing did not ebb. Nixon was deeply hurt by it. "Nixon was more sensitive . . . and wounded . . . than any figure I have known in fifty years around national politics," Pat Buchanan wrote. "The establishment disparaged and despised him for reasons I could not comprehend, given his centrist politics and even liberal policies, remarkable abilities, and extraordinary accomplishments. Yet, still, Nixon avidly sought out and welcomed their approbation and was stung by their attacks."[28]

When Rockefeller was in a hard reelection fight in 1966 and worried about losing, he sent feelers to Nixon for help and Nixon endorsed him firmly, working for him in upstate New York at a Syracuse event. Years later, I could feel some of the deep effects on Nixon of that shunning. He was helping me organize my congressional campaign back in New York for 1972. As we sat at his desk in late October 1971, he talked to me of how open California had been when he first ran, and how it still was. You could pull together a group of friends and just start building a campaign organization, raising money and knocking on doors. By contrast, he told me of how difficult it was to make your way into New York politics, how difficult the New York establishment was to crack open. He said it was a tight and tough organization, not welcoming to or easy for newcomers. "In New York, John," he told me, "you just have to kiss fanny." He still felt the painful rejection and embarrassment those years later. So, his presence at this Ripon/Javits evening with virtually the entire New York Republican establishment in the ballroom was exceptional.

Murray Kempton was a Baltimore-born journalist, inhaling H. L. Mencken's sulfurous journalism from infancy. Kempton had been a left-winger, the "Huckleberry Finn" of American journalism. He had written for the New York *Post*. Then he was editor of the *New Republic*. Kempton wrote of Nixon years later:

> The man they snatched the golden bough from, is the single most brilliant political analyst I've known in my life. . . . I had just seen John V. Lindsay, and I said to Nixon, "Lindsay has the greatest political future of anybody I've seen." And Nixon said, "Lindsay has no political future. In four years he'll have some terrible fight with Nelson Rockefeller and he'll end up a Democrat." Incredible!
>
> I've never understood him. . . . He had this incredibly keen political sense, which would just stop your breath, aethestically, but he was always a bit ashamed of it. . . . Whatever else he wanted to be, he wanted to be a great historical figure. And then he would collapse in awe before all these eastern Republicans. Intellectually, he was worth a hundred of those people.[29]

Governor Rockefeller followed Nixon and gave a short talk. Mayor John Lindsay then managed a comic turn. After he was introduced by one of the grandes dames of the New York Republican crowd, Mrs. John Hilson, Lindsay gave his greetings to "Nelson Rockefeller, Richard Nixon, and all my other fellow non-candidates." Mrs. Hilson introduced Lindsay as the "anchor man." Lindsay riffed on that, querying, "Does that mean I'm all wet or that I've been submerged for two years?"

A week later, I had brunch with Emil Frankel and Frank Samuel. Frank was another law school classmate. In the spirit of Emil's outreach as a recruiter for Ripon, as I had gotten to know Frank through an international law club, I asked him to become involved with Ripon. He had gone to Hiram College before our shared law school time. He married a wonderful Dutch/French woman, Jacqueline, and we friends gave them a twelve-volume venerable history of the Netherlands to enjoy together. Those books and countless others read with many friends in their decades-running book club, his cooking, and their two daughters they did enjoy together. Frank was to serve as a deputy assistant secretary at the Department of Health, Education and Welfare during Nixon's welfare and health-care initiatives, participating in the 1974 attempt by Nixon and Senator Edward Kennedy to join forces on a health-care bill.

The conversation that Sunday morning turned on Emil's reflections about the UK and US party mirror images. As I told my diary, "Emil, analogizing the moderate Labor Party to our own situation w/in the Rep. Party, also saying Wilson [Harold Wilson, then prime minister of Great Britain and head of the Labor Party] was a Nixonian type, having ridden left wing of Party in the way Nixon seeks to ride the right-wing of Repub. Party in this time."[30] While he might ride the Right, or at least get support from all but the Far Right, he coveted the center and the liberals for their importance in the general election. There, his rival once again was Nelson Rockefeller.

Nelson's nostrils began to flare. Others in the moderate wing of the party began to talk of him as the candidate to take up the banner, particularly as Ronald Reagan was showing every sign of inheriting the support of the conservatives, who were anxious to prove that Goldwater had been right and that his gospel could be better spread by a less impulsive and unpredictable missionary. Rockefeller's own strategy took account of Reagan. It was obvious that Nixon was the one to beat, for he held the center within the party and could bring with him most conservatives other than the core Right, which was Reagan's starting point. George Hinman was persuaded that if Rockefeller and Reagan could make common cause, from the Right and the Left, they could stop Nixon, preventing his first ballot victory at the convention. Hinman probably did not want to visualize the next scene of the drama, as it was almost inconceivable that Rockefeller could win over enough of the conservatives to outdraw the California governor on a second or later ballot.

Hinman's strategy required restraint in attacks by Rockefeller on the Right and emphasis once more on "electability." It also suggested that Rockefeller visibly exercise restraint or refusal to connect to liberal groups. The Ripon Society therefore was to lie in fallow soil, lacking the governor's support. As early as December 1964, Hinman had sought to block publication of Ripon's *Election 64* report. Ripon's board voted by one vote to proceed with publication, and Doug Bailey, a strong Rockefeller supporter, resigned, likely at Hinman's direction. Rockefeller himself, however, needed financial support, despite his vast personal resources. As the Romney collapse became more likely, Rockefeller looked ready to run. On the financial side, the "Establishment" began to coalesce.

And Then Rockefeller

In the summer of 1967, I made a decision to leave law practice. I mulled several ideas but one attracted me, as I record in my journal: "[Senator Jacob] Javits called me Thursday [September 28], saying he had not known I was available and offered me the job of project director or 'executive director' of his proposed national development corporation, charged essentially with getting it going. I will act as the liaison with him on the Bedford-Stuyvesant program, which is where I will be going to spend the next? years. Everyone thinks it is the perfect slot."

I joined and got into the spirit of it, reading the journals of David Lilienthal, who had directed the Tennessee Valley Authority (TVA) from its inception and found those "an inspiration." I went with Joel Fleischman, who was setting up an urban affairs group at Yale University, and Charles Abrams of Columbia to an intersection of streets in Brownsville, Brooklyn, which had half a century earlier been thriving. Abrams said the "bombed out quarter" of Powell and Livonia Streets was the worst urban area he had ever seen. The city had sealed up the buildings with lead. Only a few months later, John Doar was brought in to run the development corporation by Bob Kennedy, with Javits's blessing. Before the Rockefeller effort began in earnest, I found myself working for and trying in the usual fashion to understand the essentials about my new boss in Bedford-Stuyvesant.

Soon, my attention was wrenched back toward politics. On January 23, 1968, Dan Lufkin cohosted a dinner for Nixon with Bunny Lasker, who would the next year become chair of the New York Stock Exchange and who was a major fundraiser for Mayor Lindsay and now for Nixon. Another cochair was Maurice Stans, who would join Nixon's cabinet as commerce secretary. I sat between Fred Alger, a young fund manager, and George Champion, chairman of the Chase Manhattan Bank ("quite a generation contrast," I told my diary). Only while Bob Price, the architect of the 1964 Oregon Primary triumph by Rockefeller and deputy mayor of New York now, was present "was Nixon really animated, very eager for Price's every word, trying to avoid what he feared might be a negative result when Bunny asked Bob what he felt were the reasons RMN should be nominated, by saying, 'Don't put him on the spot.' Price responded very favorably to Nixon, stressing particularly his party loyalty: 'Dick was out working in '64 and '66 while others who would be the nominee were on the sidelines,' Price said."

Nixon was in full practical politics mode while Price was there, and his electricity was palpable. Here was where not only his skill but also his very being lay exposed. There was no one more knowledgeable about Republican Party politics than Nixon. Yet, ultimately, for this man, the Republican Party was an instrument. He had to remind himself every morning that he was a Republican. He was a man of endless expedience; that made him a great politician. And every first-class politician has a wider grasp. Nixon showed that in the rest of the dinner conversation, turning the talk to global oil strategy, sea lanes of communication, and other matters of geopolitical importance to the country.

Richard Nixon was not the only one looking for financial support. A week later, there was another of the many events at the home of Jock Whitney that gave a lifeline to Ripon, on this occasion five of us from Ripon, "the three angels (JHW, Paley and Thayer), and others."

> Our review with Whitney and Thayer lasted until after one in the morning. The State of the Union had occurred and the Republican response. On his second scotch upstairs, Whitney said to me that he was nonplussed by the Repub. Reply to State of the Union, and . . . he sent a letter to Geo. Murphy [Republican senator from California] saying he was sending no money to the committee [campaign finance] since the reply had "made my flesh creep."[31]

On February 1, 1968, a couple of days after the Whitney dinner, a few of us, including Petri, Marans, Walter Thayer, and I, sat in the Oak Bar of the Plaza, at the very table from which Cary Grant was kidnapped at gun point in *North by Northwest*. That morning, Rockefeller had showed Thayer a Romney/Nixon poll in New Hampshire, with Romney at 13, and Nixon at 64. An Oregon poll of Rockefeller's showed Reagan with only 13 percent of the vote there. Thayer mused aloud about Nixon, "I've got to fish or cut bait [he had given Nixon some money] and I am going to cut bait." The "Secretary General of the Eastern Republican Establishment" was about to swing to Rockefeller.

The next day, a New Jersey Republican met with Petri, Marans, and me and said he found little readiness on peoples' part to come forward and work for Nelson. He added, "The Rockefellers just don't use the power at their disposal—the Chase Manhattan, etc. They need to move NOW."[32] Four weeks later, on February 26, Whitney told me that he thought Rockefeller had over the weekend really altered course by talking of meeting a draft—a change, since earlier they were inclined to be coy until the Oregon primary. Within a week, Romney had withdrawn and Nelson was in. And then he was not. On March 21, he announced he was not running and that the party needed to choose someone who would need to be surprisingly like—Nelson Rockefeller!

Many of the Republican governors were early supporters of Rocky before this announcement, among them Spiro T. Agnew of Maryland, who was an enthusiastic cheerleader. I was dallying part time with the Rockefeller campaign during this time. I and a couple of other Rockefeller staffers met with Agnew in this phase of the campaign. But then came the bombshell.

A major ruction occurred. Agnew was stunned, and the financial friends confused. I myself was blindsided. Rockefeller had somehow concluded that he was more likely to obtain the nomination if the party came to him rather than him pursuing the nomination frontally. Agnew was outraged—and ambitious—and found ultimate revenge for his embarrassment at the Miami convention months later after he had shifted his loyalty to Nixon.

The finance people within the liberal wing of the party were more willing to overlook the ill-conceived tactic of coyness, seeing it as just that, a tactic. They would concentrate on trying to put together funding for the Rockefeller race. On Saturday, March 22, there was a three-hour lunch at the Links Club in Manhattan of Whitney, Thayer, Arch Gillies, Tim Petri, and myself. We talked about the comments made to me by the New Jersey financier that the Rockefeller people did not know how to use fully the resources of connections and power they enjoyed. Petri talked of using the correspondent bank relations Chase had all over the country, and the other ties linking establishment institutions and individuals, to lobby for the Rockefeller nomination. Whitney took it in. He commented about how the criticisms of the "Establishment" were shrill and frequent. They were getting under his skin.

As we spoke of how these levers might be exercised, Whitney became more and more animated. At last, he rose to his feet and put his arms up in the air above his head, shaking his hands in emphasis, "If we are going to suffer all this criticism for being the Establishment, then . . . LET US BE THE ESTABLISHMENT!" In the next days, Whitney and Thayer caucused with

Rockefeller and approached me to become head of the Delegate Intelligence Unit for the campaign and convention. Just a month after the Links Club lunch on March 22 with Jock, I made my decision, on April 22, to leave John Doar—he granted me a leave of absence—and to take up that job in Rockefeller's campaign.

Whitney and Thayer persuaded J. Irwin Miller of Indiana to come on as the finance chair of the Rockefeller effort. Miller was an interesting business figure, a principal owner of Cummins Engines, a major supplier to the US truck manufacturing business. A remarkable patron of the arts and architecture, he encouraged his community in Columbus, Indiana, to populate the city with commissioned buildings from leading international architects. He was profiled earlier that year in *Esquire*, with a front-page picture and a story emblazoned, "This Man Should Be President." Miller seconded one of his top executives at Cummins, Jim Henderson, to join the Rockefeller campaign full time.

The Establishment proved to be a Potemkin Village. Jim Reichley had accurately summarized the state of slow decay and eclipse of these ties, as he described the abortive efforts by Tom Dewey to rally those once in his national organization around the effort to stop the Goldwater takeover in the 1964 convention. Age, disinterest, death—all had vitiated the strength and punch of these people who once had held extraordinary influence over the party's affairs. The inexorable geographic population move south and west was also a powerful factor.

When I went to George Hinman for his list of the Rockefeller supporters, what I found did not induce optimism about our prospects. The list itself was mostly manual or occasionally typed, usually on note cards. I put a small staff together, with a remarkably resourceful and astute partner, Tanya Melich Silverman, an ABC News veteran political analyst. As we sought to contact those on the list, we found many were deceased.

As to the geographic power centers shifting in a fashion foretelling a far more conservative party, a lunch in Houston, Texas, was revealing. Warren Hellman was then a very young president of Lehman Brothers investment bank who had extensive contacts across the nation in the business community. I prevailed on Hellman to help me put together a lunch with him at the Petroleum Club in Houston to seek support for Rockefeller's candidacy. Organizing the lunch for us as an accommodation to Warren was Houstonian Robert Mosbacher. He was warm and cordial. At the same time, he made politely clear to us that he was doing this as a favor and that he would be supporting Ronald Reagan. And, so it went.

We worked hard. Even Henry Kissinger submitted to delegate hunting, being dispatched during the convention in Miami by us to lobby at poolside

John Roy Price with Governor Nelson Aldrich Rockefeller in spring 1968. John Roy Price personal collection.

Senator Jack Miller of Iowa and other wavering delegates who had shown an interest in foreign or defense policy matters. While there were hopeful moments, and Rockefeller campaigned vigorously, Nixon claimed his victory on the first ballot. Nixon relates in his memoir the congratulatory call he received from Rockefeller the next morning, during which Nixon then offered his condolences to Rockefeller. The governor said, somewhat wryly, that "Ronnie" just had not come through as Rockefeller had expected him to. After Miami, Tim Petri and I headed off for recovery to St. Thomas in the US Virgin Islands, where I took scuba diving lessons and Tim dove into the memoirs of General Charles de Gaulle. On my return to New York, I was encouraged to work for Nixon, first by Walter Thayer, who had shifted loyalty back to him; by Charlie McWhorter, whose loyalty always had been with him; and by John Doar, my Brooklyn development corporation boss, and the later chief impeachment lawyer for the House Judiciary Committee, who in September 1968 said that, as a Republican, given the alternative, I could do nothing else.

Nixon went on, in that chaotic year of the assassinations of Martin Luther King Jr. and Robert F. Kennedy, to campaign cautiously, taking account both of Vietnam and the George Wallace candidacy. The Alabama governor's bid was surprisingly strong. It was patently segregationist, though it also had broad Northern appeal among working-class men. In fact, many of those who had supported Robert F. Kennedy's bid for the Democratic nomination now moved to support Wallace. They were representative of part of the old Democratic coalition of labor and working-class and Northern Catholics. Nixon emphasized law and order and the appeals to cultural conservatism and patriotism that he and Patrick Buchanan had focused on to reach disenchanted Southerners, to those around the country who were concerned about the Vietnam War protesters, and to those concerned about job security and their futures.

Despite the law-and-order exhortations—not surprising, given the violence and divisions in America in 1968—the tenor of Nixon's acceptance speech at Miami, many remarks during the fall quest for votes, and his inaugural address all contained deep concern for the conflicts separating Americans from one another and were often uplifting, positive, and hopeful.

At the same time, he had clinched the nomination in part by assuring that Southern leaders were held close and did not shift to Reagan. I was by now working on the Nixon general election campaign, for Nixon's law partner, Leonard Garment. Two years after Nixon had come to Rockefeller's aid in the 1966 election at a Syracuse rally upstate, on October 29, 1968, Rockefeller hosted a massive rally there for Nixon. Following the rally, Governor Rockefeller asked me to sit with him on his plane back to New York. We talked of the lead up to the Miami convention. He expressed admiration for how Nixon had managed to hold out against his and Reagan's pincer movement but was impressed with my saying how tight it had been for Nixon on the Monday and Tuesday nights. His eyes closed to slits when I said I had learned of Nixon's phone call to Thurmond on the Tuesday, and he made a face when I said that, so far as I could learn, nothing specific had been promised.

Leonard Garment says that promises were made. Garment admired Nixon, although he said to me, "Nixon has an angel on one shoulder and a dark angel on the other. He is both." Garment was Nixon's law partner in New York and a liberal Democrat. Len later came into the White House, where he helped shepherd civil rights issues. In his wonderful memoir, *Crazy Rhythm*, he says that Nixon would promise Thurmond the moon and stars and the next day show him the back of his hand. Garment could be quick and could be impish. I was with Garment in his White House office on July 18, 1970. Only the day before had been "a highly significant day, since Thurmond finally lashed out at us . . . Len . . . kept looking at his office door, but said, 'Bingo!' He said that Haynes Johnson [*Washington Post* journalist] had called him with the news and asked his reaction. Len said, 'Hmmm. . . . But that's not for attribution!'"[33]

Nixon's election victory was only a plurality and a very tight one at that. Wallace carried five states and forty-six Electoral College votes. Democrat Hubert Humphrey's defeat was in part due to the division within his party over the war. Both the war and Wallace voters would be on Nixon's mind as he moved now from campaigning to governing. He had climbed to what Benjamin Disraeli termed "the top of the greasy pole."

It remained to be seen where Nixon would lead his domestic policy. So many factors would influence him. He had been an Eisenhower Republican. Nixon believed that government had a constructive role to play and thought it could function better. He saw the shift in the Republican Party base moving steadily south. He heard the anti-government mantra of the Reaganites. He had watched in the mid-1960s as many Republicans fought the creation of Medicare and Medicaid, but he had personal experience with desperate illness in the family and reflexively knew that the costs of medical care or its unavailability could be devastating. Neither he nor the opposing congressional Republicans made a multiyear campaign of trying to repeal Medicare and Medicaid. He was aware, acutely and politically, of the abuses of the welfare system as it was in 1968. He understood the balance between desperate need, pride, self-sufficiency, and the paramount importance of work.

He carried scar tissue of the many attacks on him by the liberals and the Left, first prompted by his campaigns for the House and the Senate and his own attacks on the Left and by his successful prosecutorial attack on Alger Hiss, whom many establishment figures vigorously defended. He also carried the searing memory of attacks on him by the right wing. John C. Whitaker was one of Nixon's most loyal and long-serving aides. In two long talks I had with him on October 26, 1970, John spoke to me of Nixon's aversion to the Far Right conservatives. John said, "[Nixon] just does not like the Right wing at all, and has said to him, 'They just don't like people.' He thinks Nixon 'much more moderate than the press lets him seem—at least the Eastern press.'"[34]

All of these influenced his approach to domestic and social policy issues. They would emerge in his first term, and in meeting them, he would define his presidency.

CHAPTER 5

The Oval Office Has a New Occupant

The Oval Office had a new occupant, although Lyndon Johnson's trappings and tastes there had not yet vanished—and would not in fact until summer. The soft, light-green rug and off-white sofas were still in place, and his three adjacent television consoles lined the wall. They allowed that news-hungry president to watch simultaneously the product of the three great networks, in those days still the dominant channels of news and interpretation to the American people of the day's events. The presidency had, on this day, January 20, 1969, changed in peaceful succession. The transfer of power, however, saw no clean break with the tumultuous immediate past in the nation.

The year and a half before inauguration day had seen opposition to the Vietnam war become ever more intense. A small but memorable episode in the many protests against the war occurred on January 15, 1968. It was overwhelmed by the scale of the later protests and marches on the capitol. Yet, on that day, Jeannette Rankin led a "brigade" of five thousand women to ask for an end to the war. Rankin was a suffragist and campaigner for the right to vote for American women. She was a Republican.

At a dinner she and I had in 1965, Rankin related to me her own quest for office. In 1916, she drove a station wagon all over the vast reach of Montana, before women had the vote nationally, successfully campaigning for the at-large congressional seat in the Treasure State. Seated in March 1917, she was the first woman ever to hold a seat in the United States Congress. Less than a month later, she voted against American entry into World War I.

As the only woman in that Congress, she then proudly voted for the passage of the Nineteenth Amendment to the Constitution, to provide universal suffrage. Rankin was defeated in 1918. In 1940, she once more won a seat in the House. She voted against the declaration of war on Japan and the Axis powers, in December 1941, after the attack on Pearl Harbor. This time, she was the only vote in the entire Congress against American entry into World War II. A picture after that vote shows her, frightened and huddled in a phone booth, surrounded and beset by outraged members of Congress of both parties. Her vote was a matter of conviction. Of the two Montanans honored by their state with statues in Statuary Hall in the US Capitol, one is Jeanette Rankin.[1] A consistent philosophy of pacifism like Rankin's, however, was not the principal motivation for the 1960s protestors who, often violently, were against America's war in Asia. Furthermore, it was not only the Vietnam War that was roiling the waters of American politics.

The horror of the Watts, California, race riots of 1965 was profound. The riot lasted nearly a week and led to many deaths and more than one thousand injuries. There were repeats in other cities in 1966 and 1967. Major race-related incidents, with destructive arson, theft, injury, and death, erupted in Detroit, Michigan, and Newark, New Jersey. In the spring of 1968, the assassination of Reverend Martin Luther King Jr. occurred. King had been a force for peaceful and prayerful but steady resistance to discrimination and hate. I was in my office in the Granada Hotel in central Brooklyn, working for the Bedford-Stuyvesant corporation. From my window, I could see the smoke in the distance arising from the spontaneous outpouring of rage after King's assassination in Memphis, Tennessee, by a white nationalist. In Brooklyn, the communities of East New York and Brownsville were aflame.

Violence and protest convulsed throughout one hundred urban areas in 1968. They were sparked and fanned not only by the assassination of Dr. King but also by the June murder of Senator Robert F. Kennedy, the very night of his victory in the California Democratic presidential primary. These many cities struggling with lawlessness were of all sizes and of all demographic patterns. They included Washington, DC, where riots tore through the downtown area of the Fourteenth Street corridor, only blocks from the White House, which lies at the foot of Sixteenth Street. The vestiges of the breakage, looting, and fires were still obvious and intrusive when President Nixon rode back from the Capitol on inauguration day, often jeered at and his car a target of debris, on his way to the White House, from which he would view the inaugural parade.

Racial tensions had mounted during the 1960s. Police discrimination and abusive behavior had led to the creation in many cities of civilian review boards to monitor the police actions in racially charged situations or communities. Gaps in economic attainment between white people and minorities were far more pronounced than they have come to be in succeeding decades. Employers' discrimination in hiring and trade and industrial unions' resistance to accepting minorities as union members underlay this. So, too, did dramatic gaps in educational and vocational training opportunities between the races—those very tools that could lead to securing a solid and decently compensated job. The federal effort under Lyndon Johnson's War on Poverty saw a substantial increase in job and earning opportunities for minorities. While there was a move toward closing the long-existing income gap between whites and nonwhites, there was a more substantial gain for minority middle-class poverty strategists and social service workers, partly causing the overall closure. The presumed intended beneficiaries, the poor themselves, felt benefit from these programs, but poverty was by no means eliminated.

Furthermore, the system of welfare, a child of the New Deal, born in the Social Security Act of 1935, had grown to be an ineffective and perversely incentivized offspring of that legislation. Consequently, welfare had become a political issue. It had racial overtones, as the urban, Black female-headed family was a principal recipient of the Aid to Families with Dependent Children (AFDC) program. Huge growth in the welfare rolls of Northern major cities showed no prospect of slowing. The family tragedies and incentives to family breakup in a system of state-managed AFDC programs with various requirements and levels of support added a profound human element to what was also a growing fiscal peril and political flashpoint.

The new president would face these realities as he finished taking his oath of office. Richard Nixon was sworn in on the east side of the Capitol as America's thirty-seventh president on a gray and chilly day. Former three-term Republican California governor Earl Warren was chief justice of the Supreme Court, having been appointed by President Eisenhower. Warren had once been a presidential hopeful and had run for national office as Dewey's vice-presidential nominee in 1948. He entertained hopes in 1952 of being the top spot nominee and positioned himself as the "favorite son" of the California delegation. Nixon, choosing to travel by train with most of the California delegation for two days and nights from California to Chicago, sedulously cultivated the delegates for Eisenhower, trying to undercut any Taft influence on the delegation. Doing so meant reducing any chance Warren had of emerging through an impasse. Indeed, Governor Warren's last hopes of the presidency had likely in this way been derailed on that train ride by Nixon. And this was the same Earl Warren, who a decade after that subversion by Nixon in 1952 had his revenge. Nixon, two years after his presidential defeat, was running for governor of California against the Democratic governor. Warren's son campaigned actively for Democratic Governor Pat Brown, and Warren himself, while chief justice, appeared with Nixon's opponent. With the right-wingers staying home after Nixon won the primary, and this bit of help by the Warrens, Brown won in 1962 by 300,000 votes.[2]

In the curious way of politics, it was the self-same Earl Warren who now administered the oath of office to Richard Nixon on inauguration day. The oath was spoken by Richard Nixon on the same side of the Capitol where Lincoln had taken the oath, in March 1861. The dome of the building at that time was still under construction, almost a metaphor for what Lincoln must do to perfect the Union. As with the time of Lincoln's inaugural, unrest, division, and violence in the country were all too present in Nixon's moment. There was menace in the air. At Lincoln's oath-taking, the march to war and sundering of the Union were imminent. With Nixon's January 1969 inaugural, there was another form of civil war. The combination of conflict over the Vietnam War and violence surrounding the civil rights movement was dry tinder, easily and frequently lit. The year's conflagrations around the country led to extraordinary measures. At the time of the inaugural itself, I observed on my right and left that machine guns had been placed on the concrete escarpments of the Capitol building.

The year 1968 saw a president announce that he would not seek reelection because he concluded rightly that his candidacy would provoke ever greater violent protests and end in his defeat. Even with Johnson out of the running and Robert F. Kennedy still being mourned, the Democratic Party's nominating convention exposed a chasm of differences. There were snarling attacks on speakers on the rostrum inside the convention hall itself and chaos outside it in the streets of Chicago. The violence met with violence from Chicago's police force, cheered on by an angry and orthodox Mayor Richard Daley. Jock Whitney believed television had completely affected America's view of the Vietnam War, bringing the violence and tragedy into American homes. Richard Nixon understood that the mayhem in Chicago at his rival's nomination would have dramatic implications as it unfolded on television in peoples' living rooms. "Like millions of other Americans watching television that night, I did not want to believe my eyes," Nixon writes. "It seemed as if the Democrats' convention was confirming every indictment of their leadership that I had made in my campaign speeches. Television magnified the agony of Chicago into a national debacle."[3]

The mayor of Chicago was the very embodiment of a Democratic big city machine leader, in the spirit of Tammany Hall in New York. He had been instrumental in the victory of John Kennedy in 1960. That night in 1968 he projected spleen. Fury. The Democratic Party that week seemed as riven or worse than the Republican Party had four years earlier, as it emerged from the San Francisco Goldwater convention. Nixon made much during the campaign of these divisions in America. His tactical shrewdness told him that the Democratic Party's fissures provided an opening that he could and did skillfully exploit.

Another remarkable development in the 1968 campaign involved Russia. Anatoly Dobrynin was the Soviet ambassador in Washington and was the man who revealed these events in his memoir. Dobrynin ultimately served the longest in America of any ambassador from any country, becoming dean of the diplomatic corps in Washington. Dobrynin dealt with Kennedy, Johnson, Nixon, Ford, Carter, and Reagan.

Nixon throughout his career was a consistent and articulate foe of communism and of Soviet ambitions to extend their reach and sway. Nixon, in

Moscow's eyes, writes Dobrynin, "was considered profoundly anti-Soviet. Our leadership was growing seriously concerned that he might win the election." As 1968 unfolded, discussions in Moscow turned on with whom and in what ways the Soviets might influence the election. Dobrynin was startled to receive a top-level instruction from Andrei Gromyko, the Soviet foreign minister, personally. The Politburo was growing concerned with Nixon's continued lead. "As a result, the top Soviet leaders took an extraordinary step, unprecedented in the history of Soviet-American relations, by secretly offering Humphrey any conceivable help in his election campaign—including financial aid."

Dobrynin pushed back, afraid it could backfire and ensure Humphrey's defeat, "to say nothing of the real trouble it would have caused for Soviet-American relations." He was told, "There is a decision, you carry it out." Soon after, Dobrynin was at a Sunday breakfast at Humphrey's home, where naturally they talked about the campaign, so Dobrynin tried to carry out his instructions, "as tactfully as possible." The ambassador worked the conversation around to "the state of his campaign finances." "Humphrey, I must say, was not only a very intelligent but also a very clever man," Dobrynin writes. "He knew at once what was going on. He told me it was more than enough for him to have Moscow's good wishes which he highly appreciated. The matter was thus settled to our mutual relief, never to be discussed again."[4]

Dobrynin went on to say, "This story has never been told before. The Politburo always watched American presidential elections closely for their potential effect on Soviet-American relations and usually had a preference but rarely expressed it or took sides by offering diplomatic or other help. To my knowledge this was the only time Moscow tried to intervene directly to help a favored candidate—and it got nowhere."[5] Humphrey displayed not only a shrewd perception but also a tactful rebuttal of what was being attempted and what he knew was ethically and politically improper—and illegal. The Soviet Union at the time was a strategic foe. The irony is that from the moment of his election, and in his inaugural address, Nixon specifically laid out a strategy of "negotiation, not confrontation." His détente with the Soviet Union was one of the defining points of his presidency.

On the domestic front, Nixon understood the anger and fear in many voters about the disintegration of public order and radical shifts in private behavior, including the drug culture, the burning of draft cards, and the sexual revolution. With abundant conviction, he was the candidate urging law and order and an appeal to more traditional values.

Yet at another level, he heard and seemed to understand a palpable and shared longing for domestic peace and understanding—a national cri de coeur. On a campaign train stop in Deshler, Ohio, a Nixon aide saw a young girl in the crowd holding aloft a handmade sign, "Bring us together again." Nixon would refer to it with frequency on the campaign trail thereafter, and in a Madison Square Garden rally at October's end, and yet again in his victory statement on November 6. Nixon had always believed that the general elections were ultimately won at the center. The young girl's plea resonated with Nixon's sense that not only in campaigning but even more crucially in governing, he had to heal partisan wounds, show magnanimity, and try to be the leader of more than the minority that had secured him the country's highest office.

In keeping with this, Nixon's remarks in his victory speech Election Night were deeply generous to his narrowly defeated rival. In that moment of his triumph, Nixon at length spoke to Humphrey's campaign workers and supporters, noting their dedication and hopefulness and asking that they stay involved in public life and political activism, despite the bitter discouragement of their recent defeat. He reached out to his rival. Two days after the election, Nixon flew with his family to Key Biscayne, Florida, for rest. The next day, he drove to meet both Senator and Mrs. Humphrey, and Humphrey's running mate and his wife, Senator and Mrs. Edmund Muskie of Maine, all four together in Opa Lacka, Florida, as they were on their way to a vacation in the Virgin Islands. He proposed to Humphrey that he take on the job of ambassador to the United Nations, and Humphrey reflected on it before declining some days later. This was not a victorious candidate who was vengeful or vindictive.[6]

It was a candidate who was prepared. Nixon was hardly cocksure of election. Memories of his 1960 defeat served as an antidote to any overconfidence in the autumn of 1968. He led Humphrey in double digits coming out of the Democrats' chaotic Chicago convention. He had anticipated his polling numbers to decline from their large lead over Humphrey—and they did. He understood that the George Wallace candidacy would take a bite out of Humphrey's traditional white working-class and union voter support in the North. Still, Wallace in the race was a wild card.

On September 9, 1968, Wallace came up in a discussion that Lee Huebner, Gene Marans, and I had at the home of a coworker of mine from the unsuccessful Rockefeller campaign of that year, Thomas P. Melady, who was attentive to church matters and voters. He was very close to the Roman Catholic Church, and later he held the post under President Ronald Reagan of Ambassador to the Holy See (the Vatican). He told us of his fears that white immigrants would break and vote for Wallace. The Catholic Church was the home for many of these European nationalities—from Italians, Portuguese, and Spaniards to Slavs and Hungarians—who had over several generations emigrated here, all through Ellis Island and Emma Lazarus's Golden Door to the promised land. Their parishes still filled the old textile, fishing, steel-making, automotive, and other manufacturing urban areas of the country, mostly in the North, in cities such as Fall River, Flint, Gary, and Pittsburgh. Bishop John Joseph Wright of Pittsburgh had told Melady of his own depression in the last couple of weeks at serving communion to Hungarian petitioners, who were wearing Wallace buttons.[7]

They had no truck for the liberal causes of the panjandrums of the Democratic Party. The Roosevelt Democratic coalition of Northern liberals and race-baiting Southerners was defunct. Some new political order was struggling to be born. The Wallace phenomenon was intriguing, as it was not strictly a Thurmond segregationist echo of the South Carolinian's disruptive campaign in 1948. It had a distinctly Northern resonance, and it was powerfully anti-elitist. Yet Wallace accepted an invitation to speak at Dartmouth College during that campaign and was accorded there a civil hearing, with an animated question and answer session, even though he was in hostile territory among young, Ivy League undergraduates.[8]

The Wallace phenomenon continued to draw Nixon's and Patrick J. Buchanan's attention, not only during the campaign but also throughout the first term. Buchanan, Nixon's emissary to the conservative movement, said to me in conversation in 2015, "We always had Wallace on our minds."[9] This awareness of the grievances of the Wallace voter, and the uncertainty about economic opportunities and prospects, became an important factor in the way Nixon was to approach his social policy. That policy would turn out to include a national health insurance proposal to cover all, with help on paying premiums if you could not afford them, a unified and broad-reaching food stamp program, and a radical income maintenance program, encompassing both those dependent on traditional "welfare" and, importantly, those who were working—even working full-time—but struggling to make ends meet for their families.

Before he entered the White House, there was the campaign. Policy, ideas, speeches, opinion pieces—all were important in the campaign but not central. In the candidate's and his managers' attention, the focus was on ensuring that campaign techniques were the most up-to-date. Nixon had fallen victim in 1960 to the novel medium of television and its favoring of the more glamourous and at ease Kennedy. In 1968, his team appropriated and used the most sophisticated television, advertising, and public relations (PR) techniques. He was determined to campaign as effectively in this realm as possible, and a troika of three managers, Harry Treleavan, Frank Shakespeare, and Leonard Garment, focused on the most sophisticated staging, promotional, and media events available at the time. By the Obama and Trump administrations, these would be carried to new levels and engage new social media, but Nixon's 1968 media and PR campaign was the most carefully crafted and managed of any up to its time.[10] Campaigning was not, of course, the object of Nixon's quest. To govern was the goal of campaigning. Nixon had spent his entire life and career in preparation for the opportunity to lead.

Nixon's inaugural address was the first full and formal statement of his vision for the country and his ambitions to lead the country there. Intriguingly, his speech of January 20, 1969, stood in stark contrast to that of the man who had narrowly defeated him eight years earlier. John F. Kennedy's inaugural spoke almost exclusively to foreign affairs. It staked out an ambition for Americans in terms of both military firmness and cohesive alliances for resisting the push of aggressor foes, as well as a goal of preserving and defending democracy around the world. It called for new economic initiatives, including in South and Central America, that would help our friends there and those in need around the world and for Americans to unleash their energy in these efforts. Kennedy said almost nothing about US domestic policy issues.

The inaugural address Richard Nixon gave was, in contrast, heavily oriented toward domestic matters.[11] True, the new president did assert that the "greatest honor history can bestow is the title of peace maker," the inscription carved on the headstone of his grave, next to that of his wife, in his birthplace in Yorba Linda, California. "After a period of confrontation, we are entering an era of negotiation," Nixon asserted. "Those who would be our adversaries, we invite to a peaceful competition—not in conquering territory or extending dominion, but in enriching the life of man."

At the same time, the address clearly was centered on the currents and swells in domestic concerns and politics. Nixon was seeking to calm the seething anger of the late 1960s. Trying to soothe and quiet the raucous voices, he said, "We are torn by division, wanting unity. . . . America has suffered from a fever of words; from inflated rhetoric . . . from angry rhetoric that fans discontents into hatreds."

Lower Our Voices

This was not Roger Stone's Richard Nixon.

Richard Nixon in 1937 was in West Branch, Iowa, birthplace of Herbert Hoover and site of their shared Quaker background. He toured the Hoover birthplace in that small Iowa town with his mother, his maternal grandmother, his two remaining brothers, Don and Ed, and local Quaker relatives. The family was crossing the country together, heading home to California after Nixon's graduation from Duke Law School. At Duke, where he had won a tuition scholarship, for shelter the family's tight finances meant that Nixon found and lived in an abandoned tool shed in a forest near the golf

The Nixons in Quaker Country. Richard Nixon with mother, Hanna, at far right; brother Don back left; brother Ed front row left; and his grandmother, Almira Milhous, in front of Nixon's mother, with various West Branch, Iowa, Quaker relatives. Taken June 1937, en route home from Nixon's law school graduation. Courtesy Herbert Hoover Presidential Library.

course. He was a squatter. The shed had no stove and he used corrugated cardboard for insulation—all the while studying law and emerging first in his class that year.

Decades later, as he continued his inaugural address, Nixon prescribed quiet, a Quaker notion of turning to a peaceful demeanor and inner reflection. "To lower our voices would be a simple thing," he said. "We cannot learn from one another until we stop shouting at one another—until we speak quietly enough so that our words can be heard as well as our voices." We need to listen to "the better angels of our nature." The call for quiet was accompanied by a commitment to hear the "voices of quiet anguish . . . [and] the voices that have despaired of being heard." He pledged, "Those who have been left out, we will try to bring in. Those left behind, we will help to catch up." We had to move "urgently" forward "in pursuing our goals of full employment, better housing, excellence in education; in rebuilding our cities and improving our rural areas; in protecting our environment and enhancing the quality of life." He said, "As we chart our goals, we shall be lifted by our dreams. . . . This means Black and white together, as one nation, not two.

The laws have caught up with our conscience. What remains is to give life to what is in the law."

In a passage squarely in the middle of the speech was a phrase that captures a central predicament of Richard Nixon's moment, and indeed of our own: "We will set as our goal the decent order that makes progress possible and our lives secure." Social institutions were imperiled because confidence in them was imperiled. Institutions serve a core and cohering purpose in society, and one of Nixon's greatest insights at the time of taking office was this realization. Many of his initiatives sought to remove from these institutions, including the basic institution of the family, the unsustainable stress of programs that had been poorly thought out. He recognized the fragility of the public's support for social, governmental, church, and other institutions. One of the greatest tragedies of his tenure was that his own behavior, perhaps born in part by relentless hounding and criticism by his political enemies and their total unwillingness to accept or support many of his major positive efforts, fostered a deep cynicism among the American public. Their trust in government declined on his watch.

While both the 1961 Kennedy address and the 1969 Nixon address employed lofty rhetoric, for Nixon the central issues were to tone down the rhetoric and to lay out a course toward making government responsive to the most pressing needs of the people. Nixon shared his concerns about the fragility of institutions and the need for their strengthening and legitimizing with Daniel P. Moynihan, a Democrat who came to serve the new president.

Much of my story is concerned with Moynihan and Nixon and their shared views on the institutions of government, the broader society and family, and the problem and alleviation of poverty and economic insecurity. At the beginning of Nixon's time in office, there likely was no one who so brought out the better angels in the nature of Richard Nixon than Moynihan, no one who engaged his strong intellect as powerfully, and no one who found a marriage of policy interest with Nixon's concern about those who were struggling and born without privilege and access.

The inaugural laid out sweeping visions that needed to find a footing in domestic strategy, program analysis, and initiatives. The address had been preceded by work done in the months before January 20, which described the tasks ahead and identified some program ideas and some people who would take a place in the new administration. During the autumn campaign and the transition period between Election Day and inauguration, Nixon created a number of task forces to advise him. JFK had done this. LBJ used task forces often during his presidency. Nixon's approach was most surely also an inheritance of his time in the Eisenhower regime. Nixon had spent eight years in a highly structured White House under Eisenhower, with management decision-making borrowing from a military staffing structure. Nixon was convinced that good management was a vital component of governing, even though the debates, formality, and clearance requirements in Ike's White House could drive Nixon to distraction, especially if the issue were one that he felt was urgent for either the party's election prospects for Congress in the off-year cycles or his own 1960 effort.

Twenty-one groups in all were anointed to prepare ideas for the fledgling administration. The members of the groups were a mix of academics, including many economists and a Nobel Prize–winning physicist (who chaired the space task force), business executives, bankers, and foundation leaders. Virtually all the groups focused on domestic issues, with the exception of the space group and task forces on International Trade, headed by Alan Greenspan, an economist and future chair of the Federal Reserve Board, and International Economic Policy, headed by Gottfried Haberler, a Harvard professor whose specialty was trade policy.

A task force on the organization of the executive branch, known as the Lindsay Task Force on Government Organization, underlined Nixon's interest in the organization of government. Its chair was Franklin A. Lindsay, a corporate CEO, now president of the Itek Corporation and a person with governmental experience himself.[12] Nixon never held the view that government was the problem. Despite his frequent and often picturesquely expressed disdain or resentment of federal bureaucracy, he was convinced that there were essential programs for assuring economic opportunity and security that the government must perform. To restore people's faith in government, government had to work effectively.

Lindsay's group's proposals led directly to a body created by the president in April 1969. Named for its chair, Roy Ash, the CEO of Litton Industries, the "Ash Council" was formally known as the Commission on the Reorganization of the Office of the President. It had a number of influential members, including Walter N. Thayer and John B. Connally, the former Democratic governor of Texas. The strapping Texan was to parlay his exposure to Nixon via the Ash Council's work into a position of great influence with the president. Ash built a staff whose recommendations led to some of Nixon's most lasting and major governmental reorganization moves. These included the restructuring of the Bureau of the Budget, in the Executive Office of the President, into the Office of Management and Budget[13] and the creation of the Domestic Council and the Environmental Protection Agency.

Nixon had been vice president when Eisenhower formed the Commission on Executive Organization, known as the Second Hoover Commission for its chair, the former president Herbert C. Hoover. The Hoover Commission was part of a history of examination of how to make government work better. An earlier Brownlow Commission had set the standard. A "First" Hoover Commission (1947–1949) had resulted in the Reorganization Act of 1949 that saw much usage later. It also had put the cabinet-level and presidentially chaired National Security Council into the Executive Office of the President.[14] The Second Hoover Commission focused on the role for the president of the Bureau of the Budget. It started to ask questions about oversight by the president of management of government programs.[15] These questions became the key concern of the Ash Council.

Nixon first organized his own immediate entourage. Learning from his ill-fated effort to manage his 1960 campaign, he had recruited his law partner, John Mitchell, to manage the 1968 campaign. Complementing Mitchell was Nixon's longtime aide for the electioneering side of Nixon's life, H. R. "Bob" Haldeman. Haldeman was the key whip on the campaign trail, overseeing the advance staff, scheduling, public relations, and other support.

Once the election was won, Nixon turned to Haldeman to take over the task of managing the White House for him. Mitchell was to go to the Justice Department to become the attorney general. Mitchell continued to be the crucial political advisor to the president, but Haldeman was the one who made the trains run on time. Haldeman assembled a small and young staff, many of them his colleagues at the J. Walter Thompson advertising agency, where Haldeman was a senior executive when not managing Mr. Nixon's campaigns. These young people, most under the age of thirty, filled out his organization, along with his recruitment of his occasional double-dating friend from university days, Alexander P. Butterfield. Butterfield left an active-duty Air Force colonel position, during which he had flown more than one hundred combat missions in Vietnam, to become wingman to Haldeman as his deputy. The Haldeman staff was to make things orderly. As John Farrell observes,

> They were marketers, not ideologues or policy wonks. Their job was to manage things for Nixon, not to pursue some cause or partisan purpose. . . . They never forgot what Nixon craved: a controlled clime, and time and room to think, and plot, and brood, mostly about foreign policy. Haldeman designed a system in which access to the Oval Office—by people or paper—was funneled through his office. It was efficient and met its goal.[16]

Haldeman immediately began to assert his authority over the White House paper flow, as he had over the campaign. While the seasoned campaign workers now joining White House units were accustomed to this arrangement, there were many newcomers to the White House staff for whom there was a period of learning and adaptation. At the earliest moment, Daniel

Patrick Moynihan and I unintentionally ran afoul of the Haldeman imperative that all roads lead to Rome—but through him. That was in the very first
days of the president's term, but the first impression created in Haldeman's
mind was an important factor in his and others' lasting attitudes toward us
outsiders.

Wholly apart from the tasks of executive organization, managing paper
flow, and presidential scheduling was the need to come to grips with the
policy issues that would require the president's focus. Welfare was an early
candidate for attention. One of the transition task forces had been on intergovernmental fiscal relations. It was chaired by a young (thirty-three years
old) Richard P. Nathan. Nathan had worked for Senator Kenneth B. Keating,
whose seat Robert Kennedy won from the Rochester, New York, Republican
in 1964. Nathan went on to work for Governor Nelson Rockefeller. Still later,
when selected to head the intergovernmental group, he was at the Brookings
Institution. Nathan's subsequent important role in the Nixon administration
reflected both his pedigree of Northern, big state, moderate Republicanism
and the fiscal imperatives of their governors.

As Nathan started parsing intergovernmental fiscal relations with his
group, his competence and the obvious link between big state fiscal stress
and burgeoning welfare rolls led to his being placed in charge also of the task
force on public welfare. The Nathan welfare task force's work had a lengthy
and important afterlife in policy considerations and in the roles of two of its
members in the new administration. Its conclusions were to form the basis
of one of the strenuously contesting schools of thought on how Nixon should
deal with welfare.

The Nathan task force membership illustrates that the choice of personnel
makes policy. Besides the chair, other key members included a human legacy
of the Eisenhower and even Franklin Roosevelt administrations, Marion Folsom. Folsom had served as secretary of the Department of Health, Education, and Welfare under Ike and had been one of the young draftsmen of the
original Social Security Act in the 1930s. The states that were carrying the
burden of making high welfare payments under the Aid to Families with
Dependent Children (AFDC) were well represented. The federal government made payments in partial subvention to the costs of welfare in high
cost-of-living states, like New York, yet these states still had to supplement
the federal payments to give recipients something like a living-level allot-
ment. The fiscal drag on places like New York State and New York City was
becoming herculean with what was an explosive growth of the welfare rolls
in the mid- and later 1960s.

Wilbur Schmidt, the secretary of the Wisconsin Department of Health
and Human Services, represented another high-benefit Northern state.

Mitchell I. Ginsberg was head of the Human Resources Administration for New York City. The growth in welfare population—originally thought by the new Lindsay team taking office in 1966 to be the result of slack screening by bureaucrats that would be easily remediable by new policy and supervision—ultimately proved to be rooted in far more serious issues of dependency and of the very structure of the welfare laws. Ginsberg was nationally known and was coping with the nation's largest, and most expensive, welfare program.

New York, with its thirst for fiscal relief at the heart of its desire for "welfare reform" had yet a third voice on the panel. Robert Patricelli was serving as a staff member for New York's Republican US senator Jacob K. Javits, on the Senate Education and Labor Committee, who had a strong interest in welfare and jobs.

Since he took his legislative activity very seriously, Javits was informed and attentive to welfare issues as they affected New York. As Vincent and his wife and coauthor, Vee, Burke note in their book on Nixon's welfare efforts, "The composition of this task force virtually assured a report that would not disturb the basic structure of welfare, but would merely propose more for those within it."[17] To the extent that the federal government assumed more costs for these high-benefit states, there would be both fiscal relief for the governmental bodies and possible higher benefits for the recipients. Money being fungible, that relief could be applied to anything from university campuses and highway construction to tax reductions. In support of this kind of help for their states, Nixon's 1968 rivals for the nomination, Rockefeller of New York and Reagan of California, lined up with much more speed and common purpose than they had in trying to block Nixon at Miami. Over the coming welfare battle, they were usually united in opposition to what Nixon ultimately embraced and in favor of fiscal help for their states.

Nathan's chairmanship of the task force on intergovernmental fiscal relations and then of the Welfare Task Force catapulted him into a crucial role as assistant director of the Bureau of the Budget for Human Resources. There, his staff was the repository of expertise for the president on welfare and social policy, complementing the expertise within the bureaucracy of the Department of Health, Education and Welfare, the Office of Economic Opportunity, or the Department of Labor.

Among the other task forces whose work and personnel would be important for Nixon's domestic initiatives was the Manpower-Labor/Management Relations task force, chaired by George P. Shultz, at the time dean of the Graduate School of Business at the University of Chicago. Shultz's work, and the helping hand of Nixon's friend and colleague from the Eisenhower administration, Dr. Arthur Burns, an early advocate of Shultz, were key in securing for Shultz the post of secretary of labor. From this cabinet post, Shultz would play a central role in the evolution of the strategy for Nixon's first term of "jobs and income." Shultz, with his understanding of labor markets and his quiet and persuasive analytical skills, became crucial to Nixon's decision to embrace his sweeping social policy initiative, the Family Assistance Plan.

Some 260 members of 21 task forces met for a celebratory and wider "get acquainted" dinner on January 11, 1969, at the Pierre Hotel, the transition headquarters, which was considerably more elegant than the campaign headquarters, located in more austere space in the American Bible Society building. The three task forces described were the most important for the formative period of the infant administration and for its most dramatic and disruptive grand initiatives. Other task forces helped lay the groundwork on issues, but the issues had the immediacy of neither the president's desire about organizing his office nor a strong political wind for them to be addressed. Thus, the task force on health, chaired by Professor John T. Dunlop of Harvard University, was to wait for almost a year and a half for serious attention to be paid to it.

Almost prophetically, the president-elect, at the head dinner table that night, was seated between two people whose portfolios would be linked to two of the most important moments and accomplishments of his presidency. The first was Charles H. Townes, the chair of the Space Task Group, and a professor of physics at University of California, Berkeley, who had won the Nobel Prize for the laser and was an extraterrestrial physicist. The Apollo 11 moon landing, while not linked with the work of the space task force, was nonetheless among the most memorable and spiritually uplifting moments of American history. Its roots were in Eisenhower's and Nixon's reactions to the Soviet launch of Sputnik in autumn 1957 and their formal organizing and tasking of the National Aeronautics and Space Administration (NASA) to focus on American efforts in space.

Seated to Nixon's other side was Russell E. Train. Nixon's task force on resources and environment was chaired by Train, then the president of the Conservation Foundation. Its issues were at only the threshold of broad public attention. Despite flames dancing on the Cuyahoga River in downtown Cleveland, the environment did not have as yet the political heat and pressure for attention that the burgeoning welfare rolls and perceived internal migration to obtain welfare benefits did. Train would enter the Interior Department as its deputy secretary. Train was incubating the idea of a Council on Environmental Quality (CEQ) in the Executive Office of the President and was a major force behind the National Environmental Policy Act, passed in 1969, that formalized the CEQ in the White House. Train would leave Interior to become CEQ's first head.

The soon-to-be-formed Ash Council would be attending to not only the organization of the president's office for management competence but also the organizational setting for environmental policies and programs. Within the first two years of Nixon's presidency, interest in the environment would explode. Nixon would get ahead of the tsunami and ride the wave, becoming the most important president for the environment since Theodore Roosevelt. The creation of the Environmental Protection Agency would come to be seen as one of the most forward-looking and important actions of the thirty-seventh president.

CHAPTER 6

Organizing for Domestic Policymaking
Enter Daniel P. Moynihan

While Nixon's task forces were meeting and germinating ideas for the new administration, the president-elect was weighing choices for his senior White House staff and the cabinet. On December 8, 1968, Daniel Patrick Moynihan met for the first time with Richard M. Nixon. That the meeting was held at all was remarkable. The two appeared as different as they could have been. One reason for the meeting was to address the urban unrest and profound racial tensions in 1968. Moynihan was the director of the Harvard-MIT Joint Center for Urban Studies. It was Nixon's inclination to reach out to people who could inform him about things he did not know much about. It also was in his nature to enjoy intelligence in others. He could not yet know that Moynihan would offer him those gifts in abundance.

For Nixon, the buck now stopped here, as Harry Truman famously said of the president's desk. After his decades of relentless quest, he had reached the "top of the greasy pole," as Benjamin Disraeli put it. Nixon would have to deal with urban unrest and confront the deterioration of race relations and social and economic problems in urban areas—and in the rest of the country. Finally, Nixon was ever aware of the optics and politics of everything he did; he knew he had to show concern for these matters.

The decision to meet with Moynihan also satisfied a desire on Nixon's part to engage a visible Democrat in his new administration. Nixon had Eisenhower's example—and FDR's, for that matter—of including in the cabinet or the administration one or more persons of note from the opposition party. Nixon crucially believed he was going to govern from the center. He faced Democratic Party control of both houses of Congress.

It seemed important, along with his approach to policy, that he have personal bridges to the other side. He first reached out unsuccessfully to his defeated rival Hubert Humphrey. Perhaps that was only a diplomatic courtesy or a kind gesture. He then approached Democratic US senator Henry "Scoop" Jackson, of Washington state, to become his first secretary of defense. Jackson would have been a link into the more defense-oriented, hawkish wing of the Democratic Party. Jackson demurred as well, still perhaps harboring hopes of a presidential nomination in his own party. There were early feelers sent out to Sargent Shriver, a Kennedy by marriage and head of

Richard Nixon with Daniel Patrick Moynihan, December 30, 1970. Courtesy
Richard Nixon Presidential Library.

the Office of Economic Opportunity. These were short-lived, as Shriver laid
down conditions that Nixon's team was not willing to meet.

Moynihan did not have the visibility of a presidential candidate or a senior
US senator. Nor was he a Kennedy, though he had served in that administration. But Moynihan had attributes that Nixon felt would be useful. As it

turned out, these knit them together in shared and almost reflexive reactions to what was going on around them in those waning months of the 1960s. As Nixon reflected in *RN: The Memoirs of Richard Nixon*, "Daniel Patrick Moynihan had one of the most innovative minds for domestic policy in the country. . . . Unlike so many liberal academics, Moynihan was free of professional jargon and ideological cant."[1]

Sensed perhaps only dimly at first, each of them recognized in the other a kindred spirit: someone who had been scarred by many of their life's experiences. In many respects, each was an outsider. As adults in their professional lives, each had been venomously criticized. By such criticism, each had been hardened and was often testy, defensive, and angry. As children, both of them also were raised and shaped in difficult economic circumstances. As Moynihan's widow, Elizabeth Brennan Moynihan, believes, they understood each other in some deep and sympathetic way that was not often discussed but always there.[2] She writes, "Personally I think that Pat's attitude toward RN . . . gave RN a feeling that they had similar boyhoods and neither were quite accepted by those who were the 'establishment' in either party."[3]

Nixon's biographer, John A. Farrell, says Nixon's childhood and youth were difficult because of deep family financial insecurity owing to the long, expensive, and finally fatal illnesses of two of his brothers.[4] Some early friends felt that Nixon was an idealistic young man. His college debate teammate "thought of Dick as a forward-thinking, kind and 'exemplary' idealist."[5] He was as good a Bible reader as he was a poker player in the US Navy. But the scale of his ambition produced behavior that provoked hostile reactions over the years. A Quaker elder in Whittier wrote to Nixon after the Voorhis campaign that the "petty politics" of the campaign "made me sick at heart."[6] The Quaker community was strong in Whittier. When Nixon clinched his nomination for the congressional race in 1946, the meeting was held in the William Penn Hotel.

For the rest of his life, Nixon carried the conflict within him between his religious and family upbringing and his ambition. These often ran in different directions. On a secular and political level, he also imbibed the atmosphere of his home. In that William Penn Hotel pitch for his nomination, he described himself as "a practical liberal." Farrell writes, "Dick's father, who had shaped his son's political leanings, was a latitudinarian populist, while Hannah and her family were progressive Republicans."[7]

It was Nixon's later run-in with the elites that set, as in concrete, the antagonism that would spill out into public view and onto news pages and opinion columns. He was always feeling apart, not least when he was forced by economics to attend Whittier College rather than crossing the country to attend Harvard. The Alger Hiss case in the late 1940s is always correctly cited as a crucial time in Nixon's fraught relation with liberals and the media. For his trudging, careful investigation of Alger Hiss and exposure of him as a Soviet spy at the highest levels of the American government during the Second World War, Nixon had been repaid by the contempt of those who could not fathom that a Yale graduate of fine manners, dress, and style could have consciously been a traitor. The bitterness at the manner of his treatment by American elites for exposing a long-standing Soviet spy was like an undulant fever with Nixon. That visceral memory was triggered repeatedly by criticism in the press. More than two decades later, on December 29, 1969, Nixon had an intriguing conversation in the White House with his chief of staff, H. R. Haldeman, his press secretary, Ron Ziegler, and Henry A. Kissinger. John Ehrlichman was taking notes. The conversation was about how hostile or unconvinced the press can be. Nixon said, "With Hiss, I was alone. 95% of the columns and stories—Chambers is lying." (Whitaker Chambers was a confessed undercover former communist and courier for Soviet spies in Washington. He was the main accuser of Hiss.) At this point, Henry Kissinger interjected, "Hiss was the epitome of the Eastern Establishment; Nixon and Chambers were outsiders—the wrongness of Hiss really rankled." Nixon was indelibly scarred by this experience, and the sensitivity was to emerge in his characteristic angry reaction to criticism from the liberal media and opponents.

In fact, Nixon's anti-communism was a version of the hostility felt uniformly throughout the Republican Party by the late 1940s. While there were divisions for Dewey or Taft Republicans on many other issues, the opposition to communism was a unifying glue for all factions. The presumed innocence of those like Jerry Voorhis, whom he attacked for their naivete or misjudgment, was a slender reed on which to build immunity for an Alger Hiss from the charges of espionage and perjury Nixon brought against him. The Venona intercepts of Soviet cables released decades later vindicated Nixon's— and a jury's—perjury judgment about Hiss, as did the autobiography of Kim Philby, written in exile in Moscow. Philby, the most notorious double agent of the Cold War, fled there from his very senior post—head of counter espionage against the very Soviets for whom he was working—in Britain's Secret Intelligence Service, or MI 6.[8] Philby praised Hiss for the work he had done for Stalin. The outrage and calumny Nixon received had partially crippled him by this time. When a button was pressed, through a controversial act or statement by Nixon thereafter, the predictable reaction to Nixon followed. And his reaction to the hostility in turn became predictable, too. It was almost like a Newtonian law of action and reaction—usually under control, but not always.

Pat Moynihan offered a not dissimilar tale. In Moynihan's case, his father, whom he loved, abandoned his family when young Pat was ten. The departure of his dad meant the Moynihans moved into Hell's Kitchen, an Irish part of New York City on the West side of Manhattan near Times Square. There, the times were hard and the neighborhood rough. His mother tended bar, and Pat shined shoes and worked the docks as a stevedore. He knew no one who was college bound. He knew not a single Republican. He told me he met his first of the breed, Leonard S. Zartman, in the US Navy, where Pat served from age seventeen.[9]

Moynihan, the Social-Scientist Politician

Who was Pat Moynihan, the man who became the other part, with the new president, of a not-so-odd couple? What were the life-shaping experiences and interests that caused him to become a central figure of the first years of Nixon's White House and to spur the president's interest in matters that were groundbreaking in social policy? These were policies that, had they been successfully enacted by Nixon and a Democratic Congress, which he faced throughout his presidency, might have entirely changed the shape of domestic events over the next decades. The president and his unlikely companion tried to establish a framework of economic security that would have reduced racial antagonisms and the scale of the economic divisions of which we now are so acutely aware. The strategy they pursued, consciously and articulately, might have precluded the American "polity," as Moynihan would have put it, from ever developing so severe, so divisive, so wrenching a tear in its fabric as we see today.

Moynihan was an active, engaged Democrat who, in the 1950s, had served Governor Averell Harriman of New York, a patrician titan in the Democratic Party. Averell's father was a partner in the Brown Brothers, Harriman investment firm, whose influence was such that, when Congress peeled apart the commercial banking business from investment banking through passage of the Glass-Steagall Act in the depth of the Depression in 1932 and 1933, it was grandfathered with both commercial and investment banking powers. Governor Harriman occasionally treated Moynihan with condescension. He could be cavalier in his demands on the young Moynihan, dispatching him up to his bedroom at his home to fetch a sport jacket from his closet. Yet, Moynihan had Harriman to thank for more than his job. In Harriman's campaign entourage and then in the Executive Chamber in Albany was Elizabeth Brennan. Pat fell for her. Hard.

On March 16, 2017 (Pat would have been ninety that day), when I was with her in Washington, Elizabeth told me the story: "62 years ago today, Pat Moynihan opened my door, stood in the doorway and announced to me, 'I am going to marry you!'" Elizabeth had been confined to a wheel chair because of an accident, and the door to her room was open to allow friends to help if it were needed. She and Moynihan had never been out alone on a date. Their times together in these giddy first days of the Averell Harriman administration in Albany always were spent in the company of colleagues. All together, they would push Liz in her wheelchair to the top of State Street hill, next to the Capitol building, release it, and then chase it, letting it gather speed until at the very last moment they would catch it before it roared down the hill out of control:

> The next night, he reappeared, came in, sat by my bed with his coat still on, and twirled his cap on his forefinger and repeated that he wanted to marry me. . . . The thing is, he then came around about three weeks later and asked if I had decided. I had thought I would never get married. I didn't want to give up my freedom and take on responsibilities for a husband and family. I said I could not give him an answer.
>
> Funny thing is, we went right on and got married, even though I never said "Yes."[10]

Politics knit them together. But their early shared political perch with the governor lasted only one term. Harriman was toppled by an even wealthier but far folksier Republican campaigner, Nelson Rockefeller, the comet who had lit up my sky in 1958, putting Pat and Liz out of a job. They worked for John F. Kennedy's election against Nixon in 1960, with Liz running his upstate New York campaign. Pat then served under President Kennedy and under Lyndon Johnson, in the Department of Labor as assistant secretary for policy.

It was due to work he performed while in this position that Moynihan, as Nixon had for years, suffered recriminations. In Moynihan's case, the shunning was in reaction to his work on the nature of poverty and, most particularly, the plight of the African American family. His report, *The Negro Family: The Case for National Action*, which came to be known as *The Moynihan Report*, or the *Negro Family Report*, was entirely sympathetic. It provided vast detail about the African American family, noting that it had been originally the peculiar form of American slavery that accounted for the "pathology" he described.[11] He would spend virtually his whole career trying to address these problems, especially by trying to find ways to promote family stability and to change laws and conditions that he felt increased "dependency" and the creation of a permanent urban lower class. Moynihan focused on the perverse incentives of the welfare laws, which reinforced a pattern of absent fathers in Black urban families and a consequent matriarchal culture—which, as he read the data, tended to perpetuate itself in poverty.

Following its publication, there were public disavowals and accusations from African American leaders of "racism," but in private, there was support. For example, Moynihan told me that Roy Wilkins, head of the NAACP, said to him that he thought the analysis sound but then held a press conference excoriating the report. The scathing criticism and hypocrisy scarred him. The persistent obloquy heaped on him by the "New Left" within his own party forever after made him a foe of its Far Left wing. After the *Moynihan Report*, he returned to New York from his Labor Department job for what he saw as a hopeful tilt at elective office in a New York City Democratic primary in 1965, which he lost. That unsuccessful ticket was a hearty embrace of New York's ethnic diversity: Paul Screvane, an Italian American, sought the mayoralty; Orin Lehman, a Jewish candidate from a prominent business and political family, the controllership; and Pat, an Irish American, the presidency of the City Council. This kind of ethnic balance on a New York ticket was itself not at all partisan. The Republicans four years earlier had woven an ethnic quilt for their ticket, with Louis Lefkowitz for mayor, Paul Fino for controller, and John Gilhooley for the City Council. That campaign demonstrated that law and order is a staple in political campaigns at any level of jurisdiction, from local to national. It broadcast, endlessly, a jingle over the radio, in which the vocalists sang a hummable tune, "You'll be safe in the Park / Any night after dark / with Lefkowitz, Fino, Gilhooley."

Years later, after his various tours of appointive posts with Nixon and then President Gerald Ford, Moynihan returned to elective politics. When he did, the strain was between traditional ethnic Democratic politics and a New Left. In that later bid for elective office, in 1976, he took on and defeated an ultra-liberal New York Democrat in the primary for the United States Senate seat, Congresswoman Bella Abzug. It was a near thing, very close, as another Irish Catholic Democrat, Paul O'Dwyer, was running also. Moynihan beat her and O'Dwyer, won the Senate seat, and served the next quarter century representing New York.[12]

Pat was warp and woof of a long strain of Irish politicians who had established their toehold, then control, of Democratic, anti-patrician, and anti-Yankee politics in many eastern US urban centers at the end of the nineteenth century. Discrimination had driven them from Ireland: first, the Anglican or pro-British church regime in Ireland pushed out the Presbyterians, Protestant dissidents mostly from Ulster, who constituted the overwhelming number of eighteenth-century emigrants who came here. They came to be called the Scotch-Irish or Scots-Irish. The Appalachian mountain chain largely became their destination, Pittsburgh their major city.

Then there was flight from the more Catholic parts of Ireland, propelled by the same Church of Ireland (Anglican) and absentee English landlord government.[13] The principal source of this wave of refugees was the South and Southeast of Ireland: Cork, Cobh, and the like. This was magnified by the desperate 1840s famine. Their destination became largely the coastal cities of America, where terrible slums festered and life was cheap. Masses of Catholic Irish escaped certain starvation and accepted privation in exchange. High-walled social and economic exclusion was their lot here as they arrived.

Politics became the way out of subsistence living and sidelining. Organization into tight, mutually supportive political organizations became key to Irish power and ascent in American politics. The Irish began their climb in these population centers. Some organizations were known widely, like New York's Tammany Hall (originally named for an Indian chief or sachem). County leadership had always been of consequence there. New York County's (Manhattan) first political leader was Aaron Burr, famously later the vice president of the United States and the victor in the gun duel fought with Alexander Hamilton, on July 11, 1804. By the last quarter of the nineteenth century, Tammany Hall had become the center of Democratic politics in New York County and the path to influence for the Irish immigrants. Its chair was Irish Catholic.

In 1928, a Tammany darling, Governor Al Smith of New York, himself Irish and Catholic, grasped the Democratic presidential nomination to run against Republican Herbert Hoover. Smith carried "wet," or anti-Prohibition, pockets of votes, heavily Catholic, throughout the country but won too few states to defeat the starched collared, Quaker, and Iowa-born activist Republican. That election had an intense anti-Catholic tone, which served to raise corruption and Catholic-dominated urban machines as bogey men for voters to shrink from. Around the country there were Ku Klux Klan (KKK) flaming cross burnings. The Klan was almost as intensely anti-Catholic and anti-Semitic as it was anti-Black. There also was the widely credited clear and present danger that should Al Smith enter the White House, the plan to build a tunnel beneath the Atlantic Ocean from the Vatican directly to the West Wing would be immediately implemented, allowing the Pope to secretly give the new president binding directives for America's policies.[14]

Apart from Tammany, there were other large figures within New York City, such as Edward J. Flynn of the Bronx. Flynn ran the Bronx County apparatus firmly for decades, even while holding state office or serving as Democratic National Committeeman and chair of the Democratic National Committee. In that nationwide role, Flynn succeeded another Irish Democrat, James J. Farley, whom Flynn had introduced to Franklin Roosevelt. When in the early 1940s, Roosevelt sought to thank Flynn with a diplomatic post, the Senate refused to approve FDR's nomination of Flynn as US ambassador to Australia because of his ties to New York's Tammany Hall and its perceived corruption. Flynn blithely resumed the DNC chairmanship and helped run the 1944 FDR campaign, as he had the 1940 one. In Brooklyn, another New York City fiefdom, Joseph Sharkey was the Democratic leader and parlayed his position there into a twenty-one-year stint as majority leader of the New York City Council. At lunch, with Pat Moynihan at the 1789 Restaurant in Georgetown on April 3, 1970, he told me it was "founded by the son of an Irish boss in Brooklyn from around the turn of the century."[15]

As an alert young man growing up, it was hard for Moynihan not to be aware of the powerful New York City political organizations and other Democratic satrapies throughout the Empire State and beyond. Albany, the state capitol, was in its smaller way the ne plus ultra of organization politics. Its mayor, Erastus Corning, served from 1942 to 1983, comfortably in thrall to the Democratic machine run by the remarkable Daniel P. O'Connell. A school dropout, O'Connell took over the Democratic County committee in New York's capital city in 1921, ousting the Republican organization that had long held sway. For fifty-six years, O'Connell held the reins of power. He was a legendary figure.

Further to the west, in Buffalo, a young Irishman, Peter J. Crotty, himself first-generation, formed a law firm representing many groups usually associated with Democratic politics—longshoremen, union locals of steelworkers and teamsters—and built his power base in the party. He was Erie County Democratic Chair for twenty-one years and was a powerhouse in western New York State. Tim Russert, who was Pat Moynihan's press secretary in the Senate and later chief of staff (and a beloved NBC newscaster host until his untimely death), said, "They [the Crottys] are an Irish clan in the most complete sense of the word." Crotty was instrumental in pushing the New York delegation into Jack Kennedy's column at the 1960 Democratic National Convention. Crotty was succeeded by another Irishman, Joseph Crangle.

Daniel Patrick Moynihan grew up observing the place of the Irish in American politics. To him, the vision of his own ethnic group having such wide influence held fascination. Jack Kennedy's election was one of the most elated moments in Moynihan's life, his death, too soon, one of the saddest. Moynihan later commented, "The era of the Irish politician culminated in Kennedy. . . . He served in a final moment of ascendancy. On the day he died, the President of the United States, the Speaker of the house of Representatives, the Majority Leader of the United States Senate, the Chairman of the National Committee, were all Irish, all Catholic, all Democrats. It will not come again."[16]

But his interest in ethnicity transcended a pride in the Irish and helped him grasp the rudiments of politics, including that of nations. Moynihan had an innate understanding of the tribal nature of politics. In his career, he always was sensitive to the dynamics of America's immigrants and how they become part of an American identity. He explored this as an academic and lived it as a successful office seeker. It informed his work as an advisor to presidents on social policy.

In these waves of immigration, and in the ways assimilation worked or failed and organizations responded to this, Moynihan caught the sense of enduring and socially important institutions. What he saw on the ground as a teenager in the rough Manhattan Irish West Side of Hell's Kitchen was the "organization." In the recent documentary, *Moynihan*,[17] he describes his very first time voting. He dressed in a jacket and tie and stepped down into a West Side church basement, where local Tammany poll-watchers gave him a ballot—and a list of whom to vote for.

Tammany was in Moynihan's formative years only starting to cede influence to the politically nascent Italian community. In turn, Carmine De Sapio's tenure as Tammany's leader was a brief though very important period of Italian domination before the "Harlem Fox," J. Raymond Jones, became the first African American Democratic leader of any county in the United States. I myself had a visit with Carmine DeSapio. On March 14, 1963, I attended a lunch for that controversial Tammany Democrat, who had fallen from grace over allegations about his pliancy in the hands of New York Mob bosses such as Frank Costello. I was prepared to be fascinated, and I was. I concluded that the postprandial talk he gave was ghost-written, owing to the constant allusions to Aristotle. Closer to matters concerning New York and Tammany, he made references to the gauzy visions of the liberals. Franklin D. Roosevelt Jr.'s campaign for New York governor had been torpedoed by DeSapio. In undercutting Franklin Delano Roosevelt Jr.'s candidacy for statewide office, he earned the undying and lethal enmity of FDR's widow, Eleanor, who was the lighthouse for the Democratic left for years. She was *the* key player in toppling DeSapio from his party leadership positions, including Democratic National Committeeman from New York.

My impression of DeSapio, the youngest person ever to run Tammany Hall, as we talked was that he was extremely smooth. He had very long hair, with curls at the back of his neck and grey temples, and he wore dark glasses, the result of a retina infection. They were a signature feature of his and suggested something sinister if one were unaware, as I was, of the medical reason. I engaged him in conversation about Eugene Nickerson, a Democrat who had been elected the county executive of my home county, Nassau, overcoming nearly a century of total dominance there by the Republicans. DeSapio very softly but firmly poked his forefinger into my right lapel as he told me that if Nickerson won this next round, then the Democrats were solidly in in Nassau and that in his view Nickerson was gubernatorial timber.

The importance of a Democratic victory, with a cornucopia of patronage jobs attached to the county executive position, was great. Nassau had been one of the impregnable Republican fortresses.

Throughout these shifting tides in Tammany, there were continuities. There was a sense of structure, of hierarchy, of allegiance and loyalty, of results. This must also have been Moynihan's early sense of the Church. The Catholic Church in America was dominated by the Irish, even long after the successive waves of southern and eastern European immigration had changed the demographics of the country and the Catholic population itself. The church, through its parochial schools, educated the immigrant children. Through its social services outreach, it provided help to struggling families, side by side with the political organization that was offering jobs and even heating coal and food to these families.

The church assumed commitment in faith. Tammany and its brethren asked fealty in voting. In Moynihan's time, there were towering figures in the church. Cardinal Cushing reigned in Boston, where he was a close consort of the Kennedy family, scions of "Honey Fitz" Fitzgerald, an earlier Boston mayor. In New York in Moynihan's formative years, the great presence was the Archbishop of the New York Diocese, Francis Cardinal Spellman. The church was still trying to overcome the hostility and fear that the 1928 election demonstrated about Catholics rising to the top. It sought to dissipate these fears in novel ways. Roman Catholic bishop Fulton J. Sheen was put on the air as a magnetic early televangelist in a popular weekly sermon with a national audience, competing formidably with Norman Vincent Peale and other fabled Protestant preachers. It was a new style for the Catholic Church to be reaching to the non-Catholics as Sheen did so effectively. My Protestant family watched his shows regularly.

Yet there was raw political potency as well in the church. The real power in the Roman Catholic hierarchy in New York was not its attractive TV personality but its formidable archbishop. Francis Cardinal Spellman held sway with an iron grip. He both ruled within the church and was a major presence within the broader politics of New York and even the nation. The intimate ties of faith and politics that were apparent in Boston and New York were replicated in most of New York's major cities. This was Moynihan's lineage.

Attraction of Unlikelies—Or Were They?

Edmund Burke was an Anglo-Irish figure and a contemporary and friend of late eighteenth-century luminaries the likes of David Hume, Samuel Boswell, and his subject, Dr. Johnson. He was a powerful intellect who in a measured way had opposed Britain's attempted suppression of the American colonies' rebellion. In an intriguing book, academic Greg Weiner argues that there were many analogies between the eighteenth-century conservative, Edmund Burke, and the twentieth-century liberal, Daniel Patrick Moynihan. Burke portrayed the "little platoons" of a society as the necessary institutional glue that held a culture and country together. These were basic and began with family, church, fraternal and civic associations, and community. These were the focus of most of Moynihan's searching life.[18]

Why, then, was the ultra-partisan Republican Richard Nixon interested in meeting a man heavily weighted down with partisan Democratic baggage? A man who had supported John Kennedy against him in 1960, and, in this election just held, supported first Robert Kennedy, and then Hubert Humphrey, running against him? As an Irish Catholic Democrat, he would have been a more natural ally of Chicago's boss, Mayor Richard Daley, who had eight years earlier almost singlehandedly defeated Nixon with his manipulation of the Chicago balloting.

It must have been in part because Moynihan had taken fright at the erosion of many of the natural groups, attitudes, and affiliations he—and Edmund Burke two centuries earlier—saw as essential for a healthy society. He saw a radicalization of political discourse and politics as practiced. As Greg Weiner puts it in *American Burke*, it had become a "radical moralization and total politicization, especially the variant that infected left-wing politics in the 1960s. This sanctimonious politics 'rewarded the articulation of moral purpose more than the achievement of practical good.'"[19] Here, what Moynihan saw was an intolerance by the American Left of dissent. He recalled Hannah Arendt's belief that "totalitarian propagandists succeeded in turning every question of fact into one of motive."[20]

Moynihan's central concern was the implosion or collapse of social authority, of the value and respect paid to the essential institutions of a society. He would often note that a vacuum of authority cleared the way for raw power.[21] He really saw a religious crisis: the issues were seen as political but were essentially religious. "It is a religious crisis of large numbers of intensely moral, even godly, people who no longer believe in God," Moynihan writes. This gap or space was filled with politics, where "fervor becomes pathological" and results in "the total state; the politicization of all things."[22]

Nixon, when he was savagely attacked by right-wing zealots in the losing 1962 campaign for Governor of California, had seen this intolerance and closed-mindedness on his side of American politics. He had watched the Goldwater crusades in 1964. Now, in the late 1960s, he certainly was repelled by the venom and violence of the left wing, whose excesses and zeal Moynihan felt and condemned on his side of the divide. This shared concern and Moynihan's speaking out on it provided the potential for a first tie up between the two unlikely allies.

Stephen Hess, in a fine little book bubbling with anecdotes and insights, traces the most likely history of the pas de deux at the outset between the president-elect and Moynihan.[23] Hess was the one person who knew both Richard Nixon, from having worked with Nixon on speeches and articles after the 1960 defeat, and Moynihan, through academic ties and then family friendship. Despite this, he said it was not he who cobbled the two together. He thinks the interest in Moynihan among the inner Nixon coterie centered around those more liberally inclined, such as Leonard Garment, Nixon's law partner; Raymond K. Price, former editor of the *New York Herald Tribune* and by 1967 a Nixon writer and thinker; and California's lieutenant governor Robert Finch. Hess said Finch, after the 1968 election, was repeatedly advancing Moynihan's name to Nixon. John D. Ehrlichman, who became Nixon's counsel in the White House, agreed that Finch was an enthusiastic advocate.

The spark that likely lit the fuse occurred a year before the Nixon victory. Len Garment drew to Nixon's attention a speech that Moynihan delivered in October 1967 to the Americans for Democratic Action (ADA), the High Temple of Democratic liberal politics. But Moynihan offered some stern counsel to his fellow liberals. In the talk, Moynihan expressed his concern that politics were approaching instability and that responsible people on the Left and Right should make common cause against authoritarian tendencies. The speech was titled *The Politics of Stability* and was reproduced in the *ADA World* in early 1968. Just before his speech to the ADA, Moynihan had published an article with the same title that was even more pointed in its concern. In "The Politics of Stability," which appeared in the October 9, 1967, issue of the *New Leader*, Moynihan writes, "Liberals must see their essential interest is in the stability of the social order; and given the present threats to that stability, they must seek out and make much more effective alliances with political conservatives who share their interest and recognize that unyielding rigidity is just as great a threat to continuity of the social order as an anarchic desire for change."

It is unlikely that either Moynihan or Nixon was aware of a letter John Maynard Keynes had penned to Franklin Roosevelt in December 1933, as FDR was trying to come to grips with the Great Depression. Keynes's comments to the New Deal president were apt in their concern that political leadership would not find a way within the existing system to address crucial social needs. It also anticipated what Moynihan and Nixon later came to see as Nixon's Disraeli-like effort as a conservative to advance liberal causes in order to repair the rift between the "Two Nations" of the affluent and the impoverished.

Keynes wrote, "You have made yourself the Trustee for those in every country who seek to mend the evils of our condition by reasoned experiment within the framework of the existing social system. If you fail, rational change will be gravely prejudiced throughout the world, leaving orthodoxy and revolution to fight it out."

That reflected Moynihan's late 1960s ruminations on the poverty program and political reactions to poverty. He wanted government to address the root causes. He saw these as the lack of income. To provide income therefore was the real, palpable way to help millions of destitute or dependent people. At the same time, doing so would remove the props from under the agitators for violent change. Moynihan continues,

> There is nothing whatever to be done to change the minds of the Negro nihilists and their white associates. . . . Their course is set. The only option for the nation is to deprive them of the Negro underclass which is the source of their present strength. In other words, there must be an attack on poverty itself, but in a different way. One which will lift the poorest and most dependent out of their condition, by making them less poor. Starting them on upward mobility.
>
> The Federal government is good at collecting revenues, and rather bad at disbursing services. Therefore, we should use the Federal fisc as an instrument for redistributing income between different levels of government, different regions, and different classes.

In this article, published in a liberal, anti-communist magazine read by mostly Social Democratic European emigres, Moynihan, in an almost uncanny way, anticipated two of the core elements of Richard Nixon's momentous address of August 8, 1969. There, in his "New Federalism," Nixon proposed a money-based, not services-based, attack on poverty, for the working poor as well as the dependent poor, and that the federal government share its revenues with state and local governments for them to prioritize how services—or income supplements—are provided in their areas.

Eighteen months into his service with Nixon, Moynihan said in a memorandum to the two senior White House colleagues, H. R. Haldeman and John D. Ehrlichman, that it had been his speech to the Americans for Democratic Action that attracted Nixon's attention: "As best I can tell, I got my job in the Nixon administration as the result of a speech . . . in which I proposed that American politics were approaching instability, and that liberals who understood this should seek out and make alliances with their conservative equivalents in order to preserve democratic institutions from the looming forces of the authoritarian Left and Right. It seemed to me the three-way split in the election [George Wallace] made the argument even more compelling. I took the President's offer of a job to me as an indication that he shared this view."[24]

Moynihan lost no time in returning to the theme of social dissolution. Just two days into the new year, on January 3, 1969, Moynihan wrote the president-elect: "The sense of institutions being legitimate—especially the institutions of government—is the glue that holds societies together. When it weakens, things come unstuck."

> The successful extremism of the black militants and the anti-war protestors . . . has now clearly begun to arouse fears and thoughts of extreme actions by other groups. George Wallace, a fourth-rate regional demagogue, won 13 percent of the national vote and at one point in the campaign probably had the sympathy of a quarter of the electorate.
>
> He said there had been, "for a brief period, something of a truce in the protracted struggle where the cultural elite rejected values of the larger society. . . . The leading cultural figures are going . . . into opposition again."[25]

While Moynihan's alarms about political extremism and ideological battles provided a first intellectual bond for an unlikely alliance, the initial connection derived from Moynihan's lifelong interests and Nixon's instinctive willingness to use the government to help Americans who were left out or who were struggling but failing.

The first outreach came from Moynihan. On December 20, 1967, Moynihan wrote a letter to Nixon about a *New York Times* account by Robert Semple of some of Nixon's views on urban poverty. He noted Nixon's idea of a national job census, saying the 1960 Census missed about 10 percent of the "Negro" population and probably 30 percent of "Negro" men between the ages of twenty and twenty-nine, and told Nixon he was encouraged that the president was taking an interest in these issues.[26] He then invited Nixon to come to lunch at the Harvard-MIT Joint Center, describing it as a "forum which is not without advantages for you," which shows his awareness of how the issues for Nixon are the very issues the Joint Center was focused on. He knew Nixon might appreciate both the substance and the optics of a meeting in that venue.

Months passed. In May 1968, Raymond K. Price wrote to Moynihan about an article Moynihan had written on race in COMMENTARY magazine. He allowed that he didn't expect to win Moynihan away from the Democrats, or specifically from Robert Kennedy (then running to succeed Lyndon Johnson who declined to seek renomination). But Price said he thought there was a "great kinship of aim and approach here between Mr. Nixon and yourself—and I hope that, even as the campaign develops, it won't be lost sight of."

"Much as I think you do, at this particular time especially," Moynihan wrote in reply on May 23, 1968, "I value such efforts to find common agreement enormously." He adds, in his fashion, that should Price be in the area of Moynihan's upstate New York farmstead, at Pindars Corners, he should "by all means come down for a bi-partisan meeting of talking and drinking."[27]

On October 24, 1968, in the heat of the campaign, Moynihan wrote to Nixon about Nixon's radio address on employment as the key to social stability, "a fact," Moynihan told Nixon, "which you made clear and explicit," and specifically cautioned Nixon about a Business Council call for a higher unemployment rate to combat inflation. They "do not understand what such an unemployment rate would do to the urban Negro social structure. . . . It means more broken families, more welfare recipients, more persons sent to prison . . . more of all the problems you will be trying to resolve." Contained in this brief letter to the candidate not of Moynihan's party was the weaving together of two crucial components in the thinking that Moynihan and Nixon shared and then acted together upon: first, social stability and the fragility of social institutions and, second, the implications for these institutions of poverty, welfare, and employment. Jobs and income were necessary to a sense of economic security.

In the next years, Moynihan and Nixon were to become intellectual sparring partners. They enjoyed a friendship that endured until the death of the former president in 1994. Richard Nixon longed for loyalty. For a lonely man like him and a naturally social being like Moynihan, there was an organic connection. Moynihan—with considerably more intellectual content than the New Deal's Thomas Corcoran, one of the original F.D.R. "brain trust" members, and a greatly engaging man—was the "Tommy the Cork" of the Nixon administration.

Other Early Important Nixon Advisors

In the course of President Nixon's first term, there was only a handful of individuals who had outstanding influence on the president's policy shaping and strategy. Apart from the National Security advisor, Henry A. Kissinger, who Nelson Rockefeller had recommended to Nixon, most of those whose ideas and leadership Nixon accepted and embraced were on the domestic side of the administration.

Nixon already had his efficient assistant to the president, Chief of Staff H. R. "Bob" Haldeman. But neither Haldeman nor Nixon imagined Haldeman's role to be developing policy options for the president. Rather, it was to help Nixon sift and sort those prepared by others, finding the right format and elements with which the president would be comfortable reflecting on what he asked for or was brought. Once the president had reached a decision, it was Haldeman's task to ensure that decisions were then carried out, with attendant instructions to the departments, publicity, and links with the legislature where necessary.

John D. Ehrlichman was to evolve into a critically important domestic policy figure. He had this great opportunity because of his close and lengthy relationship with H. R. Haldeman, starting as a campaign aide in 1960, working for his college friend. His career in law in Seattle was interrupted by later drafts into Nixon's campaigns. Following the 1968 election, Ehrlichman was named counsel to the president and soon emerged as a central arbiter, expediter, and shaper of domestic policy. Ehrlichman emphasized, always, that his was a "coordinating" or "managing" role in the development of initiatives in domestic affairs. He was thought by many of conservative bent, such as Patrick Buchanan and Martin Anderson, to tilt too easily to the centrist or moderate position on policy—and with good reason. He later showed his hand when he wrote in his *Witness to Power* memoir about his sympathy in 1964 with Nelson Rockefeller, Governor William Scranton, Governor George Romney, and the moderates. From the initiative on a guaranteed income, to the rightly celebrated Nixon work on the environment, Ehrlichman's hand was pressing on the scales of decision in a decidedly active way. Nixon was well aware of this. Ehrlichman in these first years was one of those who facilitated Nixon's cleaving to the tradition of Eisenhower—and Dewey—Republicanism, helping Nixon in his goal to recapture the center. Moynihan, in a memo to Nixon on November 13, 1969, mentioned, "Last night Teddy White related to me your hopes for reviving the Eisenhower-Nixon majority. . . . [It] was broad-based (Ike got 20% of the black vote in 1952 and twice that in 1956)."[28]

Two other newcomers had great influence. George P. Shultz, the head of the University of Chicago's School of Business, had been among those task force members who were noticed and advanced, in Shultz's case to the cabinet post of secretary of labor. Out of this starting gate, Shultz ran an illustrious career in government, which took him to director of the office of management and budget, which he put in business after its creation by Act of Congress in 1970; to secretary of the treasury; and then, capping his career, to secretary of state under President Ronald Reagan. His measured, balanced manner, touched with humor, appealed to the new president. In a San Clemente meeting on July 2, 1970, of the president, Kissinger, Shultz, Weinberger and some others, Ehrlichman made almost sixty numbered entries in his notes of their discussion about economists and statistics. George Shultz ventured, "An economist is a fellow who can draw a straight line from an unwarranted assumption to a foregone conclusion." Nixon loved it.

It was a style unlike that of some of the former officeholders who took posts in the cabinet. They often were territorial or boastful about their department's authorities. Shultz had the territory but avoided seeming territorial. Shultz's labor department gave him a crucial role in the income and jobs strategy that was to unfold, as labor had the bureaucratic expertise, like that of the Bureau of Labor Statistics and in its policy assistant secretary office, to inform the debate and heavily influence its outcome.

A later entrant into the leadership roles among Nixon appointees was the Democratic governor of Texas, John Bowden Connally. Connally was known nationally as the conservative Texas Democrat who had worked for, and was a protégé of, Lyndon Johnson. Edwin Weisl Sr., the Democratic National Committeeman from New York, told a close friend of mine of a conversation with John Connally about Connally's apprenticeship to Lyndon Johnson as a young congressional staff person in Johnson's office in the 1930s. Incredibly, Connally said to Weisl that his duties in the congressional office included trimming the congressman's toenails.[29]

Connally went on to become governor of Texas and was wounded riding in the car in which President Kennedy was shot and killed in Dallas, Texas, in 1963. Nixon focused on Connally after Connally served as a member of the Ash Council. He was visible and vocal in his support for creating a strong management arm for the president in the Executive Office, and Nixon was drawn to his forceful and charismatic manner. It was a long way from trimming the toenails of a congressman to cutting short the remarks of the president of the United States, but Connally made that trip. I was sitting behind Secretary John Volpe and Secretary George Romney "for a dramatic and memorable scene in the Blue Room" in the White House Residence. To either side of them in the front row was the rest of the cabinet. I was in a row of senior White House staff behind them. The purpose of the meeting was for Roy Ash to brief us on the recommendations of his Council on Executive Organization for the creation of the Office of Management and Budget, Domestic Council and Environmental Protection Agency: "The president stood in front of the group when, at the last minute, John Connally made a grand entrance, sweeping in front of RN, and shaking hands with each of the Cabinet members."[30] The president coolly, but with no obvious irritation, waited for Connally to be seated. Moments later, Connally again took the floor, as "Roy Ash followed with a terribly weak exposition, which required John Connally to rise and amplify on." Connally smoothly summarized the ideas, which were not entirely welcome to the cabinet. Nixon was to dote on Connally.

In these formative days, however, it was the unlikely New York Democrat, Pat Moynihan, who came to command the attention of the president, and of Haldeman, as they were trying to fit the jigsaw pieces together and create the right mechanism, given Nixon's and Haldeman's bent toward an organized process, for the development of policy on the domestic side of the house. As things unfolded, Pat's explosion on this very domestic Republican scene was to give the Nixon administration a large dose of paprika and panache.

Nixon and Moynihan Find the Fit

At first, the right role for Moynihan was not obvious to either the president-elect or to Moynihan. The New Yorker was identified with urban problems, namely, poverty and race relations. But his interests were wide-ranging. While at work for New York governor Averill Harriman, Moynihan took an interest in auto and highway safety and advocated the use of seat belts. He befriended Ralph Nader, the dour and iconoclastic critic of Detroit's products in his tract, *Unsafe at Any Speed*. He brought Nader into Kennedy's labor department. Pat became intrigued by the implication for American society of the Eisenhower-sponsored Interstate Highway system: its effect on residential and commercial development patterns and on the decline of cities and smaller towns as the older US or state highways and railroads became sideshows to the new multilane arteries of commerce and commutation. Moynihan's feel for urban issues and tightly knit communities also led him to lament the loss of public transportation systems in cities and rue the effect on links between home communities and work opportunities. While Moynihan's hand included cards from many suits, it was from this one, transportation, that he led his bid with Nixon representatives about a role in the new administration.

Len Garment had drawn Nixon's attention to the ADA speech that led Nixon to embrace Moynihan's themes about the failures of 1960s liberalism. Haldeman, Nixon's chief of staff, asked Len to sound out Moynihan. Garment did so in a New York restaurant, where the two began an enduring relationship. Moynihan asked for a portfolio that built on his earlier and still keen interest: transportation. He asked to run the Department of Transportation, which was among the most recently created cabinet departments.

This request surprised Nixon's people, as they did not think of Moynihan in this context. In addition, it was a nonstarter, as Nixon already had promised the secretary of the Department of Transportation (DOT) job to Governor John A. Volpe of Massachusetts. Volpe was among the cluster of moderate Republican governors, and he was Italian American, the son of first-generation immigrants, his father having started a construction business. Volpe himself had been a hod carrier, transporting bricks to the bricklayers. Volpe had been the first administrator of the new Federal Highway Administration that later became part of DOT in the Eisenhower administration, so Nixon had known him that early and in that context. The job went to Volpe.

It was well for Pat and the president that this was the case. Otherwise, rather than sparking ideas with an intellectually curious president, he might instead have been shuttling between the Budget Bureau and Capitol Hill, mustering the arguments for continuing to build the supersonic transport. At a distance from the president, as a cabinet department head, he would be violating what Pat later indoctrinated in me: "Moynihan's Iron Law of Proximity."

When the two principals met, in Stephen Hess's account in *The Professor and the President,* Moynihan found Nixon uninformed on many of the areas of social policy that were Moynihan's terrain. But Nixon displayed a keen intelligence and curiosity. Moynihan's long preparation in the bureaucracy made him fully aware of how important the ear of a president would be. They clicked. But the two still needed to figure how—and on what—they would work together.

Haldeman and Nixon had canvassed the idea of an equivalent of the National Security Council (NSC). The NSC structure in the interdepartmental coordination of foreign policy was familiar to Nixon. Created by the National Security Act of 1947 and located in the executive office of the president following a recommendation of the first Hoover Commission in 1949, the NSC consisted of the secretaries of state and defense and the directors of the Central Intelligence Agency and the Federal Civil Defense Administration. The president chaired the NSC, and the vice president was a statutory member. Nixon was instinctively a private person and a private decision maker. Yet, he was turning over an idea for a deliberative and coordinating body. As there were many more domestic cabinet departments whose interests were touched by domestic or even "urban" policy than there were those directly concerned with national security policy, such a body could be unwieldy, and Nixon and Haldeman did not yet have a clear concept for how to structure it.

The structure was discussed in Moynihan's meeting with the president-elect on December 8. As one of the architects of Lyndon Johnson's Poverty Program, Moynihan was intimately familiar with the Office of Economic Opportunity (OEO), the agency LBJ had created with congressional authorization to house many of the initiatives to combat poverty and to be a laboratory for finding, and then funding, other ideas. The OEO was to employ means to secure the "Maximum Feasible Participation" of the poor. This would become a contentious monster for Johnson's administrators and for local government officials, as the US government wound up funding or granting money to advocacy groups that were harsh, and occasionally violent, critics of mayors, county executives, and governors, many of them of the president's own party. This was repellent to Nixon. It was repellent, too, to virtually every Democratic mayor, who were the targets of the criticism and well-funded noise. The Model Cities program was in part a response to this reaction of elected officials, and Johnson created it to redirect funding to and through mayors, not to fund criticism of them.

Moynihan later wrote a searching appraisal of this approach to the elimination of poverty, which he called "maximum feasible misunderstanding." His critique was part of his growing skepticism of the strategy of providing services to the poor. Moynihan came to feel that this gave an economic boost to the consultants and social workers who were paid well to provide the reports and the social service calls (and the advocacy), but not so much to the poor themselves, the supposed intended beneficiaries of any effort to reduce poverty.

However, in the Nixon meeting in early December and after, Moynihan focused on another part of the Poverty Program apparatus, which might be said to entail the "Maximum Feasible Participation" of cabinet officers. This was the Economic Opportunity Council. In the statute creating the OEO, there was a provision for a high-level policy development body. It was to include the secretaries of all of the cabinet departments whose programs addressed poverty alleviation, from the Department of Health, Education and Welfare and Housing and Urban Development (another new Johnson-era department) to the Department of Agriculture, with its rural development programs and rural housing loans for low-income families, and the Department of Labor, with its job-training authorities and administration of the Job Corps. Under the statute, the director of the OEO was to be the chair of the Economic Opportunity Council (EOC) and to gather the cabinet members to frame and develop programs for poverty elimination. The director was to chair the EOC even though the director of OEO did not have cabinet rank.

Having not gotten his first choice heading the Transportation Department, Moynihan saw an opportunity in the availability of the Economic Opportunity Council for an even more inclusive role for himself. He later said to me, in urban affairs, "everything relates to everything else." Therefore, for policy to be comprehensive, it needed to have an institutional structure wherein all affected parties were at the table. There, they could suggest, joust, or support ideas and could see and get the response of the president. For the implementation of policy, it was important that each of them, in each other's presence, heard the president's decision so that they could be expected to comply with it.

Moynihan was still a stranger to the president and those who surrounded him. Like all of those outside the inner circle, he was relying on rumor, news stories, and perceptions about who was close to the president and could serve as an ally through whom to bring ideas to the president and to influence him. In any administration, these assumptions can quickly change as an administration spools up, and they may never have been true to begin with.

As did so many others, Moynihan assumed that the closest person to the incoming president on domestic affairs would be Nixon's old ally and aide, Robert Finch. Finch, along with Charles K. McWhorter, had been a loyal and lasting assistant during Nixon's vice presidential years. As lieutenant governor of California, Finch was at the heart of the moderate wing of California's Republican elected officials, offsetting in Sacramento the convinced conservatives who had undercut Nixon's 1962 bid and who had risen with the victory of Ronald Reagan two years earlier. In that state, the governor and lieutenant governor were elected independently of one another. Finch had outpolled Reagan by 300,000 votes, so Finch had a power base that Reagan could not entirely control. Finch was known and liked in the state capital, and he had helped Nixon on his national campaigns and so was familiar with many Republican leaders around the country. Finch was to take the Department of Health, Education and Welfare (HEW). Apart from the Defense Department, HEW had the largest budget, was the most complex of the federal departments, and was the one in which Moynihan's lifelong interests in welfare and dependency, child care and education, were most strongly focused.

Finch stood out in the new administration, in several ways. After a cabinet meeting of February 7, 1969, Jim Keogh, head of Nixon's speechwriting staff, did a brief "color" report or impressions of the meeting. He told the president, "It was apparent that there is a substantial degree of truth in the press comment that this is a conservatively dressed outfit. Not that they were all in gray flannel, but nearly all wore dark suits and quiet ties. The exception was HEW Secretary Finch. He was in iridescent green; his tie looked as if it had been designed by de Kooning in a nightmare."

Moynihan proposed that Finch become chairman of the Economic Opportunity Council, and Moynihan become the executive secretary of the cabinet-level body. In this role, Moynihan could influence its agenda, its use of the deep research resources residing in the various cabinet departments, and its coordinating role. Nixon and Moynihan were thinking along parallel tracks; both wanted an inclusive body at the cabinet level. Given his desire for privacy, Nixon was as yet uncertain about whether he would himself chair the deliberative body. Further, it was unlikely that Nixon would embrace the use of a body created under Johnson's Poverty Program, and he was poised to eradicate or redirect the OEO. Therefore, the president was going to want to create something fresh with his own stamp on it. That decision would be made before inauguration.

After they met on December 8, Pat sent a short memo to Nixon saying he also needed the White House title of special assistant to the president for domestic affairs. "The Special Assistant must be responsible for preparing the major Presidential papers on domestic affairs," he wrote, adding, "After thinking about it at some length—I hate titles—I feel also that the appendage 'for Domestic Affairs' really is necessary if I am to do for you the job I believe must and think can be done."

On December 10, 1968, Nixon announced Pat's appointment not as assistant for domestic affairs but as his assistant for urban affairs. He said a body analogous to the National Security Council for foreign policy was to be created to help shape urban policy. The right wing, along with everyone else, assumed that Finch would be paramount in influence. According to Sam Tanenhaus, their leading figures, such as William Rusher and William F. Buckley Jr., were soon taken aback, indeed astonished, at Moynihan's swift ascent in Nixon's councils.[31]

Moynihan Offers Me a Job

Ten days later, on my thirtieth birthday, Moynihan and I met for the first time. Leonard Garment, for whom I had worked in the campaign, had asked me to take soundings about whether Moynihan would work out well on the White House staff. I likely was one of many so tasked, and I came back with a very positive report: he was deeply substantive, colorful, had a strong understanding of the issues Nixon must deal with, and would very likely prove loyal, even though he was a partisan and visible Democrat. Garment thought Moynihan and I would fit well together and arranged for our meeting. It was a year to the day that Moynihan earlier had reached out in his complimentary letter to Nixon about the *New York Times* article regarding Nixon's views on urban poverty.

There were some reasons Moynihan thought I could be useful to him. I was a Republican who had worked on the Nixon campaign. But there were many of those. More unique and relevant was my recent experience. I was likely about the only one to serve in the Nixon administration who had left a Wall Street law firm to go to work at a community development corporation. At the Bedford-Stuyvesant development effort, I was Senator Javits's man, but I was also working with Sen. Robert F. Kennedy and his people, given the joint leadership of the entity.

Senator Javits was very special to me, and we seemed to have a relationship closer than his senior status and my youth and inexperience would suggest. As proof of this, in a most unexpected way, Javits involved me in one of his quests. As 1968 was drawing nigh, the senator began to dream of securing the vice presidential nomination. As quixotic as it was—Javits being a New Yorker, Nixon and Rockefeller being New Yorkers with the constitutional barrier that posed, meaning he would need to have Ronald Reagan ask him to be his vice president—he was in total earnest about it. He asked me and Jack Saloma to lunch with him and with an adman, Rosser Reeves, who was an enfant terrible in the advertising industry and who had advanced to be chair of the Ted Bates agency. He was a brilliant, early exponent of television advertising. In a sense, he and William Paley washed each other's hands, for Paley was the genius who saw the economic advantages for television stations of running programming that would attract advertisers. Reeves created the ads for his corporations that sold the products, which made the companies come for more advertising. Reeves could hardly have been more of a contrast to the cerebral, serious Jack Javits. Reeves had been a bad boy at college at the University of Virginia, from which he was expelled for drunkenness (it was Prohibition) and gambling. He was slow to settle and find his path, as he was boisterous and loved to drink and carry on. But he was great at his business and, as was I, devoted to Javits. It was only the four of us at a long, fascinating lunch. I was thrilled to be included. Javits's notion was that I might help prepare a policy book for his effort. It came to nothing, though it further cemented the relation I had with Javits.

Once established as the lone Republican and Javits man among all the Bob Kennedy aides, like Adam Walinsky and Peter Edelman and the full-timers on staff, I cobbled together a $100,000,000 pool from all the New York insurance companies and savings banks to provide mortgage finance money for "Bed-Stuy" homeowners. The equivalent amount in 2020 would be huge, a Croesus-scale sum. I got lending officers from big New York banks to get on the street for the development corporation and help overwhelmingly Black homeowners to squeeze water out of bloated second mortgages, reducing their debt burdens or secure financing to buy their homes. The dynamics were fascinating, because there were a great many Black realtors and money brokers who had been layering on extra mortgage burdens to enable Black homebuyers to pay distorted prices to fleeing whites, who were departing for the suburbs as the community changed. Thus, I was fighting a well-vested interest group but on behalf of thousands of African American families who would consolidate indebtedness, get rid of wrongly assumed debt, and pay market rates of interest, not artificially high ones, on what was left.

I think this made Moynihan quite comfortable, if not intrigued, when he was sizing me up. I very much had urban affairs experience on the ground. Upon learning it was my birthday, Moynihan ordered a half bottle of white wine to celebrate the day. It was a rushed but cheerful lunch, and Moynihan was in a robust mood. Moynihan told me he wanted me to be an assistant to him. Later, it was decided I would be his counsel, "doing the same sort of thing he is—the overview of 'domestic policy,' which means urban problems, which means the Black problem."[32] He went on at length, summarizing for me the conclusions he had reached in the *Family Report*, namely, that the American form of slavery had been the most pernicious in history, worse than the Greek, worse than the Brazilian, and that it had left deep scars on the American Black family.

After this first meeting with him, and as I walked out into the sunshine of Park Avenue from the hurried lunch at the Pierre Hotel with the offer to join him, I carried with me a phrase of Pat's that I now feel was the hope that underpinned his entire career and gave him motivation and energy. Moynihan said to me that, despite the horrors of American slavery and the lasting impact on the families and lives of Black Americans, America had it "in its gift . . . to be, not just the first multi-racial society, but the first non-racial society."[33]

These thoughts brought back a flood of memories for me of one of the more adventurous things I had done up to that point in my life. At twenty-two, between my two years of graduate school in England, I flew in a rumbling, four-engine propeller plane to Johannesburg, South Africa. We spent three days en route, with overnights in Malta, in the Mediterranean, then in Entebbe, Uganda, in the sunset time of colonialism. Britain's Tory prime minister Harold Macmillan had speeded up decolonization. While Socialist prime minister Clement Attlee had started it, massively, with Indian independence in 1947, Macmillan renewed and focused on it, which left both former British Africa and British politics in a state of perturbation. It was July 1961 when I arrived in South Africa, only weeks after the Afrikaans prime minister, Hendrik Verwoerd, the last prime minister of the Union of South Africa, had withdrawn South Africa from the British Commonwealth. He was later assassinated in Cape Town. There was massive tension as I arrived in that beautiful and troubled country. I hitchhiked more than three thousand miles all over South Africa, for nearly two months. I roomed in boarding houses, and I worked as a floor walker in a five and ten cent store in Durban, on the Indian Ocean. My hitching rides had me with Dutch farmers, Progressive Party organizers, security police, Zulu shopkeepers, prison guards who waved a Webley Revolver in my face as they drove and chewed betel nuts, and a French restauranteur from Cape Town, Maurice Webster, and his mistress, Yola Carlisle. I descended ten thousand feet into gold mines with the miners and crawled on my belly through the "stopes," as my father had in the West Virginia coal mines where he started working at age twelve. South Africa was a land where there were excellent paved roads, large gas-guzzling American cars, spectacular scenery, drive-in movies, Dairy Queens, and a horrendous race problem. Moynihan's focus on the problems of race evoked these memories and underscored the importance of my recent work in Bedford-Stuyvesant. They gave me a shared purpose with him.

Moynihan tasked me with thinking through how a deliberative body on urban affairs could best be structured and suggested that I interview former senior staffers of the National Security Council (NSC). I visited with veterans of Eisenhower's NSC apparatus. I met with Brad Patterson, the deputy to Max Rabb, Eisenhower's secretary to the cabinet, who was soon again to join the White House staff. Under Kennedy and under Lyndon Johnson, the formality and much of the process and use of the Eisenhower NSC had fallen into desuetude. The advice was simple from the Eisenhower alumni: structure the body in a way that suits the style and needs of the incumbent president but that assures he has in front of him the material and advice necessary to make an informed decision.

I sought other examples of a policy development or a decision-making body in domestic policy that would transcend departmental lines or jurisdictions. In the Department of Housing and Urban Development, created by Congress in 1965 under Johnson's presidency, there was a statutory provision for a power of the secretary. This was the "convenor" power. The secretary of HUD was empowered to "convene" his or her cabinet colleagues to discuss and determine policies that affected the cities and their development, such as housing, transportation, and commercial development. Talking to HUD senior employees and Johnson holdovers, this power, I learned, had never been invoked or exercised.

Among those who were leaving with the turnover of their departments to Republicans were Eamon Kelly, later president of Tulane University, who in his nearly twenty-year presidency there enjoyed his dedicated table at Commander's Palace restaurant, overlooking one of New Orleans's aboveground cemeteries, and John Zuccotti, later first deputy mayor of New York City and a major civic and real estate development figure. Zuccotti and Kelly were helpful in my understanding of why the convenor power of the secretary of HUD had not been used.

I turned my attention to the Office of Economic Opportunity and its Economic Opportunity Council, which had been Moynihan's first thought when he was figuring out where to position himself after DOT was denied. Here, there was a story. The OEO statute made the non–cabinet-level director the chair of the cabinet-level council. Director Shriver did initiate use of the Economic Opportunity Council. For its first meeting, he succeeded in persuading President Lyndon Johnson to attend the meeting that he, Shriver, was nominally chairing. Johnson came, of course dominated the proceedings, and left. There was never a subsequent meeting of the EOC, though apparently Shriver attempted to convene one.

In a brief memo to Nixon during the transition, I described these findings and told Nixon that Nixon's role was central and that his chairing the council was essential for the idea of coordination really to work: "Cabinet members are heliotropic—they like to turn and face the sun and not each other."[34] Without my prompting, Nixon had already reached the same conclusion.

CHAPTER 7

The Council for Urban Affairs
The Launch

Pat Moynihan completed the assembly of our small staff over the next few weeks. His friend, Stephen Hess, was a veteran of the second Eisenhower term speechwriting staff and a Washington insider. Hess had written extensively about national politics, on his own and collaborating as well with figures such as Earl Mazo and later David Broder, one of the great journalists of the time. He became Moynihan's principal deputy. Moynihan also persuaded his Republican comrade in arms from the US Navy, Story Zartman, to join. I was to be counsel and to serve as the principal support for the functioning of the Council for Urban Affairs (CUA), its formal link to all the cabinet members and their departments, assuring materials for meetings were prepared and properly distributed. I was its "rapporteur," or official minute taker, and responsible for the "Record of Action," the summaries of follow-up steps to be taken after meetings of the group with the president.

Moynihan approached two others to join the staff, both from the Task Force on Public Welfare: Richard P. Nathan, who had chaired the task force, and Robert Patricelli. Both were New Yorkers and knowledgeable about the issues in which Moynihan would take an interest. Both demurred. Nathan went to the Bureau of the Budget, where he knew he would have vast resources of data and expertise at his fingertips as the assistant director for Human Resources. Patricelli went with Finch to the Department of Health, Education and Welfare, where he was to become ultimately a deputy undersecretary. Both played central roles in the unfolding of the drama on welfare reform—and other human resources and social issues—over the first years of the Nixon administration.

Hess, Zartman, and I were the senior partners on the staff. A cluster of younger figures completed the CUA staff roster. Mike Monroe, a nephew of the musician Cab Calloway, joined. Three who were barely out of college signed on: Chester E. Finn Jr., who had been a student of Moynihan's at Harvard; Christopher DeMuth, a student of Edward Banfield at Harvard on urban problems and a veteran of the 1968 campaign; and Richard Blumenthal. Three wonderful and overworked secretaries, including one who had worked for Harry McPherson, a close friend of Moynihan's in Johnson's

White House, signed up for service in the cramped quarters in the West Wing basement.

Settling In

Moynihan's office was at the foot of the stairs leading down from the Oval Office and the offices of the chief of staff, press and appointments, and the vice president. I wound up across West Executive Alley in Room 118 of the Old Executive Office Building (EOB), as it was when we were its occupants and since renamed the Eisenhower Office Building. Nixon chose for his hideaway what had been Vice President Humphrey's office there, just at the top of the stairs coming over from the West Wing of the White House and just a few feet from my office, since I had the office of former vice president Hubert Humphrey's chief of staff, Jack West. Here Nixon would read and write quietly. The EOB formerly housed the State, War, and Navy Departments. It was a product of the Grant administration era's architectural tastes. That style having long been out of favor by 1961, Jacqueline Kennedy herself had to save it from the wrecker's ball when she was first lady and it was about to be razed. It was worth saving. Its door knobs were of brass, having engraved in them the seals of the State Department and of the military services, whose staffs their tall doors opened to (with the exception of the Air Force, which was of course not a gleam in the eye of the military in the 1870s, when the EOB was built). The spacious and high-ceilinged corridors had massive diamond-shaped slabs of marble in the floors, alternating black and white, and grand, curving staircases between the floors. A multistory library with wrought iron stairs and balcony trimmings was another relic of a bygone era. Eisenhower had held his press conferences in the EOB in its Indian Treaty Room.

Almost as soon as the small CUA staff was assembled, we gathered as a staff for a group photo in Moynihan's basement office.

The office was graced with standard government-issue furniture, including a credenza behind Moynihan's desk. The ceiling had been lowered in prior renovations and had panes of translucent glass set in large squares. When Pat swiveled his chair around, he could pluck a bottle of Black Label from the credenza to entertain his journalist guests or have a drink with White House staffers working into the evening. From that desk in front of the ground-level window, he could look out onto West Executive Alley and across to the Old Executive Office Building. Up the steps to the first floor of the EOB, Nixon would with increasing frequency climb, seeking the seclusion of his space. There, he was away—though not far—from the madding crowd that came through the Oval Office for ceremonial occasions or constant meetings with staff. He liked to put his feet up on a chair or ottoman

Daniel Patrick Moynihan's White House staff. *Left to right*: Leonard Story
Zartman, Michael Monroe, Daniel P. Moynihan, Thomas Nast, Christopher
DeMuth, Stephen Hess, Richard Blumenthal, John Roy Price. John Roy Price
personal collection.

and pick up a briefing note, or a book, or a pad of yellow paper on which to
write notes to himself or draft a statement he would make.

Moynihan from his basement redoubt sought to initiate us in the ways of
the White House. Over the coming months, he would admonish us about
the quality of our work. He would caution that we needed to take care about
leaks and to expect to be blamed for them even though, he assumed, we were
not responsible. He knew instinctively that he was a newcomer to a group
well accustomed to working with one another, and that he and we would
be subject to suspicion and scrutiny and have to feel our way carefully. Yet,
as counterpoint to all these cautionary notes, he had an exuberance and joy
about him that was infectious.

He gathered us in his office with a photographer. Before we took a group
photo, he educated us on the painting that now hung on the wall behind
us as we posed. Moynihan knew not only the pitfalls but also the influence
over policy decisions that comes with being a senior White House staffer.
He also knew and enjoyed the perquisites. For him, this included his almost
nightly dips in the swimming pool that FDR had installed for exercise and
that Nixon was soon to cover over to make additional space for the press.

It also meant he could prevail on the National Gallery of Art, the National Portrait Gallery collection, or the Smithsonian, for art for his office.
He selected a large oil painting, vertical in its axis. In the background was
Trinity Church, which was obvious to anyone who knew the Wall Street area
in New York. In the foreground was a gloomy bewhiskered older man, shoulders slumped over, deep lines in his brow. Moynihan told us this was a self-
portrait of Thomas Nast, the American political cartoonist who had made
his name and such fortune as his fame earned him by depicting in constant
and recognizable cartoons the Tammany bigwigs, including the notorious—
and, in the cartoons, bloated—Boss Tweed. Tweed had handed out lucrative
contracts to cronies with abandon. It appeared that Nast had entrusted his
savings to an advisor who turned out to be a bamboozler and a swindler. The
satirist lost all he had. Hence the palpable gloom in the picture.

I took my cue from my boss and secured a wonderful Edward Hopper oil
painting, which hung in my office until I closed shop on December 1, 1971,
to return to New York. The president himself enjoyed the abundance of the
Smithsonian and the National Portrait Gallery Collections. At one end of the
Cabinet Room, he hung an oil painting of Dwight Eisenhower. At the other
end, on opposite sides of the door leading to the Oval Office, were two of the
rivals for the 1912 presidential election, Theodore Roosevelt and Woodrow
Wilson. The curiosity of that placement occurred to me at the time. I wondered whether Nixon felt he carried traits and dreams of both—the cerebral,
would-be world-changing Wilson and the determined, charging cowboy
Roosevelt, who would assert America's interests abroad, preserve America's
greatest natural places, and do battle with powerful interests to protect ev-
eryday Americans. They were two people who did battle with one another in
1912, but perhaps within Nixon they were not at war but in harmony.

In the basement office the day of our group photo, Moynihan gathered
us in front of the Nast painting. He immediately began to mug for the camera, striking a pose. We all picked up on his cue. The photo itself is curious,
with each of us appearing to be holding our breaths and about to break into
laughter. But it suggests the humor, teamwork, and zest for getting about the
public's work that were part of Pat's gift to all of us.

Before January 20 and this basement pose, Moynihan housed himself and
us in a modern, red brick building, across the street. It was utilitarian and
bore the unglamorous title of Federal Office Building (FOB) 7, later somewhat more elegantly upgraded to the New Executive Office Building. Here
were the small, but to us, welcoming, quarters of the "Temporary Commission on Pennsylvania Avenue," the grand avenue that runs between the
White House (the Treasury Building actually) and the United States Capitol.
It is the route of inaugural parades. It also connects the three branches of

government, as the Supreme Court lies just yards from the Senate side of the Capitol, and the Library of Congress, started with the donation of Thomas Jefferson's own library collection, lies just yards from the House side. Pat had been named by Lyndon Johnson as vice chairman of the commission.

But Pennsylvania Avenue in 1969 was not so grand. It was tawdry, run-down, derelict, and dirty. The Willard Hotel, at Fourteenth Street and Pennsylvania Avenue, was a vacant hulk, awaiting demolition if no developer could be enticed to restore it to the glamor it enjoyed when its corridors witnessed the origin of the term "lobbyists": a name for those entreating—buttonholing—senior public officials who passed them in the Willard Lobby. Moynihan's dream for "America's Main Street," one that was realized, was for the Avenue, Willard and all, to be renewed and to be a fitting architectural and urban design for the grand artery. It would showcase the heart of the capital and the American government. David Childs, the commission's executive director, and Nat Owings, a name partner of Skidmore, Owings and Merrill, the Chicago-based architectural firm that advised the Commission, gladly made room there for us. David Childs was important to Moynihan in this small way, as Moynihan set out in the new administration. Childs was to be of great importance decades later to Moynihan, to Moynihan's abiding passion, and to his memory. Childs became managing partner of the Skidmore firm. Among his proudest commissions was creating plans for the rehabilitation of Manhattan's iconic Pennsylvania Station, a great public space from the grand days of passenger railroad travel and whose station in the 1960s had been razed to make way for a new Madison Square Garden. Its magnificent stone pillars wound up, in fragments, in a dump in northern New Jersey. In deference to Moynihan's decades of commitment to transportation, there is a Phoenix rising from the ashes in Manhattan. Penn Station is being redeveloped. The old station had a Baths of Caracalla–like grand hall. McKim, Mead, and White designed both the original station, and the classic, same-period Post Office on Eighth Avenue to the west, which is now the Moynihan Train Hall with a sky-lit atrium.

Moynihan, later in the Senate, rekindled his interest in transportation. In one remarkable week, he both floor-managed the Surface Transportation Act in the Senate and then departed for Oxford University, where on Thanksgiving Friday 1991, he gave the Cyril Foster Lecture, later published as *Pandemonium*. The lecture was about ethnicity in politics and postulated that ethnic rivalries and complexities were at least as much at the heart of a collapse of the Soviet Union as was a burgeoning American defense budget. I was there and listened to Moynihan, who was tired by the work in the Senate earlier that week but in fine academic fettle.

One day in early pre-inaugural January, the 1968 Nixon campaign manager and now attorney general-designate, John Mitchell, walked past my small desk in a hallway outside Childs's office and stopped, momentarily stunned. Mitchell, whether out of conviction or political dictates, had referred publicly to the Ripon Society, of which I was then chairman of the National Governing Board, as "a bunch of juvenile delinquents." As he spotted me, knowing I had worked on the fall Nixon campaign, he strolled over and greeted me with a good-humored, "How's my favorite juvenile delinquent?" When I told him I would be working with Moynihan, whose role for Nixon was by now public, Mitchell "looked mildly incredulous and asked what in the world I wanted to be involved in this part of things (the Moynihan operation) for. It was an interesting foretaste of what his attitude toward us and our work would be on many issues, for in the crime area, he became shortly very jurisdiction conscious, and, despite the fact of our creation of a Sub-Committee on Crime, and my and Pat's repeated requests to convene a meeting of it, and prepare some proposals, he never did so, and would deflect our requests."[1]

Structuring and Starting the CUA

In this period before the inauguration, Moynihan and Nixon fixed the membership of the council to include all of the domestic cabinet departments, including the Post Office, and later the Office of Economic Opportunity. For the next eighteen months, until July 1970, when the Domestic Council by statute supplanted the Council for Urban Affairs, Nixon personally chaired the Urban Affairs Council for twenty-one out of its twenty-three meetings.

Moynihan and Hess and I worked out a series of Sub-Committees of the CUA. These included Welfare, Crime, Internal Migration, the Future of the Poverty Program and the OEO, Education, Food and Nutrition, and the District of Columbia (it had not yet been accorded its self-government, which Nixon, as one of his "historic firsts," was to achieve). Each subcommittee would be chaired by a cabinet member. Each would have staff support from one of us on Moynihan's slender staff.

We also created a subcommittee on the transition to peacetime economy at the end of Vietnam hostilities.[2] Moynihan had convened a group of US mayors who met with Nixon in early January. Nixon told them that he would be thrilled to redirect billions away from the war effort to address the concerns in the cities but that there was no immediate prospect of that money becoming free.

In late winter, March 20, 1969, Haldeman wrote Ehrlichman, saying, "The President would like to have you have [Budget Director] Mayo conduct a budget briefing for all the 'spenders' on the staff, which would mean Moynihan and his top people, Burns . . . and any others that you feel would benefit from it. He feels it is imperative that the White House staff understand the necessity for cutting this year. It can also be explained to them that *next year, after the war is over* [emphasis mine], we will be able to do more in domestic programs but that they will have to go along with the cuts for now." This elusive notion of funds coming available with a winding down of the war came to be called "The Peace and Growth Dividend." It continued to be elusive. Moynihan held a press briefing in August 1969 at the San Clemente Inn, near the Western White House. In a clime accustomed to morning fog burning off and then the afternoon stream of sunshine and surfers on the coast, Moynihan announced, "The Peace and Growth Dividend is as evanescent as the morning clouds over San Clemente."

Since we staff were few in number, Moynihan asked if I, in addition to supporting the functioning of the council machinery itself, would be willing to take on one or two of the Subcommittees as my responsibility. I immediately opted for the Welfare group, which was to be chaired by Secretary of Health, Education and Welfare Robert Finch and whose members would include the secretaries of labor, agriculture, commerce, the attorney general, and later the head of the OEO. I had taken an interest in the field ever since I became aware of the work Yale Ripon was doing on welfare. I also knew of Moynihan's own intense interest in the subject. Moynihan was delighted to give me the portfolio.

As I wrote in my journal, "One of the first things I did was to show Pat a copy of a draft negative income tax statute which had been sent to me by John Topping [head of the Yale Ripon group]: it was for a forthcoming issue of the Yale Law Journal, and it prompted the first exchange Pat and I had, one where he still cleaved to the family allowance."[3] This was the very beginning of the drawn out and dramatic Nixon consideration of welfare between "national standards" for the existing welfare program, on the one hand, and a "negative income tax," or means-tested income, support for all American families, on the other. The "family allowance," more a European program in origin and use, and like the one later embraced by Senator George McGovern in his hapless campaign for the presidency against Nixon in 1972, never really figured in the internal discussions of 1969.

For my other Subcommittee assignment, I drew a Joker. I asked for the crime Subcommittee. Since it did not ever meet, my energies were not diffused. My January weeks were filled with organizational tasks for the Council for Urban Affairs, especially the drafting of an executive order that would create it. The Budget Bureau, and Arthur Focke, its general counsel in particular, were aghast at the speed with which we wanted to draft and clear the order. It was in this hasty effort, necessary because the first meeting of the CUA was to be only two days after Nixon's inauguration, that we hit the speed bump with H. R. Haldeman, the hyper-organized Nixon chief of staff.

First meeting of the Council for Urban Affairs, January 23, 1969. First executive order signed in Richard Nixon's presidency. *Left to right*: George Shultz, Robert Mayo, Arthur Burns, John Mitchell, Robert Finch (obscured), John Volpe, Vice President Agnew, Clifford Hardin, President Nixon, George Romney, Daniel Patrick Moynihan, Maurice Stans. Courtesy Richard Nixon Presidential Library.

Working with Focke at the Budget Bureau, I sent out drafts of the executive order to both the attorney general, John Mitchell, and to John D. Ehrlichman, the counsel to the president, for them to vet and edit. I drafted a like memo for Moynihan to send to the attorney general, which he did. In mine, I noted to Mitchell, "Technically, the procedure is for the Budget Director to transmit a proposed Executive Order to you; but due to the rush of events, we are handling this directly with you, and I am keeping the General Counsel of the Budget Bureau, Arthur Focke, informed, and will send him copies for their files." I noted that "the final draft . . . reflects the suggested changes and a copy has also been sent to John Ehrlichman."[4]

Moynihan's and my letters to Mitchell went to him on January 16, a week prior to the January 23 meeting of the yet-to-be-formalized CUA. I sent the Budget Bureau drafts directly to them, ad not through the Haldeman intake valve. As a consequence, both Mitchell and Ehrlichman, accustomed to the Haldeman system, likely did not take prompt notice of the drafts and the need for immediate clearance. The result was an almost Keystone Kops moment as the cabinet members were gathering for the first CUA meeting. Mitchell came with several last-minute revisions. At first, the council mem-

First meeting of the Council for Urban Affairs. John Roy Price in dark suit in front of door to Oval Office watching the signing. Courtesy Richard Nixon Presidential Library.

bers were left standing and fidgeting while Mitchell was doing handwritten changes. Smoke was curling up from his pipe, tightly clenched in his teeth, and he had beads of sweat on his brow, even though it was January. He then quickly counselled with John Ehrlichman. The decision was made to have the signing ceremony, and the members trooped to the cabinet table, where the president already sat. This was the cabinet table that FDR had installed, and I mused over how many meetings of great consequence had been held here. I joined other staffers sitting along the wall facing the president after having watched the signing ceremony with Steve Hess from the door leading to the Oval Office. Moynihan, as executive secretary, was seated at the table with the president and members of the council.

The president then signed the last, or signature, page of the executive order, "which was alright, while the middle page was out being retyped and reproduced for distribution to the press. The pens used were fountain pens, dug up from a stock somewhere in the bowels of the White House, and the President used one for each letter of his name, producing a rather curious looking signature, but one which apparently did the job. Afterwards, each of our staff got one of the pens he actually had used."[5]

This disorganization did not go unnoticed by Bob Haldeman. In his diary, he noted of that morning, January 23:

Then the first meeting of the Urban Affairs Council, and the first major breakdown of the staff system. Council Director Daniel Patrick Moynihan wanted the P to sign an Executive Order creating the Council, with pictures, etc. But he didn't pre-staff the Order [*sic*; I had indeed sent the drafts to them for clearance—just not through Haldeman], so we ended up with Council members cooling their heels in the Cabinet Room, while Ehrlichman calmly reviewed the order before approving it for P.[6]

This was the very first executive order signed in Richard Nixon's presidency. It was a shame that the event planted an impression in Haldeman's mind of an ill-prepared Moynihan and staff, offset by a calm and efficient John D. Ehrlichman. It was a first impression that would help Ehrlichman assume control over all domestic policymaking. That was but months in the future.

After this first meeting of the Council for Urban Affairs, Moynihan should have been basking in the glow of his Council meeting. The president had thoroughly digested the briefing papers done for him. His energy about having early and forceful initiatives was apparent to his department heads gathered around him. He turned to Moynihan and said he wanted a "frame of reference—a basic philosophy to affect all our decisions." In short, a strategy. The president had concluded the meeting saying, "The Urban Affairs Council should not just be a broker or coordinator of programs. Rather it should look at the cities, at everything anyone is doing on the subject, and bring together the best ideas."[7]

At its best, the council would breach the walls between departments, put a spotlight on how their programs fit into a broader than departmental approach, and reduce territoriality that the cabinet secretaries might otherwise default into. Around the cabinet table that first meeting, there were some hints of how the new department heads would play their hands. The president had asked each briefly to introduce their department to the others. I was struck by how George Romney formally recited to his peers—at some length—the statutory reach and powers of his department. Secretary Hardin of USDA showed hints of how territorial he would become. Maurice Stans, an Eisenhower veteran now at the commerce department, was not on full display yet. I wrote more than a year later, on October 28, 1970, that "he never fails to appear to want to be the first Cabinet member to land on the moon and claim it for his department. I remember Bob Finch's remark to me . . . 'If Maury had been secretary at the time the space program was being created, he would have turned the Weather Bureau into NASA.'"[8] George Shultz was called on last. He had listened to the others. He kept his counsel and kept his powder dry, saying almost nothing. To me, it showed him a cautious but shrewd newcomer, just feeling the ground under his feet and judging the president's response.

The Moynihan-Burns Rivalry at the Starting Gate

Now that the Council for Urban Affairs was formally launched, Moynihan had to wonder to himself, how wide was its mandate? "How far does MY writ run?" On the very same day, January 23, 1969, as the formal creation and first meeting of the Council for Urban Affairs, with Moynihan as executive secretary, Nixon announced Arthur Burns's appointment as counselor to the president for domestic affairs—the inclusive title that Moynihan had suggested for himself.

In the weeks before his inauguration, Nixon asked Dr. Arthur F. Burns to analyze the results of the transition task forces. Burns had known Nixon since Burns served as chairman of the Council of Economic Advisors in the Eisenhower White House. He was a conservative. He was fiscally and temperamentally cautious. Burns had been born in the eastern part of the then still Austro-Hungarian Empire, in a town now part of Ukraine. This brilliant immigrant wound up at Columbia University. His ambition was to lead the Federal Reserve, and Nixon knew this was Burns's ardent desire. The very academic professor, with his thick supply of gray hair parted in the middle and his glasses with wire frames perched firmly in place, eagerly awaited the end of the term of Fed Chair William McChesney Martin. Martin had led the board since he was appointed by President Truman in 1951 and was the longest-serving board chair in the Fed's history, his endurance record only nearly eclipsed much later by Alan Greenspan, who failed by just months to win the longevity-in-office prize. If we are to believe Burns, he demurred when Nixon first suggested that he come onto the White House staff. But Nixon was insistent.

Burns's responsibility, Nixon said, was "the coordination of the development of my domestic policies and programs." Nixon had earlier appointed two top advisors for national security and for urban affairs, both from Harvard. One, Henry Kissinger, had been close to Nelson Rockefeller. The other, Moynihan, was a known partisan Democrat. Nixon was always balancing his approach; always trying to anticipate or respond to pressures that he thought were potent in the party and beyond. Pat Moynihan could understand Nixon's need to palliate those on the conservative side of the Republican Party after Nixon's pick of Pat. Still his question must have been, "What does it mean for my role?"

It was the inception of a usually civil, but intense, adversarial advocacy relationship. The two did have some things in common. Burns, like Moynihan, was no stranger to the tools of influence and the manipulation of power in

Washington. They also were completely comfortable in the academic world, where either one might have ventured that rivalry and competition can be as ruthless, secretive, and self-centered as in business or in politics. Burns understood what Moynihan had been given with his role supporting a cabinet body of which the president was to be chair. Burns made his initial move, pushing a pawn forward on the bureaucratic chessboard. In the very first meeting of Moynihan's forum, the Council for Urban Affairs, Burns, following up on Nixon's urging of action, offered a suggestion: "The question is, what can the administration do and say now, in the next 60 days, *for the next cabinet meeting* [emphasis mine]." These first meeting minutes were not yet formalized and stored with central files as later ones were. They amounted to an aide memoire for me of the meeting, Therefore, in the next sentence I noted that Burns' attempt was "an effort I think in retrospect . . . designed in effect to change the forum of these discussions away from the Council, over which we had agenda and other control."[9]

Burns's efforts to turn Nixon and his senior staff away from the machinery that Moynihan controlled were unrelenting. Within days, Moynihan's Council for Urban Affairs held another meeting. Burns, in his *Secret Diary*, wrote an entry indicating that he, Burns, was trying to build support for a coordinating role on domestic policy elsewhere than through the CUA.

> Feb. 3d 1969
> Day began with a long meeting of Urban Affairs Council. Moynihan was the star of the occasion. We planned a meeting for next Saturday when the draft of a message on OEO [the Office of Economic Opportunity, Johnson's Poverty Program] would be unveiled. . . . At lunch I suggested to Bryce [Harlow, another conservative on Nixon's senior staff, the assistant to the president for Congressional Affairs, who had held that same role under President Eisenhower and whom Burns had known in the Eisenhower White House] that we must organize ourselves for the purpose of reducing the number of conflicts that go to R.N. Perhaps a committee with Haldeman, Ehrlichman, Bryce & myself. Bryce thought plan was good.[10]

In trying to move discussion of important matters outside of the ambit of the Moynihan council, Burns built strong relations with Spiro T. Agnew, the vice president. One reason was their shared conservative orientation. Burns also had a patronizing attitude about his own ability to lead Agnew, to help him from making false steps, a student to be tutored. Burns recognized that the new vice president did not fully grasp how important it was to be seen as accepting the president's lead and, especially in the company of outsiders, such as congressional or business leadership, not to be contradicting, even subverting, the president:

> RN is also concerned about the VP, who—undoubtedly innocently—took an independent stand at legislative leaders meeting. Agnew means well, but he lacks the instinct to realize that VP can function only through tolerance of the President; that he must not assume an independent position when Congressional leaders are around, that he must either be silent, or echo the P's voice, or reinforce the Pres' position.[11]

This stubbornness in disagreement with a decision of Nixon's was to emerge most profoundly at a meeting in August 1969 about the president's decision on his welfare reform, the Family Assistance Plan. At that climactic session, while Burns covered his own strong disagreement and disappointment by making a few points and then embracing silence, Agnew's antagonistic attitude took the breath away from a number of us present. Burns was a staunch supporter of Agnew's up until the point of Agnew's being forced to resign because of conclusive evidence of corruption.

Burns's common interest with Agnew was in trying to pull consideration of questions toward full cabinet, weakening Moynihan's role and underlining the vice president's authority. Agnew pushed in a February 8 meeting of the council to refer to the full cabinet discussion on the reorganization of the Poverty Program and on a proposal of Governor Romney's for a cabinet committee on voluntary action. Agnew got a pushback from George Shultz, the secretary of labor, and the idea collapsed. This was one of the few CUA meetings that the president did not chair, and perhaps Agnew did not want to frog-march something the president might reverse.

There were two ways for Moynihan to contend for the president's support and satisfaction. The first was administrative, namely, how Moynihan grasped and used his direction of the council. At least among the very important inner circle of Haldeman, Ehrlichman, and their closest staff, this had gotten off to a rocky start. The second was through policy itself. Over the coming months, these aspects of Moynihan's work with the president took divergent paths. Moynihan's hopes for his CUA to become the successful parallel to the NSC were ultimately dashed. Yet his influence with Nixon on policy grew dramatically. He was unique of all on the White House staff: energizing. He was able to give coherent voice to much of what the new president was trying to accomplish.

Moynihan embarked with enthusiasm and energy. He had confidence that the council machinery would be his bulwark, his bureaucratic bastion. He understood the importance for the president of coordination between all the cabinet departments and of buy-in to the policies adopted. One of his Iron Laws anchored the hopes Pat harbored for the CUA. "The Iron Law of urban affairs is that everything relates to everything. . . . The President makes a decision. All Cabinet members in his presence know he has reached it, and they know each other knows. Otherwise, isolated program goes on."

For all the coordinating potential of the CUA structure, for all of the initial bureaucratic advantage it afforded Moynihan, it was a vessel and had to be filled with content. This content had to inform the president and give him the information, analysis, and direction he needed for making major decisions. The president put the rowels of his spurs in our flanks in that first meeting. He was looking to us for results.

CHAPTER 8

A President in a Hurry

Within a month of his election, Richard Nixon formally rolled out his selection of those who would hold cabinet positions. All white, all male, all seasoned in government, academia, or business, they were ceremoniously introduced as a group, the entirety of the cabinet, front and center, at once. Nixon placed three Republican governors in cabinet posts in addition to his vice president, the former governor of Maryland, Spiro T. Agnew. One of them, George Romney, had been an early opponent of Nixon's 1968 nomination. Nixon gave the intense and intensely liberal George W. Romney of Michigan the portfolio of the newest cabinet department, Housing and Urban Development. Romney, as governor of a Northern industrial state with Detroit as its stormy, deteriorating urban center, took naturally to his brief. He was to be a determined champion of what he understood to be urban interests. He took to his advocacy with the missionary zeal that was natural for a Mormon of his solid conviction.

The vice president had earlier been somewhat sloppily—or at least too readily—dropped by the pundits into the liberal or moderate column. This was in part because of an overwhelming Black vote for him in his gubernatorial race in 1966, when he ran against a racist Democrat. It was also because of his earnest and early advocacy of Nelson Rockefeller's quest for the 1968 nomination. Even the Ripon Society in autumn 1968 endorsed the Nixon-Agnew ticket, citing Agnew's support for Maryland's open housing statute, the first of any state below the Mason-Dixon line.

But Agnew had begun to plot a different course. After the riots following the shooting of Martin Luther King Jr., while Agnew was governor, he had a confrontation with Black community leaders about the extreme and often violent rhetoric of Black Panthers and other separatists. This stirred on the Right the first pulses of excitement about him. These were to turn into great waves of support and enthusiasm.

Vice President Agnew became Richard Nixon's Richard Nixon. Pat Buchanan says that for Eisenhower, Nixon was the partisan "bayonet." As vice president, Agnew now cheerfully assumed the role of partisan in chief. He arrogated it to himself, and with increasing enthusiasm he began to cement a link with the boisterous ranks of immoderate Republicans. He had appeal for former Goldwater partisans, Southern strategists, and anti-elitist followers of Alabama's George Wallace. He found his voice. He was to grow into his role in the first year of the new administration, relishing it and trying on alliterative and provocative phrases with the same enthusiasm he enjoyed selecting his finely cut suits.

Two other governors held cabinet positions. John Volpe of Massachusetts took transportation, the relatively new department that Daniel Patrick Moynihan had coveted. Walter "Wally" Hickel of Alaska took over the old-line Department of the Interior. These two, Hickel and Volpe, had worked in the construction business. All had frontline experience in managing state governments. They were thought at the outset to be cut from the same moderate political cloth as George Romney, although neither Volpe nor Hickel had run against Nixon.

To get promptly to work on new administration priorities, the key next tier of positions—deputy secretaries or undersecretaries, even many of the assistant secretaries, on whose backs the work of the departments is done day-to-day—had been spotted, selected, and prepped for the clearance and formal nomination process. This would include FBI background checks and Senate approval. These were all presidential appointments at a level that required hearings and formal confirmation under the United States Senate's constitutional obligation to advise and consent. Nixon went about this with alacrity. At the transition offices, then the White House, the personnel vetting and selection team were connected with the Congressional relations staff to get quick and smooth confirmation by the Senate of Nixon's choices. Senate confirmation, despite control by the opposition party, followed almost immediately. It was still the guiding principle between the two relevant branches of government in 1969 that a president, having won an election, was entitled to appoint his choices for confirmable positions. The appointees might well be holding and pushing positions contrary to the views of the party controlling the Senate. It was another form of acceptance of the election's outcome. With background checks revealing nothing of a criminal or ethical nature to halt confirmation, the process moved quickly and with infrequent partisan blocking.

Whither the OEO?
The members of the Council for Urban Affairs, all to be at cabinet level, were known before inauguration. The first session of the council was held three days after inauguration and two days after those of us on the senior White House staff had been sworn in by the chief justice. Already Nixon displayed his sense of urgency. He wanted a complete inventory of where we were on urban problems, "before we take off, or before we continue people and programs." He went on. "The problem with the whole city thing is that

there is vested interest in what has been a failure. I'm concerned about the cities exploding if there is a change, but we can't fear to change or there will be a really big one. The time to take the political heat is now, whether it is on stronger law enforcement, or a change in welfare or in the OEO [Office of Economic Opportunity—the poverty program]. The magic time to change is the first couple of months."[1] He had the insight of one who had seen Dwight Eisenhower's run out of the starting gate. He wanted to capitalize on those fleeting moments at the outset of a new administration. He knew this would be even truer for a president elected only with a plurality, not a majority.

Among the first issues the president seized on was one that he thought could show his differences with Lyndon Johnson. It was also one he could find agreement on with conservatives like Ronald Reagan, now settling into his third year as governor of California. The Golden State was still electing Republicans and conservatives to statewide office. Nixon, most Republicans, and most municipal elected Democrats were appalled by the rhetoric coming from many of the groups financially supported by Johnson's poverty agency. Federal money was being used to subsidize frequently savage criticism of government.

Reagan and Nixon held common ground on this. Reagan would offer up homey if invented examples of abuses to rally opposition. Nixon understood he had to address the mismanagement of the poverty agency and OEO excesses. In that first meeting of his Council for Urban Affairs, the president spoke of the "near term issues" and said this "means our first year." Of these, "the critical one in his view was the future of the OEO."[2] Secretary of Health, Education and Welfare Robert Finch opined, "We have to put good programs in the line agencies. I think we should keep the OEO with a changed name, as a catalytic innovative agency." The president responded, saying, "I do not share the view we should keep it. At next week's meeting we should decide."[3] Nixon in his memoir confirms his initial impatience.

> From the first days of my administration I wanted to get rid of the costly failures of the Great Society—and I wanted to do it immediately. I wanted the people who had elected me to see that I was going to follow through on my campaign promises. The worst offender was the welfare system, and welfare reform was my highest domestic priority.
>
> It was Pat Moynihan who made an uncharacteristic plea for caution. . . . Moynihan wanted to take a year to consolidate our domestic situation before proposing any domestic legislation. But a year was simply too long.[4]

Secretary Finch, as the chair of the CUA subcommittee on OEO, put together a talking paper for that next meeting on February 3. Nixon as always was alert to the outside world. He mentioned that congressional committees were beginning to hold hearings on the OEO and that the National Governors Association would be meeting in DC in two weeks. He wanted to be doing something about the OEO.

Apart from the optics, Nixon was torn about a program inherited from Johnson that had a very high level of animosity toward it. He backtracked from his first desire to do away with the OEO. After the discussion of Finch's paper, his position was that we ought to "avoid giving the impression that we are dismantling OEO. . . . Rather, new life ought to be breathed into organizational activities of the poverty program to accomplish the objectives OEO was to accomplish, but has failed to."[5]

This debate put Pat Moynihan in a bit of a contortionist position. Moynihan had himself been a principal architect of the War on Poverty, working with Michael Harrington, the democratic socialist and author of *The Other America*,[6] Frank Mankiewicz, and Adam Yarmolinski, a Robert F. Kennedy aide. These four cooked up the poverty program over spaghetti dinners after work in the Moynihan house. But Moynihan later got indigestion. He turned on it. He came to question his own creation. As the poverty program geared up, he was offended, as were President Johnson and the countless mayors of cities who became the target of criticism and abuse funded by the government itself. More central to his concern about those in poverty than patching or redirecting OEO's programs was the roots of poverty, which Moynihan saw as lack of income. Still, he understood Nixon's need to deal with the OEO.

In the course of that early February meeting, the principal issue was what OEO functions might be transferred out to the major "line" departments, like Labor, Agriculture, or Health, Education and Welfare, or the Department of Housing and Urban Development. After these spin-offs, OEO would be left as an incubator, or starter, for programs that could hopefully play a future role in the alleviation of poverty. Vice President Agnew added his view that in the formative history of the OEO, "there had been no intention to have it an operational agency, but rather a 'think tank and testing station.'"[7]

Nixon directed that Moynihan and OEO subcommittee members decide what can be spun off from the OEO, and soon. His palpable sense of urgency was indicated when he said, "I would like the spin off at the earliest possible time—within this week. It would best be done at the White House."[8]

There were politics involved and jurisdictional issues. It also begged the question of how Nixon himself would assess the root causes of poverty and how he would set and navigate his own major change of course. Rightly, in Nixon's mind, welfare was uppermost in the public's mind. He had campaigned more vigorously about the failures of the nation's welfare programs

than about the excesses or failures in the Poverty program. A week before
the inaugural, Nixon wrote a scorching memo about welfare to several of
his senior aides, including Moynihan. It was triggered by news stories about
the explosive expansion of welfare rolls in New York City. The impatience
of the incoming president was readable in every paragraph. He demanded a
response within two weeks, on January 31.

Moynihan responded in a long and data-laden memorandum. It was an
important step in the building by Moynihan and the president of a relationship that was an intellectual engagement and also had a sense of reality. It
was the first of Pat's many memoranda to Nixon specifically on the subject
of welfare and dependency. Nixon read these. He was to spend more time
on reading and discussions about dependency, poverty, hunger, and welfare
reform than any other domestic issues in these first years of his presidency.

In the last moments of the February 3 CUA meeting, discussion turned
to unemployment, and those who were the casualties of unemployment,
"since," according to Dr. Paul McCracken, the president's new chairman of
the Council of Economic Advisors, "an increase of unemployment appears
to equal an increase of those on welfare." Moynihan corrected McCracken
and others around the table that the relationship McCracken described had
in fact, by the mid-1960s, fallen apart and that welfare rolls were increasing
even in times of declining unemployment.

At this point, Nixon raised the idea of a "minimum Federal standard" for
welfare—the concept embraced in his Transition Task Force on Public Welfare, or the "Nathan" plan. He ruefully noted "tremendous Congressional
opposition—especially with Dirksen [Everett McKinley Dirksen of Illinois,
the Republican leader in the Senate] in the lead position." Little could he or
others around the table know the degree to which the regular or conservative
Republican opposition in the Senate would later deprive Nixon of winning a
profound victory in social policy. But both Nixon's proposals and the ensuing congressional battles lay in the future. Nixon was only starting to focus
on welfare. He found Moynihan's long note to him informative and readable,
and he directed that all of the Council members receive a copy, telling Haldeman to be sure that future memos to him from Moynihan get wide circulation in the White House and the cabinet.

Because of his increasing impatience about OEO, he asked for a Saturday meeting on the subject, "lasting as long as necessary, to approve 'only
what we can do now.'" He went on to suggest that it should result in a statement with a timetable of April 1 for presentation to the Congress and that we
should get to the press an indication of forthcoming action, which could help
preempt Congressional moves on OEO.[9]

One of the reasons movement on OEO was not swifter was that OEO was headless. Most cabinet departments had their secretaries in place. The pressing policy changes for the agency had no input from a person who was going to have to sell them to Congress—and make them work. Nixon grew ever more frustrated, even though only three or four weeks had gone by since his inaugural parade.

The search for a director was obviously to be impacted by what any candidate thought would be the fate of the entity he or she was being asked to lead, so in a way, the debate was inconclusive. As it continued, through February and into March, the president felt slowed down on his whole domestic agenda. Nixon, as early as the first week of February, was trying to close in on a head for the agency whose future he did not see clearly. On Valentine's Day, Haldeman wrote that attention had focused on Leonard Garment for the OEO job. Garment, Nixon's former law partner, of course was very close to him. He was a Democrat and a liberal, and he would be an interesting choice. Appointing a liberal Democrat who was so close personally to the president could have a muting effect on Democratic alarms that Nixon would eviscerate the poverty program. Haldeman asked Moynihan about Garment and heard "he's interested; would be good, except not an administrator."[10] Haldeman looked elsewhere for reactions. "President wanted me to talk to Garment and test out his suitability for head of OEO. I did this at lunch,"[11] wrote Arthur Burns.

Meanwhile the freshman president continued to badger his majordomo about moving ahead on an OEO next phase, pushing Haldeman to get letters out on Head Start and the Job Corps to Secretaries Finch and Shultz "to demand changes." Haldeman says he "kept returning to these points during the day and into the evening."[12] Nixon's frustration was not only with the void at OEO but also the lack of a domestic program—at least its outlines. This was what was really nagging at him. He was of a political generation who remembered the resonance of the first hundred days from Roosevelt's whirlwind early moments of his presidency.

The Scranton Flirtation

Others—outsiders, but outsiders with very good antennae and the same kinds of memories—were beginning to ask about the domestic program as well. On February 24, Governor William Scranton—the same Scranton who had unsuccessfully sought to derail the Goldwater march to nomination in 1964, as the last-ditch candidate of the moderate wing of the GOP, and then served out his governorship—dropped by my office. After the 1968 election, Nixon had enlisted him to go on fact-finding missions both to Europe and, later, to the Middle East, relying on his independence of judgment, and, for that matter, of sources. A State Department friend of mine, who had access to Scranton's report to Nixon on his European trip on Nixon's behalf, told me that it was "refreshing." It had things you "didn't read in government documents about an incumbent," such as Scranton's characterization of the European viewpoint of LBJ as "crude and incredible." Scranton told me the way he had been useful on these trips for the new president "was by being outside, by getting info no one in the gov't was given."[13]

Scranton came into my EOB office under the guise of business, to talk a bit about the Appalachian region and the regional development commission of which he and other governors in the area were members. He then turned conversation to Nixon and said, though he generally was delighted, "I wonder when we are going to see some program?" I told him that we were working on a welfare proposal, and the president just over a week ago, "and in the presence of Dr. Burns, had told Pat he was for a federal standard." In turn, "that provoked Scranton to step back into my office and in a lowered voice to ask what the relation between Burns and Moynihan really was. . . . I told him how deferential Pat is to Burns and the other Cabinet rank people, and how we were seeking to bring Burns into the tent of the Council and make that the forum for discussions."[14]

His question about Burns was not just idle curiosity. It was understandable that he would want to know more about the liberal and conservative policymakers whom Nixon had set up in policy counterpoint to each other. But Scranton was, at this point, in fact in discussions about taking over the OEO, and that wasn't all that was being discussed.

Arthur Burns, in a diary entry of February 14, said, "I told him [the president] I'd like to have Scranton with me. He approved despite doubt expressed by Haldeman and Harlow, who feared the VP [vice president] might feel hurt. . . . President angrily said that what Scranton would do would not conflict with VP."[15] That broader notion of a Scranton role did not go away—at least in Burns's head—although focus shifted back in the next couple of weeks to Scranton taking over the OEO. Burns tells us that on February 24, "Governor Scranton came and we discussed . . . his assuming charge of OEO. Pres had expressed interest in his doing that, and Scranton showed interest."[16] This was the same day Scranton pulled me back into my office to quiz me about Moynihan's and Burns's relationship and where our domestic program stood. Scranton's name obviously was in play for either OEO or a much broader role. Nixon apparently backtracked and was not yet ready to go with Scranton.

Nixon for the moment turned his interest to a friend and mentor of mine and of the Ripon Society, Walter N. Thayer. Thayer had swung to help Nixon for the general election—and encouraged me to do so. Nixon was looking for a position in government to use Thayer's astuteness and his tough management skills, honed in the merciless world of New York newspaper publishing. The *Trib*, after bleeding red ink due to labor disputes, lived now after its New York collapse in 1966 only in its celebrated Paris offspring, the *International Herald Tribune*.

Arthur Burns was nonplussed when he learned on March 3 that Nixon was now disinclined to go with Scranton and wanted Walter Thayer for OEO. To Burns, "this sounded most extraordinary & unbelievable."[17] Likely it would sound extraordinary and unbelievable to Thayer as well. Looking at discussions of Nixon with Haldeman, and often Ehrlichman, over the first few years of his White House, one is struck by the sheer number of discussions relating to personnel questions. There were endless deliberations on the merits or demerits of both the incumbents in any visible position and the field of possible successors. The uncertainty of Nixon about the OEO post is not surprising.

The next move was on March 5, when Burns and Scranton met with Nixon, and Nixon brought himself to ask Scranton to consider the OEO. As Burns describes it,

> March 5 Meeting with President and Scranton surprised me. RN has a uniquely effective Presidential style; but he is not very effective when he invites someone to do a job. . . . I had to intervene to explain that RN was asking Scranton to take the OEO job. After that, President went overboard, told Scranton that he was not satisfied with Moynihan in the sphere of devising urban programs, that he wanted Scranton not only to take OEO but to take charge of urban programs as a whole. This looseness of assignment has caused trouble before, and I wondered how much more it would cause before RN became more precise. I later explained to Scranton what RN really had in mind (or should have had in mind).[18]

Two things are of interest here. First, Burns's comments in his secret diary are starting to take on some skepticism—later to be waspishness or crankiness—about his friend who had asked him to join the White House. Here he even sounds patronizing, feeling he had to explain to someone else what the president meant, or should have meant. While Burns's current White House role was no "holding position," he was neither happy nor comfortable with the infighting. Burns's remarks as the dates in his diary move into 1970 and beyond turn more acidic.

The second is Nixon's impatience, expressed as early as March 5, only six or seven weeks into the administration, with the efforts at shaping a domestic policy. Moynihan was feeling the pressure—and the displeasure. For someone as knowledgeable as he about securing and holding onto presidential pleasure, approval, and support, this was troubling.

But Arthur Burns was supposed to be shaping all domestic policy, as announced in the January 23 release of his new position. His diary entry noting Nixon's disappointment with Moynihan may be schadenfreude or glee at Moynihan's discomfort. But it was ignoring the fact that he himself was a target of Nixon's irritation. The president was irritated with his whole domestic policy development process. If Moynihan had not been delivering, had Arthur? Counsellor Burns would soon feel his share of the criticism, but the more public expression of the president's impatience fell on the Council for Urban Affairs members, to Moynihan's great angst.

Just a day later, on March 6, 1969, in the CUA meeting, Nixon mentioned that he felt some of the Council papers "were not grappling with the issues as much and as fast as they should be"[19] He also was concerned about the administration's work on "hunger," which was seeing lots of congressional attention. The Nixon administration would soon take dramatic steps on the issues of nutrition and hunger.

For all of his edginess, Nixon warmed minutes later to the lengthy discussion by Moynihan based on his paper on welfare, which the president had widely circulated. George Shultz added thoughts that tied in the Job Corps, then Head Start and Day Care programs, administered by other departments. Nixon reacted favorably and "asked if that was not what the Urban Affairs Council is designed to do. He asked, 'Do we have the capability to do this?'"

Moynihan had been getting some of these questions put to him. He told me the same day with irritation that Nixon is "'mad' . . . about our preparation of materials. Hard to compare us with the NSC [National Security Council—Henry Kissinger's shop], in business since 1947 and with a staff of 38 [we had eight]."[20]

It was in that CUA meeting that I felt for the first time Nixon responding to the conservative counterpressures of the first few weeks. As I was walking out of the Cabinet Room at its conclusion, I saw Governor Scranton in the Fish Room, just across a narrow hall from the Oval Office and named such by Franklin Roosevelt, who put an aquarium and various fishing paraphernalia there for display. It was renamed the Roosevelt Room, for the two Roosevelt presidents who were distant cousins, early in Nixon's presidency.

"He [Scranton] pumped me on how Pat felt about OEO, asking if he would like to abolish it—I said that he might dream that at night, but had never been explicit with us about it. Scranton said, if we did we'd have dozens of Presbyterian ministers—'and I'm a Presbyterian'—in Lafayette Square. At that very moment, Pat walked in and said, 'I usually say Episcopal Bishops.'

I learned a minute later, as we walked toward the Pres. office and Scranton went in . . . that Nixon was about to offer Scranton OEO."[21]

Unaware of the content of the Nixon/Scranton talk that Burns partici- pated in and described in his diary, and how threatening it might be to Pat's position so early in the administration, Pat and I then spent an hour with Scranton following his meeting with Nixon. I wrote in my diary, "Scranton kept at the point that the President needed someone in the White House to follow through on domestic issues, acknowledging that there were excellent thinking people. Pat agreed with the importance of this—of someone who could say no."[22] Scranton told us he had to look at this without reference to himself, while he thought about it during the week Nixon had asked him to give it. "S characterized himself as having as one of very few talents an objec- tivity greater than that of most people. 'I'm an impersonal man.'"[23]

On March 13, Haldeman sent a note to Peter Flanigan, a Dillon, Read, investment bank alumnus now on the White House staff and well acquainted with New York business circles. In it, Haldeman said, "Now that the question of Scranton and OEO has been settled, the President would like to resume our effort to see if Walter Thayer is interested in this post and if not to move to Erwin Canham [then the publisher of the *Christian Science Monitor*]."

Thayer evidently had first been offered the post of deputy secretary of the Department of Health, Education and Welfare, with Nixon and his per- sonnel shop thinking Robert Finch likely could use some strong managerial help in staying on top of that huge portfolio. Haldeman, tasked by Nixon with sounding out Thayer, had lunch with him about the OEO on March 20. Thayer was not interested.[24]

Burns apparently felt he could maneuver and have Scranton report to him, which would cement his control over the formation of domestic policy and marginalize Moynihan. What he did not grasp was the unhappiness of Nixon about the evolution of a domestic program, and Burns did not go untainted. This unfolded in Haldeman's account. Haldeman, whose detailed, daily dia- ries are surprisingly objective, with a frequent ability to step back and put things in a context, must be almost unique in the annals of White House senior staff. In his own behavior, Haldeman reflects Nixon's petulance at times; he also shows, in the course of entries in these first weeks, the growth of impatience and irritation with Arthur Burns. It was born partly no doubt of style. On Lincoln's birthday, 1969, just three weeks into Nixon's presi- dency, Haldeman noted that Moynihan, Finch, Bryce Harlow, Haldeman, and Burns met in yet another of many all hands meetings on the question of the OEO that ended inconclusively. The next day, Haldeman commented briefly, "Arthur Burns drives me nuts."

Domestic Policy Oversight Starts to Move to Ehrlichman

A week later, on February 21, Haldeman related a "long hassle with Burns, et al, about domestic planning. Upshot, made him Chairman of 6:00 PM Group to meet daily to coordinate. Should help." This was not unlike the Burns idea, floated two weeks earlier to Harlow, to have a group for vetting or filtering issues to go to the president for decision. However, even in these few days, the ground was beginning to shift under both Moynihan and Burns. On March 6, Haldeman wrote again of his irritation that Moynihan "had not properly staffed the agenda, and had sneaked in a four-page release and a new [volunteer action] plan." Writing of the "P's" irritation, for the first time there is an intimation of a new arrangement.

Likely, Haldeman had seen the Burns and Moynihan shops much as they looked to the outside world and much as Nixon may have initially wanted them to be: repositories of ideologically clashing, or at least different, ideas. Haldeman did not know Moynihan, and Moynihan did not know the ins and outs of the staff, nor their links to particular pools of influence on Capitol Hill, nor their way of handling the public relations side of policy. Haldeman did doubtless know Burns. He may have regarded him as I did. Burns was an older school, dignified, deliberate, cautious economist. He also could be vexing in his stiff manner and in his use of his best prop, his pipe, to exact time between sentences—or the thoughts that underlay them—to give him more opportunity to rebut or to frame an argument.

Moynihan never, in Haldeman's mind, was dull or sententious. His color, in fact his off-color, was a difference to the West Wing standard or regulation issue. In his very first Council for Urban Affairs meeting, when Burns asked, in his rather reedy, slightly nasal drawl, that Moynihan develop an urban policy, Moynihan stunned the assembled dignitaries by saying, after a brief pause, that he would, "providing no one would take it seriously."

There was a silence. Nixon chuckled, and the release of tension in the room was palpable. Perhaps it was not unlike that around a dinner table with General Secretary Josef Stalin of his mandarins, or a demanding corporate CEO, when all awaited a signal from the leader. But then they began to laugh. For all the Sturm und Drang over the next two years, Haldeman never lost his respect for Moynihan or his sense that Moynihan was a spark plug for the president and for the staff, and he took pleasure in Moynihan's sense of humor.

Still, all that being true, what was happening in these earliest days to lessen Moynihan's organizational control over policy formulation was also laying the foundation for more formal action soon. For both Moynihan and Burns, the impact would be felt. None of the rest of us knew yet what was going on in Haldeman's and Ehrlichman's minds. But planning was being put in place that would displace both the Moynihan and the Burns shops. As early as the first week of March, in the same entry as his indication of pique at Moynihan's staff work on March 6, and saying "P pretty upset," Haldeman tips his hand: "Hope our plan for E to oversee domestic matters will overcome this."[25]

So, six weeks in, the master plan is being developed for a takeover by the counsel, John D. Ehrlichman, of all domestic matters. This would mean Moynihan would lose the direction of policy on urban affairs. Burns would lose his authority over broader matters than urban affairs. Haldeman had not yet convinced the president of this. However, within the week, he and Ehrlichman met with Moynihan and with Burns, separately, giving Haldeman a sense of "some progress on domestic policy coordination." Burns and Moynihan are set to go. Haldeman wrote in his diary: "Will put E in overall charge. Now have to get to work that way. Hard to get P to stay on the big issues. He keeps hacking away at PR concerns, especially in the domestic policy area. Moynihan points out that he can't have a domestic program. Not any money available, and politically impossible anyway. Better just to try to get rid of the things that don't work, and try to build up the few that do."[26]

A day later, on March 12, Haldeman pens in his diary, "Got the E plan finalized." Obviously, Moynihan understood. The day before, March 11, I observed that "DPM [is] a little down, says RN has not responded for the last 5 days to anything Pat has sent to him. Also told me last evening it is obvious who is running the place—Haldeman and Ehrlichman who spends nearly three hours per day [with the President]."[27]

For Burns, it meant he would have to face an Ehrlichman who found Burns petulant and difficult. Haldeman observed on March 17, "Poor E has to untangle all this, and Arthur Burns is now driving him nuts, as he did me (and still does)." Burns did not go gentle into that good night. He raged, raged, against the dying of the light. On March 25, Ehrlichman and Haldeman "had a knock-down with Arthur Burns at lunch. Pretty bitter discussion. Still didn't settle the problem of getting a domestic program. Burns determined to run the show, but it's obvious he can't manage. Tough one for John. P later said E has to ride hard on this because Arthur will never get it done. We are about at a point of internal dissension."

Only weeks later, amid Haldeman's positive reaction to progress on a domestic program that Ehrlichman had helped to clarify at a lengthy Key Biscayne meeting, Haldeman observed some shortcomings in his protégé. Ehrlichman had not followed the Haldeman system for clearances. While Moynihan's earlier peccadilloes had earned comments like "sneaked in" from Haldeman, Ehrlichman received a kinder, gentler rebuke. Noting that Ehrlichman was not following the rules, Haldeman offered, "John goes on his merry way, ignoring the staff system. But it'll work out, as he sees his need for the system."[28]

For Moynihan, his minimalist earlier comments to the president about what would be possible proved too cramped for his energetic persona and for his ambitions for what Nixon not only could do but must do. Crucially, Nixon was feeling the same way. He felt he must do the work to have the social structure repaired and the American people filled with confidence in the ability of institutions to deliver what they need.

One reason Moynihan may have felt constrained was a feeling that possibly he and Burns shared (although they likely never discussed it together). As Haldeman wrote after his lunch with Thayer, "Still a stir about domestic program, not organized yet. Burns and Moynihan both feel strongly that P not putting enough time or attention on this and that nothing will be settled until he does. I think they are right." This was about to change. Nixon had not yet been exposed to an idea that would mark him as a major social innovator. He had not yet seen, saddled and bridled, "the charger" he would like to ride.

My Early Sense of Nixon

I was still forming my impressions of my boss. Snapshots of Nixon's behavior and attitudes were coming in from all directions and going in all directions. One morning, just weeks into the new administration, I was sitting in the White House Mess at breakfast with a friend and Al Haig sat down to join. Haig was in civilian clothes. He had joined the National Security Council staff as Henry Kissinger's deputy and as a colonel. In about the same number of years, Haig was to have four stars on each shoulder. This morning Haig seemed to be trying to show how important he was in his role. He mentioned the president's reaction the prior night to news about North Vietnamese aggression. Haig told us, "It was all I could do to keep him from 'nuking' Hanoi!" Over his waffles, he meant to leave the impression that he was able to control the commander in chief's worst impulses.

At about the same time, also on Vietnam, a very different message about the president came to me. Lee Huebner was at a reception after a White House dinner in those first weeks, standing with Mrs. Nixon, as she spoke with someone whose connection with the Nixons went back at least to 1960. The guest spoke consolingly about how the loss in 1960 "was possibly a blessing in disguise in that President Nixon could now take on the even more difficult challenges of the current era." Mrs. Nixon disagreed. "If her husband had been elected in 1960, she said, a lot of things might have been very different: 'for one thing, we never would have had the Vietnam War."[29]

Only more than forty years later did I learn of yet another Nixon in his handling Vietnam. My seatmate on Air Force Two in early July 1969, for the flight to and from the launch of Apollo 11, was a Frenchman, Jean Saintenay, a Gaullist cabinet member and now an Air France director. He had decades of experience living in Vietnam, tutoring the young emperor Bao Dai, being interned by the Japanese during the war, and knowing many nationalists, who were to become Viet Cong. His being at the launch was a cover. He saw Nixon before and after our trip, to handle secret correspondence between Nixon and Ho Chi Minh, as Nixon sought to start negotiations directly with Ho to end the war. The first meeting between Henry Kissinger and Ho's emissaries was held in Saintenay's Paris apartment. This was the off-camera, peacemaker side of Nixon.

A more personal side of Nixon was on display one morning in those first weeks. Dr. Paul McCracken and I were sitting in the "Fish Room," which Nixon was soon to rename. As we sat there waiting to see the president, a steward from the US Navy asked us if we wished to have some coffee. Dr. McCracken asked him how he liked the new president. The steward answered, "Oh, I like him very much. He is so nice to you. The other man, he shouted at you all the time." Nixon may never have had the radiant charm of an FDR, but he was a man of common courtesy. I kept hearing anecdotes like this as I settled in. Nixon had empathy, which was so outside the normal picture of this unstoppably ambitious man.

And the OEO Prize Goes to Donald Rumsfeld!

By now, Moynihan had a general approach for the OEO that the president bought. A draft statement that Moynihan had prepared for release by Secretary Finch about the new concept for OEO was so liked by Nixon that Nixon issued it under his own name. The sales job for it fell to a new figure. The problem of finding the right person to manage OEO was happily resolved, after Moynihan and the president zeroed in on Donald H. Rumsfeld.

Rumsfeld, or "Rummy" was an ambitious, smart, and highly energetic Republican member of Congress. When the idea of his taking on OEO was first mooted, he thought it almost daft: his district in the Chicago suburbs was the second highest in income of any congressional district in the United States. He was an Ivy League grad (a wrestler at Princeton). He had voted against the creation of the OEO. He concluded that the job the White House wanted done was the "liquidation of the Johnson poverty approach. The development of the Nixon approach to these problems would essentially be the responsibility not of OEO but of [other] Departments."[30] These were the arguments Rumsfeld made to the Nixon team to argue why he should not take the job.

Moynihan felt differently. First, Rumsfeld was an activist and had, within the House of Representatives, been a leader of a group of "Young Turks" who were impatient for change and responsiveness in the Republican hierarchy and the House as a whole. Also, Rumsfeld, despite his sharp edges and often exuberant and enthusiastic partisanship, was one who reached across party lines. One of his closest friends for a time in the House was Democrat Allard Lowenstein, representing a district in suburban New York and a former community organizer and celebrated rabble-rouser. Rumsfeld even defended him for reelection against his Republican opponent at a time when Rumsfeld had joined the Nixon administration. He withdrew his support only when both the White House and the juggernaut Nassau County, New York, Republican organization, with significant power in state and national elections, piled onto him.

Rumsfeld was influenced by Moynihan's reasoning as to why a young, ambitious politician like himself should invest his energy in this seeming dead end. As Rumsfeld reconstructs it, "Moynihan had keen political instincts. Who better, he proposed, to run an agency disliked by Republicans in Congress than . . . a conservative Republican from Congress? Pat knew I had voted against OEO but that I had supported civil rights legislation and had shown an interest in tackling reform. He strongly recommended that Nixon appoint me. It was an unorthodox choice."[31] Nixon worked hard to convince Rumsfeld. "Nixon persuaded me to take on an assignment I didn't want, at an agency I had voted against, with a mission that Nixon didn't like, for a purpose that was still unclear."[32]

But take it he did. He recruited strong staff, including his assistant Richard Cheney. He also persuaded his Princeton wrestling friend, Frank Carlucci, to leave the Foreign Service and come on to take hold of the most problematic and publicly visible parts of the OEO, the Community Action Agencies. Christie Todd Whitman and Bill Bradley signed on. She was later the Republican governor of New Jersey and an administrator of the Environmental Protection Agency, which Nixon created. Bill Bradley was later a distinguished Democratic US senator, himself able to reach across party lines. OEO started to come together.

Rumsfeld's relationship with Moynihan was very positive, since Rumsfeld felt that "Pat Moynihan was creative, entertaining, and one of the smartest individuals I had ever met. . . . I thought that it said something laudatory of Nixon that he saw the merit of bringing Moynihan into his confidence."[33]

Moynihan and our staff worked at flank speed to generate policy proposals Moynihan took with him to an Easter weekend meeting in Key Biscayne. Principal among them was a welfare reform initiative. It was to evolve into the Family Assistance Plan. The battle for Nixon's decision about welfare, or "income maintenance," began immediately and raged throughout the spring and summer, up until the last moment, in early August, when the president made clear that he had embraced a transformative idea.

While the control of the machinery for policy coordination would ebb from Moynihan's hands, what he would influence was Nixon's attention in policy. With input and ideas from the departments, but with his inimitable stamp and his strategic sense, from Moynihan was about to emerge the centerpiece of Nixon's domestic policy. Nixon later took to calling it, in conversation or letters with Moynihan, "Our Monument."

CHAPTER 9

"Our Monument"
Laying the Foundation

In the winter 1968 issue of the *Public Interest*, Patrick Moynihan wrote an article titled "The Crisis in Welfare." About welfare he said, "The nation is not likely to do anything much to change it."[1] The irony—and inaccuracy—of this forecast stemmed from the job Moynihan never envisioned he would have, working for a president he had not supported on a strategy they built together. As things turned out, early in 1969, President Nixon and he put the lie to that resigned tone about the status quo that Moynihan had struck only a year earlier.

The roots of the Nixon proposal of a guaranteed income included an important book by the Nobel Prize–winning economist Milton Friedman. His *Capitalism and Freedom* (1962) proposed an income-tested payment for families to place a floor under their income, the very idea that Moynihan was in the new administration to put in front of Nixon.[2] The Ripon Society had done detailed work on this negative income tax, taking account of liberal economists' similar interest in the idea. Based on Ripon's work, I put the idea in front of Nixon during a late January 1968 small dinner with him. I then, a year later, pressed my new boss, Pat Moynihan, to turn to the negative income tax and forgo his romance with the more costly "family allowance."

In spring 1967, it appeared that conservatives and liberals might find common cause on this issue. In a March 1967 issue of *National Review*, Milton Friedman renewed his 1962 call for change from the current welfare system. He said that the system "involves a tremendous bureaucracy, widespread intervention into the operation of the market system in areas that have nothing to do with poverty, and inexcusable interference with the individual freedom and dignity of the truly poor who receive assistance."[3] His remedy was the negative income tax.

Not a month later, the April 1967 issue of the *Ripon Forum* carried a six-page detailed proposal and argument for the negative income tax.[4] It invoked the call of the deceased but still revered Senator Robert Taft for a minimum income for American families. The Ripon proposal said flatly that this should be the "cornerstone" of an alternative to Lyndon Johnson's War on Poverty. A draft statute by Ripon members appeared in the *Yale Law Journal*, and the idea was embraced by Rep. Richard Whalen from Taft country in the heart of Ohio and became the first detailed and defensible ready-for-action Republican social initiative in this policy area.

A similar citation of Robert Taft occurred a year later upon the release of the report of the National Advisory Commission on Civil Disorders in March 1968. Known as the Kerner Commission for its chairman, the Democratic governor of Illinois, its vice-chair was John V. Lindsay, the then Republican mayor of New York City. Lindsay asked Richard Nathan to help, and Nathan joined as associate director for program research. He oversaw a proposal that looked strikingly like Richard Nixon's Family Assistance Plan of 1969. It called for a "National System of Income Supplementation" to aid both the working poor and the dependent poor. Taft was recalled for having proposed, in 1949, a "minimum standard floor under subsistence" to guarantee all Americans a minimum standard of decent living and "all children . . . a fair opportunity to get a start in life."[5]

The Nixon administration labored over numerous issues around a negative income tax (NIT), many of them quite detailed or technical. These included "marginal tax rates," namely, how much the federal payment decreases as earnings for the family increase. A dollar-for-dollar reduction would amount to a 100 percent marginal tax rate, so it must be something less. Powerful questions of incentives are in play here. There also are questions of administration. What is the right governmental entity to administer this? Is it the Internal Revenue Service, which would send out checks rather than receiving them? Or is it the welfare agencies, which are more accustomed to dealing with the dependent poor but not the working poor?

There were many more philosophical issues surrounding the new concept of "supplementing" or "maintaining" income. One paramount concept was work itself. Should individuals or families be required to work in order to receive a base amount or supplements? On whom should the work requirement be imposed? What limitations will there be on work requirements? These issues are hardy perennials and were front and center not just in 1970 but also in the 1990s, when a massive shift in welfare policy was put in place. The Republicans, Democrats, libertarians, and liberals who were debating welfare reform in 1969 were struggling to find a rational path for assisting those in need. Nixon sought to thread the needle through politically fraught and technically difficult issues.

An Early Earful for Nixon on the Negative Income Tax

On January 28, 1968, just days before Nixon declared his candidacy for the 1968 Republican presidential nomination, I was with him for a small dinner for eight at the Links Club in Manhattan. I suggested that Nixon take an interest in the negative income tax. I invoked the name of Milton Friedman, as a philosophical conservative who saw the NIT as a crucial element for social policy and the right way to correct the current skewed and controversial welfare system. I might, in hindsight, have been less forceful in arguing Friedman's support of it as authority for the NIT. Years later, in a conversation with John Ehrlichman, the president exclaimed, as Friedman's name came up, "I wish I were as sure about anything as Milton Friedman is about everything!"[6]

The point I made that evening at dinner was that there was an intriguing convergence of conservative and liberal opinions on the idea. *National Review* ran the piece of Friedman's on the NIT, and on its heels, there was the extensive Ripon proposal, including a full draft statute. On the liberal side, in support were a number of Democratic economists, such as Joseph Pechman and James Tobin.[7] As a political matter, I thought Friedman's arguments would help a president Nixon, if not a candidate Nixon, propose a radical departure from the current welfare policy worldview and legislative structure. Friedman had advised Goldwater and was popular among conservatives.

One thing Nixon was certain of in 1968 was that the current welfare system was flawed. He saw also that it was producing a political backlash that had profoundly negative repercussions for race relations. As his inaugural address and welfare messages were to show, despite the increasing pull in the Republican Party away from its historic support of civil rights and racial progress, there was a side of Nixon that hoped and strove to reduce the discord between the races. As a clear example, Nixon took concrete and ameliorating steps in his management of Southern school desegregation, despite a lot of resistance in his own White House.

As to welfare, in the 1968 campaign, Nixon was by no means ready to embrace a negative income tax publicly. In fact, he opposed it, publicly. Because a NIT, like a "family allowance" as practiced in Europe, Canada, or elsewhere, was a form of guaranteed income, there was a political liability in speaking of it:

> The term "guaranteed income" had become ideologically charged. It had come to stand for the proposition that people ought not to have to work for a living. American public opinion has shown a persistent tendency to associate political radicalism with the abolition of the wage system, an essentially utopian ideal, with bohemian disdain for the work ethic. Any president proposing a "guaranteed income" in those terms would press that button, and that would be the end of his proposal. But nothing required that a guaranteed income be called a guaranteed income. . . . "Guaranteed income" was the lone label that said "Poison."[8]

Nixon may not have thought the phrase "negative income tax" was toxic, but it did sound complicated. His main concern was to focus on the need to reform public assistance and to make clear that the existing political authorities were not doing so. He was not ready, yet, to think through what form these changes might take. Even as he moved to embrace a landmark proposal for change in social policy, he was careful to avoid the use of terms that would puzzle or provoke controversy. In fact, great pains were taken throughout the development and rollout in 1969 of Nixon's plan to call it neither a "negative income tax" nor a "Guaranteed Income," although it was both.

My point was not lost on Nixon, however. Whatever the clothes in which it was dressed, the idea would not be unrecognizable. When the concept crystallized a year later and was presented to him as one of several ideas provoking war among his aides, he was conceptually familiar with it. The key was Nixon's conviction that something had to be done about welfare.

The New Deal's Dependent Children Program
Just Grows and Grows

In his mining of the data on welfare, incomes, and dependency during the early 1960s, Pat Moynihan detected the beginnings of the unexpected pattern of growth in the welfare rolls that clearly had emerged by 1965. In a chart that he created, he was able to show dramatically that the correlation that had existed for years—decades—between unemployment rates and the expansion and contraction of the welfare rolls, had broken down. Even when the unemployment rate was falling, indeed when the number of persons classified as poor was falling, the enrollment in the Aid to Families with Dependent Children program was continuing to trend upward. In a steep climb.

New York City was the epicenter of this increase by 1965. Four years later, the president-elect wrote his angry memo to Moynihan and others in his infant administration, spurred by a news story about the continued burgeoning of the New York welfare rolls. It was accurate. Richard Blumenthal was a very young man, just twenty-two, on Moynihan's new staff and many years later a US senator. He wrote for Moynihan only two days after inauguration that the best estimates were that one in every eight New Yorkers would be on public assistance in 1969, at a cost then of $2 billion. For New York City alone. For welfare alone. Moynihan replied to Nixon's sharp memo in his own, instructive memo of January 31, 1969. From it, Moynihan gave the first of a series of primers or "seminars" for the president and the CUA on the welfare situation. On February 4, Moynihan told the CUA that national data were good enough to have seen the welfare explosion coming, and government could have done more to head off the current racial situation in cities like New York. "The number of persons classified as poor in the span 1959 to 1968 decreased by 36 percent. The number of public assistance recipients rose 41 percent. This is about the gist of it."[9]

Moynihan saw the linkage between the patchwork of social or safety net programs and the increasing tensions that often broke along racial lines. With George C. Wallace in the race, running on overtly racial issues, these questions took on strong political implications as well. According to Moynihan, "older ethnic working and lower middle-class groups found . . . they appeared to be paying for . . . a vast dependent population of female headed families, and a shadow population made up of the presumably absent fathers.[10] They resented that "a dependent family which optimized its situation—public housing, Medicaid, food stamps, and such-like—could have an equivalent income at least equal to and probably above that of the average New York family."[11] This was to be the focus later that spring of a piece by Pete Hamill, on which Moynihan was to comment to the president.

Gareth Davies analyzed the tensions between the Great Society aspirations for eliminating poverty, with its emphasis on "opportunity" and providing services, on the one hand, and the growing interest in addressing poverty directly, through income maintenance, on the other. He, as Moynihan did, saw the stress in race relations that the mid-1960s array of programs prompted.

> At a time when riots, the open housing issue, school desegregation, and the Black Power movement were already alienating white America from the aspirations of the minority poor, welfare chiseling provided an attractive campaigning theme for conservatives who were happy to exploit the backlash yet reluctant to adopt an explicitly race-based message. *America* magazine observed that "although in most cases the critics of welfare don't talk openly about race, most of them regard relief programs as the special preserve of shiftless and morally obtuse Negroes." It added that such resentment was prevalent among all classes, but that "lower-middle-class" Americans "reserve a special scorn for those who don't support themselves."[12]

In the 1960s, the 1970s, and the 1980s, the median recipient of welfare was a white child, but the perceptions and the resultant politics did not reflect the reality. One goal at the center of Moynihan's and Nixon's "Monument," the Family Assistance Plan, was to reduce the racial focus or implications of the welfare discussion by broadening their effort to all poor families, including the full-time working poor. Poverty itself, rather than a particular subset, such as the minority mothers and their offspring in Northern cities, was their target. Crucially, they intended that the incentives to family breakup for artificial economic reasons would be eliminated, as they shared the belief that family cohesion and stability have salutary effects, giving children a more successful start. They saw that FAP would provide dramatic economic development in the South, where most of the poor lived. This could over time eliminate incentives for "welfare migration" that itself prompted stereotypes of Black immigration from the South. FAP would target the poor, more than two-thirds of whom were whites. All of us hoped that Nixon's Family Assistance Plan of 1969 would reduce the febrile racial tensions over welfare.

The Aid to Families with Dependent Children (AFDC) program, at the heart of the matter, was a New Deal creation, a part of the Social Security Act of 1935. Its original intent was to provide assistance to families whose wage earner was temporarily out of work or had died. It was conceived as a state program, where the federal government would help defray the costs to cities or counties at a level set by the local authorities. The federal government would not impose a benefit level but would respect and assist the state in providing a benefit.

As Vince Burke and his wife, Vee Burke, note in *Nixon's Good Deed*:

Franklin D. Roosevelt . . . planted the seeds of the welfare problem of the 1960s and 1970. . . . Federal funds [were] offered to states by the Social Security Act to encourage them to make welfare payments to two groups of the needy who everyone agreed should not work, even if jobs were available . . . persons over 65 years of age and members of broken families— dependent children and their mothers who had been deprived by death, or other cause of a male breadwinner. These programs . . . it was thought, would largely wither away, unneeded, once Social Security began paying our retirement and survivor benefits and once unemployment insurance took hold for the jobless.

Instead, the little-noticed federal program of aid for broken families, launched in 1935, grew into a monster. By providing welfare funds for fatherless families (and later, beginning in 1961, for families of jobless fathers), yet denying funds for families headed by working poor fathers, Congress inadvertently encouraged creation of mother-headed families.[13]

By the 1960s, the benefit levels between the different states had become wildly disparate. In Mississippi, the AFDC monthly payment for a statistical family of four (a mother and three children) was a maximum of $50 a month and often lower. In New York, it was a $278 maximum; in New Jersey, not much different; in Wisconsin, also high. In Mississippi, the federal government paid about $41 of the $50; in New York, it paid $139 of the $278.

This vast regional discrepancy ran counter to the reality of where poverty resided. The minimal levels of assistance in most Southern states did not address the fact that most of the nation's poverty was located there. As Moynihan observed, geography, more than race, family size, or family structure, was the most powerful indicator of poverty status.[14] Even there, when a state would set a formal minimum level of subsistence, its setting of a level for welfare payments often did not even come close to its own definition of a minimum subsistence level. Half the population of America's poor lived in the South, as defined by the federal government.

While some questioned the data that suggested this difference in benefits payable between Mississippi and New York led to welfare "migration," a prima facie case could certainly be made with those disparities, and there was no question that it became a powerful political issue. Northern politicians began to campaign to deny benefits to in-migrants. The mayor of Newburgh, New York, a town up the Hudson River from New York City, found celebrity among conservative critics of welfare. He pushed through an ordinance denying benefits to families who had arrived from low benefit states such as Mississippi and Alabama and who attempted to enroll for New York–level AFDC benefits in Newburgh. Another officeholder in a town to which a family with eleven children had arrived from Alabama directed the city to purchase tickets to send them back home.

Moynihan by now was convinced that there was a pathology of dependency at play. The most visible flaw in the AFDC benefit was that a man, even an unemployed father, in the house, to say nothing of a man not married to the mother of the children, could not expect his family to qualify for benefits under the AFDC program. This encouraged the male parent to absent himself from the family. This might have reminded Moynihan of his own family situation, in which his father had left the family—though never in his case to return, unlike many men in their shadowy presence in AFDC situations. Family cohesion—family intactness—was one of Moynihan's most powerful concerns. He believed deeply in family stability and knew it influenced family members' ability to achieve their potential. This belief informed his concern about the stability of the institutions of society as a whole.

There was some recognition of the "man in the house" issue in Congress, and it led to a legislative attempt in 1961 that modified the AFDC program somewhat. This was the change known as the AFDC-UP, or unemployed parent (father), program. But the program did not "bend the curve." That curve had been discussed in 1965 by Moynihan with the incoming municipal administration of Mayor John Vliet Lindsay. Moynihan advanced his notion there was a perverse incentive that had taken hold in public welfare and that major changes in the programs were required to arrest a further explosion in the rolls. The new Republican administration in New York, now elected after decades of Democrats, was inclined to embrace a "withering away" notion.

Moynihan's Early Favorite: The Family Allowance

In Catholic social thought, Moynihan concluded, "the family is seen as the basic social unit whose interests take priority . . . over those of the market-place . . . but also . . . of the state and the individual."[15] Conversant with Catholic social policy, and convinced of the central role of the family, Moyni-han embraced one of the responses to the linked problem of poverty and a flawed system of delivery of assistance to families with children. As early as his tenure in the Department of Labor, he fastened on to a European model. He still favored it into the spring of his first year in the White House.

The idea to which he gravitated was the "family allowance." In the early 1960s, the United States, alone among the industrial democracies, did not have a system of family allowances. This was a per capita grant for every fam-ily of parents and children in a society. Its theory in Europe, much influenced by Catholic thought, was that it is "the responsibility of society to provide families with an adequate income. . . . A married man with five children . . . can be said to need, and . . . to deserve, more income than does a bachelor."[16] The history of the policy, as Moynihan observed, could be traced often to conservative, pro-natalist, Catholic regimes in Europe, countries with de-clining birth rates, to try to increase fertility. In these places, it was thought of not so much as an anti-poverty device but as an inducement to have chil-dren and to strengthen the family or the "nation." Most recently in 2007, in Russia, where population was falling by seven hundred thousand every year, President Putin introduced cash grants to women giving birth to a second or third child and giving a woman 40 percent of her prior wages if she left the workforce to raise a child. Family or children's grants were popular in European countries, and Canada introduced family allowances during World War II, partly as a gesture to Catholic French Canadians, and it took hold and became highly popular. Most of these programs were not so pointedly natalist as the Russian one. The name for the grants varied—sometimes "family allowance," sometimes "children's allowance"—but the form was the same. It was not related to income of the family but was a cash, per capita grant to everyone, including parents, or based on the number of children. It was simple. And it reached all. But it was not an efficient means to attack poverty. The allowances go to families of any and all income levels. Both the rich and the indigent get the grants. This is like the recent per capita grants in the first round of COVID-19 relief assistance in 2020—it was sent to all without any distinction between no need and great need.

Moynihan became identified with this solution and—for him—the linked issue of family stability. He tended to see it as supporting family income and thereby averting family stress and breakup. He proselytized constantly. While still in government under Lyndon Johnson, he had the Policy Planning Staff at Labor develop a paper on "Family Allowances in the United States." Once he left government, he lectured and wrote on it. He authored a persuasive piece in the *New York Times Magazine* of February 5, 1967. It was a summary of testimony Moynihan had given before New York senators Jacob K. Javits (R) and Robert F. Kennedy (D) and Connecticut senator Abraham Ribicoff (D) in hearings on the cities. In the committee there was not yet an inclination to shift from the notion of OEO-style services programs and toward an approach based on directly raising the incomes of the poor. Indeed, the approach of the liberal Democrats was to double down and suggest multitudes of additional categorical aid programs of services for the needy, not money directly paid to them.

Kennedy himself rejected the notion of a guaranteed income for families and favored an employment strategy with tax credits for the private sector to create jobs. Kennedy—and Jacob K. Javits, his Republican colleague on the panel—had created, together, the Bedford-Stuyvesant Development Corporation, in which Javits had placed me to work on housing finance and job development issues. The development entity was designed to lure corporations to this Black and Hispanic part of Brooklyn, to help stimulate jobs. It was driven by the concept of opportunity, not an income maintenance policy. This emphasis on opportunity was the same conceptual underpinning as the Poverty program and the Department of Labor's Job Opportunities in the Business Sector (JOBS) program.

They had Kennedy's attention. Senator Eugene McCarthy, on the other hand, favored a guaranteed minimum income, campaigning on it in his brief 1968 run against President Johnson. Alas, in his crucial seat later on the Senate Finance Committee, as Nixon's Family Assistance Plan came before it, McCarthy did not lend his support. Nor did other liberal Democrats. Since Republican senator John Williams was undercutting Republican support among conservatives on the panel, the lack of liberal help that Nixon had almost assumed, given the extraordinary ambition and liberal nature of his proposal, meant that the center did not hold and Nixon was to be denied an important victory.

Moynihan's testimony and his *Times Magazine* piece triggered dozens of positive responses from diverse sources. These included Lewis Mumford, the noted expert on cities, who told Moynihan it was the last word on the subject. In his February 5, 1967, letter to Moynihan, Mumford said, "The massive good sense of your proposals for dealing with poverty . . . undercuts all the devious plans that have so far been put forward." A touching result of the article was a letter to Moynihan from his former social studies teacher at Benjamin Franklin High School in East Harlem, New York. Samuel I. Schweitzer wrote Moynihan on February 7, 1967, that there is a "great danger attention will be diverted from the basic problems you have stressed, i.e., the economic instability and social insecurity which have afflicted so many of our Negro families."

A more influential supportive reaction came five days after the *New York Times Magazine* piece when the *Catholic Century* ran a strong, positive editorial under the title "Money as a Cure for Poverty." Which, of course, was Moynihan's very point.

By the middle 1960s, it was not only a social scientist like Moynihan, an ambitious politician like the Mayor of Newburgh, New York, or economists like Milton Friedman or Joseph Pechman who were worrying about the disconnect between unemployment rates and welfare rolls. The business community took an interest in the issue.

Nelson Rockefeller into the Fray

Governor Nelson Rockefeller of New York saw that the welfare system was broken and that most likely the social-welfare administrators and gatekeepers were not going to call for the end of the system and its replacement with something new. He therefore did what came naturally for the governor of New York. He convened business leaders to listen to academics. For years, Nelson Rockefeller had called together experts on subjects he wanted to explore. He would give the ideas of the scholars and specialists heft by having them discussed and their proposals adopted by visible business and nonprofit sector leaders. Over the decades, even before he jumped into elective politics, this had been a modus operandi for Rockefeller. It was these libraries full of studies that he had opened to Walter DeVries, George Romney's senior aide, when Rockefeller was an early backer of the Michigan governor for the 1968 nomination. As DeVries told me, the volume and the quality of the policy research had staggered him. He had spent days and days trolling through what was on offer to Romney. It all went back to Nelson's conceit that well-researched, well-considered, well-publicized "right" answers will excite public support for the proposals—and for the candidate embracing them.

In this case, Rockefeller got a blue-ribbon group of leaders to focus on why public assistance was not working and what could set it right. The governor convened a meeting in the winter of 1967 to mark the centennial of the New York Board of Social Welfare. He pulled together a group including the CEO of upstate New York's dynamic Xerox Corporation. Joining Joseph Wilson were the senior partner of Goldman Sachs, Gus Levy; the CEO of Mobil Oil (still based on East Forty-Second Street in Manhattan at the time); the chair of the Marine Midland Bank (based in Buffalo); the chair of the executive committee of Inland Steel Company; and others, including, notably, Arjay Miller, vice chairman of the Ford Motor Company, and later Ford's president, and still later, head of the Stanford School of Business.[17] They met at Arden

House, a magnificent property once owned by the Harriman family that had been converted into a conference center up the Hudson River north of the Palisades. Averell Harriman had been Rockefeller's target as the incumbent when Rockefeller first ran for New York governor in 1958. This was a region of Eastern Establishment geography: The Palisades, running as sheer cliffs and dense parkland for miles and miles on the west bank of the Hudson River, had been Rockefeller property, in the tens of thousands of acres, until they turned it over to public ownership to preserve its forested and undeveloped nature. The massive former Rockefeller property ran north to a point not many miles from where the former Harriman property commenced.

The task force members started to grapple with a problem about which the businessmen quickly realized there were few facts firmly known, and they were skeptical about the advocates or administrators of the current welfare institutional structure. The group heard from Moynihan and from Milton Friedman, advocates of the family allowance and the negative income tax, respectively. They leaned toward the negative income tax and did opine that there needed to be strong incentives to continue work if there were to be income supplements. As debate intensified in the spring of 1969 in the White House, Rockefeller put in an appearance, aware of the Arden House analysis of welfare's misfunction and its proposal for a path forward, even though it was not the governor's first choice, as he wanted fiscal relief from New York State's burden of welfare costs.

Grudging Moves against the Grain for President Johnson

The Arden House meeting was preceded that winter by an announcement in Lyndon Johnson's Economic Message of January 1967. The president said he would establish a Commission on Income Maintenance Programs. Then Johnson dragged his feet, not committed to an idea that seemed to question or subvert the whole approach of the Office of Economic Opportunity and the strategy of services for the poor. At the highest levels of the Johnson administration, they were constantly conceiving of additional niche programs to support the services strategy with which they were identified. Johnson did nothing for more than a year.

Meanwhile, his Office of Economic Opportunity almost stealthily started an experiment on the negative income tax in New Jersey. A pilot effort, with small funding, it was to test whether an income supplement program would encourage people to work, as they could retain most of the earnings, or would incent them to relax efforts to find or keep work. Also, it was to explore whether it could reduce incentives to family breakup. The interest in an alternative or a complement to the "services" strategy operated initially at subterranean levels in the bureaucracy and among lower-level appointees in the dwindling days of the Johnson administration. It did finally get the interest of Sargent Shriver, the head of the OEO, but he could not gain a beachhead for it on higher ground—at the White House.

As the Nixon administration hit the ground, there was a positive combustion between these ideas for income maintenance in the OEO and lower bureaucratic levels of the HEW, on the one hand, and the ideas of some of us arriving with the new administration, on the other. Robert Patricelli from Javits's staff on the Hill and I were initiates into the negative income tax concept through Ripon's embrace of the concept and draft of a model statute. George Shultz, incoming secretary of labor, certainly was familiar with it as well, being a colleague of Milton Friedman at the University of Chicago, and as a cabinet member with a relevant portfolio, he was to have great impact. Moynihan himself, while a staunch and continuing advocate of another brand of income maintenance, was nonetheless determined to get an income maintenance program adopted. At the Arden House discussions and elsewhere, he was regularly exposed to the NIT ideas.

Meanwhile, the business community kept worrying the bone of welfare reform and would not let it go, as they saw disruption and huge social costs in current welfare arrangements. A group of senior businesspeople called the Committee for Economic Development (CED) took interest in public policy issues, both economically centered and social policy oriented. While its staff was based in New York, its membership was geographically broad and composed of prominent figures in industry, commerce, and finance. The work initiated at the Arden House conference was passed on to the CED, as a way of not letting the spark of an idea at a single conference simply die but continuing to fan it into a proposal that would catch fire and result in action.

The staff director of the Arden House Conference, Victor Weingarten, leapt from one trapeze to another. He now stirred the interest of the CED group of businessmen and was instrumental in preparing for an important set of congressional hearings before the Joint Economic Committee of Congress that occurred for more than a week in June 1968. Those hearings were presented with a raft of studies and statements both for and against family allowances and negative income tax schemes, analyzing urban and rural poverty, and generally starting to lay a foundation for more informed discussion of the welfare issues being decried in the 1968 presidential campaigns.

The Republicans on Capitol Hill were not wholly somnolent during this time. Representative Melvin R. Laird of Wisconsin now headed the House Republican Conference, in a party that had long languished in downtrodden status, and was to do so for another twenty-five years. Laird was a Wisconsin conservative Republican. He was extremely intelligent, a successful candidate on his own upper Midwest turf—he was a Carleton College, Minnesota, undergrad—and securely held his House seat for eight terms. Laird was known better for his wiles and tactical adroitness than his marriage to substantive proposals. Henry Kissinger, who later faced him when Kissinger was Nixon's national security assistant and Laird was Nixon's secretary of defense, was in constant paroxysms of paranoia about Laird's maneuvering. On February 16, 1971, I attended a cabinet meeting where Nixon's health-care proposals, on which I was working, were to be presented to the cabinet. It was the first meeting at which John Connally was present. Admiral Thomas Moorer, "the chairman of the joint chiefs of staff . . . with frequent interruption by Melvin Laird, conducted a briefing on the [Laotian offensive]." Secretary Laird was seated next to the president and said that we were not going to train the South Vietnamese in the image of the American army, that they would not need certain capabilities. "He continued, while Henry Kissinger, who was sitting next to me, began to stir." Laird said, "They could have done this on the ground without us." At this point, Kissinger elbowed me in the ribs and said in a husky whisper that I immediately feared could be heard at least to the other side of the cabinet table, "Bull shit. It's not possible. How this man LIES." I thought at that point of what David Young had told me—that Kissinger fears Laird more than any other man in the town and thinks he is completely devious.[18] Anecdotes abounded in the administration of the amusement Laird got from twisting the tail of the Bavarian national security advisor, who reciprocated with great ferocity and frequency in his efforts to disparage or discredit Laird with the president. Nixon regarded Laird as "sneaky but manageable."[19]

While he was still a Republican doyen in the Congress, Laird watched the attempts at opposition by Republicans to the Great Society and to the poverty program. In his "Republican Papers," Laird made a game effort to assemble some initiatives so the Republican Party would not be seen simply as intransigent nay-sayers, like the "Do-Nothing" Congress of 1947–1949 that had been thus colorfully tagged by Truman and lamented by Dewey. As Moynihan captured it,

> The Congressional Republicans, debilitated and in ways corrupted by having been out of power for the better part of four decades, were no match for the dazzle of the New Frontier or the Great Barbecue that followed. By all indications, an entire generation of middle- and upper-class youth, offspring of Republican parents, moved during this period to the Democratic party or beyond. It may surely be argued that this occurred in part because the Democrats gave them something to do.[20]

Laird understood this and pushed the Republican Papers as an idea piece to get Republicans to be in favor of something. Among the essays was "The

Case for the Negative Income Tax" by none other than Milton Friedman. While the Ripon paper and draft statute had been the first promotion of the NIT by any political organization, the embrace by Laird and the Conference of this paper carried much weight. Laird entered the administration as Nixon's secretary of defense but maintained his interest in the NIT idea, and Moynihan and he were later to make common cause with the concept.

In January 1968, President Johnson finally and reluctantly got around to naming the members of the Commission on Income Maintenance. He made the announcement when, without other comment, he signed the Social Security Amendments of 1967.

The Commission was a balanced group of the great and the good, so typical of the blue-ribbon panels formed to analyze and reflect on major problems bedeviling the nation. Its chair, Ben Heineman, the CEO of Northwest Industries, was accompanied by other Democrats like the former governor of California, Edmund "Pat" Brown, who had defeated Richard Nixon in California in 1962; Lyndon Johnson's incumbent secretary of HEW, Wilbur J. Cohen, who had deflected efforts within his department to advance an income maintenance proposal on to the White House; Clifford Alexander, an African American Johnson office holder, as head of the Economic Employment Opportunity Commission; and other African American leaders, including State Senator Barbara Jordan of Texas, businessman Asa Spaulding, and A. Philip Randolph, head of the Brotherhood of Sleeping Car Porters union, a long-serving and greatly respected labor leader. It included a sprinkling of Republicans, such as New York lawyer Maxwell Rabb, who had been secretary to the cabinet in Eisenhower's White House, and some academics, such as Harry Rowan of Santa Monica's RAND Corporation and Otto Eckstein, a member of the Council of Economic Advisors under President Johnson. This group was gearing up during the election year, and the timing and content of its contribution to the discussion would prove to spur Nixon as the new administration was deep into deliberation about what form changes in welfare should take.

The last gasp of the Johnson administration on the subject was an interdepartmental task force, pulled together at the end of July 1968, by Joseph Califano, Johnson's top White House aide on domestic affairs. It was to look at the broader question of income maintenance. It had some negative income tax advocates on board and was headed by Merton Peck, of Johnson's Council of Economic Advisors.[21] The action now turned to the new Republican appointees and their receptiveness to the career and holdover executives, who were deep into their own concepts of what would make for meaningful reform of welfare.

CHAPTER 10

The Battle for Nixon's Decision

The Johnson administration was running on an empty gas tank in its closing months, as it ignored both the ideas on welfare policy percolating within its own ranks, the boiling of interest in the business community, and the politics of 1968. LBJ struck down proposals for a refashioning of the welfare system and did the same to ideas about dramatic expansion of the Food Stamp program. Richard Nixon was to take both and make them centerpieces of his social policy, which would radically reorient and strengthen the federal government's approach to the safety net for low-income Americans. As Moynihan pointed out, "It is perhaps the ultimate irony that the Nixon proposal for a negative income tax was drafted by Democratic advocates who not months earlier had had the same proposal rejected by the Johnson Administration."[1] While previously such a proposal had been blocked at the Department of Health, Education and Welfare, with the knowledge that the president would dismiss it, now that was no longer the case.

What a difference an election made.

The process of forming a Nixon policy on welfare had started first with a broad campaign call for reform. This was followed by the transition task force report, given to the president before his inauguration. Within days of the inauguration, the Council for Urban Affairs formed a cabinet subcommittee on the subject, and it met in the first days of the new administration, setting about to offer options to the new president. Thus, consideration of public assistance issues had begun in an orderly, structured way. It did not last that way for long.

Around mid-December, Nixon had in hand the "Nathan Task Force" transition report chaired by Richard Nathan of the Brookings Institution, formerly an aide to Nelson Rockefeller. Nathan tells a tale that illustrates in its way the attitude of Rockefeller toward his staff and their talents. Nathan had long left Rockefeller for the Brookings Institution when George Hinman, Rockefeller's close political confidant, in a conversation with Nixon after his nomination, said that Rockefeller was pleased to offer to Nixon the talents of Dick Nathan. Nixon was interested. Hinman called to let Nathan know that the governor was willing to have Nathan be released to go to work for the president-elect. Nathan said to Hinman that while he was pleased the governor thought well of him and was indeed interested, it was not within Nelson's gift to offer him to Nixon, as Nathan was no longer an employee of Rockefeller's but a fellow at Brookings.[2]

Nathan had chosen members so that the "composition of this task force virtually assured a report that would not disturb the basic structure of welfare, but would merely propose more for those within it."[3] This was not entirely the case, as the Nathan task force would establish a nationwide minimum floor for welfare beneficiaries—of existing programs, not of a large new universe of beneficiaries—that would be fully paid for by the federal government. This move, which Nathan's group called an "incremental" step, would in reality be dramatic. Under Eisenhower, welfare was held to be a state and local responsibility. Nathan's group urged that welfare become a national duty for the first time, with "complete Federal financing of welfare."[4] The impact on many, especially in the South, where often the states paid less than their own definition of subsistence to welfare recipients, would be salutary. But the main dollar help would be for the treasuries of the states where payments were higher, and relief would come to state and county budgets, not so much to the welfare beneficiaries there themselves. What the Burkes saw as not disturbing the basic structure of welfare was correct, as Nathan would not change the basic definitions of the program. But the federal financing and federal fixing of a minimum level to be paid in all states amounted to major change.

At this very early stage, even Pat Moynihan, associated with a far more extensive concept of universal income maintenance, became a supporter of the Nathan plan. As was the case with Moynihan, I was pleased by the chance of a major shift in current programs to benefit especially the lowest-income and most indigent recipients. As Moynihan put it, "My God, I didn't think any Republican administration would go for any more than that."[5]

I was the staff support in the White House for the Subcommittee of the Urban Affairs Council on Welfare. Secretary Finch was its chair, and the other members were the secretaries of Labor, Agriculture, and Commerce, and the attorney general. A meeting was scheduled for February 6, 1969, and Nathan and I were the editors of a short paper that condensed the Nathan plan. The February 4 draft was titled *Staff Paper: Reform of Public Assistance; National Standard for Payments and Related Recommendations.* Nathan's staff helped me to put the paper together, and one of those staff was particularly dedicated. Often in Washington, there is a pride, an egoism, in how hard one works. In this case, there was a sad note on that point. One of Nathan's people, an eager career public servant named Greg Barlous, was so touched that he was working on such a high-level project, certain to be seen at some point by the president, that he literally worked himself to death.

The Nathan-Price paper would give $300 million more in larger benefits to recipients; it also showed that states and localities would get $1.1 billion in fiscal relief, substituting federal money for what the states had been putting in. The paper drew many questions and some hostile comments at the first meeting of the cabinet-level subcommittee. Nathan's bureaucratic reaction to this resistance to his idea was understandable: it was to go around, or rather under, the cabinet-level group. To Nathan's ultimate chagrin, this opened the way for the resurrection of an idea that had been pushed for several years by Democratic staffers in the Department of Health, Education and Welfare, and especially the Office of Economic Opportunity, but had met no enthusiasm or support from their superiors or the Johnson White House.

The Players at Health, Education, and Welfare

Secretary Finch had known Nixon when the latter was a young House member after World War II. He then served as Nixon's vice presidential chief of staff for the two Eisenhower terms in the 1950s and as Nixon's titular campaign manager in the 1960 presidential campaign. He sought and got the secretary post of the lead social program department (HEW) after Nixon's election.

Finch brought with him a cluster of Californians who were close politically, some of whom had a detailed knowledge of the principal HEW programs, including health policy and welfare. Foremost among these was John A. ("Jack") Veneman. Veneman was a farmer from Modesto, in the California "Valley," where he grew peaches. (His daughter, Ann, years later in the George W. Bush administration was to serve as the US secretary of agriculture.) Jack was also a highly effective liberal Republican legislator in the lower house in Sacramento and had become an expert on social welfare issues. He was tough-minded and facile politically, so much so that the notoriously political Democrat who ruled many of these years as Speaker, Jess Unruh, found it obligatory to work with Veneman and a handful of other like-minded Republicans for the California legislature to function well. And it did.

Veneman was close to Finch, and as much as Finch wanted him, he was concerned about there being two Californians as the top two figures in the department. He was convinced otherwise by yet another Californian. Lewis Butler, a Bay Area environmental activist and lawyer, became the assistant secretary for policy and persuaded Finch to bring Jack Veneman in, making three liberal Republican Californians in the three top management and policy jobs.

Another liberal became part of the front office at HEW. James Farmer, one of the most important of America's civil rights leaders, joined as assistant secretary for administration. Farmer had headed the Congress on Racial Equality (CORE). Chris Demuth had been Farmer's campaign manager when he ran for Congress in 1968 against Shirley Chisholm, and Demuth and I poll-watched election night for Farmer in Bedford-Stuyvesant in Brooklyn. I sat and visited with Farmer on a "Shuttle" flight from New York to DC in late February 1974, after which I wrote in my diary:

> Jim had first come front and center to my attention in 1968, when he had the Liberal nomination for the new 12th Congressional District, and the Brooklyn Republican leaders gave him the Republican line. I first heard him speak during Rockefeller's campaign at a rally staged just off Broadway at a discotheque (the Cheetah I think it was). It was an anomalous place in which to hear this man speak. I had not by then ever heard at close hand the cadence of one of the great rights leaders (except for watching King's I have a dream with my father in the den over our garage during which both of us wept at the power and vision of that speech). Jim was spellbinding. The resonance of the voice; the precision of the diction, and the movement of the lines: not just waves, but the more subtle changes in mid-sentence. I felt I was listening to one of the greatest orators of my time. It is interesting to speculate why the great bulk of our current politicians today have no oratorical ability. Even rather extreme positions such as Goldwater's in 1964 or McGovern's were delivered flat and, ultimately, boringly. Yet Farmer was uplifting. No doubt it has something to do with a philosophical or political bent: if I were an ideologue of the right, I might have found Barry or Reagan spellbinding. But I think it's more, and it has to do with what is in your viscera. Where powerful emotions are at play, and where they are the product of direct personal experience, and where furthermore, the rhetoric is polished in front of groups who feel equally strongly, something very beautiful and moving can happen.[6]

These were the early days. Farmer was later to leave in disagreement with the administration and in the end to die in sad circumstances, including blindness brought about by severe diabetes. Lew Butler later also left with few positive feelings. But for now, it was "Camelot." We were indeed about to do serious things.

Veneman had benefited in his California legislative work from the advice of a brilliant, blind Korean American, Tom Joe, who navigated his way with a walking stick and with a voluminous amount of knowledge in his head, some obscure, all useful, about social welfare programs and their arcana of details. Veneman brought Joe with him to Washington, and his became a familiar presence not only at HEW but also in Nathan's office in "F.O.B. 7" (a modern, reddish-colored nondescript building hulking behind Blair House) and mine in the Old Executive Office Building. He was vastly more sophisticated and proficient at program details than I was, but we shared the same concern about eliminating the perverse incentives in the existing system and about trying to reach those truly in need, whether working and still poor or not able to work and poor. He also had a singularly upbeat, enthusiastic manner, almost perky, which cheered us on.

Tom Joe became the key conduit to the new top fellow-Californian management of the Department of Health, Education and Welfare, on the one hand, and, on the other, those in the Office of Economic Opportunity who had been pushing hard, but without success, on the negative income tax. The OEO advocates had a couple of sympathizers who were holdovers in HEW. It was to Tom Joe that Worth Bateman, a soon-to-depart program analyst at HEW, gave his critique of the Nathan-Price plan. Bateman argued, "Many persons consider a national standard in Public Assistance a step in the right direction. However . . . such a change would intensify present inequities in the treatment of male and female headed families and provide increased financial incentives to break up intact households, particularly those low income families headed by a man who works."

Bateman continued, "You may want to trade higher payment levels in the Public Assistance program [AFDC] for broader coverage and propose a modest new program which is income tested but provides supplementary income to all families with children. The program could be staged in a way which could result in some State savings. (This is a Negative Income Tax plan for families with children, but it could be called by a different name)."[7] Joe put the Bateman proposal in a large policy book he was assembling for his former boss, now Under Secretary Jack Veneman, and Secretary Finch, and it was presented to them on February 17, less than a month into the new Nixon presidency.

Earlier that very day, in a meeting of the new Council for Urban Affairs (CUA), John Gardner, now head of the Urban Coalition, made a presentation to the president and council members. Gardner was a former secretary of HEW under President Johnson, and he was a Republican. He was there to talk about urban policy and the Urban Coalition. Nixon said the discussion "show[ed] the wisdom of the creation of the Urban Affairs Council, for in the discussion of housing in and out of the cities, Mr. [Walter] Reuther [Detroit, head of the AFL-CIO] touched on transportation, housing and labor. He stressed how valuable it is for the members of the Cabinet to see the urban problems as being related and not broken down neatly along departmental lines."[8]

But it was welfare that was on Nixon's mind. He noted that this meeting was probably the first time that three secretaries of HEW had met in the same room (Bob Finch, the new tenant, John Gardner, and Arthur S. Flemming, who held that post the last two years of the Eisenhower administration). Gardner noted that "probably just two of them are smiling" but then plunged into welfare. He said he was "familiar with and generally approved of the Nathan Task Force Report."

This was not surprising. Gardner knew Richard Nathan. In fact, Gardner had received a call just after the election from Nixon's campaign manager, John Mitchell. Mitchell told Gardner he was concerned that the transition task forces did not include one on poverty or the poor. Gardner suggested that Dick Nathan undertake a poverty task force, telling Mitchell that Nathan worked fast and well, having just completed the management of a preelection task force on federalism. Mitchell and Nixon took Gardner's suggestion.[9]

The president pressed Gardner on his proposal that "the AFDC-UP [unemployed parent] program be made mandatory in those States where it is not now being applied."[10] This was one of dozens of detailed interventions by Nixon on welfare in meetings of the Council, and the president adverted several more times in this meeting to AFDC and was interested to hear Gardner say that the AFDC-UP addresses cases where there is an unemployed husband. It was one of the prior, if half-hearted, legislative efforts to reduce incentives to family breakup, a recurring criticism of the current programs. It was one path, as yet undiscerned, toward the broad approach Nixon was to take. Interestingly, it also was the final bunker into which Arthur Burns was to settle, having fallen back from one defensive trench to another in his unrelenting opposition to the Moynihan/Finch approach that Nixon was to embrace.

Rockefeller Appearance before the Council for Urban Affairs

Less than a week earlier, the Council had its first guest from outside. Governor Nelson Rockefeller, Nixon's perennial but always vanquished competitor for the Republican presidential nomination, laid out a domestic five-point proposal, all of which, Dr. Arthur Burns noted in his *Secret Diary*, would require heavy federal expenditure. Three of them became part of President Nixon's domestic program. Variants on two of them, with Nixon's own crucial ingredients, were to become highlights of Nixon's social safety net approach. Rockefeller urged federal standards and more federal financial help for welfare and a national contributory health insurance scheme. Rockefeller noted that welfare rolls were increasing by nearly 20,000 a month in New York and that probably 350,000 persons were eligible to be on welfare but were not. He urged that growth in federal revenue be used to provide complete federal financing for public assistance cases throughout the country, holding harmless the States at their present levels of welfare expenditures.[11]

I recorded in my diary, "Nixon's demeanor was not easy to read things into. He looked at me once or twice while NAR was speaking, and I wondered if he were asking himself if I were still making comparisons."[12]

After Rockefeller left, Moynihan made a presentation on new census data, but the conversation veered back toward issues of welfare, such as spousal desertion and forced contribution to support the family they leave behind, which Dr. Burns raised. The attorney general said there were no personnel to enforce these laws. Moynihan made the point that there were still many voluntary desertions and "that income flows to the lower classes are just not working."[13]

Later in the meeting, discussing a draft statement about the future of the OEO, Moynihan once again attempted to flag the problems of the racial antagonisms provoked by the current welfare system. He was trying to get a blessing for the OEO to address the problems of the "near poor," who often were working-class whites. The vice president objected strenuously to the term "near poor," to which Moynihan replied, "There is a feeling that there is a racial division due to the fact the poorest of the poor are only Black and Puerto Rican, while the whites making $90 a week see efforts directed only to the former and say—'To hell with it.'" The attorney general felt that the use of the phrase "opens Pandora's box." When the secretary of commerce said we should strike the expression of concern about the near poor, Moynihan objected, saying, "That's offering something to those who voted for Nixon." His increasingly antagonistic rival, Dr. Burns, said, "Offer them something else." Moynihan asked that we find "other language to express the same thing to try to include the near poor whites within the concern of OEO."[14] Moynihan was wrestling with the early stages of conceiving a strategy that would leech out some of the racial antagonisms provoked by AFDC and its problems, looking toward a flow of incomes more efficient at reaching more of those in need—many more than only those benefiting from the current public assistance structure.

After the meeting, I lunched with Moynihan, Rockefeller, and Alton Marshall, a longtime Rockefeller aide and later president of Rockefeller Center. As we were "walking out, someone lit up with recognition, walked over to NAR & me, and introduced his companion to 'Governor Romney.' I said, as we walked away, 'You're brushing your hair back straighter these days, or something,' and he said, 'You know, George belongs down here. I don't,' and was silent and reflective for just a couple of instants."[15]

But Romney in many ways did not belong "down here." It was very difficult for this proud, self-made man who had run a company and governed a major industrial state to adjust to being in a subordinate role. This was made worse by Gov. Romney's extraordinary sensitivity to slights and his emotionalism. Some months later, at the conclusion of a Council meeting, I walked over to where the president, Moynihan, and Romney were standing, near the door leading to the Oval Office. The president was just asking Pat to come with him into his office, and he then saw me and asked me to come along. Romney stood there, with his color deepening, and started to ask if he could join but stopped almost before the words could come out, as the president had turned and started away. Nixon was unable to see what then occurred. Romney's jaw and lower lip began literally to quiver with emotion. His whole body then started to shake. I walked past him feeling deep embarrassment. I wondered how Nixon might have felt if he had seen Romney's face, since the president himself had felt such crushing hurt and rejection so often in his own life, not the least in his treatment at times by President Eisenhower. I can only speculate about that, but it is clear from endless episodes recorded in Ehrlichman's or Haldeman's notes of meetings with the president, that Romney, with his demands, his sense of self-righteousness, and often his substantive directions for his department, gave them frequent moments of heartburn.

Moynihan was buoyed in a separate meeting later the same day of our lunch with Rockefeller. Nixon, in an Oval Office session with Moynihan, Secretary Finch, and Counselor Arthur Burns, declared that he wanted to establish national standards. Burns, before the Rockefeller meeting and fearing that Rocky would bulldoze the new administration, had cautioned the president in a memo that "the desire to do something—such as setting up national welfare standards—should be resisted until we have a clearer idea of what the results may be."[16]

Burns was crestfallen, Moynihan exhilarated. Finch was steady on course. Moynihan immediately called me to his office and said he was replying to Burns's earlier warning memo to the president, citing again for Burns and recording for the president that which Nixon had just announced to them. Moynihan told me, "You have to seize such opportunities with a president."

Work on Two Levels. I Discover and Join the Conspirators.

While these back-to-back council meetings with the president were going on where welfare was a central part of the discussion, Finch and Veneman lost no time moving ahead with their welfare reform project. The day after Tom Joe presented the Bateman proposal to his bosses, Veneman had a meeting of the subcabinet "task force," of which I was an ex officio member, along with Dick Nathan and Wilbur Schmidt, welfare director of Wisconsin who had been on the Nathan Transition Task Force. Veneman named Bateman head of a "working group" of technical experts from HEW and Nathan's shop at the Budget Bureau.

Bateman misinterpreted his appointment as a green light for him to move ahead with his negative income tax idea. Bateman took it as a signal to try to inter the Nathan-Price plan's proposal for the Council, thus making way for the sub-rosa NIT plan to become the only proposal. To help move in this direction, Bateman got the approval to add James Lyday of OEO to the group. Lyday was "the leading architect of the poverty war's abortive negative income tax proposals."[17]

As I got to know him, I found that Lyday was intense—really intense—in his commitment to economic issues of the poor. He had come from his Oklahoma home to Washington to work for Wright Patman, the longtime Texas chair of the House Banking Committee. But he also had a light and humorous touch. Lyday was gregarious. He was an enthusiastic string player, picking banjos and playing the guitar, and singing along. We clicked. Because I grew comfortable with him and he with me, he soon learned of my earlier interest in the NIT and slipped out to me that this was what he and Bateman were working toward in this "working group" of technical experts, on which Veneman had sprinkled holy water.

When Veneman, the new undersecretary, approved his joining the working group, "Lyday thought he must be dreaming. At the poverty agency he had spent four years helping to design negative income tax plans to combat poverty, all to no avail. Was it possible that the conservative Nixon administration might buy what Lyndon Johnson had spurned?"[18] Now, in early February, as Bateman saw it, "it was clear to three or four of us . . . that the name of the game was structural reform. I saw the creation of the task force as a maneuver to get key people—Price and Nathan—committed to structural reform, rather than simply the Nathan plan."[19]

Arthur Burns had told President-Elect Nixon that of all his transition task force reports, the worst was on welfare, and he said, "Burn it up! Burn it up!"[20] Burns had no seat at the table of the CUA Task Force or on its working group. Nathan's experts from the Budget Bureau were working with Bateman on the one half of his effort—fleshing out the national standards for AFDC that Nathan thought was the whole task—while Lyday and others on the clandestine side were working on the NIT proposal. However, in the weeks to come, Burns and his copilot Martin Anderson would fly frequent sorties strafing the emerging notion of a broad income maintenance scheme to replace the existing welfare legal and administrative structure.

An occasional participant in the sub-rosa group was Robert Harris, the staff director of President Johnson's Commission on Income Maintenance that Johnson had only grudgingly allowed to begin work a year after he announced it. Harris's involvement meant that there was mutual tracking and awareness of the evolution of analysis and proposals. Moynihan himself kept in touch with Heineman, its chair, and Harris.

A Road to Damascus Moment for Moynihan

Moynihan for the moment was still tantalized by the idea of a universal Family Allowance, or per capita grant for all. He exchanged correspondence with a fellow social scientist at Brandeis University while all this furious paddling was going on beneath the water over at HEW about a negative income tax. In the letters back and forth, in February 1969, Moynihan told his friend that he would ask OEO if it would undertake a study about the effects and manner of administration of a family allowance. He was not aware that OEO had already begun an experiment looking at the same kinds of questions but with a very different approach to income maintenance—the negative income tax. He also was unaware—as was I—that Secretary of Defense Melvin Laird, while in Congress, had taken some interest in the OEO pilot program. The moment of truth came for him soon. As the glorious Welsh hymn, "Tony-Botel," says in its most familiar lyrics, "Once to Every Man and Nation, Comes the Moment to Decide."

I had been taken into Bateman's and Lyday's confidence. They had struggled with how to propose a universal floor on family income and still come within the cost that the Nathan plan carried. They were struggling with how to manage politically the radical change of direction they were pursuing. The road there was tortuous, even hilarious. Among the persistent issues Veneman and others at HEW were facing was the phrase itself, "negative income tax." It had put Nixon off when I suggested it to him in late January 1968, at the intimate Links Club dinner. It was a political land mine for many, even though an academic like Milton Friedman had found it tripping logically off his lips ever since he envisioned the Treasury simply sending checks to those eligible for an income supplement based on income statements—the reverse of collecting tax payments from those better off, hence his term "negative income tax."

Lewis Butler had groaned when he saw the title page in the proposal. "The first thing I saw was 'negative income tax.' It looked like a red flag to me. I knew people were violently for and against that." Caucuses were held. The J. Walter Thompson or Ted Bates ad agencies would have been proud of the creative product that emerged. As Butler opened the meeting on March 3, 1969, for presentation of the plan to the secretary, he entreated Finch, who had flipped to the summary, to return to the title page. He did. There he read, "Christian Working Man's Anti-Communist National Defense Rivers and Harbors Act of 1969."[21] Even with the nonsense nomenclature, Robert E. Patricelli, new to HEW from the committee staff of Senator Jacob K. Javits, warned that it was a negative income tax and that "the president will never buy it." A rose is a rose is a rose. Finch bought it, however. He relied on Veneman and felt that if the group thought it was workable, it was important to get something up to Congress "with the President's name on it and start a national debate."

On the other side of the compartmented policy development, the Nathan plan for national standards had been priced out in two versions, costing just over $2 billion. Each would raise benefit levels in the many low-paying states, and each would lighten the load of the more generous states through a higher federal participation. But the group concluded both would further disturb family stability and harm a work incentive and would exacerbate racial disunity.

The Veneman task force met on March 7, and Nathan said that there was not a way that these issues could be addressed within cost limits that would satisfy those objections. It was a perfect invitation for an alternative—which in fact had already been prepared! The assignment was made to cover the working poor, with work incentives and at a cost of no more than $2 billion.

It was time to bring Moynihan fully on board. He and I went together for a late dinner to New York Avenue NE to the *A. V. Ristorante*, which was a legendary Italian family place popular with not just Capitol Hill but also the other end of Pennsylvania Avenue, as well as Supreme Court Justices and Hollywood types when they were in town. We walked past a plaster version of the Tower of Pisa to a small table. We ordered veal scaloppini and some wine, and I outlined for Pat the proposal that the HEW senior officials wanted to bring to the welfare subcommittee of the Urban Affairs Council. As I talked through the expansion of help to millions more, based on eligibility for the working poor, higher floors in low-paying states that would bring in more dependent poor, and the degree of relief as well for the large, high-effort Northern states, Moynihan was intent and then elated. He was totally focused and staggered that there would be a serious option brought to the Council to guarantee incomes of all families with children. He had been pursuing this option with passion for more than half a decade. He said to me with emotion and with determination, "You've got it! That's it!" He was exultant. He did not look back on the broader, costlier, more-European-style family allowance again (even though he would later occasionally use the term to describe Nixon's plan).

Pat was on board. I had worked toward that end from the moment, in January 1969, when he asked me to take on welfare and I raised the NIT proposal and Yale-drafted NIT stature with him. The path to Nixon's approval would not be smooth. Based on the Veneman group's draft of the NIT (and its further work on the Nathan-Price plan), I was tasked to write the decision paper, which would go first to the Finch-chaired Council for Urban Affairs welfare group. I rejected frantic pleas from the Bateman/Lyday faction that I exclude the "national standards" option—the one that was the revised recommendation of the transition task force. They urged that I put before the CUA welfare subcommittee only the negative income tax proposal.

I wrote in 1974 to Vee Burke, coauthor with her by-then deceased husband, Vince, in detail of my reactions to their book, *Nixon's Good Deed: Welfare Reform*. As I described it to her, the paper to go forward for the March 24 meeting "was a product of the machinery of the Urban Affairs Council. . . . The 'report' was a 'Draft Decision Paper for the President' a Memorandum for the President from the Sub-committee, and . . . I had drafted it from the materials prepared by Lyday, Bateman, Patricelli, USDA, DOL and BOB." I added in handwritten marginalia, "Actually, I was involved in endless Saturday and Sunday sessions with Lyday & Bateman as we struggled over formulation."[22] I told her, "I insisted, over the vehement objection of Lyday, and only somewhat less objection of Bateman and Patricelli, on including the 'repellent' national standards for AFDC option. The purpose of the March 24 meeting was for the Sub-committee to suggest revisions of its draft decision paper for the President." In this I had the support of Finch and Veneman, but I did indicate a plain preference. I called the NIT idea, which had now been christened the family security system, the "preferred option" and the Nathan, or national standards idea, the "less preferred option."

Finch scheduled his meeting for March 24. The draft of the lengthy decision paper included a proposal for a $1 billion food stamp plan to accompany the cash payments. I put my March 23 draft on Moynihan's desk. Late that afternoon, I got a summons to his basement office and came across West Executive Alley to the West Wing. I sat in front of his regulation-issue government desk. He slammed my paper down on his desk in front of me. "Price, your prose is OPAQUE!" he bellowed.

Chastened and intimidated, I took his suggestions and retired to my office. I worked through the night and put a new draft on his desk before he came in. The towering cumulonimbus storm clouds of his temper, unleashing lightning bolts and hurling hailstones, dissipated. After the cold front passed, sunshine radiated and warm zephyrs blew. Moynihan was a joy to work for not only because of his remarkable taste for policy as a crucial part of politics but also because he was generous and warm. The storms rarely lasted long and were followed by wonderful weather.

After we had worked together that first year, Pat gave each of us senior staff at Christmas handsome cuff links from Shreve jewelers in Boston. Each was fashioned with our own initials on the outside of the link and, on the inside, in the same font but smaller engraving, were the initials "D.P.M." It was Pat who threw my bachelor party for me, at the Iron Gate Inn, a converted stable and a Washington icon, when I was getting married at the end of 1970.

His instinctive warmth and regard for his staff became obvious one day in the midst of this welfare combat. Pat and I walked out together from his office at the base of the stairs leading up to the second floor of the West Wing, where the Oval Office is. At the very moment we emerged, we literally physically collided with President Nixon, who was just reaching the foot of the stairs, coming down from his office. As we all three recovered our balance, Pat immediately put his hand on my back side and pushed me forward toward the president, at the same time saying, "Mr. President, you remember John Price, who is doing the work for you on the welfare issue!" As I have thought about it over these decades, I remember my gratitude for Moynihan. So quick to give credit—and in almost a reflex action. In a flash I thought at that moment, Nixon still standing in front of me, of a likely contrast with what Henry Kissinger would have done. I admired Henry's intellect and religiously read his briefings, but his approach would likely have been to share no credit. Pat was different.

Pat would need all his warmth, congeniality, and wit. Until now, welfare had been a campaign issue. A transition task force paper. A focus for a cabinet-level subcommittee of Nixon's new domestic policy formulation body. Now there was a formal decision paper to be considered by the welfare subcommittee and then taken to the president. It went far beyond anything the transition work, or the Nathan-Price paper, had contemplated. It would be an untested and radical change in American social policy.

Just three days before the all-important meeting of Finch's Welfare Sub-Committee, Ben Heineman, the industrialist who was chair of the now very much alive Commission on Income Maintenance, spoke at a dinner at a poverty conference in New York. Arthur Burns had worried that the Commission would be a spur to some sort of extravagant Nixon welfare proposal. Indeed Moynihan hoped it would spur Nixon to action. He later used its imminent report to urge Nixon toward a swift decision and then to urge action on Nixon's proposals. Burns had tried to get Nixon to terminate the Commission's writ right away, to disband it. Burns was right to have been concerned, as that night Heineman announced that he, personally (the Commission had not yet made any recommendations), favored a guaranteed income for all America's poor.

While the earlier meeting of the Finch CUA subcommittee had been restless and critical of the Nathan plan, which was the only option at the time, this one promised to be incendiary. In the preliminary meeting with his staff where he was first presented with the broad income maintenance proposal, Finch, at the end of the presentation, "asked the dread question: 'How are we going to explain why we have to add six million persons to the welfare rolls?'" It was right after this probe by Finch that Robert Patricelli said that "this was a negative income tax and the president will never buy it."[23]

The Council for Urban Affairs machinery had caused things to reach this point. The fact that we were looking at a negative income tax was due not only to the tireless work and then lobbying by the holdover Democratic career staff at OEO and HEW. At that first meeting of Finch's subcommittee on welfare,

> The key thing to come out of it . . . was a question George Shultz raised after reading the draft which Barlous and Nathan prepared and I put into final shape for the meeting. "*What about the working poor?*" The Subcommittee process can therefore, arguably, be said to have been working very well indeed. The establishment of the Veneman task force was therefore, at staff level, to explore, among other questions, this one, which was to become the central one of the whole exercise. Moynihan was informed by me of the fact Shultz had asked this question.
>
> Nathan [had been] disturbed by something that was happening . . . *in the Subcommittee process.* Instructions to staff meant they *had* to look beyond a proposal just to provide national standards for AFDC. Some version of the Lyday-Bateman NIT had to emerge.[24]

Veneman urged Finch just to keep taking it forward, and Finch finally approved the advance to his council subcommittee, since his staff thought it workable.

Direct Lobbying of the President

As the CUA welfare group convened on March 24, Moynihan had qualms as such a dramatic departure from current welfare policy was put in front of this group of conservative cabinet officers. This was even though the "preferred option" answered the question Secretary of Labor Shultz had raised in the February 6 meeting when he asked about the "working poor," who would not be aided under simply a reworking of the existing AFDC program. Moynihan attempted a preemptive strike and said that it was a bold and historic move and should go to the president immediately. He said that if we were to work on it for five years, it would likely not be improved upon.

Moynihan felt this was an historic opportunity for Nixon—and for social policy. Moynihan's mode of persuading Nixon stimulated Nixon's own sense of history and the importance of daring, indeed liberal or even radical moves, from an essentially conservative politician. In this he famously cast Nixon in the role of Benjamin Disraeli, the nineteenth-century Tory prime minister who took sweeping steps to assure that the forgotten were included in the Tories' policies. In 1845, Disraeli—a novelist as well as a politician—published *Sybil, or The Two Nations.* Interestingly, it was preceded a year earlier by Friedrich Engels's *The Condition of the Working Class in England*. Disraeli was a conservative, taking radical steps to improve living standards of the workers in the interests of maintaining social tranquility and justice—all within the capitalist, free market system. Engels took quite another path with Karl Marx, when they joined efforts on writing the *Communist Manifesto*. Moynihan repeatedly encouraged Nixon to respond to recognized needs with far-reaching but ultimately conservative solutions, preempting those more radical on the Left who would be less invested in trying to maintain self-reliance in the population and a free market system.

I argued to Vee Burke in my 1974 letter,

> You perhaps do not completely capture the full thrust of his effort not alone to play to the President's sense of history, but to *educate* the President. Jim [Lyday] and Worth [Bateman] were not in the Urban Affairs Council meetings those first and frantic four or five months. Not only on the occasion of the Rockefeller or Lindsay, or Don Kendall presentation, during which welfare was the principal subject, but on other occasions, Pat was professorial and didactic in the best sense. He would do chart talks on dependency; he did a capsule version of the analysis of the Family Report, and continued the graphs whose disjunction had led to his original thesis in 1964–65. His was, in short, not alone an appeal to ego.[25]

Moynihan's second point in that March 24 meeting, that further delay was pointless, was canny. Many skeptics or outright enemies of the negative income tax or guaranteed income proposed delay or lengthy studies and tests to prove its merits as a way to kill the idea. Even some who were conceptually open, like Melvin Laird, were a few weeks later to suggest in-depth additional study. Heineman's speech of three days before, the pendency of the Commission report sometime in autumn, the desire not to fall behind and to appear to be playing catch-up with what might emerge from Democrats in the House or Senate all caused Moynihan to urge Nixon to swift movement.

In the Congress, one House member, a strong liberal from Manhattan's upper west side, William Ryan—with drafting help from Jim Lyday—had introduced NIT legislation. Some Ripon-aligned Republicans were intending to do so. On the Senate side, Gene McCarthy had embraced a guaranteed income and Bob Kennedy had not. Liberal Democrat senator Fred Harris of Oklahoma introduced a welfare reform bill with a floor far higher than the one Nixon's was to begin with, but he was derided for it being too cheap by the most liberal and high-cost advocacy group of all, the National Welfare Rights Organization whose bill was the costliest. Harris's was not a NIT, however. Instead, like Nathan's national standards approach, it stuck to the current law, and Harris's proposed vast increases went largely to exist-ing beneficiaries and had positive fiscal consequences for the high-benefit states. It was precisely what the NWRO was seeking but was also too little for them. Senator Long, the Louisiana Democrat chairing the Senate Finance Committee, wanted none of the above. Wilbur Mills, the Arkansas Democrat chair of Ways and Means, had not yet tipped his hand. Conservative opposi-tion had not yet formed because there was as yet no presidential decision. However, later in the spring and summer, Bryce Harlow, Nixon's congres-sional liaison, begin to bring back to the president tales of mystification or abject horror on the part of stalwart conservative Republicans, as word began to leak out about the direction of the president's thinking.

Nixon faced competing ideas. Into this he would have to insert clarity and leadership. And he desired to do it with speed. Increasingly restless and goaded by both Democratic and Republican politicians and by journalists, ever ready to needle Nixon, and their questions about where his domestic program was, he was pushing Moynihan, Finch, and Burns for results. He set a deadline of April 15 for a domestic program.

The CUA welfare subcommittee meeting on March 24 had the anticipated fireworks, despite Moynihan's effort to push ahead on what were essentially political considerations. Martin Anderson, Burns's principal deputy, said that Nixon had campaigned against a negative income tax. Moynihan replied that whatever the *candidate* said was less important than what the *president* wants, and he wanted a proposal now.

Anderson and Moynihan were to spar at length. Anderson reached back to the English Poor Laws and a nineteenth-century program called Speenham-land, which Anderson argued was a universal program of assistance to the poor that experts argued had failed. Moynihan for the moment turned this aside with a witticism, but a debate raged for some weeks to come in memo-randa to the president, filling his in-box about this nearly two-hundred-year-old, recondite social program. In them were the kind of abstruse arguments that Lyndon Johnson's aides would never have dreamed of putting in front of him. But in Nixon they found a willing Oval Office reader of the arguments, rebuttals, rejoinders, and surrejoinders. Martin Anderson worked hard to prepare this assault on the idea. He located a friend who was researching the English Poor Laws and persuaded her to rush a copy of her work to him at the White House. Moynihan turned to his friend, Professor J. H. Plumb of Cambridge University, and I turned to my friend from boyhood, historian Reed St. Clair Browning, of Kenyon College in Ohio, for help in these lively debates for the president's benefit.

Commerce Secretary Stans had chuckled in that March 24 meeting at some of Moynihan's bons mots. He was appalled, however, at the core idea and the cost of the family security system (FSS), a federally guaranteed family income. As Eisenhower's budget director, Stans had pushed not to increase, even by a small amount, the federal share of the AFDC costs in welfare.

The agriculture secretary was concerned that the Nixon initiative on food stamps not be put on a siding until the family security system could steam past it on its way to enactment. That food stamp initiative was then being hammered out and finally embraced by the president in his powerful and fluent proposal in May.

Finch repeated what Moynihan had said about the April 15 deadline set by the president and suggested they take the proposal to a full cabinet meeting before then. The attorney general and Stans said they needed to know more about it, even though Mitchell conceded he thought that Finch and Moynihan were on the right track.

Earlier, Richard Nathan had decided he needed to go "under" the Urban Affairs Council process; now Moynihan and Finch decided they had to go "over" the process. Moynihan, two days later, on March 26, sent a strong memo to the president.

> The essential fact about the Family Security System is that it will abolish poverty for dependent children and the working poor. The cost is not very great. Because it is a direct payment system. The tremendous costs of the poverty program comes [sic] from services i.e., year-round Head Start costs $1,000 per child. Almost all this money goes to middle class teachers, and the like. Ditto Community Action.
>
> The Family Security System would enable you to begin cutting back sharply on these costly and questionable services and yet to assert with full validity that it was under your Presidency that poverty was abolished in America.[26]

Finch told the president there would be widespread political support for the FSS, not only from big states that would have fiscal savings but also from both beneficiaries and conservatives, because it provides incentives for family stability and work. He argued, inaccurately, that FSS was neither a negative income tax nor a guaranteed income because it did not do away with all other income-support and service mechanisms and because it still holds to the need or ability to work.

Feeling the presidential push, Moynihan doubled down in his pressure on us staff to put together a package of domestic policy proposals for an Easter weekend meeting on Key Biscayne with the president, himself, Burns, and Finch. We prepared a thick multipart document, with a light blue paper cover, stapled together with industrial strength staples.

In his cover note, Moynihan summarized our eight proposals, including one on the "First Five Years of Life," another on home rule and congressional representation for the District of Columbia, a commission on Goals for 1976 (the national bicentennial), transportation trust funds, and a couple of others.

The first proposal mentioned was the family security system. My final, April 4 draft was now twenty-five pages. It constituted our material in the packet for Nixon for the summit weekend and was headed the "Report of the Committee on Welfare of the Council for Urban Affairs." Moynihan's table of contents called it the "Draft Report." An asterisk at the bottom of the page noted "*Not approved by Council for Urban Affairs." This final draft had the "Preferred Option" and the "Secondary Option." It said, "market incentives and not compulsion determine participation in the new manpower program" to accompany the cash payments. In a bow to Agriculture Secretary Hardin's concern, a family would, for now, receive both cash and food stamps. "Political considerations would appear to dictate that we must move first and soon with a food program. However, we should look toward the integration of the two programs by the time the Family Security System is enacted."[27]

Two key issues would be wrestled with for the rest of the spring and much of the summer. The first was the "work requirement." The second was the integration of the many existing programs for the welfare population or cohorts of the poor, such as medical assistance, housing assistance, food stamps, or surplus food, with AFDC, or any "adult category" welfare payments, such as to the blind or disabled.

Moynihan put three short sentences at the bottom of his one-page summary of the package: "I call your attention, above all, to the Family Security System. For two weeks' growth in the Gross National Product you can all but eliminate family poverty in America. And make history." The time had come to take sides, as Moynihan confessed later: "No one could be neutral about it: to seek to appear so would have been an exercise more in duplicity than of discipline."[28]

Key Biscayne Domestic Policy Summit:
Easter Weekend, 1969

Just two days after the tumultuous welfare meeting, Moynihan and I had lunch in the White House Mess with US senator Paul Douglas, Democrat of Illinois. Douglas had been defeated for reelection to the Senate by Charles Percy. He was "a grand old man—an intellectual patriarch. Very strong grasp of detail," as my diary recalled of the luncheon.[29] We talked of welfare, though with no intimation to him yet of what we hoped Nixon would decide. Douglas "mentioned to DPM as he was leaving, 'You and I should talk sometime about family allowances—I wrote the first book on it, in 1928. But [wistfully] I made one mistake. I assumed the stability of the industrial workers' population—I just did not anticipate the movement of the Negroes from the South.'"[30] With this last, likely nostalgic nod by Moynihan to his attachment to the family allowance, the presidential assistant turned to full support of the negative income tax he was presenting to Nixon near the waters of Biscayne Bay in Miami that Easter weekend.

It was only a year earlier exactly, on April 4, that Martin Luther King Jr. was assassinated. King, in the later days of his pastorate and leadership in the rights movement, had come to embrace the war on poverty and advocated a universal income floor for the poor, to be financed by the federal government—a cash program such as Moynihan and Finch were proposing to Nixon. Neither Moynihan's nor Burns's nor others' notes of the weekend discussion record that mention was made of this. However, in a Council meeting just days later, on Easter Monday, it was noted that the anniversary had passed peacefully. Certainly, there was awareness at Key Biscayne of King's death and legacy. In that Council meeting on Monday morning, April 7, the president asked what the explanation was for the relatively quiet weekend, and Moynihan said, "It was not surprising since the American people are not trying to tear this country down, but want to build it up. The president said, 'It seems most editorial writers seemed disappointed.'"[31]

During the Good Friday and Saturday meetings, H. R. Haldeman, the usually omnipresent chief of staff, was taking some well-earned relaxation, although on site if ever needed. His alternates attending to the president's requests at various times were John Ehrlichman and Bryce Harlow. The jousting began. Nixon again read the decision paper I wrote, and Moynihan and Finch argued for it, with Burns against. Burns was still opposing even the secondary option of national standards for the existing AFDC program. When Nixon did not reject the income maintenance proposal out of hand, Burns was stunned, as it struck him as out of character for Nixon. But when he kept objecting, Nixon said in effect, don't just oppose but show me something better. Burns could not fight something with nothing.

Moynihan's optimism coming out of the Key Biscayne conclave meant that "Moynihan set me to work on a draft presidential message to the Congress. I completed it after countless iterations and sent it to Ray Price, speechwriter, to be put in final form. Ray started, and then demurred, saying that he had to [be] sure there had been a final Presidential decision before he finished the message."[32] Therefore, while my drafts could have papered a wall, they could not paper over the differences remaining among top staff.

Moynihan's instinct that Nixon had been convinced was justified. Alex

Butterfield, Haldeman's deputy (and later famous for his disclosure of the taping system in the Oval Office), sent a "Very Confidential" memorandum to John Ehrlichman, dated April 14, 1969, just ten days after the Key Biscayne conclave. On a memorandum (about the family security system), "the President wrote in the strictest confidence the following note to you: 'John—I have decided to go ahead on this program. Please do not tell Finch, Moynihan et al; but get a plan ready for implementation by the first of next week.'"

Burns was not supine. He was surprised. He immediately realized he had to mount a substantive counteroffensive if he was to fend off the president's embrace of an idea Burns considered dangerous and radical. In the counterattack, Martin Anderson was his principal adjutant. But Burns also enlisted help from Richard P. Nathan. Burns said to them, "Now the president is going to do this fancy Democratic national income [maintenance idea]." Nathan told me in 2018 that Burns told him he didn't like it, saying, "now what I want you to do Dick, is I want you to take your report and beef it up a little bit. Put some more money into it. I want to use that as a counter to argue against Finch and Moynihan because they were advised by people who had very wrong ideas."[33]

Burns said he wanted to use the main point of the Nathan-authored transition report on welfare, that is, the need for national standards for the existing program of AFDC. But, he told Nathan, to give it more of a chance to offset the Finch/Moynihan idea, Burns wanted it "richer and more distributive."[34] With Nathan's help, Burns and Anderson produced a proposal that leaned heavily on trying to expand and make mandatory for all states the program to help fathers in their families who were unemployed: the "UP" program, which was embraced by only a minority of states. Burns was now advocating the "national standards" option he had opposed, having told Nixon he should "burn" the task force report. This strategic retreat of theirs, to be followed by others, likely was influenced by the discussion of the "UP" program in the Urban Affairs Council meeting with John Gardner, Arthur Fleming, Walter Reuther, and others. The "Burns paper" was dated April 21, a week after Nixon had told Ehrlichman that he had decided to go with Family Security and not to tell Finch and Moynihan.

In *Welfare*, Martin Anderson notes that historically there were three "philosophical" approaches to welfare in the United States. The first was private charity or philanthropy—the approach of the McKinley era and, for some, ever since. Anderson conceded that "few support this approach as the total answer to poverty." The second was the "needy-only" approach. Here he correctly concluded that an overwhelming majority of Americans, at least at the time in question of the late 1960s, were in favor of assistance for those who, "through no fault of their own, are unable to care for themselves or their families. . . . The role of government is seen as a limited one."[35]

The third form that he, along with Moynihan, saw as a "relative newcomer" to the United States was the "guaranteed income" approach, the idea "that the government should guarantee to every citizen a level of cash income high enough for him or her to live in moderate comfort, and that no restrictions whatsoever should be placed on the use of the money."[36] Anderson took note of, in his view, a frightening incoming tide of belief in a guaranteed income. He cited as an example that 1,300 economists at almost 150 institutions (spearheaded by Robert Lampman at the University of Wisconsin's Institute for Research on Poverty) signed a petition to the Congress in 1968 urging the adoption of a national system of income guarantees and supplements.[37] Closer to home, Ben Heineman, chair of the Presidential Commission on Income Maintenance, had declared his commitment to an income floor, the Republican Ripon Society had drafted a negative income tax statute, and the idea had been floated in Melvin Laird's Republican Papers.

The framework of reform for Burns and Anderson was quite within the existing system. They thought, wrongly as it turned out, that Nixon would in the end simply shudder at the idea of adding millions more persons, as the family security system (soon rechristened the Family Assistance Plan [FAP]) would do, to those receiving payments from the federal government. They had likely been encouraged by an exchange at an earlier council meeting of March 6, on welfare.

In that meeting, after a discussion of youth unemployment, this dialogue ensued, as noted in my minutes of the meeting:

> The President said the key to the problem is that the social acceptability, as Dr. Moynihan points out, of going onto welfare, has increased, and this increase is directly related to the time the Great Society programs came out with the themes that "the less fortunate people—it's not their fault, etc." were developing. The circle begins to move. This gets us back to the whole business of incentives. We're on a spot—we want to be humanitarian, and be aware of these needs, yet the natural tendency of man is not what many academics say—"the natural tendency of man is to work, if the obstacles are removed"—rather, the President said, the "natural tendency of man is to sit on his fanny." You don't have to whip him, but if this social acceptability factor goes up, that is the problem.
>
> Dr. Moynihan said, "We'd be fools not to see a welfare subculture growing up in our cities."
>
> The President said, "Jack Veneman is right to say that it is not leniency responsible for this [lax administration of admittance to welfare rolls]—I

buy that—but it is this other. . . . We get into the whole business of moral-
ity, of one's background, church and family."

Dr. Moynihan said that the increase may in part be because people who
apply are now more in need. They are "atomized individuals" that arrive
in the city. Women arrive with children and have no visible connection to
relatives. People aren't glued together by the connections we assume.

The President said, "Everything we do to help people may hurt them.
. . . It has happened to a lot of societies before—if we get $20 billion from
a letup in the Vietnam war, maybe it's the wrong thing to spread it around
this way."[38]

The discussion about the attitudes toward welfare led Moynihan to write
a lengthy memo on the subject to the president. He had me take a first crack
at it, and I did a draft. I was unsuccessful. I felt the same dejection when
my later boss, Gabriel Hauge, chairman of the bank where I worked in New
York, asked me to draft a speech for him to give to the Regional Plan Association in New York. I labored on it. It was then eviscerated. Yet, I thought,
Hauge was a principal speechwriter for President Eisenhower, and economic
advisor to him. I had given him an idea or two, or a phrase or two. In this
case, Moynihan wrote almost every day of his life. It was his métier. And the
subject was his. I gave him an idea or two and a phrase or two.

Burns and Anderson took these "obiter dicta," or musings of Nixon from
the council meeting, as an indication that Nixon would be most comfortable
just proposing something that addressed the AFDC program and its ills.
Nothing beyond.

The almost wistful references to background, church, and family conjure
up the "little platoons of society" of Edmund Burke's view of institutions and
their purpose. Moynihan and Nixon shared the Burkean notion of society
and of community needing to be knit together. Moynihan at the outset of
the administration had argued forcefully to the new president that he must
repair damaged institutions and restore the peoples' trust in them; he must
convince them anew that the country's leaders were acting wisely and that
government was responsive to real and felt need.

In a lengthy and thoughtful memorandum of January 3, 1969, to the president-elect, Moynihan said, "In one form or another all of the major domestic
problems facing you derive from the erosion of the authority of the institutions of American society. This is a mysterious process of which the most
that can be said is that once it starts it tends not to stop."

He continued, noting that "the term 'authority' has acquired for many a
sinister cast. . . . Yet it remains the case that relationships based on authority are consensual ones: that is to say they are based on common agreement

to behave in certain ways. It is said that freedom lives in the interstices of authority: when the structure collapses, freedom disappears, and society is governed by relationships based on power."

Moynihan then enjoined Nixon: "Your task, then, is clear: to restore the authority of American institutions . . . with a clear sense that what is at issue is the continued acceptance by the great mass of the people of the legitimacy and efficacy of the present arrangements of American society, and of our processes for changing those arrangements."[39]

Both were realists and at the same time sensitive to the sweep of history. Burns and Anderson were in the end stunned by the willingness of Nixon and Moynihan—against most of Nixon's cabinet, save for Robert Finch, George Shultz, and Don Rumsfeld—to embrace the Family Assistance Plan. As Nixon was to put it, it was "to take a gamble on human nature."

CHAPTER 11

The Fencing Moves from
Épées to Sabers

The combat grew more tense. It was during this phase, at one of those moments when we thought the president had decided for certain to go with us, that Moynihan told me, "You have drawn your first blood!" But Burns and Anderson had not yet laid down their weapons. For now, they labored away on their more circumscribed and cautious ideas. I labored away on the vastly broader plan that would put in place a national floor on family income.

Years later, Richard Nixon made remarks at Dr. Burns's memorial service on July 22, 1987. Dr. Moynihan wrote to the former president: "You spoke so beautifully of Arthur Burns yesterday, and how I do remember that 'titanic' battle. How extraordinarily generous he was in any such encounter so long as he felt decent rules of engagement were observed on both sides, which is to say some modicum of respect for fact!"

One bright Sunday in April following the Key Biscayne discussion with Nixon, I happened to walk from my first-floor office downstairs and out of the basement of the Old Executive Office Building (EOB) at precisely the same moment Dr. Burns did. We started strolling and talking together and then turned north on Seventeenth Street, up to K Street, where we entered a Sholl's Cafeteria. As we were exhorted to do by the staff, we moved speedily along the steam table and had our money ready, because, as an employee said, "It keeps the prices down." We sat down for a light lunch together. At each seat was a laminated card with a suggested preprandial prayer on it. Clergy ate free at Sholl's. I enjoyed the signature rhubarb pie. Not a word was spoken of welfare reform. Rather, the conversation was exclusively about Vietnam, and to my surprise, Burns held forth on a sustained criticism of our involvement in the war, on economic, moral, and geostrategic grounds.

After lunch, we walked back together to the EOB and returned to our desks to renew combat over welfare. That Sholl's moment was not unlike the famous Christmas Eve truce in a December of World War I, with Christmas carols sung in English and German across the lines: "O Tanenbaum" becoming "O Christmas Tree" sung together; indeed, there was fraternization among soldiers crossing no man's land to visit each other. Following it was an immediate return to shelling and trench warfare.

Not a week later, I was in my office on Saturday morning when I received a call from Haldeman's office, asking for a copy of my April 4 options paper ("That's the one the president saw in Key Biscayne, isn't it?"). I looked and said I had only the file copy. The peremptory order came barking down the phone, "Bring it! Now!"

I walked out onto the White House lawn with the only copy I could lay my hands on and went up to Bob Haldeman, standing by the stairs leading up to Marine One, the presidential helicopter. Haldeman took it and handed it to the waiting president, who tucked it under his shoulder as he stepped up and into the helicopter, planning, Haldeman told me, to read it at Camp David for a weekend of reflection.

This moved me to reflect. I went to Grinnell College, a small liberal arts college that had, at the turn of the twentieth century, been a fountainhead of the "Social Gospel Movement." As its name implies, it saw the purpose of education and of the college in particular as imbuing graduates with a strong sense of civic duty and involvement in the public arena, especially on behalf of those less fortunate than those of us attending Grinnell. As George Drake, a professor emeritus of Grinnell, writes, "It was an ethical, outward focused, activist kind of Christianity—for social justice."[1] It had as goals such specific reforms as abolishing child labor and providing a living wage to workers. It was infused with a strongly and specifically Christian ethos. Harry Hopkins, a graduate of Grinnell at a time when the Social Gospel movement was a major force on the campus, went on to be president of the National Association of Social Workers for nearly a decade. Following this was his commanding role in FDR's New Deal, running the Works Progress Administration, the program of federal employment for the jobless. His relationship to FDR came to surpass that of any other advisor, and he lived with the Roosevelts in the family quarters. Drake writes, "The New Deal was led by Roosevelt's 'alter ego' Harry Hopkins, 1912 graduate, who enlisted Halley Flanagan, class of 1911, Chester Davis, 1911, and Florence Kerr, 1912. The historical consensus is that the intellectual fabric of the New Deal was drawn from three collegiate institutions: Harvard, Columbia, and Grinnell."[2]

I never had an occasion to talk with Richard Nixon about his time at Whittier and mine at Grinnell, two sectarian liberal arts colleges, one Quaker and one Congregationalist. In both of them, the consciousness of the Social Gospel movement was present. There was an atmosphere in which, even by osmosis, we were encouraged to think of service. I would love to have had such a conversation.

At the moment I saw Nixon going up the steps into Marine One with my paper tucked under his arm, I was deeply moved. I felt that my inchoate concern as an undergraduate, my work as Ripon's research director, and my interest in welfare and poverty had brought me to this moment. I thought that my work and words, distilling the ideas of others far more knowledge-able than I was, might influence the president of the United States to a deci-sion that would dramatically change the lives of more than thirteen million Americans for the better. I hoped that my prose had moved beyond "opaque" and would be clear and convincing.

The president asked to have reactions to the Burns plan by May 9 and for Paul McCracken, head of the Council of Economic Advisors, to chair a tech-nical group further to vet the proposed family security system. On it with me were Marty Anderson from the White House, Barlous and James Storey from the Bureau of the Budget, the usual suspects from OEO and HEW, and others from the Treasury and CEA itself.

The group further compared and costed the family security system, the "Burns Plan," and a straw man known as a Universal Security System (USS) "to provide income support for virtually all poor people, included here for comparison purposes."[3] The latter, while not pursued and used only for cost-ing comparison purposes, was the very first "Universal Basic Income (UBI)" idea looked at by any president and his cabinet, certainly in any formal fash-ion. It was in the form of a negative income tax. It included individuals and not only families with children, as a means-tested program. It was therefore universal for all Americans at or below the poverty line, working, unem-ployed, or dependent. Strikingly, its cost was only incrementally greater than the family security system cost (later the FAP) itself, which supported all families with children.[4] Nixon was reading every memo coming through this lengthy debate, and he read this one. Since this full-blown "UBI" had no advocates, it remained simply a comparison against which the other two pro-posals in the game could be weighed as to coverage and cost. The focus for both Moynihan and the president was on the family and reducing incentives for its instability. Yet, fifty years ago, a full Universal Basic Income proposal was before a president and his government, and Richard Nixon did propose and fought for two years to get a nearly universal plan.

For my part, trying to chip us out of the sand trap, I wrestled with the notion of creating a new category for the working poor while leaving AFDC alive. I raised this option with Dick Nathan. Earlier I had chewed on this with Tom Joe over a dinner lasting more than three hours. Burns had great respect for Nathan, as their instincts were much alike in not wishing to wan-der too far from the existing public assistance structure. Burns in fact was tethered to it. My diary for May 2, 1969, notes, "In talking with Bramson from the CEA, I learned that the Burns proposal will provide incentives to family separation higher in every instance than the Family Security Sys-tem would." Nathan thought a possible compromise could be obtained with Burns by doing something like what Tom Joe and I were thinking of, namely, the creation of a new category for the working poor. But the key to bringing Burns along would be "by treating anyone assisted under this new category as eligible only so long as he continues to work. If he were to stop working, he would lose his benefits under this category, but would be eligible for either unemployment compensation or the UP program which Burns would mandate in his proposal."[5] The income-tested Earned Income Tax Credit (EITC) was passed during Gerald Ford's presidency. EITC did some of what Nixon's FAP sought to do for the working poor, though FAP was broader than touching only working parents. EITC is the progeny of Richard Nixon, although one that has in recent years been disinherited by many conservatives, especially in the crest of the Tea Party movement. It is flexible and increases as incomes decline, or do not keep up, so it is costly. The stated reason for attempts to cut EITC is cost, as when the Republicans failed to support their own Speaker John Boehner when he worked on an agreement with President Obama for its updating. The other reason is that it is an entitlement. For whatever reason, Republicans still do not have enthusiasm for Nixon's support for the working poor.

The other issue that is not avoidable in any discussion of the UP program, or welfare more generally, was the "work requirement." The president was to insist upon bringing his proposal more in alignment with his own views. He shared the then widespread public willingness to help those in real need. He, like so many of his generation, was aware of a stigma about the "dole" and felt embarrassment to go on relief. Yet unlike what most conservatives thought, he recognized that there were millions striving and still poor, still unable to feed their family. All of this came together as he turned FAP over and over in his mind. He embraced a vigorous requirement for work for those able to but, along with it, training and day care better to enable men and women to find job opportunities. His insistence on a work requirement was born of personal conviction, but it also, no doubt, was intended to make FAP more palatable to conservatives.

At a meeting chaired by Dr. Burns on revenue sharing, on May 1, C. D. Ward, the staff person on whom Vice President Spiro Agnew relied for interaction with the Council for Urban Affairs, "came up to me and, in a rather confidential tone, suggested that the Vice President might be the figure to put together the compromise. I was non-committal."[6] Perhaps too readily, I brushed aside the suggestion. His boss, the vice president, was later to emerge as one of the most implacable foes of Family Assistance (and, I might add, a strenuous critic of the February 1971 Nixon proposals on health insurance and health services delivery on which I labored).

I in the end opposed Nathan's various suggestions for deviating from the Family Security (soon renamed FAP) proposal, even though some of it was congruent with my thinking. At this juncture, "Nathan was moving toward a 'compromise' which would have kept AFDC and creating a separate categorical assistance program for the working poor. I insisted to Nathan there would be *no* compromise, and should be none (I was secure in the knowledge that Moynihan felt we had made a sale with the President)."[7]

On a Saturday at the end of April, the Urban Affairs Council spent a morning talking through the Family Security proposal, as Nixon had requested. He was not present and Finch plopped down into his chair, with its back to the Rose Garden. There was an almost audible inhaling of breath when Finch did this and proceeded to lead the discussion.

All of the arguments for and against a guaranteed income, a term "that dare not speak its name" in the debate, were advanced. From the almost libertarian preference of the chairman of the Council of Economic Advisors, who favored only cash grants, to the fiscal cautionary tales of the budget director, Bob Mayo, and the sceptics who feared all would be spent on beer, whiskey, gambling, and beyond, everyone was heard.

Mel Laird got into the act at this point. Laird told the president in a May 7, 1969, letter that he hand carried to Nixon for a meeting that afternoon that "he was a reasonably close student of the problem . . . [and] had something to do with the pilot program that is currently being conducted in New Jersey on the negative income tax." He said he strongly supported the need for substantial changes and looked at both the Family Security Plan and the Burns proposal. What concerned him most, he told Nixon, was that adoption of the Burns approach "would essentially lock the Nixon Administration into an affirmation of the basic philosophy of the past." At the same time, he cautioned about family security that it "would launch us into a sharp break that I am not certain would be politically palatable or salable in its present form." Laird was prophetic. His finger stayed on the pulse of Capitol Hill and especially on Republican politics.

Laird basically fell in with a proposal from Paul McCracken for further study, but Laird emphasized that there should be a "clear statement of the Administration's intent to abandon patchwork reform and to advance a thoroughly thought-out welfare package to be presented to the Congress in 1970."

Curiously, in light of his later crucial role in pushing Family Assistance over the finish line, Secretary of Labor George Shultz also urged caution and suggested a further dive into the subject. In a memo of May 9, 1969, he said Nixon should *not* choose one of the proposals in front of him, nor a combination of them. Shultz raised four points:

- the marginal rate of taxation in the family security system proposal was too high to meet adequately the family dissolution problem.

- the possible responses of the working poor were not really accounted for; they might choose to forego some of their existing income in significant measure in preference for FSS payments of training allowances.
- the costs of transition from welfare to work were unrealistic.
- the need for a child care system, let alone its relation to the "first five years" efforts (Nixon's initiative in early child development), was not adequately explored.

Shultz's outline of what a system needed to contain became the basis of the final Nixon version, announced almost exactly three months later to the day, on August 8. Here he was urging further work and the additional trappings of a cabinet committee on welfare reform, which Moynihan or I would say he already had in the Urban Affairs Council Welfare Subcommittee. Shultz said that the Heineman Commission on Income Maintenance report would be out in October and that Shultz's proposed cabinet committee should work with its staff and report by year-end.

Moynihan adopted a different approach with the president about the pending Heineman Commission. Moynihan urged that Nixon move quickly so that the proposal debated would be *his* proposal, not that of a Johnson-appointed commission. He said that we needed to seize the initiative, fight for it, and not have a repeat of a situation of just a few weeks prior, where we sent up a first-rate and powerful set of proposals around hunger and then heard nothing more of them. Moynihan was appealing to Nixon's leadership, to his place in history. He was urging the president to mount his charger and go into battle.

Shultz was urging step-by-step, cautious movement, but toward what, if his requirements were followed, would indeed turn out to be a far-reaching reform. In his May 9 memo to the president, Shultz said the report of his proposed committee should set national minimum standards. It should move the maximum number of adult welfare recipients into productive work through incentives for training and employment. There should be quality day care facilities so that mothers of small children would be able to take advantage of training and work. Current incentives to family dissolution should be removed. Finally, and crucially, "the welfare system should be extended to cover working poor, male-headed families as well as the female-headed poor families now covered." On this point, he was repeating the concern he expressed at the very first meeting of the CUA welfare subcommittee. His steady advocacy of this aspect was to bear fruit.

Things were heating up. Only two days earlier, before the due date for the flurry of memos giving conflicting responses to the Burns plan, there was scrambling for a response to another critical memo Nixon had read, Martin Anderson's memo about the English nineteenth-century poor law, Speenhamland. Anderson called his memorandum "A Short History of the Family Security System." Shultz, as part of his rebuttal of Anderson, made the same point he would make two days later about the urgency of welfare programs taxing income at something less than 100 percent in order to maintain incentives for low-income people to increase earnings. Shultz asserted, "In effect, [under Speenhamland] his income was taxed at a 100 percent marginal rate because every shilling earned was offset by a shilling subtracted from the welfare payment. The identical situation has existed under the AFDC program as it has been administered in many States."

As this debate went on, Moynihan kept looking for signals that the president was resolute in his support of the Moynihan/Finch proposal, which he appeared to give the nod to at the Easter weekend meeting in Key Biscayne. After one such signal, Moynihan called me into his office in mid-May, at the time all this kerfuffle was going on, with multiple memos reaching the president—and many others in government, who were reading the same memos because of the wide and open circulation of this debate.

My diary for May 15 noted, "DPM tells me in confidence that RN decided over weekend to go w FSS. 'You've drawn your first blood.'"[8] After my adrenaline rush following his congratulations on my drawing blood in this most truly universal blood sport of politics, I told Moynihan two days later that it clearly was not settled yet. I had just learned that Nixon had sent my paper and the Burns proposal to Walter Thayer and to Roy Ash, chair of the Ash Council, of which Thayer was also a member. Thayer called me to tell me Nixon had asked them both to read both papers and, by June 10, to "take sides."

By now, Nixon had the Shultz reaction. He also on May 9 had Paul McCracken's task force analysis and a promise by McCracken that "since the new Food Stamp Plan is in important respects similar to FSS, we are also preparing a statement showing the interrelationship between FSS and the Burns proposals on the other."

Haldeman sent a memo to Ehrlichman on May 13. He said, "The President asks that you slow down Moynihan and the others on the Family Security Program. He wants a complete game plan developed before any announcement is made. The game plan should cover a day-by-day build-up before, during and after the announcement of the Family Security thing so that we know we are getting the maximum advantage out of it." This and Haldeman's next paragraph imply clearly that Nixon had reached a decision, since Haldeman was talking to Ehrlichman of what he knows best, that is, a rollout of a public relations program. They also said Nixon wanted more analytics. Haldeman continued, "For your private knowledge, as you may already know, he does not intend to move on Family Security until the first ABM [anti-ballistic missile] vote. He now wants two weeks of intense study, analysis, and costing done on the whole program, but he does not want to take on the Family Security battle until the first ABM battle has been put behind us."

Just four days later, Moynihan was in an irrepressible mood but also deeply reflective about the Wallace voter and the racial divisions that were besetting the country. My diary recalls for me a special moment.

May 17th was gloriously warm and the day clear. Most of the Janissaries were somewhere else, and the Oval Office was left in our custody. Pat Moynihan collected Story Zartman, Dick Blumenthal and me and decided that we were going to seize the metal porch furniture right outside the President's entrance off the Rose Garden into the Oval Office. Pat with an unerring instinct due to considerable practice, magically produced four glasses, and even more magically some ice shavings, and poured a libation over it. We sat down tasting not just the Black Label but also the hush and glow of knowing exactly where we were sitting. There was also a sense of camaraderie which was notable among Pat's staff.

Moynihan told us about his fifteen-page memo to RN, which he had sent to the president that morning, on Pete Hamill's piece in *New York Magazine* about the revolt of the lower middle class. Looking back, this long conversation laid out the strategy of the income-maintenance proposals and their relation to the alienation of the Wallace voters.

He told us that there were two approaches, one easier and one more complex. The first was to underscore the importance of the jobs and income strategy and to explain it systematically to the public. To do so would defuse some of the animosity felt toward "welfare." The second was to recognize that there has been, "in a curious way," a role reversal. This was manifested in several ways. First, the attitude of Black militants had become "ferocious." Second, the children of privilege, the students at the elite institutions, had decided they were now to dictate behavior on campuses and were upending norms. "It's going to the point where the students are saying to the faculty, 'It's 9:00 pm; go up to bed,'" Moynihan said. He emphasized that we had to make helping people with their basic needs less contentious and less divided along racial lines. As Moynihan had put it in his memo of that morning to Nixon,

How is the great mass of white working people to regain a sense of positive advantage from the operation of American government, and retain a steady loyalty to the processes of American society, at a time when those above and below them in the social hierarchy seem simultaneously to be robbing the system blind and contemptuously dismissing all its rules. It seemed to me this is just what you were talking about during the campaign. . . . "These forgotten Americans finally have become angry." We must cease defining social problems in such a way as to separate blacks (and to a degree Hispanic Americans) from the rest of the society.

A services strategy, Moynihan told us as we looked out onto the spring blossoms in the Rose Garden, tended not only to exclude working-class white Americans but also to set up a great many middle-class white, and Black, Americans in the "resentment business." Pat told us that "on social services and the resentment business . . . all Richard Nixon now knows is that he doesn't like it." Pat said he hoped "to have at least gotten him to try to analyze it rather than simply be frightened by it."

As to student attitudes, there was a "class prejudice of the college population from which the service dispensers are drawn." Today, they are "really rather fiercely contemptuous of Hamill's folk. (And mine! My relatives are New York cops, plumbers, bartenders and the like)."

The income strategy sought to provide adequate incomes for all so that as much as possible, everyone purchases services in a single market. Thus, the government would not seem to be playing favorites while ignoring the needs of others who are only marginally better off. He said he told Nixon that his tax reform proposals, which would exempt five million persons in poor families from income taxation, was the first step. His hunger program of food stamps, a form of currency, was the second step. The FSS, which would aid the working poor (60 percent of whom are white) as well as the wholly dependent poor and do so as one system of income maintenance, would be the third step. Revenue sharing, if large enough, could begin to ease the ferocious burden of regressive sales taxes and the like on Hamill's urban working class. A final component would be manpower-training on the level and with the structure then being prepared by DOL.

Together "these measures have the making of a social revolution which preserves the fabric of American society, rather than tearing it to shreds. At long last the people-in-between would begin benefiting from the efforts of government to redress the long standing and fully documented grievances of the people at the bottom." Almost eerily, these comments of Moynihan's in May provided all the elements of the speech that Nixon was to deliver three months later, on August 8, 1969, termed "The New Federalism." Virtually every point Moynihan outlined in his memo to Nixon addressing Hamill's picture of white and working-class frustration was addressed in the New Federalism speech.

His May 17 memo to the president ended by saying, "We must dissolve the black urban lower class, turning it into a 'black lower middle class' in its own right, and simultaneously seek the ethical and political formulations that will restore legitimacy to our society in the eyes of its elite youth."

Mayor John V. Lindsay of New York must also have read the Pete Hamill article in *New York Magazine*. As Moynihan notes in *The Politics of a Guaranteed Income*, Lindsay, taking office in 1966, initially thought that merely more efficient administration would halt the growth in welfare rolls. Moynihan said that the task force looking at it for the newly elected mayor concluded that with tighter scrutiny of applicants and less permissive administrators, there would be a "withering away" of the number of people on the welfare rolls. As Moynihan tells it, "This was an agreeable view. The task force went on to other matters." But the growth in welfare rolls had continued. Reality about the reasons for the growth in welfare cases may have set in during these past three years for the mayor. And the reality of the politics of welfare was harsh. The Hamill piece had run in early May. Mayor Lindsay came to the Urban Affairs Council for a meeting with the president and council members on May 26, 1969.

By this point, like Moynihan, I had become an advocate for the family security system, or Family Assistance Plan (FAP). Looking back from 1974 to the frantic struggles of the spring of 1969, I wrote Vee Burke, "I saw myself as a non-technical person—a galvanizer, a catalyst, a salesman." This was by now true even though I had earlier tenaciously kept in my options paper for the president the Nathan national standards option, a form of which became the principal alternative opponents offered to stop FAP.

On the Saturday before the vitally important meeting of the Council on May 26 with Lindsay, I went up to Gracie Mansion, on Manhattan's East Side along the East River. The mansion, the mayor's official residence, besides a view of the river, of Hell Gate, and the Triboro Bridge, offered a tranquil spot of green lawn, shade trees, and classical architecture amid high-rise apartments and a nearby looming Sanitation Department facility. I spent most of the day with the mayor and two people who would be accompanying him as he presented to the president and the Council. They were Mitch Ginsberg, a leading figure in the social services world as an academic and practitioner and now Lindsay's head of the Human Resources Administration, and Jack Goldberg, the welfare administrator of New York City. Both were in the thick of the struggle with ever-increasing caseloads and cost. I worked with them, "helping them phrase their presentation in such a way so as to be most effective given the audience they would have. After soup and sandwiches with Mary [the mayor's wife] serving them, back to work."

After the premature conclusion that Nixon had fully agreed to the Finch-

Moynihan approach by mid-May, the Lindsay meeting was important. It was important to Lindsay, as well. This Council meeting would be a presentation from a man whom Nixon was obliged to deal with—or not: the Republican mayor of New York, a city at the epicenter of the welfare morass. Lindsay's Republican affiliation was sorely tested, and in only days, he would be defeated in the Republican primary for renomination by a conservative Staten Island Republican legislator, State Senator John Marchi. Lindsay had seen off William F. Buckley's challenge to him four years earlier. The articulate, amusing, and amused Bill Buckley could not carry the day on the Conservative line. When asked the counterfactual question of what he would have done had he won, Buckley immediately answered, "Demand a recount."

State Senator Marchi from the "outer borough" of Staten Island did not have Buckley's charm, style, Yale lineage (which he shared with Lindsay), or money. He did savor victory over Lindsay in the party primary, however. No recount was requested. After defeat on the Republican line, Lindsay would run and be elected, but on the Liberal Party line (conservatives might argue it was the last refuge of a scoundrel), on his road to conversion to being a Democrat, as Nixon had predicted four years earlier to Murray Kempton.

Whether Lindsay should even be invited on the very eve of the Republican voting was therefore a question up for debate within Nixon's White House. Advocates lined up on both sides, with Ehrlichman thinking he should not be asked in so close to the primary date. Curiously, the president's political advisor in the White House, Harry Dent, felt that since Lindsay was the incumbent Republican mayor of New York, he should be asked to come in, since he wished to be heard on the welfare issue. This was of interest if for no other reason than that Dent was Strom Thurmond's man. Dent represented the Southern strategy in White House counsels if anyone did. The mayor asked that, one way or another, he at least have the chance to get his word in before a decision was made. Lindsay was invited to the Council meeting.

Just before it began, the president, with the New York mayor present, swore in Don Rumsfeld as the new director of the Office of Economic Opportunity and a member of the cabinet. Speaking on the steps to the Rose Garden outside the Oval Office and Cabinet Room, Nixon said, "He is a very brave man to have left a safe Congressional seat and taken all of this on."

Lindsay opened by noting that everybody knew the need for reform of the welfare system: "It is felicitous that the Administration considers it such a high priority item. We in the mayoring business take heart at that."[9] Lindsay then proceeded to note the pattern of increase in caseloads, not only in New York City but also in the surrounding suburban counties, like Nassau and Westchester, and even in areas such as Cook County, Illinois, which includes Chicago. The conversation anticipated several elements that Nixon,

Moynihan, Finch, and Shultz would focus on in the final proposal for Family Assistance. Lindsay mentioned the New York "home relief program," which was an income supplement to many New York families whose average size was six and whose earnings were below $4,000. He argued that "the supplement is not a disincentive to work. It does not encourage people not to seek work." Ginsburg added that varying with the size of the family, incomes of up to $6,000 were supplemented. Shultz probed about the marginal rate of taxation, and Ginsburg said it was about 55 percent. Lindsay mentioned that in the next year's budget for the city, expenditures for welfare would exceed those for education.

One reason Lindsay had primary opposition was his apparent lack of understanding of the very constituency Hamill was drawing to his attention. Murray Kempton, after an initial infatuation with the mayor, said that Lindsay had a "St. Paul's Chapel style." A gulf was there because Lindsay was "unduly superior to his electorate." Lindsay had calmed the city down but not mastered income and ethnic politics.

Showing his attempted digestion of the message that Pete Hamill had been offering, Lindsay said, "Imagine the middle-class resentment at this—also that of the poor because of the welfare apparatus. The reason it is a hot political issue is that it has such terrific impact, not in the South but in the North. The message about the inequities of the burden is beginning to get through to the northern middle-class taxpayer. They have less government services, and they pay more per income earned."[10]

Lindsay outlined a six-point set of guidelines, among them that "there has to be some neutralization of taxpayer resentment so that there is help where the effort is greatest." This was a call for the federal government to take a larger share of the payments in the high-benefit-level states. Here, he and his frequent nemesis, fellow Republican Nelson Rockefeller, the New York governor, were on the same page. Otherwise, the points were akin to what we were suggesting, such as that "the working poor should get Federal aid with incentives to work," that "in low grant states, individual payment levels should be brought up," and that "there should be a greater incentive to intact families to stay together."

The mayor boxed with the vice president over several points and found agreement on labor issues around case workers; Lindsay mentioned the union requirements for case workers, such as master's degrees, and that they are highly organized with "red tape" and requirements layered in to protect the caseworkers.

As to the administration's idea of a federal floor under the income of all families with children, Lindsay said they embraced it, with caveats, some due to the payment level. This meant some thirty-three to thirty-five states would have to keep a residual payment that supplemented the federal floor if they were to maintain payments at their current level. Also, there was not a provision for poor individuals or couples with no children. The straw man Universal Security System in Prof. McCracken's paper would have covered these.

As to the adult categories proposal in the family security system, Mayor Lindsay said, "We endorse it completely." This proposal was to combine as one the Aid to the Blind, Aid to the Partially and Totally Disabled, and Old Age Assistance and to provide a federal floor under the income of these people. This did finally become law. It was the only part of Nixon's proposal that made it over the finish line. It was known as Supplemental Security Income (SSI). As to individuals and couples who were childless, the mayor suggested that the federal government create a program to cover them and have a federal sharing of 20 percent of that. The mayor had his input into the decision-making process.

The next Council for Urban Affairs meeting, its thirteenth, was a couple of weeks later, on June 13. It featured a man whom Nixon liked and whose company he enjoyed socially, Donald Kendall, the CEO of Pepsi Cola. Nixon had even played the piano at Kendall's wedding. Kendall was a close friend of Nixon's, one with whom he shared an interest in the Soviet Union. Kendall at this time was trying to bring Pepsi to the Soviets, and Nixon was, as always, calculating his moves and relations with the Soviet Union. In this instance, Kendall was at the Council as chairman of the National Alliance of Businessmen, as was the chair of the group called Plans for Progress, and they were to talk merger of their two nonprofit groups.

The timing of Kendall's appearance at the Urban Affairs Council was crucial, as we were fine-tuning the family security system, and Kendall could be a key to convincing Nixon. Vic Weingarten had helped prepare Kendall. The three of us sat up on the floor of Kendall's suite in the Madison Hotel until two o'clock in the morning, drinking Pepsi Cola and working over his charts on FSS and the kind of savings it would afford and its impact on work and jobs. Kendall did a forceful and convincing job the next morning as I listened and took my regular Council minutes, bleary-eyed but happy.

Kendall told the Council we should not spend money protecting against cheating, arguing that "it's cheaper to give the people the money." He said the combination of a NAB jobs effort and the Finch family security proposal can make a major impact on underemployment. Nixon said, "We are still debating it, but if we move on Family Security, I feel—we all agree—that we need a strong work incentive. George Shultz is working on this question right now."[11] Nixon had intimated a crucial next step and turning point in the fate of the Family Assistance Plan, in his reference to Secretary of Labor Shultz's effort to provide a strong work incentive.

In this CUA meeting, I enjoyed a sense of Nixon that I had frequently in these settings. It was as though he were an appellate judge. He had read the "briefs" or preparation papers thoroughly. Now he was hearing the "oral arguments." Where two people were making pitches, as the NAB spokesman, Don Kendall, and the Plans for Progress president were, Nixon would move his attention from one to the other. I regularly observed in the president this same attention swivel to follow an argument. It reminded me of a line referee in a professional tennis match watching the ball move back and forth over the net. But the president often would intervene, as does a Supreme Court justice, questioning counsel.

By this point, I had become edgy. I reached out to Finch, who some of his staffers said was overwhelmed with everything going on at his massive department and who was not bird-dogging the welfare proposal as much as seemed warranted. Finch and I turned to Moynihan and asked that he cobble together a missionary trip to some disparate leaders in New York, whose supportive voices seemed crucial at this point. Moynihan lined up meetings with David Rockefeller, the president of the Chase Manhattan Bank; Terence Cardinal Cooke, the archbishop of the Diocese of New York; and William F. Buckley Jr., the central figure among conservative intellectuals.

I made the trip with Moynihan, as did Story Zartmann. David Rockefeller was the youngest of all the children of "Junior," who had taken a philanthropic turn, likely to soften the harsh image of the founder of the family fortune, which had become so ingrained in public consciousness. "Junior" started the Rockefeller Foundation, the Blood Bank, restored colonial Williamsburg, and created the Rockefeller University with its remarkable feats in areas of fruitful research such as agricultural productivity, thereby reducing the incidence of hunger around the world. Nelson, the governor of New York, had arrogated leadership to himself of the Rockefeller brothers. David disclosed in his memoir some of the resentment that he—and most of his siblings—felt toward the ambitious, forceful Nelson. Also, David was still chafing at Chase Manhattan under the chairmanship of George Champion, a Texas-born conservative and tough leader of the bank that always was associated with the Rockefeller name. Nonetheless, David was a central figure in the New York and national business, civic, and nonprofit communities and had disproportionate influence over discussions of public policy, even if he did not yet exercise full control over the Chase Manhattan. He was most receptive to us and familiar with the debates about family allowances.

Our next stop was at Madison Avenue and Fifty-Second Street, at the back entrance to Saint Patrick's Cathedral, for tea with the cardinal at his residence. I had never met a prince of the church and was most curious. The residence was at the southeast corner of the whole city block occupied by the cathedral. Walking in, I observed that the furnishing was very simple, late Victorian or Edwardian, with straight, high-backed chairs, heavy rugs and draperies without ornament, and very little bric-a-brac. We took tea with Cooke. He was most interested and in fact wrote a follow-up letter to Moynihan indicating his support of the Nixon proposal owing to his perception that it would help support the integrity of families.

As we left, still in June late-afternoon sunshine, Moynihan turned to me on the corner of Madison and said, "Well, what did you think?" I searched for words. Somewhat tentatively I said I thought he was a lovely man, very caring and seemingly thoughtful. I ventured that I was not sure how forceful a leader he might be. Moynihan replied, "He came up through the education and social services side of the archdiocese, for almost his whole career, under Francis Cardinal Spellman. Not many acorns grew in the shade of that mighty oak."

A couple of years later, I was on the dais in the Waldorf Ballroom at the annual Al Smith dinner, seated between Frank O'Connor, president of the New York City Council and Governor Rockefeller's opponent in that tight 1966 race, and Leonard Hall, the former Eisenhower campaign manager, former RNC chair, and son of Theodore Roosevelt's coachman at Sagamore Hill. Cardinal Cooke came over and invited me to come by the residence, which I did the next morning. He and I talked about Pope Pius XII, whose portrait I took note of on the wall, calling him "Pacelli" and being corrected to use his papal name. Cooke told me that he had been the original mover for the Second Vatican Council, to be held in 1939. The war stopped that and Pius XII again tried in the 1950s, unsuccessfully. Pope John XXIII finally convened it. My conclusion about Cooke after this second visit was that he was more confident and stronger than had been my impression eighteen months earlier.

From the curb outside the cardinal's residence, Moynihan, Zartmann, and I went to the Upper East Side, to the townhouse of Bill Buckley at 778 Park Avenue. This had become a shrine for movement conservatives. Moynihan had never met Buckley. The first meeting was absorbing for me, since I was sizing up their reaction as the two of them were sizing up each other. They had much to bind them, including a deeply shared Roman Catholic creed and practice and a broad intellectual awareness of the church's teaching on family and social policy. In this specific mission of securing Buckley's support—or at least his interest, or at least his non-opposition—for the family security system, I suspect Moynihan felt this was where he could establish his beachhead.

Buckley invited to the dinner party William Rusher, another of the most consequential leaders of the now flourishing conservative movement. In addition, I told my diary, "There was a small number of epicene young men, one of whom strummed on a Jew's harp, playing 'Danny Boy.'" We sat down to dinner, which commenced with a cold soup, it being late spring and hot outside. Moynihan dipped his spoon in, and after one sip exclaimed, "There are apples in this soup!" Buckley almost purred with amusement, assuring Pat that indeed there were. Conversation then turned to social policy and the welfare idea. Pat was eloquent. Buckley was largely noncommittal but showed engagement in the arguments Moynihan advanced. Moynihan seemed greatly to have enjoyed this first encounter. From it grew a long acquaintance, with sparring, humor, and brief strains on the relation owing to the successful run by Moynihan against Buckley's brother, James Buckley, the incumbent, for the United States Senate in 1976.

CHAPTER 12

The Hunger Issue and
the Food Stamp Revolution

Only three days after the inauguration, at the Council for Urban Affairs's first meeting, Secretary Hardin spoke up about the hunger issue after the formal agenda had been concluded: "He, the President and Dr. Moynihan had an exchange in which the President expressed concern that it is 'not constructive to say that people here are starving—that our friends on the other side of the Curtain would eat this up.' But Secretary Hardin insisted that it is a problem for millions of people, and the President probed him, and Dr. Moynihan on how accurate the estimates are, expressing more concern, and saying 'Let's get the facts.'"[1] What were the drivers and the politics of the hunger issue in 1969?

National attention had been generated almost two years earlier, in the spring of 1967, as a consequence of a Mississippi trip led by Democratic senator Robert F. Kennedy of New York and Pennsylvania senator Joseph Clark, accompanied by Republican senators Jacob K. Javits of New York and conservative Republican George Murphy of California. These senators were members of the Labor Committee's Sub-Committee on Employment, Manpower and Poverty—not of the Agriculture Committee. The institutional framework in the Senate and the House—the committee structure—had historic roots and program histories and was not always hospitable to new purpose. The Agriculture Committees—as well as their Appropriations Committee cousins—in both the Senate and the House were chaired by Southern and farming-state legislators, and the response of most members with respect to nutrition or hunger issues, if they responded at all, lay in "tweaking" the surplus-food distribution programs. Geography was less important than the influence on legislators of product interests—tobacco, peanuts, cotton, rice, grains, or dairy interests crossed state, and to some extent regional, boundaries. George McGovern of South Dakota was the only non-Southerner of seven Democrats on the Senate Agriculture Committee. The historic purpose was to take market pressures off of crops that were a glut on the market, depressing prices farmers could realize at sale. This was done through government purchase of these surplus crops and its inconsistent distribution of them throughout many—but not all—counties around the country.

The Food Stamp Program was first authorized in a trial program in 1962.

In 1964, it was formalized, with the rhetoric of President Johnson's Poverty Program. It suffered similar shortcomings. Food stamps were designed to give additional purchasing power to low-income families and individuals in buying foodstuffs. The Food Stamp Program was even sketchier and more varied from jurisdiction to jurisdiction than was the surplus food distribution program. A great number of counties offered no program at all. At the time Nixon took office, the administration and collaboration between state and federal responsibilities for the welfare program, namely, Aid to Families with Dependent Children (AFDC), and the food programs were related. The food stamps were distributed through state welfare offices. The federal government would pay for the program, but the states determined who was eligible and did all the audits and vendor checks.

The Johnson administration in these waning days, as with the welfare issue, was uninterested in major change in food programs. There were differences. With welfare, there was a bubbling interest below staff at the presidential appointee level. They were to find receptivity with the new top Republican appointees in their departments.

At the Department of Agriculture (USDA), there was little such interest or agitation at staff levels about any transformative improvement of the food distribution or purchase (stamps) programs. The USDA was remarkably in thrall to their authorization and appropriations committees of the House and Senate. The Democratic committee chairs exercised virtual veto power over the department and the secretary. Johnson's secretary of agriculture, Minnesotan Orville Freeman, was provoked to an outburst of temper in questioning by New York's Republican senator Javits, who probed about why the department's programs were in only two-thirds of the country's counties and providing relief to only a part of the poor, even where the programs were nominally available. In an interesting precursor to the Nixon White House debate about Food Stamps interacting with Family Assistance to provide some tangible part of income maintenance, Secretary Freeman argued in 1967 testimony against liberalizing the Food Stamp program to enable the very poorest to afford the stamps. His rationale was that free stamps or less costly ones would mean the states would contribute less to "relief." He argued that Food Stamps must remain a "food" program and not be a "welfare" break for the poor. Freeman testified, "They [the states] cannot use the Food Stamp program as a backdoor method of shifting that responsibility [i.e., welfare] to the Department of Agriculture."[2]

With the welfare issue, the Johnson White House and the president himself had become the roadblock to reform. The same presidential resistance blocked reform of the food programs. There were two strong political reasons why Johnson put the issue in a bottom drawer for 1967 and 1968. One was Robert F. Kennedy. There was smoldering ongoing animosity between the two, lasting until Kennedy's assassination. Kennedy's very visible Mississippi trip with Clark to the homes of destitute families there (Senators Javits and Murphy had returned to DC after a hearing in Jackson) came when Johnson suspected that Kennedy might move against him for the 1968 nomination, using poverty and the failure of Johnson's War on Poverty as a central issue. Johnson had no desire to be drawn by Kennedy.

The second reason was institutional. Senators Allen Ellender of Louisiana and Spessard Holland of Florida and Representatives W. R. Pogue of Texas and George Mahon of Texas were committee barons, Mahon at the helm of Appropriations. In this case they were almost omnipotent in representing interests of producers. Johnson was disposed not to do anything to incite these powerful chairmen. The president was seeking passage of a surtax that would help him pay for the ongoing Vietnam War and the many Great Society initiatives. Southern Democrats chaired the Ways and Means Committee and Appropriations Committee in the House and the Finance Committee in the Senate.

There was also interdepartmental strife. Freeman by now was fending off a move by the Office of Economic Opportunity (OEO) to move into the hunger and nutrition area. Pushed by the Clark subcommittee, he sought a meeting with Joe Califano, the same Johnson aide in the White House who tried to referee an effort to get an income maintenance or NIT proposal ready to put in front of Johnson and gave up. The OEO and USDA continued their wrangling and only at the end of the year sent an innocuous and watered-down report to Clark. As this struggle was going on, Califano tasked Charles Zwick of the Budget Bureau to head a Nutrition Task Force to make suggestions for LBJ's 1968 budget and program. What they came up with was, for the second straight year, refused by the president. But not by Nixon.

As with the income maintenance ideas that were turned aside by Johnson, these core ideas about nutrition, hunger, and poverty were picked up on by Nixon's administration. Nixon championed them and saw them enacted. They included:

- More bonus stamps "to provide all participants with an opportunity to have at least better than a 'poor diet'"
- Uniform national eligibility standards to protect millions from exclusion from the program by state and local governments
- Nutritional supplements for pregnant and nursing mothers and babies.

Even more startling, there was a linkup between the Johnson administration's ill-fated income maintenance idea and the food programs. The Zwick committee said that, in the unlikely event $1.5 billion were to become available for a food program, it should be used to start a "minimum income" plan rather than to improve food programs.

The Zwick committee had both OEO and USDA members. Recall the bubbling cauldron of income-maintenance enthusiasts at OEO. It is no great reach to imagine the OEO carried the day on this idea with Zwick. Agriculture probably figured the likelihood of getting $1.5 billion was illusory and did not put up much of a fight. So, on the eve of the Nixon administration, LBJ had repeatedly quashed two social policy ideas that were related and that spoke directly to the reality of poverty, about which the Great Society had made so much.

The issue of hunger and poor nutrition was not as long embedded in the public consciousness as was the "welfare" problem. Concern about welfare was like a chronic ailment—at least for the past half dozen years. It already had wide public awareness. There were political fault lines that had developed around it and, by now, also lobbies, such as the National Welfare Rights Organization, which had become well established. With hunger, the issue was more like an acute outbreak of concern. Following the field trip by the members of the Joseph Clark subcommittee, there was a flurry of academic and media attention to the issue. These included a hard-hitting "Field Report" and "Hunger in America," a CBS television special, narrated by the popular Charles Kuralt, better known for documentaries on more soothing topics, such as the most scenic highways in America. The upshot was a successful bipartisan effort in 1968 to create a specially dedicated Select Committee of the Senate on Nutrition and Human Needs. It was chaired by South Dakota senator George F. McGovern, and its ranking member was New York Republican senator Jacob K. Javits.

That election year began without a deep partisan divide over the hunger issue. On McGovern's committee, as it began to hold national hearings on the subject, there was active Republican participation. New York's Javits was of course a liberal Republican and represented a heavily urban state (as did newly elected Charles Percy, Republican of Illinois). Other Republicans on the panel were from more rural states. They included Marlow Cook of Kentucky and, as the junior Republican member, Robert Dole of Kansas. Dole in the coming years was to prove instrumental to helping Nixon and succeeding presidents to shape food programs. He remained a champion of the reforms and their purpose throughout his long Senate career.

The idea that Jacob Javits would call attention to need would not surprise or rankle Nixon. It would seem normal. Nixon's view of Javits was that he was a thoughtful liberal, even if always more liberal than Nixon. Javits's involvement on the McGovern committee likely gave Nixon an early warning of the reality and the importance of the issue of hunger. Soon, the bipartisan approach to the hunger issue began to fray. A number of the more formidable and very liberal lobbies focused on the issue. The United Auto Workers was among them.

The issue was not long in arriving in the president-elect's in-box. One of the advocacy energizers on hunger and malnutrition issues was Robert B. Choate. Within a week of New Year's Day, 1969, Choate gave John C. Whitaker, who was Nixon's incoming secretary to the cabinet, a bundle of materials. These included articles by a well-respected journalist, Elizabeth Drew, for the *Atlantic,* and another by Choate himself for the November 1968 issue of the *Ripon Forum.* Choate called his Ripon article "The Politics of Starvation."

Just a month later, Chris DeMuth sent our boss, Dr. Moynihan, a terse memorandum on "the politics of the hunger issue." In that February 11, 1969, memo, DeMuth noted first that it was becoming increasingly evident that "there is a clear relationship between malnutrition and mental ability. . . . Just how widespread malnutrition is among the American poor, nobody knows, but it is far greater than anyone realized a few years ago. . . . The more one knows about it, the more desperate one becomes over its true dimensions."

DeMuth noted this would become a critical political issue in the course of this administration, as the press was showing increasing interest. He added that recent "findings by the Public Health Service's study are incredible, and they will be releasing periodic reports over the next few months." He concluded, "If we do not construct a major program to alleviate hunger, the President is going to get hurt badly."

Moynihan had anticipated the urgency of the issue and had tasked one of the Sub-Committees of the Council for Urban Affairs to look at "Surplus Food and Nutrition." The laboring oar—as well as formal ties to the congressional committee purview—lay with the US Department of Agriculture, so the Sub-Committee had its secretary, Clifford Hardin, as chair, and included the secretary of Health, Education and Welfare, Robert Finch, and the secretary of Commerce, Maurice Stans, as members. Once Donald Rumsfeld had been selected as OEO director with cabinet rank a couple of months later, he, too, became a member. DeMuth told Moynihan that Hardin was deeply involved already in the issue, getting extensive briefings from his staff on current USDA efforts.

The politics of the McGovern/Javits Select Committee was followed closely by Secretary Finch. There were California hearings on hunger by the Committee, of which Governor Reagan and his cabinet kept abreast. Lawsuits were filed there by advocates to force the offering of food programs by the many counties that did not do so. After that first Council for Urban Affairs meeting, Finch briefed and leaned hard on Nixon to take an interest in the hunger issue. Nixon came to Finch's department only a couple of weeks later and made a forceful talk on hunger to the employees of HEW. A week after that, before the end of the first month of his presidency, Nixon went to the USDA and gave a similarly strong commitment to working on the hunger issue. He told them that their department would have the "lead responsibility" on the issue, for the moment blunting the move by HEW, spurred by Choate, to take over the food distribution programs from a nonresponsive USDA.

It was at USDA that substantial internal division over the hunger issue in the new administration could be found. The secretary, a pipe-smoking Nebraskan, was from an academic background, including a degree from the University of Chicago in agricultural economics. He was a long-serving chancellor of the University of Nebraska when Nixon tapped him to be his secretary of agriculture. He and I had many dealings, and I joked with him that even though he was the secretary of agriculture, thanks to my Iowa summers on my granddad's dairy farm, I had doubtless hand-milked more Holstein cows than he ever had. Had Hardin had a better sense of humor, he might have told me that while it did not increase my grasp of food stamp policy, it had given me a firm handshake.

He was a traditional midwestern Republican with moderate to liberal views on social concerns. Rather than calluses from coaxing raw milk from Holstein or Guernsey cows, he had grown calluses from political infighting in the groves of academe. These hardened him for the emerging struggles about nutrition programs. He displayed considerable political aptitude in how he negotiated the politics in the infant administration and in Washington circles.

Hardin was very quick off the mark. Attention—including Senator McGovern's—had focused on a couple of coastal South Carolina counties, where there was documented hunger. On February 20, Hardin announced that the department would take some funds from a recent appropriations act that had a small amount of supplemental funds for feeding the poor. He would target it on a pilot basis to the two counties. For the first time since the Congress approved a permanent food stamp program in 1964, this pilot effort would allow for the free distribution of food stamps to the lowest-income families.

Johnson's secretary, Orville Freeman, after being pounded by Kennedy and Senator Clark, privately acknowledged that he had the power to do a pilot program. However, he went as a supplicant to Jamie Whitten, chair of Appropriations for USDA. Whitten simply said no to having free stamps and blocked any availability of both Food Stamps and commodity distribution in the same county. The veto was agreed to by the other Southern committee chairs.

With the new Republican secretary, things were different. Hardin secured a change in the legal interpretation of the supplemental legislation.

While Hardin would ultimately win the internal battles, there were ructions. Some within his department, including Phil Campbell, the undersecretary, were insisting that the Food Stamp law itself precluded this. They urged that a change in law was necessary. The same concern had impeded LBJ's secretary.[3] Hardin's undersecretary, whom he had not personally selected, was a farmer from Georgia whose career had included elective office in the Georgia House of Representatives. He capped that with a fifteen-year stint as Georgia's commissioner of agriculture, all as a Democrat. In conformity with the long line of Democratic conversions, which began in earnest four years earlier with Barry Goldwater's appeal in the South, Campbell in 1968 renounced his former faith, crying "Hallelujah!" and became a Republican, in time enough to become the second-in-command at the Agriculture Department. The undersecretary opposed any moves away from the existing system, including its emphasis on surplus food distribution. Evans and Novak, two celebrated and often well-informed columnists of the day, said that Hardin made the decision over Campbell's "violent (but private) protest."[4]

Apart from a more "green-light" lawyer, more important for Hardin was a political shift by an important Southerner. Senator Ernest F. "Fritz" Hollings of South Carolina, a former governor, now publicly conceded that there existed serious hunger in his state. He admitted that having just been elected to a six-year term to the Senate gave him the elbow room to speak with candor. The issue became ever more visible, and even the arch conservative and race-baiting Herman Talmadge of Georgia announced he would begin a hunger crusade in his state.[5]

With the change of administration and the receptivity of the Nebraska Republican secretary, the proposals became more ambitious. Senator McGovern, who had urged Hardin to launch the program, met with Secretary Hardin at the time of the pilot program announcement. McGovern in days announced his own proposal for all seven million Americans then estimated to be living on less than $1,000 a year to receive free food stamps. While McGovern offered no cost estimate for his proposal, the Agriculture Department said it might amount to $2.1 billion per year.

Meanwhile, in Beaufort County, South Carolina, where the pilot was started, failures of the existing system came into sharp focus. Critics said that the new opportunity was reaching only those few who had been on food stamps before and had to pay only a token fee. Both the pilot counties already had a food stamp program in effect, unlike hundreds of counties throughout the country that had none. Hardin—and the president—were to attempt to fill these gaps in help for the most indigent.

The president kept pushing about the hunger issue. In the opening moments of the Council for Urban Affairs meeting on March 6, he asked about the work of the Subcommittee on Food and Nutrition. Moynihan and Hardin said they hoped to have something by the end of the following week. The discussion turned to welfare and dependency, and Nixon noted at the end of the meeting, "We have to find some new directions. As we look at the charts, we see that the poverty program is not a success. . . . Time may be running out on our coming up with some new initiatives." At the next CUA meeting, he was presented with some.

On St. Patrick's Day, March 17, the Council for Urban Affairs met, and discussion was about the report of the Subcommittee on Food and Nutrition. Hardin and Assistant Secretary Richard Lyng called it a "program for poverty-related malnutrition." The president probed the information about hunger and malnutrition and the impacts on health, including mental health and intellectual disability, asking, "Why is there such a lack of information on this problem?" The secretary said one reason was that the typical curriculum of a medical school has no course on nutrition, and doctors do not recognize cases at the margin, to which Nixon replied, "So it is just a lack of knowledge."

Hardin said, "There is great urgency about this. This is the hottest item on the domestic front, and we must take the leadership ourselves." Hardin noted that the proposal favored Food Stamps over commodity distribution, while a special package of distribution would get right at the one-to-five-year-olds, where damage most often can be done. When Nixon queried Hardin again on how widespread the problem in fact was, Hardin replied, "We *know* that there are six million persons in families with less than $300 per capita income. Twenty-five million persons live in families of under $3000 income, and there might be ten million people with poverty-related nutritional problems. . . . We are absolutely convinced this is a serious problem in the United States, and one that with our abundance should not be permitted to exist. Our policy should be to wipe that from our land."[6]

Secretary of Commerce Maurice Stans chimed in, "A man ran against you for President and made an issue of it, saying there were 35 million Americans who went to bed hungry every night." The president said, "I remember it; but then they did nothing about it. They had no program."

Hardin said he was scheduled for three speeches this week, the first one the next night, and that he needed to say he was speaking within the policy of the administration. Nixon told him he could say that this administration will have the first comprehensive, far-reaching attack on the problem of hunger in history, then added "so long as it doesn't cost any money." The phrase has been cited to suggest that Nixon was not serious. Of course, he had budget problems, but he would figure out how to pay for this necessary change in approach. In the next breath, he was suggesting to Hardin that he pay for this by having flexible farm price supports. The administration was in fact going to spend sums that far exceeded previous expenditures and put in place a series of reform measures so that every place in the United States would have a program when they had not before, and much else.

The relationship of hunger and of lack of income and the specific responses there should be to each was to become a line of tension in the forthcoming debate on welfare reform. It would affect the timing and emphasis of programs designed specifically to abate hunger versus the issue of more broadly getting income in the hands of the poor, through cash income-maintenance programs and work opportunities. It was to force front and center the question of whether with a new Nixon family income support program, things like Food Stamps should be "cashed out" or eliminated and replaced by cash transfers. My April 4 draft on the options for welfare reform mentioned formally for the first time that the Food Stamp program would at some future point be integrated with and likely replaced by payments under the proposed family security system (soon the Family Assistance Plan).

Secretary Robert Finch embraced the hunger issue. In classic Washington fashion, he worked to enlarge the writ of his Department of Health, Education and Welfare. He brought on Robert Choate to help him draw up plans for HEW participation in the war on hunger. Choate, the author of the piece for the *Ripon Forum* and a veteran of Senator McGovern's efforts, was later to provoke some of Moynihan's most inflamed feelings of grievance about the mindset and hauteur on the part of the cadre of critics who Moynihan thought were condescending elitists. Despite the president's announcement at the Department of Agriculture that USDA would have the lead responsibility in the war on hunger, Secretary Finch began to lay plans for HEW to take over surplus food distribution nationwide.

At the same time, another issue illuminated how central to Moynihan was the focus on income or cash transfers, and not on a services-centered strategy. McGovern had shown interest in a program that would provide nutritional education services. In fact, nutrition education became one of the lasting results of the various Nixon reforms. Among the ideas immediately in play after the March 17 CUA meeting was a small program for nutrition education centers. Moynihan remarked on it in an April 23, 1969, memo for the staff secretary. He said that the idea "once again falls into the basic pattern of our anti-poverty efforts which have been so counterproductive. Once again we are to hire a large number of middle-class persons to give advice to poor persons." Moynihan had by now fully converted to an income strategy that would put cash in the hands of the poor. Months later, after the New Federalism speech in which Family Assistance was announced, Evans and Novak ran a syndicated column, on August 27, titled "Administration Accepts Food Stamps—But Only as Temporary Measure." In it, they said that recent weeks "have made clear that Pat Moynihan's analysis of what ails the poor—a lack of money—is now administration policy."

There was not yet a positive response to the CUA St. Patrick's Day meeting series of recommendations, and over the next six weeks, there were meetings between Hardin and White House staff, with a conclusive meeting in John Ehrlichman's office on May 5. Those present were Secretaries Hardin and Finch and Director Rumsfeld. Pat Moynihan, Budget Director Robert Mayo, and John Whitaker were also there. Hardin and Whitaker were pushing for a food program, but Whitaker told me later that the meeting seemed to be drifting toward the conclusion that there would not be one. In the middle of it, Ehrlichman had a call from Nixon, who asked him to come to him. Ehrlichman said he would ask one more time. Ehrlichman returned. Nixon had made a crucial decision to get the money from somewhere other than the Department of Agriculture. They would poach an additional $270 million for fiscal year 1970 and $1 billion for fiscal year 1971 to spend on the food programs. It would come from funds for the manned orbital space station. This would begin implementing the recommendations of the March 17 Council for Urban Affairs report.

The president sent his message on hunger to the Congress on May 6. Forty-four years later, Dorothy Samuels, in a *New York Times* piece of May 20, 2013, titled "There Was a Time When Ending Hunger Was a National Goal for Republicans and Democrats," spoke both of the significance of Nixon's commitment early in his presidency and of it being little noted at the time. She writes:

"That hunger and malnutrition should persist in a land such as ours is embarrassing and intolerable." So declared Richard Nixon in May 1969 in his now widely forgotten "Special Message to the Congress Recommending a Program to End Hunger in America." In that document, he summoned the country to a new level of generosity and concern and laid out a series of strong legislative steps and executive actions, including a significant expansion of the food-stamps program.

The May 6 message made another announcement: there would be a White House Conference on Food, Nutrition, and Health, to be held later in 1969. To manage the conference, the president turned to one of the world's most prominent nutritionists, Dr. Jean Meyer, then at Harvard University and later president of Tufts University. Meyer was a blender of discovery science with global public health practices. Meyer was also a Frenchman. He had fought with thirty thousand other French soldiers at Dunkirk, covering the British evacuation of their army. Captured, he escaped by shooting a guard.

Recaptured by the SS, he escaped with an injury whose effects remained in his gait. He then fought in Morocco and Algiers during the North African campaign and, finally, as a partisan or Resistance fighter in Metropolitan France. Meyer was driven and a driving force.

After Nixon's May announcement, in a regular staff meeting of our Moynihan staff on July 2, Dr. Jean Meyer joined us. Discussion turned to the political environment for issues of hunger and nutrition. Talking of the skeptical greeting of Nixon's new focus on hunger, Moynihan, in an irascible and even sarcastic way, instructed my assistant, Christine Miller, to phone Assistant Secretary of Agriculture Dick Lyng and tell him, "If the president is going to send up these socialist measures, against the advice of three-quarters of his staff, he ought to get credit for it."[7]

Moynihan's lament was that they appeared to have been swallowed immediately in a black hole of media and political inattention. In the same staff meeting of July 2, Moynihan decried the lack of attention—and respect— paid to the proposed changes Nixon made in April to the tax system to relieve the poor of federal income tax liability. He told us "that the tax reform was the first major reform proposed by the administration, and it was 'as if it hadn't happened' (a theme that he was to repeat often)."[8] This was the crux of his lament about the fate of the May 6 Message.

As the Burkes note of that message in *Nixon's Good Deed*, "As usual, the rhetoric of the proposition was extravagant, but this time the substance matched the rhetoric."[9] It became clear only later in the context of that other income guarantee, the Family Assistance Plan, which was struggling for its birth, that Nixon was the father of the nation's first true income guarantee. The Burkes write, "Instead of proposing simply to give the states and counties more food stamps for distribution to those whom they ruled eligible, in the old fashion of cash welfare, Nixon wound up proposing that food stamps become a form of *national income guarantee*. The plan had the three basic elements of a negative income tax. First was the income guarantee—the cost of the USDA economy diet of $1,200 a year; a 30% tax which was applied to income; and finally, as a result, a benefit cut-off of $4,000 in income."[10]

This income guarantee of Nixon's would persist through the decades, along with his combining of aid to the aged, aid to the blind, and aid to the partially and totally disabled in the Supplemental Security Income (SSI) program. SSI was also a negative income tax. Between SSI and the Food Stamp reform, his successful social reforms aided tens of millions of marginal or wholly indigent individuals and families.

The Hunger Conference met in early December with some five thousand participants over three tumultuous days. There was a potentially combustible mix of academics, nutrition and health professionals, young people, and

activists, along with organized advocacy groups, such as the National Welfare Rights Organization. It met at a highwater mark for student activism,
following by only two weeks the nearly one-million-person demonstration
against the Vietnam War. There was risk politically for Nixon, and it would
be uphill for him to achieve credit from this group for what he was trying to
do. As Andre Meyer, Jean's son, conceded five decades later: "It was Richard
Nixon. It was the wrong side."

Nixon opened the conference with a stirring speech. The twenty-six panels proceeded to their work. The conference issued a massive report with recommendations for legislative and executive action. One of the commitments
Nixon made was accountability. He promised a follow up mini-conference
in a year to examine the consequences and steps taken on conference recommendations. On Christmas Eve 1969, Meyer and I met with the president in
his office, and Meyer burdened the chief executive with the volumes of the
report, which Nixon took in his arms and then turned over to me as we sat
down at his desk. I was to follow up on the implementation of the proposals.

The heavy volumes contained 1,800 recommendations. The follow-up
conference was one year late, but as promised, it was held. Speaking half a
century later to the lasting importance of Nixon's conference and what came
of it, there was a conference at Tufts and Harvard Universities to review
the significance of achievements flowing from that December 1969 convoca-
tion. On October 3 and 4, 2019, Keynoter Dean Cathie Woteki, professor at
Iowa State University, summarized it, saying that Nixon did a wise thing in
requiring a follow-up. She reminded the audience that of the 1,800 recommendations that Meyer turned over to Nixon and me, two years later, by the
accountability meeting that Nixon had imposed, 1,560 of the recommendations had been implemented.

In Professor Wotecki's view, the top four lasting effects of the conference were the legislation of national food programs, the establishment by the
USDA and HEW of surveys that were to monitor national nutrition, the initially voluntary, then codified efforts at food labeling for nutritional content,
and the focus on the family, especially on poverty-related hunger.

Weeks after the 1969 White House Conference, Pat Moynihan wrote a
warm letter to Senator George McGovern:

Dear George: It was splendidly—and characteristically—generous of you
to issue that statement on the Administration's efforts this past year to
overcome the problem of hunger. I think you are right. It has been perhaps
our most important accomplishment, in the sense of things actually done
as against merely proposed. . . . What has gratified me, and I expect you
also, is that the subject has not become partisan. There has been an atmo-

sphere of accusation, even denunciation on the fringes of the subject, but those with the ability and responsibility to act have kept their heads, and I think we can all be proud of the result.[11]

On New Year's Eve 1969, the Congress passed amendments to the Food Stamp Act that ensured an adequate diet and relief for the poorest from any cash requirement to acquire food stamps, and for others a cap on outlays. They were what Nixon's May 1969 Message on Hunger had called for. Another early step taken was passage of H.R. 515, the National School Lunch and Child Nutrition Act, signed by the president on May 14, 1970. This set a federal minimum family income standard and was warp and woof with the move by Nixon toward clarifying, making uniform, and liberalizing eligibility for these types of assistance programs. FAP and the Food Stamp proposals were the same in character.

In the decade following the conference, there were first pilot programs, then legislation for the Meals on Wheels program (1972); the 1974 Food Stamp Act; the 1975 School Breakfast Act; and nutritional help for pregnant and nursing mothers, which became the Women, Infants, and Children (WIC) program.

At the 1969 conference, one of the most dramatic recommendations adopted was promoted by the National Welfare Rights Organization, a group lobbying for mothers on welfare, especially where they were numerous, such as in large, Northern urban areas. George Wiley, its leader, who tragically died young in a freak boating accident, urged a $5,500 floor under income for a family of four. It became a hurdle for any other proposal to be measured against. It was an outlier and all other income guarantee proposals would seem parsimonious by comparison. As to the income guarantee, as the keynoter, Dr. Wotecki, said fifty years later, "Richard Nixon was in favor of it, before he wasn't in favor of it." This was the very tale of the fate of the Family Assistance Plan.

Food assistance programs were central in the conference calls for action. They were crucial in what Nixon managed to accomplish. Wotecki said, "The food assistance programs have done their job," noting that the Supplemental Nutritional Assistance Program (SNAP), which food stamps have evolved into, "mirrors unemployment data with a slight lag." This is to be paused over for two reasons. First, this then is an income maintenance program that reaches virtually all the needy. It does not have a perverse disconnect with the unemployment rate data, which Moynihan first observed in 1962 or thereabouts about welfare rolls and unemployment graphs going in opposite directions. Rather it tracks unemployment well, even to this day, and is an utterly crucial means of support for tens of millions of American individuals and families.

Dr. Jean Meyer presents White House Conference on Food, Nutrition, and Health recommendations to the president. December 24, 1969. Courtesy Richard Nixon Presidential Library.

The second, and sad, reason is that this is no longer a program supported strongly by Republicans. As Dorothy Samuel's *New York Times* article notes,

The modern food-stamps program, built with Republican and Democratic support, succeeded in eliminating the most extreme pockets of hunger in parts of the country. Today, the program remains an immensely important source of support for low-income families and children living below or near the poverty line. Still, some 50 million Americans live in households that cannot consistently afford enough food, even with the food-stamps program . . . now called SNAP, for Supplemental Nutritional Assistance Program.

Nixon signs School Lunch Act, May 14, 1970. Director Rumsfeld of OEO and Secretary Hardin of USDA behind president. John Roy Price at far right. Courtesy Richard Nixon Presidential Library.

The origin of the SNAP program was Nixon's Food Stamp reform. A central struggle both before and after the Hunger Conference became Food Stamps. Jean Meyer had been appointed by Nixon on June 7 to prepare the December conference. The internal jousting over Food Stamps and the cash income FAP, turning on total costs and preference for types of aid, continued. The results of the head-knocking became public at a press conference about the Family Assistance Plan after its early August announcement by the president in his New Federalism speech to the nation. Richard Nathan of the Budget Bureau was sent out to brief the press on FAP. He was asked whether families drawing cash under FAP would still get food stamps. Dick said what Ehrlichman instructed him to: "No." A reporter then pushed to clarify that it meant the food stamp program would be phased out when FAP was enacted. Moynihan understood that would mean a reduction in assistance levels and immediately worked with Ehrlichman to patch together a "hold harmless" set of proposals that accompanied the president's message to Congress a few days later. Jean Meyer, his prestige committed to a strong food program coming out of the pending conference and then becoming administration policy, also began to fight behind the scenes for the preservation of food stamps. Nixon said there would be "an orderly substitution of food stamps by the new direct monetary payments."

In the afterglow of the August announcement of FAP, at the Council for Urban Affairs meeting on August 25 in San Clemente, the president, as usual in the chair, referred to his bill sent up in April that would take the poor off the tax rolls. He had not only called for a "minimum income tax," saying that tax preferences "permit far too many Americans to pay less than their fair share of taxes [and] too many other Americans [to] bear too much of the tax burden" but also requested the enactment of a "low income allowance," which would "remove more than 2,000,000 of our low-income families from the Federal tax rolls and assure that persons or families in poverty pay no Federal income taxes." Moynihan, later putting this in the context of "income strategy," said the income tax relief for the poor of $1.5 billion paid between 1965 and 1969 by persons with income below the poverty level would almost be the same as the cost of Nixon's FAP per year.[12] In effect, this would mean almost double the impact of the FAP proposal alone on improvement of the financial plight of the poor. The president then said of the uproar at the press briefing by Dick Nathan a couple of weeks earlier, "We're not throwing malnutrition out the window. We stick with our hunger program unless and until we get Family Assistance." Moynihan piped up, noting, "Our critics say we have two bills which work in conflicting ways. The fact is they are both ours."[13]

The discussion was coming to grips with the problem of meshing food stamps and FAP. Dr. Burns said, "The critics have a case against us. Very many families are worse off if food stamps are displaced for all Family Assistance recipients. . . . We can't be in the posture that millions will be worse off than at present with the welfare plan in operation and our proposed food stamp plan." Secretary Shultz interjected, "I thought we were moving to cash equivalence as against food stamps?" The president said, "Yes, but in the transition period we must go with food stamps." Shultz worried about the work incentive being changed, putting his finger on the issue made complex by many separate, interacting income-support programs.

Nixon said, "Nobody's going to get less than under the present program. I'm not concerned as a big state man that New York doesn't get as much as Mississippi." He turned to Rumsfeld and said, "How does all this relate to the tax thing? By removing the poor from the rolls, does that mean that no one under Family Assistance would be on the tax rolls?" The president and his cabinet were talking about and teething on the interrelation and effect on the impoverished of three of their own revolutionary initiatives.

The bipartisan character in most of 1968 on the hunger issue (most of the conflict then was within the Democratic Party itself) quickly changed. Senator McGovern and the advocacy lobbyists went after the administration. Both houses of Congress were in Democratic control, and Nixon was an opposition-party punching bag most hours of the day. Moynihan was upset at the attacks on Nixon given the powerful commitments on hunger Nixon had made in his May address. Moynihan's by now well-trained reflexes triggered testy reactions to charges from those he regarded as overprivileged and partisan. He later commented that groups like the Council on Hunger and Malnutrition and the farm block had a "notably abusive, accusatory lobby."[14]

Meyer came to be seen by some on the White House staff as an antagonist. Len Garment on April 1, 1970, told me of recently getting frequent calls from Nixon, at home and at all hours: "Ehrlichman works for a tough boss—a very complicated one. He hasn't changed at all. Still a split man, with good and bad things. Courtier problem, tends to lead to marshalling evidence in favor of an attitude, as with outlook on Jean Meyer." I remember Meyer in a positive light, and his relentless pushing for the food stamp program as a key to Nixon's full embrace of it. A lot of the five thousand attendees at the conference were very rough on Nixon, in comments and press releases, though, and some aides said it "shamed" him. Nonetheless, the president had set his course of dramatic expansion and improvement of hunger programs. He fought for and got these changes.

Republicans later left the path and programs Nixon set out on. They no longer focused on those falling through the safety net or working in jobs that could not support their families. This was true certainly of the Republican moves on welfare, as it was amended in the 1980s and 1990s. The 1996 "reform" was to reduce the numbers and costs of those on welfare, much like the early Reagan California moves had been. It was work-oriented and was intended to "end welfare as we know it." It was to incent, or, more realistically, to push, welfare recipients off the rolls. The principal cash welfare system from the Social Security Act, the Aid to Families with Dependent Children (AFDC) was abolished, with both Clinton and the Republicans agreeing to it. For the first time in sixty years, there was no specific federal program supporting poor and dependent children. This caused outrage on the part of Senator Daniel P. Moynihan, and several prominent Clinton administration members resigned in protest. Some insiders felt the Republicans, controlling Congress, had passed and sent the bill to President Clinton thinking he would never sign it and been stunned when he did. The Personal Responsibility and Work Opportunity Reconciliation Act (PRWORA) of 1996 became law. The number on welfare rolls did decline, as benefits ceased at certain points.

But the risk was great that the incidence of poverty would ramp up dramatically, as job training might lead to no jobs or to destitution for those removed from the rolls after the new statutory limit on years, imposed by the changes, with no alternative. It transpired that a quarter of poor households with children started to live virtually cashless lives, in extreme poverty. Two

Nixon programs provided partial but crucial protection; both were to see major increases in expenditures for the poor, but both then were to be subjected to persistent and strong attacks by Republicans. In the 1990s and until now, the Earned Income Tax Credit and the Food Stamp Program, one inspired by and the other signed into law by Richard Nixon, ramped up and filled in as income decreased and were automatic in operation, being income tested.

The Food Stamp program delivered for those most in need. When all was said and done, when FAP had failed, food stamps were now available all across the country. Some years later, Dick Nathan, by now the director of the Rockefeller Institute of Government, was at a conference on poverty at the University of Wisconsin's Institute for Research on Poverty. This had been the base for Robert Lampman, one of the fathers of the negative income tax. The institute's work had inspired James Lyday and many others. On this occasion, Nathan was talking about income maintenance and food stamps. He said he had always called the Food Stamp program a Negative Income Tax with "funny money." Milton Friedman, an iconic NIT figure himself, was in the room. Nathan said to Friedman that the Food Stamp program was better than Friedman's NIT plan for intact families. "He looked around the room and said, 'Is Dick right?,' and the others said, 'Yes.'"[15]

In the years closely following the financial collapse of 2008, when food stamps proved essential for millions, Republicans led the way toward cutting billions in authorization, meaning that millions of people, mostly low-income working families or the dependent poor and the elderly, would be cut out. Today in the pandemic, the lifeline of Food Stamps is, if anything, more crucial. The Earned Income Tax Credit (EITC) was also under attack. The EITC was a direct descendant of Nixon's negative income tax covering the working poor. It functioned through disbursements to those filing a declaration showing work earnings below the poverty level. Periodic checks were mailed by Treasury in a mirror image of estimated tax payments or withholding by affluent Americans. Conservative Republicans turned against it. The Tea Party, with EITC as with Food Stamps, pushed for cuts in the programs. In the case of EITC, Republicans spurned a tentative deal struck by their own Speaker of the House, John Boehner, with President Obama for its expansion and improvement.

Nixon would be saddened, but not surprised, by conservative—indeed, almost all—Republicans trying to open holes in the safety net he sought to tighten.

CHAPTER 13

"A Gamble on Human Nature"

Nixon in a Minority in His Cabinet

Jerome Rosow, Ed Morgan, Martin Anderson, and I sat in front of Nixon's clean desk. It was Saturday at noon on August 9, 1969, the day after his address to the nation on welfare reform. Sunshine was pouring in the windows looking out to the South Lawn. As we sat down, he was hanging up the phone with Governor Rhodes of Ohio. He replaced the green receiver into its cradle on the corner of the desk somewhat awkwardly, requiring a few nudges to get it to settle in place.

"Isn't it wonderful that your idea has been given birth to?" the president asked the three of us. "Yes! and you made a wonderful midwife," I immediately replied. Martin Anderson, sitting next to me, was silent. He had wished it stillborn.

Jerry Rosow was assistant secretary of labor for policy and was George Shultz's right arm in analyzing the expansion of the Family Assistance Plan to the working poor. He was now working with Finch's people at the Department of HEW to understand how it would be run and integrated with the job-training components of the New Federalism.

Arriving late at the gathering was Richard Nathan. The meeting had been hastily called, and Nathan was out shopping at the hardware store on that Saturday morning, arriving in his Bermuda shorts and short-sleeved shirt almost too late for the "laying on of hands" by the president. He and his staff at the Bureau of the Budget (BOB) were the source of technical program analysis and cost scrutiny of the proposals. Despite his consistent preference for national standards for the existing welfare system, he had played the BOB's role of neutrality and was a good soldier, despite his misgivings.

In 2018, Nathan recalled with me the president talking to us that morning about the politics of the proposal. Nixon told us that the Democrats would have to go with him on this. They would recognize this was an issue he would win on. Since the Democrats controlled both the House and the Senate, in the president's view, this meant Family Assistance would have a very good chance of passage. This proved to be an optimistic reading by Nixon of the liberals. Offsetting this were early alarm bells from Governor Ronald Reagan. These aroused Nixon's more sensitive, astute, and accurate antennae about the Right. When Nathan and I had earlier met with some visiting

Sacramento staffers to outline Family Assistance to them, there was wariness of engaging with us.

This Oval Office meeting, though, was one of optimism and purpose. We were embarking on a national marketing foray across party and geography. Dick Nathan was to be teamed with Ed Morgan, and Jerry and I were to be paired. Our mission was to fan out, making stops across the country, to brief editorial boards on the Family Assistance Plan and the other elements of the New Federalism, including revenue sharing and job training. We would wind up in California, where Morgan and I would be part of a group that would meet Governor Ronald Reagan with the president at Nixon's San Clemente Western White House.

As he talked to us, the president reviewed what had been some of the main arguments in the contest for his decision. He stressed what had made him more comfortable. He also acknowledged that he had a sense of reliance on fate about his plan. It was now in the lap of the gods—although he was dispatching us to help them with their task. Nixon said the proposal had, through the work requirement, become "more refined, and more in accord with my own prejudices." He went on to say, "Now it is in the hands of God and the people who will benefit from it—[that] it was a gamble on human nature."[1]

Before this meeting in the Oval Office, from later June to early August, there had been many steps toward a final decision. The problem of including the "working poor" had been resolved. But another gnawing problem involved the "effective tax rates" on this broad program of support for all families with children. The current AFDC law held that any increase in income would be offset significantly, or entirely, by a reduction in federal payments. The tax "bracket," or the effective tax rate on the lowest income recipients of the proposed FAP, could be up to 100 percent. That would be higher than the marginal tax rate for the most affluent Americans. These in 1969 were nominally taxed at 70 percent of their marginal income in the highest bracket, though deductions allowable to them typically brought the effective tax rate for the very high income to a level far below 70 percent. Therefore, the tax rate on very low income would be very high in comparison. This disincentive was the one on which Martin Anderson pounced in the spring of 1969. It was made even more perverse when one looked at the combined effect of trying to integrate FAP with other existing income-maintenance or subsidy programs of value, such as Food Stamps or Medicaid or housing subsidies. There at the same time was the problem about whether the combined impact of various of these programs meant that poor families could wind up with more than some lower-middle-income families not on the government programs—just above their eligibility limits. This was the gist of the Pete Hamill column in May 1969 and Moynihan's long memo to Nixon on it.

Beyond these political issues was the mechanical one of how the programs fit together and whether a person or family might become ineligible for something they were already receiving. Interconnected with the marginal tax rate issue, this "Notch" problem meant a recipient could be worse off as FAP payments interacted with these other preexisting programs, causing eligibility to be at risk. As FAP finally foundered two years later in the Senate, these proved to have been the most effective technical arguments against it.

To reduce the negative effect of high marginal tax rates on the earnings of the poor, Secretary Shultz, the avatar for the working poor, reacted by proposing a "set-aside" of some amount of their earnings. This would allow them to retain part of their earnings (or additional earnings) without losing the base of family income that FAP would provide. It was also called an "earnings disregard." The set-aside or disregard became part of the FAP. Former Secretary Shultz, still with notable pride fifty years later when talking with me, referred to it as "what is known as the Shultz set-aside."[2] I bumped into Ehrlichman outside the West Basement on June 16, 1969, as Nixon was close to his decision, and he told me there was "something new—George Shultz has done an analysis of the whole thing—he took the book with all the submissions, and has done a thorough job of costing—he gooses the cost up by about a billion, also analyzed how many people would be drawn onto assistance, then thru the training, moved out." Ehrlichman then spoke of a matter raised in the Yale Ripon paper: "The one thing not covered yet was government as employer of last resort. Not decided whether to patch that on."[3]

There was discussion with Nixon on the subject of "employer of last resort" at a meeting on June 20, and it prompted Arthur Burns to send a memo to Nixon the next day saying that, in the absence of private jobs, there was much to commend it. He noted that the labor market was currently tight (unemployment was to be the lowest then for the next fifty years) but that preplanning was a good idea for when jobs were not plentiful. He raised points both about levels of pay and about labor mobility. After the meeting and the Burns memo, Ehrlichman sent a memo to Moynihan, Burns, Finch, and Shultz calling a meeting for Saturday morning, June 26. The Office of Economic Opportunity had begun a small pilot project on the issue, and Ehrlichman asked Rumsfeld to discuss the question with the small group. In a sense, it had a fate like that of the Universal Security System straw man in the Council of Economic Advisors' paper of a month earlier. It was mooted; it was discussed; it was not embraced. Ehrlichman did raise the idea again later, calling it a "Permanent W.P.A.," referring to the Works Progress Administration, the jobs program Harry Hopkins ran for FDR. The issue kept popping up in discussion, even in October 1970, as Nixon was hammering away at the Senate and Democratic senator Ribicoff was still suggesting public employment, while Senator Long was holding out for an employer wage supplement.[4]

On July 7, Ehrlichman told us Nixon had decided to go with the family security system. Later that day, he told us that Nixon wanted to take the general line of George Shultz but that he likes Burns's work requirements. When I told Moynihan at ten o'clock that night, he said, "We don't care about these things around the fringes—I'm concerned only about the income maintenance."[5] Fascinatingly, since Nixon made much of a work requirement—mainly to avoid calling FAP a "guaranteed income"—he said to Moynihan in the Oval Office on August 7, the day before his public announcement of FAP, "I don't give a damn about the work requirement. This is the price of getting the $1600" (the floor in FAP for a family of four).[6] Martin Anderson suggested in *Welfare* that Nixon was saying this simply because he thought it would resonate with Moynihan: "The statement was probably the price of getting Moynihan to stop lobbying him."[7] I think while he preferred some kind of effective and humane work requirement, Nixon was so keen to achieve the breakthrough, the breakout if you will, that he would have negotiated his way to simply the basic income guarantee if it meant FAP would pass both houses. Moynihan spoke to me on July 12 about the hostility from some Nixon aides to Finch and some of these ideas. "They just don't agree with his politics," he said. "These people just don't understand what the American middle class and lower middle classes are thinking. They don't understand them."[8] The president and Moynihan did.

At the president's behest, Ehrlichman called me for data for the president to see on the effect of FSS (FAP) in the South and the respective incidence of benefit between white and nonwhite populations. It was very clear that FAP would be of enormous economic benefit in that region. The lowest levels of welfare payments in the country were in the South at the same time that there was the most widespread poverty there, even among those working full-time.

Melvin Laird's interest in welfare and especially the negative income tax finally came into critical play. Laird had, weeks earlier, favored a test run before a full welfare proposal. Now, he changed course mid-July and came down squarely on the side of FAP. Moynihan in his notes writes, "Laird spoke to RN for an hour before he left for moonshot and for an hour on his return/supporting FAP."[9] Days later, the president departed on an overseas tour, including Bucharest, with the subplot of enlisting the aid of Romanian President Nicholae Ceausescu in the diplomatic engagement with China, toward the realization of Nixon's long-held dream of normalizing relations with China.

John Ehrlichman flew to Romania to brief the president on the final details of Family Assistance. While he was with the president, Ehrlichman phoned us for an answer to a question Nixon was asking him. The White House operator tracked down Pat Moynihan, me, Ed Morgan, and Dick Nathan, where we were all together in the Executive Chambers of the grand, nineteenth-century statehouse in Albany, New York. My time working for Governor Rockefeller had been in his cramped Manhattan offices at 22 West Fifty-Fifth Street, Rockefeller family townhouses near the Museum of Modern Art that had been converted to office use upon his election as governor. There, beside his own office and a small conference room, he housed Henry Kissinger, Roswell Perkins, John Deardourff, Mary McAniffe, and other researchers and the press offices. In Albany that summer day, as I sat in the high-ceilinged corner office, I looked over at Pat Moynihan. Moynihan knew this office intimately. Here, he had served Averell Harriman, ultimately as secretary to the governor. The tall windows looked out onto State Street, which started there and plunged steeply down toward the old New York Central Railroad's grand station. Here, Moynihan and Elizabeth Brennan had met and married.

All these thoughts must have hurtled through Moynihan's mind. Our mission today was to brief Governor Rockefeller on the president's pending address on welfare and revenue sharing. As Nixon and Ehrlichman had anticipated, the Northern and big-state governors were not pleased with the prospect of FAP directing most of the new federal money to the working poor and relieving the Southern states of what they were now doing in very limited versions of public assistance, and paying for the higher levels of assistance with federal money, too. Rockefeller had consistently asked for fiscal relief for the much greater levels of support—and infusions of state money—in states such as New York.

Nathan himself had favored more fiscal relief for the heavy-lifting states. When we told the governor that there would be hundreds of millions in fiscal relief for the high-benefit states, including New York, Rockefeller almost snorted. His budget director, Norman T. Hurd, was sitting with me on a sofa. Rockefeller turned to Hurd, and said, "Norm spills that much on the way to the bank every day!" This dismissal was not going to surprise Nixon, as he had said that these governors would decide on fiscal and political grounds. We, including the two of us who had worked for this governor, had paid our respects and made our best case.

Meanwhile, walking together through an outdoor garden four thousand miles away in communist Romania, Nixon gave his final approval for FAP, and Ehrlichman headed home to prepare the logistics for rolling out the related programs in the New Federalism address for the president to give upon his return. Ehrlichman came back and marshalled the arguments, both substantive and political. He convened a meeting including Secretary of the Treasury David Kennedy, Director of BOB Robert Mayo, Finch, Shultz, the vice president, Rumsfeld, and Moynihan. Herb Klein from communications, Bill Safire from the speech-writing staff, Martin Anderson, and myself were also on hand, as were Ed Morgan, Jerry Rosow, Dick Nathan, and Bob Patricelli.

In this "all hands" meeting, two points were especially interesting. The first was Ehrlichman's remark that the cost was not as material as the importance of getting FAP in place. He sought to make this point more palatable, especially when the secretary of the treasury and the director of the budget were listening, by noting that we should make it clear that this will not be this year's cost. The other point he pounded was that "we oppose a negative income tax"—as if FAP were not one. He rightly recognized that FAP will change the system. He very politically pointed out that the "work thing is the bait . . . go fairly far, w/o destroying the whole thing."

Agnew was the spoiler. He told the group that governors are in unanimous opposition. He mentioned "Rocky, Reagan, Rhodes (Ohio), Sargeant (Massachusetts), Shaeffer (Pennsylvania), because this adds 13 mm to the welfare rolls." Agnew said, "Why bring new people in?" Ehrlichman's response was clear and aggressive: "Accept that the decision is made. Don't expect support from governors. 40 to 50 governors will oppose." Agnew kept pushing, advising against adding new people to the welfare rolls, citing the stigma of the dole and that people want their checks larger. There are vested interests in the welfare makeup.

Finch cautioned against labeling those working poor being added as "recipients." But George Romney piled on and said that once these new members are on, there will be pressure to keep them on, and "middle income people will resent it." Arthur Burns raised the issue of the effects of FAP on wage levels, and Secretary Shultz conceded that he did not know and that it might raise unemployment. This was in the context of talking about the amount of the "set-aside" or the "earnings disregard." Shultz planted his flag on behalf of the working poor, saying, "Too nice to the working poor? What's wrong with that? We should encourage work."

Cost always was in play. There was a detailed discussion of raising the floor and "cashing out" food stamps, which had been a constant in any discussion since the very first meeting about food and nutrition on St. Patrick's Day and was to be a contest that would continue over the next two years of debate. Ehrlichman, in his usual sardonic fashion, said that for fiscal year 1972, FAP would "cost exactly $3 to $10 billion."

In a small early morning meeting just days before the public announcement, the president was with Henry Kissinger, Bryce Harlow, Ehrlichman, and Bob Haldeman. Nixon spoke in detail about the public relations rollout of the welfare reform, including suggested editorials, which should be "not too long—assume they won't read it all." There was also a plan devised for briefing on Capitol Hill, and it was bipartisan. As part of this preannouncement one-on-one briefing of key legislators, I was dispatched to brief Democratic senator Walter Mondale, who was crucial to us on Senate Finance. He was very open and cordial, as he was years later when I visited him in Tokyo while he was the US ambassador to Japan. Mondale had a keen interest in the issues of working-class and middle-class families and was quite intrigued by what I told him of FAP's focus on the "working poor."

Shifting from editorials and congressional briefings, the president took up the topic of the governors and said there would be high levels of support from them because the polls have us high. Tellingly, he then said, "The VP doesn't play them well. We need to cultivate Rocky more—though never with Agnew. Agnew should work the conservative governors, except Reagan who is a personality in his own right, and who is only with us on questions of principle, while the others are motivated by political considerations."

The same afternoon, August 5, Nixon convened many of us at Camp David. The meeting included the cabinet, those of us on staff involved in FAP, presidential speechwriters, and Gerald Ford. The dynamics of that meeting were as surreal as the museum of Salvador Dali's work in his home town in Catalonia. Nixon had made his decision and he had a presentation made by Robert Patricelli for the FAP team. He countenanced Martin Anderson making some critical points centering on the negative incentives of marginal tax rates. Dr. Burns himself understood that the horse was out of the barn and contented himself largely with puffs on his pipe.

Others did not appear to grasp that the alea jacta est. Secretary Hardin for one spoke up very critically. He was motivated by alarm that FAP and its complexities might push aside an otherwise fairly straight path for a robust improvement in the food stamp program. Whatever his reasons, his opposition was shrill. The director of the budget, Robert Mayo, was repetitively carping, to the point that Haldeman said to the person next to him that if Mayo attacked once more, he should be fired. Of all the critics, the most egregious was the vice president. He nagged the president in front of the rest of us, saying the liberals would oppose it, the conservatives would oppose it, and there were no votes in it. He needed to return to the Capitol, as there was to be a crucial vote on the Anti-Ballistic Missile Treaty, one that was thought so close it might come down to the vice president casting the dispositive vote. In what others considered an effort at humor, but I thought had an edge to it, Agnew turned around to the president before going through the door and said he would phone Nixon again before the vote and see if he had changed his mind about the family security system. The tension was broken when Mel Laird turned the topic to terminology: what is better than "family security?" His effort to defuse the situation worked.

In almost a providential piece of timing the day after the Camp David scene, on August 6, 1969, the *Christian Century* ran a piece, "Public Attitudes Toward Proposals for Guaranteed Annual Income." In it, Rev. J. Philip Wogaman wrote, "The opposition to guaranteed income needs to be deprived of its good conscience—a task in which Christians have a role to play." The Protestants were linking arms with the New York archbishop, Terence Cardinal Cooke, in seeing a moral basis for this social policy that hoped to stabilize families and lighten poverty.

Nixon reflected later to Moynihan on the battle before the Camp David cabinet session on August 5, and the cabinet briefing there itself: "As you know, only three members of the Cabinet were with me." He noted the vice president's petulant behavior there, which had also astonished me: "Why was the Vice President so whiney? The first thing he said to me before the nomination was the need for national welfare standards!" This lack of support kept nagging at Nixon. Before and after August 8, Moynihan noticed a degree of passion in the president about what he was embarking on. He was a man committed. He told Moynihan in the next breath, "I have been reading of Disraeli, and Winston Churchill's father. Tory men and liberal principles are what have changed the world."[10] Moynihan's repeated invocation of Disraeli and the similarity of Nixon's and the nineteenth-century conservative leader's response to the ills of their society had taken root in fertile soil.

On October 24, when much of the early outpouring of strong editorial and considerable political support started to dissipate, the president told Moynihan, "The Cabinet cannot sell our programs because they don't believe in them."[11] Nixon at Camp David admitted, "It is full of holes, but you have done the best you can given the fiscal constraints." Nixon confessed privately to Moynihan, "I have doubts . . . but we will do it anyway. . . . I did this because it had to be done."[12]

Three days after Camp David, I wound up in Jim Lyday's home, for the dramatic moment of Nixon's August 8, 1969, announcement of his New Federalism welfare reform. I settled in the basement to watch the president's television description of Family Assistance with Jim and other members of the "Thursday club." These were staffers from HEW, OEO, and Treasury who were tasked with welfare reform analysis at their various departments and met regularly at Jim's home starting in 1967 most Thursday afternoons. The night of the unveiling of Nixon's Family Assistance Plan was boisterous and celebratory at that location and among those knowledgeable folks. I was welcomed as an honorary member of the group. Resentments about my earlier insistence on a true "options paper" for Nixon were left behind. The people in this room were overjoyed, if still stunned by the outcome. There was a disbelief that this proposal could have been born of a president with such a conservative reputation.

Following his address, Nixon deployed a dutiful Burns and an exuberant Moynihan to the Sunday television news shows. Pat was on *Meet the Press*. Len Garment, Steve Hess, I, and my history-loving friend Mavis Jackson, who had gone to high school in Liverpool, England, with the Beatles, watched Moynihan face Lawrence Spivak, the moderator of that longest-running show in TV network history, and the other panelists, live in the NBC Studios near American University. We then went to Steve's home. Bob Finch called ("he's manic," said Pat) and wanted to send up a bill to Congress by Wednesday.

Then the president phoned from San Clemente. He and his wife, Pat, were having martinis watching surfers off the beach, and obviously, as Len said, "feeling no pain." Given the time on the East Coast, the sun had come over the yardarm very early indeed in Southern California. Nixon was simply jubilant. Len informed him we were having crabs and beer. Moynihan, himself a bit aglow when he took the receiver from Garment to talk with the president, "was irrepressible. He told Nixon that the press was euphoric— and that it wouldn't last. He said, 'How nice of you to call on your vacation.' And ended with, 'Go swimming now!'"[13]

Days later, at the summer White House in San Clemente, California, Moynihan told the Council for Urban Affairs that with Congress coming back, we will see the beginning of opposition from the liberal Left, whose main criticism will be that this is not enough and that it is regional in nature.

I came back from San Clemente a couple of days after Moynihan, since I had met with Governor Reagan there and he did not. He called me to his office and marched me upstairs to the Oval Office. The president was still in California, soon to return and to inhabit the Oval Office redecorated from the Lyndon Johnson furnishing that had been in place half a year into Nixon's presidency. Moynihan walked in, pointed to the sofa, and said, "Look at that. Not only is there a presidential seal on the floor in the center of the carpet. Look at those seat cushions on the sofas. There is a presidential seal on every cushion. Just think of it. Before the year is over, half the members of the U.S. Senate will have farted upon the presidential seal!"

He must have told Haldeman the same. Before Nixon returned to his new, fresh office, the seat cushions were exchanged for ones with no seal. It was for reasons like this that Haldeman so enjoyed Moynihan. "Pat is great, because he provides the upbeat shot in the arm that the rest of the staff lacks."[14]

Moynihan plunged into the fight. He and I met one evening only weeks after the FAP announcement with the Leadership Conference on Civil Rights, a broad umbrella group of most of the major liberal lobbies in Washington, including the American Friends Society, the National Conference of Negro Women, the ACLU, the American Jewish Committee, AIPEC, the NAACP, and others. Moynihan had me lay out the details of FAP and then he launched into passionate support of the plan. He said it was a liberal proposal coming from a conservative president. He said they should not fail to support it just because it was Richard Nixon's. He said a failure of FAP would mean there would be no welfare reform for a generation. One of the few voices to speak up in support was that of Hyman Bookbinder. "Bookie" was a bow-tied, long-time lobbyist for the American Jewish Committee. He entreated the group, "Don't let the best be the enemy of the good." It was to no avail. Not only did a deeply embedded hostility toward Richard Nixon have powerful impact here, but the group numbered as one of its own the National Welfare Rights Organization (NWRO). As it did in the push for recommendations at the White House Conference on Food, Nutrition and health, NWRO here in the Leadership Conference held out a high, indeed impossible, bar of benefit levels largely to aid existing recipients, and these like-minded organizations did not wish to appear anemic in their response to an issue that was the rice bowl for one of their own.

Nixon still was ebullient. In a Republican Congressional Leadership meeting on September 15, he told Senator Scott and the others, "This is the first time in memory that the Republican Party has come out for a program with wide popular support." Nixon added, "I wouldn't like to be a Republican candidate running in 1970 if there is no action on FAP."[15] A week later with Moynihan in the Oval Office, Nixon said of FAP: "This is the Big Game. . . . This will be our monument."[16] On September 18, Nixon said, "Democrats don't want to pass anything that will give credit to a Republican administration. . . . The Great Society was a welfare strategy. We have an income strategy. This has great political potency."[17]

In the midst of the push for Family Assistance, Moynihan's and Ehrlichman's respective roles clarified. As Moynihan had early inferred, Ehrlichman would now be the "go-to" man on domestic policy. Pat was persuaded by the president to stay on, principally to deploy his skills and nourish his contacts to get FAP through the Congress. Since Nixon feared Moynihan's departure upon Ehrlichman's ascension, he turned over ideas for a new role for Moynihan, and there was extensive discussion about it. What he thought Pat should take over was the emerging field of the environment. Moynihan had on September 17, 1969, written a memo to John Ehrlichman, who Pat knew to be interested in environmental matters and concerns of land use. Moynihan drew his attention to climate change. It was remarkably prescient, warning of the impact of rising temperature levels.[18] Nixon also understood the energizing character of Moynihan's focus on a topic or project and his ability to frame issues in a strategic context.

Nixon aired his idea with Haldeman, Ehrlichman, and Bryce Harlow as early as October 1, 1969, in a discussion about the environment. Nixon waxed more enthusiastic as he went on, saying that Moynihan is "creative" and that he wanted to keep him as a presidential assistant with a portfolio to include environment. He said that would make it "exciting" and told them he wanted Moynihan to come in "today" about environment. A week later, he was talking with Ehrlichman and Haldeman about vetoing a bill of Senator Muskie's (Muskie was an early environmentalist and a looming possibility for the Democratic 1972 presidential nomination), and he again asked that Moynihan come in so they could talk about his tenure, the staff he would need, and the duties.

This came to nothing, as a more powerful motive for Moynihan staying was to support the president's welfare initiative and see it through to passage. They finally agreed this would be his focus. Later, in May 1970, when Finch collapsed and moved out of HEW, Nixon did discuss Moynihan as his replacement as secretary of the department. On May 25, Nixon told Haldeman and Ehrlichman he was thinking about Moynihan as secretary and moving Ed Morgan over to support him on the administrative side. He repeated this idea just a week or so later on June 3. But on June 5, Bob Finch told Nixon that he did not think Moynihan was right for the job and thought Elliot Richardson, a Republican with strong administrative skills, would be the best choice.

Nixon pivoted and offered Moynihan the ambassadorship to the United Nations later that day. Moynihan informed Nixon on June 8 that he was not interested and if he was to stay, he wished to focus on Family Assistance. In any case, Ehrlichman formally took over domestic policy. In his memoir, Ehrlichman describes how he inherited this important role. He goes back to the roots in the Burns/Moynihan rivalry.

> They were ideological adversaries, but the competition went beyond doctrine. Arthur's staff was created in his conservative image, whereas Pat's was younger and much more liberal. . . . Their assignments were virtually co-terminous; there was hardly a subject one began to deal with that the other wasn't involved in. . . . At first Nixon played one off against the other. Burns's memoranda were sent to Moynihan for criticism and vice versa. But both men were playing for keeps—they were arguing social philosophy they both cared about passionately, and the responsive criticism was often deadly.

Both men were old Washington hands, wise in the ways of the press leak and the bureaucracy. Before long each was seeing the President behind the back of the other, hoping to gain the final favorable decision on some disputed issue. Neither had an inside track, however. It was a fair, equal and brutal battle.

Pat . . . worked tirelessly to produce the Family Assistance Plan. Burns argued that Pat's FAP plan would just give more money to the layabouts. Any reform, Burns said, should include a draconian work requirement. Nixon agreed with that, instinctively. Moynihan urged that the system be bottomed on incentives, not penalties. Nixon could also see the desirability of that.[19]

Ehrlichman confirmed that by the summer of 1969, Nixon wanted Ehrlichman to "coordinate the two—'to become a buffer between the President and his two contending advisers.'" Then, Nixon decided to move Burns into the chairmanship of the Federal Reserve. Ehrlichman writes in *Witness to Power*, "About that same time Nixon decided to create the Domestic Council organization. Without Burns to balance Moynihan, Moynihan could not be put in charge of the domestic-policy apparatus; he'd run away with it." As part of the reorganization, Pat and Bryce Harlow—both, coincidentally, born in Oklahoma—stood in a press conference in November 1969, as they were named counselors to the President. Moynihan, with his shock of lengthy untamed hair, towered over his shorter and more kempt colleague as they spiritedly greeted the press.

Despite his being elevated to cabinet rank and despite Nixon's obvious caring for him—having wanted to give him the portfolio for the next big emerging issue of the environment—Pat felt demoted, disfranchised.

Two of Pat's youngest aides, Checker Finn and Art Klebanoff came in to my office on December 18 and talked to me about Pat and what they both perceive as a change of his attitude. Art felt it was quite personal and noted a difference between his behavior of a couple of weeks prior, when he was nearly impossible—praising Art for nothing and blaming him for everything—a bit like the experience I had in June for the two weeks that Steve Hess was away. This week, however, Art says that Pat is remarkably gentle. At the same time, he has been taking long walks by himself. Checker says that for the first time he has the distinct feeling that Pat is not in the central part of things here any longer.[20]

On December 5, 1969, the president announced that I would take the place of Moynihan as the executive secretary of the Council for Urban Affairs, and

John Roy Price with President Nixon in the Oval Office, with John D. Ehrlichman in foreground. Courtesy Richard Nixon Presidential Library.

I was named special assistant to the president for Urban Affairs. That day, I sat for the first time at the cabinet table, bracketed by Pat Moynihan to my left and John Ehrlichman to my right. I was thirty years old. I would report to the president through John Ehrlichman.

There followed a melding of the staffs "from the Urban Affairs Council, Burns's doughty conservatives and my several young lawyers." When Burns was confirmed for the Fed in December 1969, "he turned over to me, Martin Anderson, Richard Burris, Roger Freeman and the rest of his staff. Assimilating those wiry right-wingers along with some of Pat Moynihan's young liberals was enough to give a rock python indigestion."[21]

Perhaps with the aid of Pepto-Bismol upon awaking, Ehrlichman appeared to hold indigestion at bay as he and I started to meet mornings at 7 a.m. in the White House Mess, usually with his executive assistant, Tod Hullin, present, and John would consume three soft-boiled eggs as he laid out the day's chores for me.

Swallowing disappointment, and pursuing what was his life's work, Moynihan turned his attention back to issues of family stability and income and immediately was in full-court press for FAP. He brought in Ben Heineman for a visit with Nixon. Heineman had a corporate investment going into Louisiana for which Senator Russell Long was heaping praise on him. Senator Long, as chair of Senate Finance, would be crucial to the passage of FAP.

Council for Urban Affairs meeting, December 5, 1969. John Roy Price back to camera, between Moynihan and Ehrlichman. Courtesy Richard Nixon Presidential Library.

They were seeking Heineman's help with Senate Finance, since FAP and the Commission proposals were so akin.

Moynihan then turned all his power of charm and flattery to the court-ship of Wilbur Mills, the chairman of the House Ways and Means Committee. The Arkansas congressman was a power in the House to be reckoned with. He straddled trade, taxes, Social Security, and welfare legislation like a colossus. Coming to Congress in the year I was born, 1938, he was the young-est member ever elected to the US House from Arkansas, and the second youngest in the House when he joined. This type of "youngster/achieve-ment" record kept being set by the Ozarks legislator, as he was appointed at age thirty-three by "Speaker Sam" Rayburn to Ways and Means, the young-est ever placed on that hallowed committee. When he stepped up to the chair, he was the youngest ever. He was a King of the Hill. His stewardship of Ways and Means was marked by both a grasp of the substance of its work equal to that of any committee chair and a manner of collegiality and accommodation that reduced partisanship and that bred a pattern of productivity and well-drafted legislation.

It was little wonder that Mills thought himself special and distinctive within the House. His head now was turned by dreams of advancing to the top post of Speaker of the House and even beyond that, possibly to the presidency. Moynihan was tireless in his attention to the chairman, sedulous in his courtship. Moynihan agreed to give the commencement speech at Hendrix College, Mills's alma mater. There, he delivered an important speech on the significance of "policy" as a context in which specific programs should be placed.

Moynihan had great respect for Mills's grip on the material over which Ways and Means held sway. He also had respect for the pure political skill with which Mills managed. But Moynihan's courtier skills also were brought into play. My irrepressible boss, because of his passionate conviction about the importance of the income maintenance program he had helped design, was now selling hard. He employed brazen flattery. He was over the top. Moynihan told me of addressing Mills as "Mr. Speaker, uh, um, I mean Mr. Chairman."

Ways and Means and then the House itself soon passed Nixon's bill. That was cause for happy tumult in the Moynihan staff. Moynihan's basement office had a ceiling of translucent glass panels, each more than a foot square. On learning of passage by the House, we pulled corks from bottles of champagne for the staff. The corks burst through the ceiling glass and, inches from their entry, came to rest. I poured champagne for all amid whoops and laughter. Pat himself announced in a triumphant growl, "No more Dr. Pepper for those poor folks down South anymore. It's the bubbly from now on!"

Those dark cork silhouettes remained in the ceiling through Moynihan's time in that office—until December 30, 1970. The metaphor, alas, was apt. We had broken through the first barrier and celebrated it. However, the process from there on became less clear as it moved to the Senate. The corks heartened us with that early victory. The victory, but not the champagne, was repeated once more a year later as Chairman Mills guided H.R. 1, or House Resolution One in the new Congress, out of his committee on May 26 and on to House passage on June 22.

The Senate Finance Committee ultimately would not pass Family Assistance. Democrats said it was too little. It failed to satisfy many of the natural constituencies of the Democratic Party of the time. Republicans faulted its mechanics and its cost. They also found ideological error, even heresy, in its apparent redistributive philosophy and argued it was just a vast expansion of "welfare." But that is the story of the rising Republican resistance to FAP and, more broadly, to Nixon's liberal, activist domestic policy.

CHAPTER 14

Briefing Ronald Reagan
The Beginnings of the Conservative Rebellion

At the end of the transcontinental sales mission I made on FAP with Jerry Rosow, while Dick Nathan and Ed Morgan had been hitting different cities, I landed at El Toro airbase in Orange County. On the next afternoon, August 13, 1969, just steps from the Marine Corps helipad, a few of us joined the president in his San Clemente office overlooking the best surfing location along the entire US Pacific Coast, where the president was going to do his best to persuade Ronald Reagan to embrace his welfare initiative. The warm-up act for the pending presidential performance was Frank Borman, the astronaut. Borman had been with Nixon interpreting technically for him much of the Apollo 11 launch and then the landing on the moon just three weeks earlier. He was in San Clemente to recount much of this for Nixon's guest, Governor Ronald Reagan. Borman then went offstage and Nixon's supporting actors strode in: John Ehrlichman, Arthur Burns, Don Rumsfeld, Bob Patricelli from HEW, Ed Morgan from Ehrlichman's staff, and I.

This was the meeting where the two Californians, one an incumbent and one a future president, discussed a program soon seized on by Reagan as a crucial argument against Nixon's view of where the country should be going. We may have been at sea level, yards away from the surf; however, I felt as though they were atop a continental divide. From one side—the president's—the streams would continue to flow in the direction of the national government, using its authority and resources to meet the economic needs of destitute, dependent, or economically at-risk citizens and to protect us from risks to health or the environment. FAP was the paramount example, although other initiatives, like Nixon's universal health-care proposals and dramatic reform of Food Stamps, illustrated his activist social policy. Apart from social policy, creating the Environmental Protection Agency and the Occupational Safety and Health Administration were willing expansions on a grand scale of federal leadership and regulation. Together, these strong roles for the federal government define Nixon's approach in domestic affairs. He was a man of government.

From the other side of the summit—the governor's—the flow was downward toward Reagan's view that government had come to do too much and address more needs than it had business doing. Nixon was the last Republican president to pursue an array of liberal policies aiming to expand and complete the social safety net and to build more protections for public goods for the country, against risk through environmental damage and assuring greater public health. Reagan's worldview was wholly different. It was indeed a continental divide, even more clearly discernible fifty years later.

I was at this summit. Notably absent was my boss, Daniel Patrick Moynihan. The president was very concerned about Reagan's attitude to the Family Assistance Plan. Nixon understood that Moynihan's presence would only underscore for Reagan how an impetus for the welfare initiative had come not just from Milton Friedman articles in Melvin Laird's Republican Papers. He was anxious to debunk the notion that this was a "guaranteed income," so he wanted to obscure the early and crucial effect on his thinking of a partisan liberal Democrat, one housed in the West Wing, no less, only yards from his office. Moynihan was an intellectual whose wide-ranging historical and policy interests appealed to this president with a conservative carapace but definitely with a thirst for history, a taste for boldness and transformative ideas. In an interview on NET some months later, the interviewer, Paul Niven, said of Moynihan that he was the "only advisor to a Republican President ever to quote the turn-of-the-century German socialist Rosa Luxembourg, in a television interview."[1]

The briefing by the president of California's conservative Republican governor would prove to be a fateful meeting, not only for the future of Nixon's Family Assistance Plan but also for the broad direction the Republican Party would pursue on social policy. Nixon recognized its importance because of the resistance he encountered internally from some within his cabinet and White House staff about where he wished to go with welfare reform. Later that fall, on October 24, he unburdened himself to Pat Moynihan and me, saying, "Many in the Cabinet do not think this way. . . . You know, I had made up my mind about Family Assistance three months before I announced my decision. . . . The purpose had been to have a debate which would give people time to grasp what it was we were trying to do—a long period of debate, which he said he thought was good. He then said that the Camp David Cabinet Meeting had been historic. 'We broke the backs of some of the Cabinet, but they came around.'"[2]

Just three weeks earlier, I had driven Moynihan to the airport on October 3 and he said to me, "The only thing the Pres. has done so far that has really caught on is his welfare reform, and he knows it. He is feeling very alone up there these days, in an awful mood. He feels no one is *for him* or with him."[3]

Nixon knew there was a visceral conservative opposition to his concept, despite considerable conservative intellectual investment in an income-maintenance idea of this kind. Going into his August meeting with Rea-

President Nixon and Governor Reagan, San Clemente, August 13, 1969. Courtesy Richard Nixon Presidential Library.

gan, Nixon understood what the governor's defense of his corner within the Republican Party would be. Reagan saw his strength lying in the territory Goldwater had taken five years earlier—the South. Within the South, the rich soil to till would be the Wallace vote, even more the shifting Southern conservative establishment. Nixon well remembered the Reagan preconvention 1968 moves in the old Confederacy. They were not quixotic, just late, and they were thwarted by Nixon's cultivation of Clarke Reed of Mississippi and Strom Thurmond. The South held for Nixon in Miami. All that was likely in part behind Ehrlichman's question to me of a few weeks prior about the demographic impact of FAP.

In FAP's content and its geography, Nixon thought he had an answer to the Wallace vote. Nixon's postmaster general, Winton Blount, on his return from his native Alabama and conversations with Wallace supporters, described alarmed reactions to FAP within Wallace's inner circle. He told Nixon in a congressional leadership meeting on September 15, "In the South they asked us—Wallace people—'are you trying to put us out of business?.' YES! [shouted Blount]." Nixon himself noted that in Mississippi, John Bell Williams, the governor, and two senators were "as conservative as you get—all for it."[4] He told the group that the Wallace supporters realized that from an economic and political point of view, the Nixon plan would be hurting their 1972 ambitions as it would have appeal to his more populist base. They were not thinking through with Blount the social implications or the disruption that a sudden infusion of economic strength into the working and lower middle classes, both whites and African Americans, would mean for the long-static social infrastructure of the South.

Nixon thought FAP also could erase much of the racial animosity and perceptions of the current welfare structure. In this he was in lock step with Moynihan. So, in the San Clemente summit with Reagan, Nixon was trying to show how FAP should have broad appeal in the South and hoped to get Reagan to understand both its merits and its politics.

The charts I prepared for him went to the president the day after his New Federalism speech and were relied on by Nixon as he discussed FAP with his guest. I recorded, "The president took considerable pains to analyze the rural impact of this and stressed to Reagan that the major impact of this was going to be in the South, and at least half among whites. . . . While he was roughly accurate in his description of it to Reagan, it seemed that he made the point at the expense of many others that he could have made about FAP."[5] The demographic distribution of FAP benefits was weighted heavily to the South simply because, as Moynihan pointed out, that was where the poor people were. There the distribution of FAP benefits would flow almost two-thirds to white indigent and working poor people and one-third to Black poor people. That was owing to the profile of poverty in the South. Professor John F. Kain of Harvard soon published a paper on the economic development effect that FAP would have in the South. He projected it would be not just beneficial but also dramatic.

Reagan had possibly not thought through the national economic implications of FAP, but he was aware that California would not get significant fiscal relief. More importantly, the governor was beginning to see it clash with a conservative ideological framework. The main sticking point was the dramatic increase in the number of those benefited. Secretary Finch had cautioned us that the additional thirteen million beneficiaries of FAP (principally the working poor, but also many who would be welfare eligible owing to raised minimums in the parsimonious Southern states) should not be called "recipients."[6] Finch grasped that, politically, calling them "recipients" made it easier for conservative opponents to say the "welfare rolls" were being bloated by FAP instead of shrunk. Do not forget that Reagan and Finch were a bit like scorpions in a bottle in California Republican circles.

Reagan was to plant his flag on reducing the numbers of those receiving public assistance, putting emphasis on weeding out the ineligibles who, he told Nixon, had been flooding the lists due to complicit social service workers. Reagan echoed Lyndon Johnson's unwillingness to support cash dispensation to the "working poor." This was in direct contrast to the strategy of "income" in the hands of the poor that Nixon, Finch, Shultz, and Moynihan supported.

Discussion then turned to one of the central issues about an income-maintenance plan: work. It was central in the struggle for FAP with Nixon. It defined the Personal Responsibility and Work Opportunity Reconciliation Act of 1996, and the 1997 abolition of AFDC and its replacement with Temporary Assistance to Needy Families (TANF). In any discussion today about the universal basic income, "work requirements" or work opportunities will occupy a central role. What is the relation of cash benefit payments to a work ethic? Does their cluster of incentives lead either to indolence or to greater work effort?

Nixon moved to both work incentives and a work requirement. "With regard to the work requirement, he [Nixon] was equally pointed. Reagan responded to this by saying that the requirement should be firm, and spoke of the social workers as 'the enemy in our midst.' He said that in California and elsewhere, no doubt, the 'social workers have been going out and recruiting welfare clientele.' At this point Williams [Carl Williams, aide to Reagan who accompanied the governor] raised the question of whether we as a state can make them take public jobs."[7] Neither Ehrlichman nor the president mentioned the internal discussion about considering the government as employer of last resort as a complement to the income maintenance part of FAP.

Reagan asked if there was any work requirement for the adult categories, and was told no. Arthur Burns, who was also present, said we must look next year at the rehabilitation of the disabled. I recalled in my diary, "Reagan noted that this was a great opportunity to get rid of farm price supports, due to the heavy rural impact of this. 'You can pay for this program.' [This had been one of Nixon's first ideas about how to pay for broadening the Food Stamp program.] He went on to say. 'Welfare should be in the business to put itself out of business.'"[8]

Reagan, as did other governors of major states, had a massive welfare problem to deal with. The man who became Reagan's key welfare advisor, Robert Carleson, in his memoir *Government IS the Problem*, noted that in ten years' time, "during periods of great prosperity, California's welfare rolls had soared from 600,000 to over 2.2 million persons."[9] Carleson went on to express astonishment that "we found that the welfare system, which originally had been primarily intended to provide social services to people, had grown into a huge fiscal operation where 80 percent of the money spent was in the form of un-restricted, direct money grants to welfare recipients. Expenditures for social services accounted for only 20 percent of the total welfare budget."[10]

To his credit, Governor Reagan did raise the benefit levels for the "truly needy" AFDC recipients, who had not had an increase for thirteen years. This was paid for by harshly winnowing the rolls. The professionals, Carleson says, had "used their discretion solely to broaden eligibility for welfare benefits. . . . Work related expense deductions were accepted for everything . . . [and] in combination with the federally mandated work incentive income disregards, permitted thousands of non-needy persons to be on the welfare rolls by reducing their apparent earned income."[11]

Nixon came away from the San Clemente summit knowing that the wheels in Reagan's mind would be turning, not only about the substance of FAP, and its direct and administrative implications for California, but also about the politics of it. This despite Nixon having earlier announced that while Rocky, Sargeant of Massachusetts, Ogilvie of Illinois, and other Republican governors would be moved by fiscal and political considerations, Reagan's views would be moved by ideology. In fact, Reagan fused ideology and practical politics in a seamless fashion.

Following the August announcement of Family Assistance, Nixon began an intense campaign in support of it. Endless meeting notes by Ehrlichman and Haldeman during these early months show Nixon urging his aides and members of Congress to get behind it. There began almost two years of strong-arming, persuasion, constant chiding of his inner circle for more ways to move it forward, and even slick names for it or slogans.

Ehrlichman toyed with themes of family/work/security, in handwritten charts:

Labor/Incentive/Family/Training/Security
Incentive
Family
Training

Lift system
LIFTS.

The issues were hashed and rehashed. There were discussions, in almost all of which the president himself participated, about raising the floor, increasing the purchasing power of Food Stamps, of phasing out Food Stamps, and of lowering the "disregard." This was the Shultz "disregard" of a part of earnings before cash benefits would be reduced. Secretary of Labor Shultz argued that this method recognized the costs of going to work, such as bus fares. This set-aside, or disregard of costs of working, was deemed to keep an incentive to work and to make this incentive visible. It had been embodied in some of Wilbur Mills's changes in 1967 legislation, called the "Thirty and a Third" rule. Any allowance of expenses would mean the net figure for a welfare client would show that much less income when compared to the "standard of need." Therefore, the cash benefit would not be reduced. Astounding as it may seem, the president actually sat through discussions in this much detail. The Mills revision, for AFDC recipients, allowed for the deduction of work expenses plus the first thirty dollars and the next 33 percent in income from work, "that is," as Richard Nathan explains, "not treating them as an obligation out of disposable income. Labor Secretary George Shultz wanted to disregard more income as an incentive to work but that didn't happen. We disregarded Shultz instead."[12]

To protect existing benefits in high-cost states, there was a firm conclusion to require a "maintenance of effort" by the high-benefit-paying states to maintain their supplement and ensure that beneficiaries would not get reduced payments. FAP would provide $100 million as a "hold-harmless" to such states (the olive branch to the high payers that Nelson Rockefeller had dismissed as a pittance when we met with him in Albany).

Nixon Quarterbacks the FAP Game

Nixon immediately took charge of the lobbying effort. Twelve days after the meeting with Reagan, the president chaired a Council for Urban Affairs meeting on August 25 at San Clemente. In an echo of one of Reagan's points, Dr. Burns opined, "Family Assistance opens up opportunities we ought to lose no time in exploring. For example, we ought to revise our agricultural programs drastically." Secretary of Commerce Maurice Stans said, "We need a study of what categorical grant programs could be withdrawn on an orderly basis as a result of Family Assistance." Likely this was responding to the president's comments some minutes earlier about the fiscal constraints under which FAP had to operate.

The president asserted that follow-up was crucial, saying, "This is a critical period because the counterattack now begins. Others have lost because they became confused or compromised. A lot of work has gone into this. It is now very refined. In the Family Assistance program, there is a delicate relationship between the work requirement and the work incentives. We need a continuing public relations program in the country . . . and the Congress." He urged that we "stick to our own line. It is the right one. We must not be forced into saying $4 billion is not enough, and we need $40 billion. Sixteen hundred is too little, and we need $3,200. They are out to destroy it. These numbers are the outer limit of what is possible. We must sell this program and constantly resell it. We must remind the country that this is our program and not somebody else's. . . . All this is like a campaign—it is a continuing battle."[13]

Secretary Finch observed that Wilbur Mills was for the program, and the president replied, "He should be. He's from Arkansas. . . . This may have been a Democratic idea, but they are usually for the non-working poor. The working poor is the real zinger in this." Finch pushed back, "We shouldn't concede these are Democratic ideas." His was an important point. He was well aware of the Milton Friedman advocacy, Melvin Laird's support of it, and, through Bob Patricelli and me, the early Ripon Society negative income tax plan and statute.

On September 5, 1969, the president again emphasized pushing FAP with Haldeman, Bryce Harlow, and Ehrlichman. Nixon noted that so far there was a high support level among governors "because the polls have us high," and he assigned Harry Dent to work Oregon's Governor McCall and Minnesota's Governor "Hap" Levander, while insisting that we "cultivate Rocky more—though never with Agnew." He assigned work with Washington State's Governor Dan Evans and Florida's Claude Kirk. He instructed Harlow to push the Republican leaders such as Senators Dole and Griffin and to add a few Democrats.

He declined putting much work into Senators Percy (Illinois), Saxbe (Ohio), or Schweiker (Pennsylvania) and said not to waste time on Mathias or Goodell, from Maryland and New York, respectively. Such a progressive proposal would, at first blush, appeal to these liberal Republican senators. This calculation of Nixon's might be due to their representing higher benefit states, which would not see fiscal relief of any magnitude in FAP, as most of the money goes to the lower-paying states to bring benefits up to the new federal "floor" and to the new eligible population of the "working poor." Or more likely he thought they would ultimately fall in line and that the energy should be spent on winning over the conservatives and the Democratic House and Senate leadership. If this was his reasoning, he was absolutely right. This was early in the struggle and the editorial swooning and the initial polling on FAP did not foretell how the Right and the Left would harden in opposition over the next couple of years.

Nixon sought to rally the Republican legislative leaders again in a meeting with them on October 7, asking Moynihan to do a page of briefing notes and a couple of minutes of presentation to the legislators on each of "the great things we've sent up." One of the truly novel features of the FAP was aid to the non-welfare or the "working" poor. It was a heavy portion of the total cost. When arguments were heard about so much of FAP going to the working poor, the reaction of Ehrlichman and Finch was as Shultz's, "Too nice to the working poor? What's wrong with that? Encourage work."

Deep into the lobbying effort and with a mounting conservative resistance, Nixon, on April 21, 1970, brought into the Oval Office the domestic policy staff and held forth in a lengthy monologue, emphasizing history and calling for FAP's passage and stressing its importance. This mood, this fight for his program, and this confidence was ongoing. Four months earlier, on Christmas Eve 1969, the president had promoted Family Assistance. As Professor Jean Meyer and I sat in front of the president at his desk in the Oval Office, with the massive tomes of the report of the White House Conference of Food, Nutrition and Health pushed over to one side, Nixon turned to his income strategy. He said to us that we would get Family Assistance, and we needed to get it.

He gave a bow to the political realities. He had only recently called for indexing increases in Social Security benefit levels to advances in a Cost of Living base calculation. He did so to avoid an annual political battle over increases, which would regularly define Republicans by their opposition to increases or to the amount of the increase.

He conceded there would be battles over the levels of benefit payments under Family Assistance, once we had gotten it legislated. (Wilbur Mills later that fall in a strategy session with Nixon on FAP made the same point.) Nixon admitted to Meyer and me that the Democrats regularly would call for healthier increases, which would trigger Republican rebellion, and that the Democrats regularly would win. He said that was "alright." In words that have stayed in my head to this day, he said, "The important thing is we will have established the principle."

"Benign Neglect"

Already the "Far Right," as Nixon spoke of it, was launching its assault on FAP. *Human Events*—a principal media organ of the conservatives, on December 5, 1969, the day I took over from Pat Moynihan as executive secretary of the Council for Urban Affairs, ran a front-page piece listing and lamenting the many Ripon Society liberals in positions of influence in Nixon's White House and administration. *Human Events* and its co-owner and editor, Allan Ryskind, were to mount a steady campaign of opposition to FAP, and Ryskind worked closely with Reagan's Bob Carlson. Martin Anderson also continued a rearguard action. Anderson brought Milton Friedman in during the autumn and walked him through the mechanics of Nixon's FAP. Friedman concluded that his own negative income tax was good and FAP was bad. This was quickly made known to conservative outlets and further fortified the opposition to Nixon's idea.

Moynihan, in the *New Leader* piece of 1967, had decried the ferocity of extremes of the Right and of the Left. He now observed unfolding an only somewhat less militant version in the battle lines over FAP. The poles in both parties were now beginning to strengthen in opposition to Nixon's liberal reform effort. Just days after his note to George McGovern, thanking him for his praise of Nixon's hunger initiatives, when he had drawn some solace from the moments of bipartisanship, Moynihan wrote a lengthy memorandum for the president. It came to be known as the "Benign Neglect" memo. It was leaked soon after it was written, for Nixon had left standing an earlier instruction that memos to him from Moynihan should have broad circulation within the White House staff because of their instructive value.

This memo had political value. It became a handy weapon for those who wished to quash Nixon's Family Assistance Plan. The reasoning was that Moynihan would be instrumental in wooing and winning the liberals over to Nixon's income-maintenance program. After all, Nixon himself seemed to believe that the liberals would come along—had to come along. When he had the FAP briefing team in to the Oval Office that August Saturday morning before sending us out to sell FAP, he had told us that the "Democrats would have to go with [us]" and that it was an "issue [we] would win on." Given Moynihan's and my sour and unproductive experience with the Civil Rights Leadership conference a month or so later, that proposition had hardly been proven.

Therefore, the reasoning went, if Moynihan could be discredited among the liberals, his ability to muster support for Nixon across the aisle would be weakened. This strategy recognized that Moynihan had suffered shunning among the liberals and Left-leaning critics in reaction to his "Negro Family Report" five years earlier. The "benign neglect" memo could, if read only for its all-too-cute and catchy two words, revive suspicions about Moynihan among the Democrats on the Hill and help to minimize the support he could draw for Nixon from even the more practical or objective of the liberal Democrats. This carom shot by conservative opponents of FAP in the White House on potential liberal support was ingenious.

In the January 16, 1970, memorandum, Moynihan pointed out current and recent data on trends in the situation of the Black population, urban and rural, noting steady gains through the 1960s in employment and income—although the South was still a problem, and one that Family Assistance would have a major role in ameliorating. Related to the welfare reform, he took note that the female-headed dependent family situation was still worsening, with ever-increasing rates of illegitimacy. The data were beginning to show rising rates of illegitimacy of white children as well, albeit at lower rates at the time. Because of de facto segregation in schools and neighborhoods, "socially stable elements of the black population cannot escape the socially pathological ones. Routinely their children get caught up in the anti-social patterns of the others." He spoke as well of social alienation, not only among Black lower-class citizens but also among portions of the large and prospering Black middle class.

> During the past year intense efforts have been made by the administration to develop programs that will be of help to the Blacks. I dare say, as much or more time and attention goes into this effort in this administration than any in history. But little has come of it. There has been a great deal of political ineptness in some Departments, and you have been the loser.

Moynihan was thought, accurately, to be indicting the Justice Department, which he felt had ineptly handled issues like the Black Panthers. He told me at one point, with his usual sarcastic growl, that when the mayhem and police overreaction with violence in racial situations occurred, "it was under the repressive, racist Justice Department of——Attorney General Ramsey Clark!" In LBJ's administration. The facts bore him out. Still, in Pat's view, the tone struck and the rhetoric of Mitchell and others was wrongheaded and counterproductive. Moynihan also was paying attention to Nixon's vice president, Spiro Agnew, who was finding his voice—and enjoying hearing it—on issues of protest and decrying what quickly had come to be known by the epithet, "Limousine Liberalism." Agnew was fanning racial reaction, in Moynihan's view, in a way that was as irresponsible as that of some of the leading voices on the Far Left.

Agnew began to be viewed with some concern by the president. Discussing school desegregation in the South, Nixon told Bryce Harlow and John Ehrlichman in their meeting of February 12, 1970, that "he'd rather have Finch or Shultz [his liberals] step up to busing rather than Agnew. Or the president rather than Agnew. Agnew can go too far, with a McCarthyite tinge."[14] Whatever his concerns about the vice president, the retention of Agnew on the ticket was to be one of the demands that the "Manhattan Twelve" group of archconservatives were to make later of Nixon going into the 1972 election cycle, in exchange for their support.

Moynihan's plea was turned against him by enemies he had within the White House.

The time may have come when the issue of race could benefit from a period of "benign neglect." The subject has been too much talked about. The forum has been too much taken over to hysterics, paranoids, and boodlers on all sides. We may need a period in which Negro progress continues and racial rhetoric fades. The administration can help bring this about by paying close attention to such progress—as we are doing—while seeking to avoid situations in which extremists of either race are given opportunities for martyrdom, heroics, histrionics or whatever.[15]

Moynihan's anthologist and friend, Steven R. Weisman, says that Moynihan came up with this catchy phrase on his own, although both Steven Hess and I dimly recall Moynihan telling us that it was in the middle of some nineteenth-century report back to the Foreign Office in London by a governor-general of Canada, arguing for London to relax about Canadian federal issues. Of course, this being Pat Moynihan, it is entirely possible that he had scanned such a report for some obscure purpose and the phrase lodged in his semiconsciousness. Whatever the source, an aging diplomatic document or Moynihan's fertile imagination, the phrase and the memo did become a cross to bear.

Moynihan Is Not the Only Target

The internal White House forces from the Right were not calling in airstrikes on the Liberal Democrat in the basement alone. On March 17, 1970, resident conservative Patrick J. Buchanan sent a memorandum to H. R. Haldeman. In it, he compiled editorials and columns from the Ripon Society, saying, "We have an excellent opportunity with this list to pull the teeth out of Ripon attacks on the President. . . . Right here on the White House Staff, we have four individuals—Lee Huebner, John Price, Tim Petri and Chris Demuth and I think Peter Wallison—who were formerly the top men . . . in the Society. A joint letter by these to the Washington Post repudiating the Ripon attacks on the Administration would really draw the wind out of their sails; it would indicate that the Ripon posture of criticism and hostility was not shared by the top membership of the society."

On April 25, 1970, I raised this with Ehrlichman. "I said we had been asked to recant. He asked, 'In Lafayette Sq? The conservatives have a lemming-like instinct, and Pat [Buchanan] and Mollenhof [former *Des Moines Register* reporter, now working for Haldeman] want to lop off heads. . . . He agreed with my point that he and Cole had to pursue a balancing act and mentioned his concurrence with a request by YAF for an appointment with the President. He also mentioned that the right wing had been killing the President on welfare."[16]

I myself almost became a victim of the focus on Ripon. After the Bu-chanan memo noting Ripon's criticisms and suggesting public sackcloth and ashes for us, there was a Ripon event at a nearby conference center, Airlie House. Senator Bob Packwood of Oregon spoke, and news stories indicated that Ripon and he were critical of the administration. I happened to be more in the line of sight of the president, or more visible, than other Riponers at that moment, owing to my overseeing now not only the Urban Affairs Coun-cil but the Rural Affairs Council, both of which Nixon chaired. Nixon created this cabinet body devoted to rural development and national growth policy in autumn 1969 and appointed me its executive secretary. In a meeting some days after the Airlie House event, on May 5, 1970, the president mentioned the Ripon event and told Haldeman and Ehrlichman to "get rid of Ripon people—John Price—in about two weeks." In another meeting around the same time, he told Ehrlichman, "Price to go—ASAP." As with Moynihan's occasional moments of temper with me and towering thunderstorm clouds, this outburst of Nixon's quickly quieted. Nothing came of it, either for me or for other Riponers in the White House. I was there for another year and a half, at the end of which Nixon took the time and effort to strategize with me and get Ehrlichman and John Mitchell to help me as I sought the nomination for Congress in my home area of Long Island, New York.

As for getting us to do penance, Ken Cole was assigned by Haldeman the task of leading us to recant. Huebner went to work on a memo from us that closely analyzed the charges Buchanan—his close colleague in the speechwriting department of the White House—had made. Huebner wrote a compact eleven-page memo showing how the charges were usually inac-curate, dated, or about positions that had turned to support. The cry for us to shrive ourselves was muted when Huebner suggested that Haldeman ask the two leading conservatives in the White House, Pat Buchanan and Tom Huston, publicly to recant the hostile criticisms of Nixon and his policies by the Young Americans for Freedom and the American Conservative Union.

All went quiet on the internecine front. Cole wrote DeMuth, Huebner, and myself on June 13, "The points you raised are good ones. I have reviewed them with several of the resident critics and we agree that it would not make much sense to pursue this endeavor at this time. Thank you for putting up with this exercise."

When Huebner passed his colleague Buchanan in the hall the next day, Buchanan, with a broad grin on his face said, "Touché."

CHAPTER 15

The Center Does Not Hold
Nixon Folds His Hand on FAP

By August and September 1970, Nixon was back in focus on FAP and was again directing the lobbying efforts. On August 11, Bryce Harlow told the president that he had again told Senator Hugh Scott that the president was strongly for Family Assistance. Harlow told Nixon, Ehrlichman, Finch, and Shultz that a FAP bill would come out of the Senate Finance Committee and that it would be written in conference committee in a form that could be signed.[1] Harlow was being disingenuous. Harlow's heart was never in Family Assistance, and conservatives knew it. Harlow was also an intransigent internal critic of Nixon's desegregation of Southern schools after the Supreme Court decision that required immediate compliance. On April 21, 1970, I recorded, "Lee Huebner tells of the two hour plus meeting of the speechwriting staff with #1 on a Friday afternoon sometime before the school message, in which he said Harlow . . . kept urging a course to which the President would reply, 'John Mitchell can't do that; he has to enforce the law.'"[2] Pat Buchanan, in *Nixon's White House Wars*, pictures Harlow as one of only a few true conservatives in Nixon's senior circle of advisors.

Just as he was slowing down Nixon's welfare reform and trying to curb the president's enthusiasm for it, so Harlow had tried to hold Eisenhower back from President Eisenhower's instinct to push a very liberal health-care proposal in early 1960. Health care was an issue eating up the attention of top White House staff in Ike's last year, and Eisenhower himself kept saying, "Make it liberal." It was Ike's proposal for what he called "Medicare" for the elderly. Nixon was squarely in the camp of moving ahead. According to Ike's secretary, Ann Whitman (who later was secretary to Governor Nelson Rockefeller), Eisenhower seemed predisposed to action but, after talking with Bryce Harlow, returned to his eternal query: "How much can be allocated to the Federal Government to do."[3]

So, as Buchanan assumed of him, Harlow always had his foot near the brake on more liberal social policies. Had he still been around during Watergate, Harlow might have pulled the emergency brake on politics, not policy. Buchanan says Nixon often would call Buchanan the next day after he had ordered him to respond and strike out at an attacker, saying he had slept on it and decided to drop it. Buchanan quotes Harlow, "Watergate happened when some damn fool came out of the Oval Office—and did exactly what the President told him to do."[4] Harlow, while he was around, was hitting the brakes on Nixon's social policy instincts. He, like so many others around Nixon, failed to apprehend how driven the president was to do things of profound consequence for people to whom most of his staff and cabinet did not relate.

Harlow was a Washington veteran. For us White House neophytes in the first days, he cautioned us to respect where we were and to adhere to high standards of conduct, as we would be targets for approaches by those seeking to influence presidential action through us. Perhaps Harlow's highest aim was to be a top Republican lobbyist. At this, he was successful. But his return after eight years to his old spot in the White House was in a world different from the 1950s, and he was serving a different president.

My first moment of doubt about Harlow's understanding of Nixon—and of the current makeup of the Congress—came at the end of a cabinet meeting. Harlow and I were seated next to each other along the wall. The president was about to go through the door to his office. Nixon turned and, with a delightful smile on his face, said to us, "Tomorrow marks the last of my series of Congressional breakfasts. I will have given breakfast to all the members of the House and Senate. But tomorrow, I am really looking forward to it, because tomorrow, BELLA'S COMING!" Several folks chuckled. But Harlow, the head of congressional relations for the president, turned to me and said, "Who's Bella?" I told him she was a West Side Manhattan ultraliberal congresswoman who always wore a distinctive hat and was a brawler. He was innocent of any knowledge of her.

Two years later, back in New York, I was on a radio show during the 1972 campaign. Barry Gray had invited me and Bella Abzug to represent Nixon and McGovern. I brought with me a friend, E. L. "Bud" Stewart, of Muscogee, Oklahoma. Bud in 1968 was the Republican Party chair of Oklahoma and the first state chair to announce for Nixon. He sat in a small audience area behind a soundproof large glass partition looking into the tiny studio. Bella had come armed to the teeth, with volumes of books with place marks in them so she could quickly cite Nixon's sins. I disarmed her, left her speechless, if only momentarily, when I told her of Nixon's comment about how he looked forward to meeting her. The battle then began, and the charges flew. At one point, Bud was on his feet, waving his arms soundlessly behind the heavy partition, and yelling, almost pounding the glass, at her comments. It reminded me of the scene with Dustin Hoffman behind the glass partition overlooking the wedding in the sanctuary of the church at the end of the film *The Graduate*.

Harlow's attitude toward FAP, what Nixon saw as "The Big Game" or "Our Monument," showed how so many on the president's staff simply did not grasp the determination, the need, the hunger to create that Nixon had. They would understand and vigorously concur in his complaints about the bureaucracy. Tropes about the wrongs and the resistance of the bureaucracy even then were popular among Republicans and would become central to the rhetoric of the Reagan era and beyond. They agreed with, fed, and worked to implement his most partisan instincts. They concurred with his irritation and frustration, even rage, with the mainstream press and commentariat. His associates knew he could be energized by knowing many wanted him to land flat on his face.

But most had no real grasp of the visceral drive this man had to leave his mark on history. They did not see the longing to change things fundamentally. There was a religious underpinning to Nixon's concern about the struggling and hungry and those lacking health care. He had imbibed this in his home and in Meeting. His ambition and sheer brilliance meant he was a tough, canny man at the game of politics, the Nixon that was the political machine. Behind the furious political intriguing, though, he had made invisible this larger-hearted part of himself. Even those who served him well in working for his announced goals, like John Ehrlichman, thought he was a man with no principles; Ehrlichman never understood that Nixon could not face the spirit of his mother without knowing he was on the case for doing good things.

Hill conservatives often read Harlow's lukewarm advocacy of FAP to mean that Nixon did not really want it. It went well beyond that. Harlow was subverting Nixon's effort. On September 10, 1970, a friend, close to Senator Wallace Bennett, told me that two days earlier, Harlow had told the senator that "Pat [Moynihan] was out in left field and that FAP was not that important to the president. The president would be agreeable to a Long-Bennett income subsidy proposal, but, in any case do not feel too much on the spot about supporting FAP."[5] This was a crucial moment, and Moynihan had called me out of a meeting to tell me the Senate would vote in executive session within hours about whether to debate it in October. It went down. I should have known Harlow was a slender reed on which to rely when it came to him pushing the welfare reform of the president. On the first Earth Day, April 22, 1970, I wrote in my diary, "Harlow objected so strenuously to Family Security last Spring, after I had briefed him.[6]

Nixon still did not waver. On October 12, with Secretary Elliot Richardson and John Ehrlichman, he spent the whole meeting on the Senate, walking through the head count in detail, as there was to be another committee vote the next day. He inquired about the exact content of discussions by his staff or HEW with every senator. He agreed to make several calls himself and noted particularly Wallace Bennett's loyal support. The president was hoping to ensure that the FAP amendment would be included in consideration with other Social Security Act amendments. The hope was that the nine senators they were focusing on were a majority of the full committee and that if three others were absent, "we [could] win with eight."[7] This was the shirtsleeves in the boiler room kind of work that Nixon was expending for his welfare idea.

Earlier he strategized about getting more labor support. On August 11, regarding the administration and labor, he said there was a "snob attitude by Republicans." Nixon noted that he was "closer to their leaders in makeup and experience." He did not often identify himself this way, but it was an important ingredient of his self-image. In another argument for why labor should be well disposed to him, Nixon was against the "Right to Work" laws. This alone placed Nixon in an altogether more moderate or liberal position than that of the evolving conservative Republican Party, which was trying to pass these laws intended to inhibit union organization ability all over the country. He remembered 1962 when the Far Right's push for right to work was an issue on which they had fought Nixon in the nomination battle and that had hurt him in the general election. It also indicated that he was anxious to build the broadest base of support for FAP that he could and to pull organized labor onboard.

Nixon asked to get Senator Long in for coffee the next morning before his Finance Committee meeting and talked with his advisors about Long's idea of a test or pilot for an employer supplement to the working poor (as opposed to the "negative income tax" approach of using either the Treasury or the Social Security Administration to administer the income makeup). The "employer of last resort" idea surfaced once more because Senator Ribicoff of Connecticut was interested in it.[8]

By now, very preliminary results had been developed from the "Income Maintenance" experiment that the OEO had embarked on in Trenton, New Jersey. These early returns appeared positively to answer the question, as John Ehrlichman put it, "does FAP encourage them to work or to lie by?" He told Nixon that the pilot data, so far, with only partial results in, suggested that FAP "will be an incentive to work up and out." He added, "We'll find out how people will react." Nixon told Ehrlichman to spend some time with this group and "get ideas to modify the Administration program. Make it a joint venture—we're not here for therapy. We really want the best program."

In the same meeting, Nixon said that there were no jobs to require people to take and that "work training is a bust—there are no jobs at the end." That was his reason again to talk about public and quasi-public service employment. He mused about whether the Wallace Bennett–Russell Long approach of employer supplements might be put into a pilot program. He said, "If Bennett and Long agree, we can write a bill and pass it without major amendments. I'm a liberal. Wally's a conservative. Russell's a populist." There. It had slipped out. Nixon was "a liberal."

On August 19, with Shultz and Ehrlichman, Nixon ruminated on his "liberal assistants." He said they must be effective and get things done. He said that Finch is "a poet." Moynihan, too. But we also need doers. Shultz "does" and Ehrlichman "does." He continued, "Listen to the Poets—then the prose guys get things done." He wanted FAP done.[9]

Ehrlichman's activities reflected this. In the July 9, 1970, morning meeting of Ehrlichman and Shultz top staff of the now nine-day-old Domestic Council and the Office of Management and Budget (OMB), FAP had much discussion. Focus was on the Hill. Gene Cowan, the White House liaison to the Senate, reported that Senator Carl Curtis of Nebraska was "unalterably opposed." Cowan described the widespread hostility to welfare or relief. Curtis had said, "In Nebraska, people refuse their relief checks and still keep their heads above water." This hesitation or reluctance about relief was something Nixon himself felt and why he believed in the linkage of work and job opportunities with any income maintenance proposal. Cowan noted that "the only ones with us are the soldiers, like Bennett, who is with us only because it is the president." Ehrlichman asked if White House and department people had "done absolutely all they could." He and Shultz asked if the Committee members were being met with individually and if Secretary Richardson had met with them yet. Ehrlichman said, "This is an administration flagship, and we must do all we can."[10]

There were one or two "false dawns." Moynihan took me to lunch on August 3, 1970, at the 1789 restaurant in Georgetown, and before we sat down, "showed me a clipping from the day's *[Evening] Star* showing that Williams of Del. indicated he thought the FAP would get out of committee. Pat regarded this as a real breakthrough."[11] It was not to be. California's governor was on the move.

Reagan's First Moves

At the very same time, Governor Reagan was putting together a secret task force on welfare, excluding the agency that contained the Department of Social Welfare. The professionals, according to Bob Carleson, who was to become administrator for the governor of California's welfare programs, had "used their discretion solely to broaden eligibility for welfare benefits[,] . . . work related expense deductions were accepted for everything[,] . . . [and] in combination with the federally mandated work incentive income disregards, permitted thousands of non-needy persons to be on the welfare rolls by reducing their apparent earned income." Carleson also helped to think through and manage the politics that would result from Reagan's welfare position.[12]

Carleson and the governor embarked on a change in welfare that would bend the budget line. The change did increase benefits for those in the AFDC program—by 26 percent—which was important, as there had been no increase in benefits for years. It was paid for by ruthlessly going after eligibility through audits—something John Mitchell, the attorney general, and his friend Don Kendall had told Nixon would have limited effect and be difficult to administer. Carleson admits that when the decline in welfare rolls began in California in January 1971, there had been a national decline in birth rates. Also, abortion had become widely available. He asserted that the drop was due to the excision of ineligibles from the rolls and not to these collateral reasons. Carleson's and Reagan's move was hostile to Nixon's inclusion of the working poor and near poor, and it limited recipients to the AFDC categorical program for dependent families. Carleson characterized FAP as the plan Joe Califano tried to bring to LBJ, who rejected it. He says that Moynihan sold it to Nixon with "conservative rhetoric."

> The cash benefits plan was a cover for a move toward universal eligibility, and the work incentives plan was a cover for adding millions of workers to the income redistribution system. Nixon and many conservatives bought these arguments. . . .
> An efficient system for redistributing income needs three features to be workable—universal eligibility, a national number, and benefits in the form of cash. . . . The Food Stamp Program already has two of the three legs in place: universal eligibility and benefit levels set by Congress. If benefits were to be given in cash instead of food stamps, the last leg would be in place, and off we would go to efficient income redistribution (which is why it is imperative to block-grant these two federal programs to the states, and end their entitlement nature).[13]

Moynihan and Nixon were anxious that the presidential appointees throughout the domestic side of the government have an accurate appreciation of the strategy of Nixon's programs. He and Nixon would convene the assistant secretaries of the domestic departments and attempt to place proposals like FAP and Food Stamps into a conceptual framework so that these important leaders in the administration could better interpret and sell the programs. Nixon and Moynihan lamented that even their own administration did not understand.

Carleson did understand. He saw that Food Stamps were cut from the same cloth as FAP and that the two were both a negative income tax and an entitlement. He was wrong that they were pushed by the welfare establishment. If food stamps were cashed out, innumerable county and state administrators of food distribution and Food Stamp Programs would also be without a reason for their jobs. If FAP passed, the administration of FAP itself would be through either the Treasury or the Social Security Administration. In Nixon's and Moynihan's thinking, FAP was a move to *reduce* bureaucracy. In one of the paramount ironies, the welfare establishment were the beneficiaries of the Reagan approach, which meant keeping in place the existing administrative structure. It anticipated the main structure of the 1996 Personal Responsibility and Work Opportunity Reconciliation Act (PRWORA). This had a cutoff of welfare support after a number of years. It had a deference for state determination of benefit levels and for the way social workers would interact with welfare recipients having a work plan that had to be met. It was a reverse direction from that of FAP. Savings were to be achieved by culling out low-wage earners who were claiming expenses for work—in other words, the working poor Nixon was trying to aid. For a "conservative," the PRWORA meant increasing social workers and their control over their cases. This was not Milton Friedman's approach to income support. Nor was it Nixon's. But it was Reagan's.

Nixon began to hear rolling thunder from the Right, while he continued to press for FAP. In a meeting on August 27, 1970, with Finch, Moynihan, Undersecretary Veneman of HEW, Shultz, and Rumsfeld, Nixon began to realize he would lose Senator Carl Curtis of Nebraska and now saw Senator Williams of Delaware emerging as the key Republican Senate opponent to his FAP.

First, the liberals had attacked Nixon, in reflex reaction, even before his plan was public. On July 31, 1969, Moynihan noted that Ted Kennedy was sending a letter to Nixon, signed by him and several other Democrats, opposing the family security system (FAP), even though it had not been announced.[14] Now it was the conservatives' turn. Trying to figure ways to blunt the opposition, Nixon and Veneman talked about a year's delay in effective date, to January 1972, saving money in the current budget, which, the president said, "was my date all along, as Ehrlichman will tell you." Nixon kept coming back to how important his welfare reform was: "Just get something done. This is the only major social reform of this Administration. We must be for it—it is not enough to blame the Senate (the Republicans blocking it)." He then ticked off the "PR" points starting with the fact that "it's reform." He admitted that it had a high starting cost but noted that there are no more "give-aways" and that it should appeal to the blue-collar workers. It would help the working poor part of the workforce with their total take home pay, which keeps them from poverty when the supplement is added to their earnings. And, said the president, "it'll work."

A few days later, on September 2, Nixon brought in Senate Finance Committee members Long, Byrd, and Ribicoff, from the Democrats, Bennett, the ranking Republican, Paul Fannin of Arizona, and Jack Miller of Iowa. With him were Moynihan, Finch, Shultz, Ehrlichman, Bill Timmons, who would soon replace Bryce Harlow as the president's liaison with Congress, Veneman, and Bob Patricelli from HEW. He told them that he knew many Republicans were "without enthusiasm" for FAP, but he argued that there was a good chance the idea would work and a certainty of difficulty under continuing AFDC as is and encouraged them to weigh the two. "The future of FAP is in this room," he said.

Chairman Russell Long told Nixon that we could get a bill, although Long emphasized that the ranking member, Republican John Williams of Delaware, was against FAP. Bennett said Williams was lining up the Republicans to oppose it. They noted the public antipathy to a "guaranteed income" and flushed up the issue that ultimately sank FAP in Senate Finance: the inability to plot a path by which FAP could be integrated with Food Stamps, Medicaid, and the Family Health Insurance Plan (FHIP), which was at this stage only a Department of HEW proposal but was about to become part of the February 1971 Nixon message to Congress on health care. But already both the department and the leaders in Senate Finance were aware of these issues of integrating the various programs for those in need. Patricelli, who was in this meeting, later in testimony before Senate Finance was stumped when asked to show how the inconsistencies or roadblocks to the amalgamation of these programs could be resolved. These were not just "notch" problems. They were "cliff" problems. You could fall right off. Williams was to ask Patricelli, "So you earn $1 more and you lose $5,560, is that right?" Given the question about a particular program interaction as they then stood, Patricelli was obliged to say, "That is correct, Senator." Paul O'Neill, Nathan's deputy at the time at the OMB, remained convinced fifty years later, as he and I talked over breakfast in a Greek diner in Pittsburgh, that the meshing could have been worked out. But the way the question was framed and its narrow focus were devastating.

This meeting of Nixon with Senate Finance leaders occurred long before the final curtain fell on FAP, but the rumblings were already clear. As some of the senators in this September 2, 1970, meeting noted, FAP was a "highly vulnerable bill."

A Salvo from the "Sunbelt" Guru

John Ehrlichman, in *Witness to Power*, says of this time, "The conservatives were militant battlers who would take my scalp . . . if I gave them half a chance. In the fall of 1970, the conservatives nearly got me."[15] Kevin Phillips on September 25 wrote a column, "Post Southern Strategy," attacking the direction of domestic policy, and argued that Nixon needed to change direction. Phillips had been among the earliest to use granular demographic data to suggest voting proclivities and targeting of issues to voters. His book that followed his work on the 1968 campaign with John Mitchell, Nixon's campaign manager, was *The Emerging Republican Majority*.[16] Nixon sent a copy of Phillips's article to John Ehrlichman with a handwritten note in the margin, saying it was a correct view and Ehrlichman should "take action to correct it." Phillips was asserting that what Ehrlichman had been leading Nixon to embrace was wrong. Nixon was looking to Ehrlichman to rebut Phillips or to acknowledge the error of Ehrlichman's ways and change course. Ehrlichman had been mystified and frustrated for a period of time during which he had heard virtually nothing from the president. Now he understood why. Nixon was being pushed by conservatives to reverse the direction he was being encouraged in by Moynihan, Ehrlichman, Finch, and George Shultz. The "Counter Reformation," as Pat Buchanan described it to me, was the conservative reaction against Eisenhower "moderation" or "moderate Republicanism." The Counter Reformation was now holding an inquisition on the heresy of Nixon's even more aggressive efforts in domestic policy.

Ehrlichman came out swinging. He responded on October 20 with a memo to the president "flatly disagreeing." In it he sought to undermine Phillips. Ehrlichman was condescending, patronizing of Phillips. He referred to Kevin as "Young Phillips." He said Phillips was trying to trap us on the Far Right and staked out a strong defense for the path Nixon was on—a path of moderation and of broad social benefit. Haldeman two days later wrote to Ehrlichman, "You really scored with that memo," and a day later Haldeman wrote to the attorney general, regarded as Phillips's main access to the administration, that "Kevin Phillips has flipped." Ehrlichman spent one and a half hours with the president on domestic policy for the first time in about ten days.[17]

During that autumn of 1970, Moynihan was slowly gliding to the moment when he would return to Harvard to resume his post. He could not help but have complicated feelings. He had won the distrust, even enmity, of academic colleagues for having come to Washington to assist Richard Nixon. At one point during his work in the Nixon White House, his family and his home in Cambridge were threatened with violence and arson by the Students for a Democratic Society (SDS). David Stockman, who was a live-in babysitter for the Moynihan children, mobilized a corps of watchers and protectors from the Harvard Divinity School to surround their house and stave off any attack. Stockman was later to serve as Ronald Reagan's director of the OMB. Moynihan and he then had a pointed duel over the Reagan tax cuts, which Stockman defended. Stockman was sitting next to Elizabeth Moynihan at the head table when Senator Moynihan gave his answer in a speech at the Gridiron Club. He characterized the cuts as efforts to "starve the beast," thereby to hollow out the federal budget for social services and other human needs by saying there was no revenue to pay for them. This was the fault line between a Nixon approach and the Reagan Republicans. Mrs. Moynihan told me that to her recollection, Pat and Stockman were to speak only once again. "When David was returning from NY and signing with his publisher—he arranged to meet with Pat on arrival in DC. He said to Pat—'How do you write a book?' and Pat said, 'In the morning.'"[18] In 1970, Moynihan was also under steady attack from the Right for the paths he encouraged Nixon to follow.

But so was Nixon, as shown by the Kevin Phillips attack that John Ehrlichman repulsed in late October. So were we more liberal staff members, as with Buchanan's abortive effort to have us publicly shrive ourselves. As Election Day approached, Nixon was also feeling rising enmity and more hostile protests from the Left. The war had not gone away, as Haldeman had so hopefully predicted it would in his memo in the early weeks of 1969, talking about resources for other concerns consequently coming available. The intensity and occasional violent behavior of anti-Nixon demonstrators showed that his imploring of the country in his inaugural address to listen to one another and lower our voices had not taken root. Nixon in his own turn became more angry and bitter that his efforts to end the war were not understood and credited.

At the very end of the midterm campaign, there was a rally in San Jose, California, held just five days before the election. The rally in a large hall had been boisterous, pro-Nixon. Outside, angry anti-Nixon crowds swirled about. The combined, sustained assault by the Right about his social initiatives, and the seething mass of yelling, pushing antagonists on the Left principally about the war, though with a good dose of plain old Nixon hate, were building to a point where Nixon yielded to his angrier, darker side. Further pushing him to an explosive outburst was the fact that he had been forced by protestors to abandon plans to attend the college graduation of his daughter, Julie, that spring, and of his son-in-law, David Eisenhower, that same week. Rennie Davis of the "Chicago Seven," who had disrupted the Democratic Convention there in 1968, Jerry Rubin, an antiwar protest leader and founder of the "Yippies," and the Black Panthers were all threatening violence if the president came for the commencement. Julie had to write to her father telling him that if he came to Smith College, it would get ugly, and she asked him to forgo being with her for graduation. For two years, he had been trying to be open, reaching out to critics. He had met with proponents of views across the spectrum. He had proposed sweeping and liberal initiatives. In his view, he was trying to exit Vietnam. Nothing seemed to avail him to gain support of the liberals or the major press newsrooms, editorial boards, or pundits. Pat Buchanan remarked on how anxious, even emotionally needy, he was for the approval and appreciation of the elites, the liberals. He was getting none. Instead, the antiwar chorus was louder and angrier. He was under relentless pressure from conservatives. He found it ever harder to hold the center.

All of these elements were swirling in Nixon. Emotionally he shifted gears and footing. With a sense almost of release, he gave way to his impulse to taunt the crowd of hostile demonstrators in San Jose. He walked, as antiwar cries and hostile jeers echoed, to his waiting motorcade and the press headed for their bus. He climbed up on the trunk of his limousine. He relished the antagonism in the air. Several of his aides, including H. R. Haldeman, stood by the car. Nixon thrust his two arms in the air with his signature "V" for Victory sign. The White House correspondent for *Newsday* was next to Haldeman, his Sony recorder in hand, and it captured Nixon, as the crowd roared with anger, when he said to Haldeman, "That's what they hate to see!" Nixon curdled at San Jose. He became what many thought he was. It was a turning point. He did pull his way up toward the "sunlit uplands" again, especially with his efforts to secure universal healthcare for the American people. But he changed.

His departing limousine was pelted with rocks, and windows of the press bus were smashed. In the campaign wrap-up television address, he invoked the San Jose violence to arouse the country against the "anti-democratic elements in society." Grizzled Nixon watchers would say he provoked it and used it.

Two of Nixon's young lieutenants agree that this was a defining moment, in some sense an inflexion point, in the Nixon presidency. Dwight Chapin, Nixon's appointments secretary during these White House years, and Tod Hullin, executive assistant to John Ehrlichman, were eyewitnesses to the event. They felt that there was an emotional shift in the president. It was not just a momentary, emotional reaction or a political tactic of capitalizing on an angry mob reaction. Chapin told my son, John Mason Price, and me in Yorba Linda on July 20, 2019, that Nixon had been very open in the first year of his presidency. As I knew, he had invited in every member of the Congress for coffee during that year. He had flooded his calendar with appointments with diverse men and women and met with groups that were not always friendly, indeed even rude and angry. For a Council for Urban Affairs (CUA) meeting in the spring of 1970, I had invited James W. Rouse in. The CUA was looking at land use and urban growth, and Rouse was the developer of the planned community of Columbia, Maryland, as well as the South Street Seaport in New York City and Faneuil Hall in Boston. The week before Rouse was to come in, John Ehrlichman called me and asked, "Is this your Jim

Rouse who has just run the Anti-Vietnam War ad in the Washington Post." I said that it was. Ehrlichman checked with Nixon, and the president agreed to go ahead and give the meeting to Rouse and his people with the whole domestic cabinet and the president. In that May 19, 1970, meeting he gave to a man who was running ads against him over Nixon's Vietnam War conduct, he even displayed humor. In a discussion of urban congestion, Nixon alluded to Goldwater's disparagement of New York in his campaign: "'I remember that in 1964 there was a solution proposed as to New York, which was to cut it loose and let it drift out to sea; but, I guess it was decided we could not do that.' (He made this allusion to Goldwater's 1964 quip with a broad grin, and a sigh as he interpreted the election result on the question)."[19]

That was not to be the case later.

Dwight told my son and me that after San Jose, Nixon altered. He grew less willing to reach out. He began to hoard his time more to himself and to reduce the array and difference in points of view of those with whom he would allow himself to be scheduled.

After the 1970 election was behind us, on November 6, I asked Pat Moynihan what he thought the election results might mean for me, and he told me that it would depend on how those results were read in the White House.

He said the President came into the Cabinet meeting yesterday looking as though he himself had been defeated. He looked down, and softly said, "Let's hear about the '72 budget" and then did nothing for almost the next hour and a half. Pat went on to say that he has concluded they won the '68 election pretty much by accident. He agrees with me that Nixon's policy awareness is amazingly good, and his judgment good, it's only the politics that hurts. Pat feels he has no influence whatsoever on that. He's right. Nor do I. And, the schizophrenia between policy and politics will get more and more unnerving, until one of them has to go, a point that Auspitz [Lee Auspitz, Ripon president] has made.[20]

Lee Auspitz at this moment wrote an article, "For a Moderate Majority," that ran at election time in *Playboy* magazine. On November 9, I was assailed by Egil "Bud" Krogh, an Ehrlichman assistant, about the Auspitz article. I defended its point about the disconnect between Nixon's policies and the election politics, and he reluctantly agreed but said, "It should not be openly discussed." I was feeling pretty lonely by now in this White House setting.

Len Garment, on November 13, gave me counsel. He told me, "The President could be going through another change of attitude. That is the remarkable thing about him—his changes. They are so natural, and they so accurately reflect the evil and the good that is in all of us, and in the country as a whole. He moves from rage to generosity, and from eloquence to something other. It's not at all like Johnson, where it was so calculated. It is just the way he is."[21]

Things did not immediately improve from the president's point of view. Despite Nixon's efforts, on November 20, Senate Finance voted against FAP 10 to 6, and an effort by the White House to attach it to a broad bill on Social Security and Medicare and Medicaid was quashed by a filibuster. The full Senate voted to recommit the bill with instructions to report out only the non-FAP pieces. The House refused to conference the bill without FAP, and it died for that Congress.

On November 23, Nixon demanded Ehrlichman and Shultz "clean out the bugs" in FAP and get a revised bill moving. On December 5, in a meeting with Ehrlichman, Shultz, Casper Weinberger, who had moved to OMB as deputy to Shultz, and Ed Harper, the president said, "The country needs to be shaken—a bold stroke. I feel strongly about FAP. . . . FAP was no help in '70 but we either get it or we are in trouble."[22]

At the very end of the year, Nixon was still struggling with FAP. On December 28, Nixon talked with Shultz and Ehrlichman saying, "They [the Leadership] should come down and commit to me personally it will come up early in the new Congress." Ron Ziegler, his press secretary, joined the meeting, and Nixon spoke of the FAP recommittal, saying it was a step to prevent a vote: "This is a motion to kill FAP. Over the weekend I discussed it with Elliot Richardson and some Members. If the Senate acts to kill FAP we must get the leadership—bi-partisan in both houses—to make FAP the first order of business."[23]

Nixon's View of Leadership

Earlier that month, on December 6, 1970, the president met with Shultz, Ehrlichman, Casper Weinberger, and Treasury Secretary John Connolly. He had tasted bile at the end of the 1970 campaign. Now he was pulling his way back up toward the mountaintop. Nixon mused that a president must get their own image and have an effect not just as a manager but also because he understands the problems and the source of people's concern and discontent and must act with compassion and concern. "The President owes it to the country," Nixon said. "What do you want to do—what mark will you leave? It is better to go whole hog. Defeat is not fatal. Leadership has to come in here." He continued, "Tidy, careful, cautious, it is the accountant's way. It is not psychologically what the US needs. They are so frustrated with government. The hell with careful."

Later in the same meeting, the president talked at length of the *Disraeli* biography by Robert Blake, which Moynihan had given him eighteen months earlier, mentioning that he had reread it the prior weekend. He concluded that Disraeli "was the ablest politician of the late 1800s in Britain. But he also was a novelist. A poet. We need a little more poetry. We need new concepts. We need something more. The more I'm here, my reading is nearly all about ideas and history. Churchill's history—his early work is best, the First World War, especially one in 1931 about the Eastern Front. It's about people. Like *War and Peace*." He closed with yet another reference to the need for "poetry" in what we do and how we narrate it.[24] Nixon had a "dreamer" or "poet" place in him, too, despite being a man of endless expedience.

On December 30, 1970, with Shultz and Ehrlichman on hand to recognize Moynihan's last day in the White House, the president said he wanted Moynihan to come down with whatever frequency he could muster and help "on the liberals." Nixon addressed three other problems. He felt we had to change the name of Family Assistance and a few other details. More urgently, he said, "Agnew must be sold." Ronald Reagan must be for it—"let him claim a scalp." Nixon was feeling the heavy weight of opposition on this issue by the California governor. There was more to come.[25]

Robert Carleson, Reagan's man, worked closely with Allan Ryskind, the co-owner and Capitol Hill editor of *Human Events* (*HE*), in opposition to FAP. Ryskind wrote to me, "We believed there was *already* a terrific answer to the skyrocketing welfare costs that were troubling to so many states: the Carleson/Reagan welfare reform in California."[26] That California welfare reform was being floated in January 1971, right after the failure of FAP in Senate Finance in December 1970. It was blocked in California by the Democrats controlling the legislature in Sacramento. They would not even allow Reagan to address the legislature on it. But Reagan's tactical response was brilliant. Reagan announced a huge and detailed proposal for change in front of City Hall on live TV in Los Angeles on March 3, 1971. He said the legislature should pass it, "or else." They did not. It had been quickly killed by the first legislative committee to look at it. The "or else" was a secret initiative petition that Carleson's group had prepared. It would be submitted to the people for signatures and then put on the ballot in the 1972 primaries in both parties. Reagan would lead the charge and there would be primary opponents in both parties. Carleson described the Reagan strategy:

> Supporters of FAP knew that if Reagan succeeded in welfare reform in California, the largest state, their efforts to nationalize welfare were dead. Therefore, we were fighting not only the Democrats in Sacramento; we were fighting the Nixon Republicans in Sacramento and Washington. This situation made a Reagan-led welfare reform initiative in the 1972 primary election a threat to all of his opponents—Democrat and Repub-

lican, state and federal. We code-named the secret initiative plan "Operation Crossfire."[27]

Even as he was seeing a mounting opposition to his centerpiece domestic policy, Nixon was seeing resistance to his revenue-sharing proposal, the other cornerstone of his New Federalism. On January 15, 1971, Nixon met with Governors Shaeffer, Nunn, and Rockefeller (this time with Agnew in the same room with the NY governor in violation of Nixon's rule not to have Agnew around Rockefeller). Also there were Finch, Rumsfeld, William Safire, and Ehrlichman. The National Governors Conference had just again called for revenue sharing. The Congressional opposition, however, was implacable. Both Ways and Means Chairman Mills and ranking Republican Byrnes were opposed, even though Nixon wanted it again to be a centerpiece of the State of the Union. Nixon ruefully observed, "Congress loves the categorical grant system"—members loved, in other words, to announce the money going to projects in their districts and to deny their governors that bragging right.

He tried to pump up the enthusiasm of the governors in the meeting, saying that revenue sharing would be more than $500 million. Then, remembering what we had told him about Rockefeller's reaction in Albany when Dick Nathan and I had spoken about what New York would get in relief under FAP, he turned to Rockefeller and said, "Smile."

Nixon's prescient forecast to Murray Kempton about Lindsay's future comes to mind. Nixon had foreseen Lindsay and Rockefeller falling out and Lindsay becoming a Democrat. The governor, talking of New York City's welfare rolls still going up thirty thousand per month, said of Lindsay, "Let's just get a good movie for our mayor—get him out of there!" Nixon said, "Maybe the Supreme Court?" and Rockefeller said, "No. Just a good movie [to get him to act in]."[28]

But Family Assistance still was the center of the president's concern. The constant attacks from the Right and the lack of support from the liberals were chipping away at Nixon's resolve about Family Assistance. On March 30, Ehrlichman noted Nixon musing that "welfare reform is a winner, FAP a loser." He conceded that Reagan was having a "good play." Nixon saw hardening the work requirement as politically safer; he said "meaningful" work should be out, "for sure," and everyone should take any open job. Nixon and Ehrlichman tried to persuade themselves that FAP was not a guaranteed income, as they prepared to meet with the California governor the next day.

On April Fool's Day, Nixon met with Governor Reagan, along with Secretary Richardson and Director Weinberger of the OMB, who had been in Reagan's administration in Sacramento. The next day, April 2, marked a turning point for Nixon on his welfare proposal. He was almost ready to throw in his cards. Nixon said to Ehrlichman and Haldeman that "we're on a bad wicket, and Reagan is on a good one." He saw "work," and attitudes toward it by the public, as the key issue politically supporting Reagan's approach. The conservatives coalesced in opposition to FAP. Through the spring there was a drumbeat from *Human Events*, the Heritage Foundation, Paul Weyrich (a mobilizer of conservative funding), and the American Conservative Union, all protesting FAP. In the House, the Right, led by Congressman Sam Devine, tried to choke FAP by getting an "open" rule on bringing Mills's H.R. 1 to the floor. Devine wanted to "roll Wilbur Mills" since Devine "can't take FAP."[29]

Soon the president was pushed even harder by the Right. The conservatives found grievance not only in Nixon's FAP but also in his trade policy, his negotiations with the Soviets over Strategic Arms, and his initial moves toward Communist China and apparent abandonment of Taiwan, which had been a bedrock relationship for the Republicans after the Democrats "lost China" in the late 1940s.

Still, Allan Ryskind told me, "FAP was the biggest domestic bone in our throats." Because of broad conservative dyspepsia about Nixon, they begin to coordinate. Ryskind described the cohering of resistance in the form of the "Manhattan Twelve."

> So a number of conservatives . . . encouraged John Ashbrook, a prominent conservative congressman from Ohio, to run against Nixon in the 1972 GOP primary . . . *National Review* editor William F. Buckley was coaxed into this rebellious contingent, and a number of us, the so-called Manhattan 12, wound up in New York at *NR's* headquarters to issue a statement on July 26, 1971, "suspending support" of Nixon, which was rightly seen as an encouraging signal to Rep. John Ashbrook, the prominent Ohio Republican conservative, to challenge Nixon in the 1972 GOP presidential primaries. . . . Buckley decided to rewrite [the initial "declaration"] reorienting the group's resentment more toward foreign policy than domestic policy, which caused me plenty of grief.[30]

The Ashbrook threat was important in the White House calculations. Pat Buchanan was tasked with reaching out through Allan Ryskind to the "Twelve" and did so in December 1971. In a memo to the attorney general and H. R. Haldeman of December 3, 1971, Buchanan reported on the latest gathering of the Manhattan Twelve and noted that among the anti-Nixon hawks who could not, "under conceivable circumstances, be brought back into the fold" was William Rusher.[31] Buchanan understood how furious the anger was on the Right about FAP. "FAP, and its successor, Big FAP, as Human Events called it . . . was always an irritant with the Right. They wanted it dead. It was Moby Dick."[32]

It was agreed that Ryskind would come to the White House soon after the New Year and meet with Charles Colson, who would be coordinating with Ehrlichman and others, as many of the demands were about the defense budget and for Nixon to keep Spiro Agnew as his vice president. In an end of year memo, Charles "Chuck" Colson reported back to Buchanan that the attorney general had said there was a major need to "care and feed" the conservatives. "He thinks we have substantively neglected our own constituency. . . . Obviously our strategy with respect to FAP is a key item."[33]

Ashbrook was willing to cool his heels, "though [he was] chomping at the bit to challenge Nixon . . . and would be willing to at least look at the Colson offer before he charged into the primaries."[34]

> We could not ask Ashbrook to withdraw unless the Administration gave us an iron-clad pledge to sink FAP, since we couldn't assure Ashbrook that Long had the clout or the conviction to keep the legislation buried. Indeed, Jeff [Bell] came up with a unique idea: The Administration, he said, should publicly declare it would no longer press Republicans to fasten Nixon's guaranteed annual income plan on the entire country, but that, in exchange for this concession, the Congress would have to agree to fund a pilot FAP program in the District of Columbia. The Administration turned the idea down.

But it met the underlying demand. The White House was concerned that "'those nuts in California' might go for Ashbrook (Buchanan's phrase, for he too recalled Joe Shell's devastating shots against Nixon in 1962)."[35] Nixon finally threw in his cards on FAP.

> They decided to give the conservatives the three concessions that Colson had offered from the beginning: Agnew, an increase in defense spending, and permitting Long to bury FAP in his committee. Looking back, I think the Ashbrook challenge—which I felt was an extremely dubious idea—paid off, even though Ashbrook received about half the votes that the more liberal Pete McCloskey got. From my point of view, the death of FAP was worth the disappointment of the Ohio conservative.[36]

The real stake through the heart of FAP was driven by Ronald Reagan. He appeared before Senate Finance on February 2, 1972, at the same time the negotiations were proceeding with the "Twelve." According to Bob Carleson, who sat with him at the witness table, Reagan proposed "a long list of legislative changes—opposed by the income redistribution establishment." He then criticized FAP as a "guaranteed income." Reagan's criticisms hit the mark with Long, and Long borrowed Bob Carleson once a month for the rest of the year in helping to draft—or deflect—legislation for Senate Finance on welfare.[37]

The intransigent opposition of conservative groups in the Manhattan Twelve centered on FAP. That and Reagan's steady and public opposition meant that Nixon could not carry the Republicans in the Congress for his reform. He had no support from the liberals. Hopes for FAP's success were fading. It was becoming an orphan, and Nixon's sense of political reality told him it was over. With a taste of bitterness, Nixon met with Ehrlichman about FAP on April 21, 1972, and told him, "Flush it! Blame it on the budget."[38]

It would not, after all, be his Monument.

FAP finally died in Senate Finance on October 4, 1972. I had left the White House almost a year earlier. That day, I was in Syracuse, New York, at the university, debating Nixon/McGovern with Dean Campbell of the Maxwell School of Government. I wrote later in a letter to Vee Burke, "I walked out in time to see the evening news on a television set in the lobby of the G.E. office building in which the debate had been held, and saw Senator Long's smug smile. My heart sank."[39]

Reagan had claimed his scalp.

So, the curtain fell on Nixon's push for Family Assistance. The 1972 campaign against George McGovern featured a replay of some of the issues debated in the White House in 1969. Nixon harshly attacked McGovern, who embraced a full European-style "Family Allowance" of the type that had so long appealed to Moynihan. McGovern called it a "demo-grant." He would give every man, woman, and child an annual grant of $1,000. It suffered the vulnerabilities that I in January 1969 had told Moynihan would preclude Republican support: the cost was stratospheric, and the inefficiency in reaching the poor was demonstrable. McGovern lived to rue his embrace of it, saying he wished he'd never heard of it.

When conservatives announced their "Suspension of Support" for Nixon on August 7, 1971, *Human Events* wrote, "Today we fear the President . . . advocating policies at almost total variance with conservative sentiment on the domestic front (the Family Assistance Plan being the most glaring example)."[40]

The tone was to change after the 1972 election. Looking back after Nixon's January 1973 inaugural and budget message, Jeffrey Bell, a leading conservative, said,

For me, the last four years were the most politically unpleasant in 11 years of . . . constant activism. . . . Now, rather suddenly, the clouds are beginning to lift. . . . The Nixon budget for FY 1974 does not, for the first time in four years, mention the Family Assistance Plan. . . . On a single page of the [budget message] . . . he mentions five times the need not to raise federal taxes.[41]

Bell continued,

[Nixon] . . . is less an opportunist than an enthusiast; in his first term he was enthusiastic about FAP. . . . The evidence is that Nixon is a man easily excited by ideas, both good and bad. The tragedy of the first term lay partly in the fact that liberals like . . . Pat Moynihan were the first to see this. . . . Moynihan told Nixon he could became a latter-day Disraeli, the Tory man of liberal measures, passing domestic schemes too radical for any Democrat to contemplate. . . . Nixon *was* enthusiastic about FAP.[42]

Accurately summing up Nixon's steady if ever more frustrated effort to get Family Assistance, Bell concludes, "The truth is that for two solid years and part of a third, Nixon and his government worked very hard, and not at all incompetently, to achieve enactment of a guaranteed income."[43]

"Big FAP"

In the election year, the president's political instinct had told him that FAP was a dead-end. Pat Buchanan, in an email to me, sums it up well: "By 1972, RN was prepared to Deep Six it, . . . knew it no longer had political juice for him, and thus the deal with the Manhattan Twelve was easy to cut: Keep Agnew, which RN had decided to do, abandon FAP which was in trouble anyway, and increase for defense."[44] But another look at FAP was taken by a new secretary of HEW, Casper Weinberger, when he took over in February 1973. There was a touch of irony in Weinberger's interest in FAP. Weinberger had served as Governor Reagan's director of finance and had been familiar with FAP as early as Nixon's briefing of Reagan in August 1969. Weinberger had early and deep ties to Nixon as well, having been appointed by Nixon as Republican state chairman in California in 1962, as Nixon sought the governorship. Weinberger brought William Howard Taft IV to HEW as his chief of staff, Taft having worked with Weinberger in key roles in the secretary's prior positions in the Nixon administration, including at OMB. Knowing well how influential Bob Carleson was on Governor Reagan, Weinberger brought Carleson in as welfare commissioner of the United States in 1973. "We tried to co-opt him!" Will Taft told me, ruefully, as Taft and I recalled the time.[45] What had changed was Watergate.

There commenced a reprise of the FAP initiative. Frank Carlucci was, in autumn 1973, the deputy to Weinberger, in only one of the many key domestic and national security jobs he held, up to and including national security advisor, then secretary of defense under Reagan. Frank had become a close friend, and on a trip up to see me in New York, he told me in October that "in a perverse way Watergate has been good from the viewpoint of the Department, since it has given them more autonomy, but in . . . the next breath he indicated some concern that the scandal was paralyzing the White House to the extent that it would not be possible to get a program decision out of the president."[46] The talk then turned to welfare reform. What he then told me addressed many of the questions that had caused FAP's demise in the Senate a year earlier.

> Frank showed me an October 20th draft memo from Cap Weinberger to the President, which had been prepared by Mr. Morrill, the new assistant secretary for policy. Frank said that only the three of them and now the four of us were aware of it. It is a call for sweeping welfare reform in the form, at last, of a pure negative income tax. They had arranged a long session with Milton Friedman, which they found fascinating, and convincing. The memo recognizes the problem of mere categorical welfare reform, and proposes a federal floor of around $3,000 [double the floor level of the original Nixon proposal] with a marginal tax rate of 50 per cent. The idea is to be able to eliminate other forms of in kind or welfare assistance, such as food stamps and housing. States could supplement as they could under FAP.[47]

I was delighted, and I told Carlucci of a letter I had sent to Melvin Laird earlier in the summer, pointing out the notch problems that FAP had suffered from. Cashing out or otherwise integrating these other programs, would ease the problem. Medicaid (I was not aware of the pending health proposals by Nixon), Food Stamps, and housing allowances were all needing to be pulled together into a real statement of need.

The new HEW memo also faced the issue of the work requirement head-on. Nixon had mused a couple of years back about how training might be illusory unless a job was waiting. He grasped the need for there to be jobs and had flirted with the idea of a government role in providing jobs if there were none in the private sector with which people could be linked. This memo "concluded that any work requirement would be largely an exercise in futility unless it were accompanied by a program guaranteeing jobs."[48] I recalled my initial feeling against the work requirement, "but, having gone before [Cong.] Sam Devine's group . . . on the Hill with Bryce and our road show team one fine afternoon, I appreciated the president's political wisdom of having insisted on the work requirement, so that Bryce could say, 'This is not a guaranteed income."[49] But work requirements would be empty with no jobs to be filled.

Simultaneously, Secretary James Lynn, of the Department of Housing and Urban Development (HUD), was asking that the housing message, itself about to go up, tie housing allowances to a suggestion for a much broader welfare reform. The president went round and round, and some ten days before the message finally went up,

> Lynn managed to build a head of steam into the president, who immediately insisted that Moynihan be brought back into the picture. Pat started drafting and did a five- or six-page section of the message, which Lee Huebner said was excellent. At this point, however, our old nemesis, Bryce Harlow, reappeared and much like Banquo's ghost, caused the loss of appetite. . . . He and Haig, alternating with Cole, played the heavies, against the broader construction. . . . Over the weekend [when Harlow flew with the president to Key Biscayne] their view prevailed, but the first of the week, Weinberger managed to see the president, and once again there was a signal, though more muted, of his desire to try something broader. At this point, Harlow and Haig again, with Cole, began trying to turn it back. Without saying that they had the approval of the president, but that he was just terribly busy, and could not get into it personally, they changed the entire emphasis and direction. In the last day, mainly Cole was trying to counter Jim Lynn's strong representations. At least twice in that last day, Jim got up and threatened resignation.[50]

I was puzzled by the absence of Laird in these discussions. And I was discouraged by the repeated sabotage by Harlow of something the president had given clear indications not only that he favored, but that he felt might be important to him politically since it was large and bold. I told Carlucci of the undercutting role that Bryce had played in 1969 and 1970, of his reaction to my briefing him, and of the next Saturday morning at the summit meeting in the Cabinet Room when he made his remark about the entire Republican establishment rising up and running the president out of town if he sent this proposal to the Congress. "Frank recognizes that in order to get the president's approval, he and Cap must somehow circumvent Harlow."[51]

The reprise of the Family Assistance Plan, "Big FAP" as the Right termed it, failed. The efforts to enrich its levels and to connect it with other safety net programs, eliminating many of the flaws that led it earlier to collapse in the Senate, were thwarted. Instead, Weinberger and the president were to pivot back to health care and dramatically enhance Nixon's February 1971 proposals for universal health coverage. Here, they nearly made history together.

CHAPTER 16

Richard Nixon and a Health Strategy

Senator Robert Dole of Kansas overcame heavy odds to rise in American politics—chief among which was surviving World War II. His right arm had been mangled in combat, requiring a lengthy and agonizing convalescence, and he never recovered the use of it. He took to placing a pencil in his right hand to deflect proffered handshakes. One of the weapons he kept after the war was wit. Dole was spontaneous, often succumbing to the temptation of an easy laugh line. If a target popped up, he drew and shot. In 1991, Egyptian leader Anwar Sadat had been assassinated, and President Bush dispatched three of his predecessors to his funeral, former presidents Ford, Carter, and a reemergent Richard Nixon. At a Gridiron dinner in DC soon after their return, Dole referred to the three as "See no evil. Hear no evil. And evil."

Three years later, Dole was present for the state funeral service and interment, at his childhood California home, of Richard Nixon. On that occasion, in a tear-streaked farewell, Dole said of Nixon, "He leap-frogged the conventional wisdom to propose revolutionary solutions to health care and welfare reform, anticipating by a full generation the debates now raging on Capitol Hill." Dole was speaking at Nixon's graveside in 1994. The Republican leader, who was to be his party's presidential nominee against Clinton in two years, spoke then as the Clinton health-care proposals were being aired before a skeptical Congress. Those few elements of Clinton's that were enacted owe their lineage to Richard Nixon's strategy and proposals on health care. Many years later, the Affordable Care Act under President Barack Obama passed without a single Republican vote. Since that moment, we have been subjected to a decade of denigration by Republicans of "Obamacare." But Obamacare's core features had been advanced by Richard Nixon nearly a half century before.

In their book *The Heart of Power: Health and Politics in the Oval Office*, David Blumenthal and James A. Morone say of the groundbreaking nature of Nixon's ideas that "he left a richer health policy legacy than almost any other president."[1] Nixon's efforts at broadening health insurance and expanding the kinds of coverage and care, his push to place doctors and health services into underserved inner cities and rural areas, and his intense focus on a cure for cancer secure his place in the pantheon of the most determined and committed presidents in health policy.

In Nixon's first year as president, the Family Assistance Plan became his early domestic priority. Nixon was a relative latecomer to issues and politics of welfare and public assistance, but he was not so with health policy, where he had a much longer history and deep understanding. Nixon had a visceral empathy for those families overwhelmed by serious health problems and by the emotional and financial carnage they brought. Nixon, upon leaving the White House, emotionally referred to his mother, Hannah, as a "saint." He and the rest of the family had to get along without her for long durations, when she went with Richard's brothers to a sanatorium in Arizona, in the vain hope that their tuberculosis would be cured. Both died. They had no health insurance. She had to tend to other invalids in order to pay for her sons' treatments. This had a potent emotional effect on the young Richard Nixon. It gave him a deep understanding of families with insufficient means to care for their loved ones' illnesses. Dr. James Cavanaugh, who worked on Nixon's health-care proposals, tells of many meetings he was in with Nixon in which the president would at length speak of the strain of his brothers' illnesses and deaths.[2]

Apart from his personal and emotional awareness of what it meant to have no health insurance, Nixon's attitudes were further shaped by his involvement in the far-reaching changes to health care and health insurance enacted or attempted under Dwight Eisenhower. On Eisenhower's watch, one of the two most significant postwar decisions in health policy occurred. Ike oversaw the creation of the most expansive health care and private insurance coverage of the latter twentieth century: employer-sponsored insurance (ESI).

The medium for the reshaping of health insurance of Ike's time was the Internal Revenue Code—the tax law. In 1954, the Eisenhower administration, as part of a wholesale overhaul of the code, clarified and expanded the availability of tax deductions—and freedom from tax liability—of employers offering and employees receiving health insurance. Eisenhower's characteristic budgetary constraint was abandoned—but that was concealed. This was a "tax expenditure," not a line in the budget showing "outlays." Nearly everybody was happy. The private health insurance market was the means for coverage, not a single-payer government program nor a mixed private program with a public provider option. Medicare still lay in the future. The Eisenhower expansion through ESI of health coverage did provide a crucial sense of economic security. Jobs were more stable then. Unions were more powerful, representing as they did a much larger percent of the total workforce, and supported this employer approach.

Still left out were the elderly, the unemployed, and the indigent. At the apogee of the New Deal, in 1934 and 1935, Harry Hopkins was at Roosevelt's side and urged that Roosevelt do both social insurance (Social Security) and health coverage, but the health issue did not animate FDR. Nearly a decade on, Senator Wagner of New York, Senator James Murray of Montana, and, in the House, John Dingell of Michigan, teamed up on a health-care bill with coverage for all. It was structured as a contributory plan, to be administered by the federal government. The liberals at the time opposed programs directed at the poor only, worrying it would drain support or reduce pressure for a universal plan. Roosevelt was willing to separate care for the poor from everybody else. Truman, his successor in 1945, was not.[3] Truman favored a complete federal program of health care for all.

Nixon first stepped into the health-care debates in 1949, when Harry Truman, after his unexpected reelection in 1948, was again trying to promote his vision of universal, federally run health care. Congressman Richard Nixon, in only his second term, joined the most liberal member of his party in the House, his colleague, New York's Jacob K. Javits, and two liberal Republican senators, Ralph Flanders of Vermont and Irving Ives of New York, in introducing a private insurance system that would cover all, regardless of whether they could afford the premiums.

Nixon did not align himself on health with the conservative lion, Robert Taft, in Taft's constrained response to Truman's proposal of fully federal-funded and managed medical care. Taft's route was to allow the states to point the way, at their own pace and with their own often-meager percentage of participants in health insurance programs. Taft's approach of the 1940s has eerie similarities to the preference of Republicans after their takeover of the House of Representatives in the sweep election of 1994 and, more recently, in the first decades of the twenty-first century. Taft would defer to the states and oppose a leading federal role in health insurance in prescribing eligibility or benefits. Speaker Newt Gingrich in the 1990s led Republican efforts to provide block grants of funding to the states for them to do with what they wished in health care for the needy. These moves to abdicate a federal responsibility for defining eligibility and requiring minimum benefits, which also greatly reduced funding for Medicaid, were vetoed by President Clinton. In more recent years, the efforts of Republicans have likewise been deferential to the states, much like the Taft approach.

Nixon, in clear distinction to the Taft and regular Republican approach, was not passive or willing to accept holes and gaps in eligibility or benefits. Rather, in the 1940s, he was a marquee name on activist legislation with Republican liberals. Theirs was an aggressive alternative, using the private sector, to a government-does-all proposal. It assumed a far more meaningful role for the federal government in standard setting than did the Taft formula. From this, authors Blumenthal and Morone conclude, "This was the first intimation that the ambiguous Nixon would eventually stand alongside Harry

Truman—two presidents who cared about health care, failed to win their own signature program, and yet decisively shaped the policy debates long after their troubled days in the White House."[4]

Despite their differences in geography—California and New York—and the fact that Javits was the most liberal of the Republican members of Congress, Nixon and he were on good terms. They had both entered the House of Representatives in the postwar 1946 elections, along with Jack Kennedy, and all did so as veterans; Nixon and Kennedy in the navy; Javits rising to Lt. Colonel in the army in his four years serving in the Chemical Warfare Department. As Thomas Dewey and his shotgun, Herbert Brownell, did, Javits had entered the Republican Party as a reformer, in opposition to the corruption of the Tammany Hall Democrats in New York City.

Javits represented the West side of Manhattan, a very liberal redoubt. It became even more so with Democrats William Ryan and then the larger-than-life Bella Abzug taking the one-time Javits House seat. Abzug was the incumbent at the time of Nixon's inauguration in 1969. She was later defeated by Daniel Patrick Moynihan in a bruising primary in 1976 for the Democratic nomination for US senator.

Javits was a self-made man and had a drive, intelligence, and tenacity a great deal like Nixon's. Like Nixon, Javits had ascended from an inauspicious beginning, on the edge of poverty as the child of poor immigrants on New York's Lower East Side. His mother supplemented the family income by peddling ribbons from a pushcart. Unlike his fellow Jewish Republican colleague, Louis J. Lefkowitz, who earned the accolade, "The Peoples' Attorney General" with a combination of diffidence and folksiness, Javits was not one to hide his mental gifts under a bushel. Nor was he affable and backslapping. He was brilliant and he was serious.

Javits also was a vote getter. In his four Senate elections, he racked up record-setting margins of victory; in two instances, more than a million votes separated him from his opponent. Despite his outlying liberal positions for a Republican—both in the House and later in the Senate—Nixon held him in high regard. Javits was industrious and thoughtful, a good man to have on your side. On October 2, 1969, according to notes John Ehrlichman made, the president, while discussing court appointments with Senate Republican Leader Hugh Scott, said of the New York senator, "He is very intelligent—a fighter." These qualities drew Nixon to Javits, as they were features of his own makeup of which he was proud. Javits was a party man. He believed the Republicans should have a broad church, and he was defiantly not a Democrat. Javits had opposed funding for the House Un-American Activities Committee when Nixon was finding his path to prominence, as he exposed Alger Hiss through its work. But Javits was also an internationalist, as was

Congressman Nixon and President Nixon. Nixon did not regard Javits as one of those New Yorkers who lived on an island (Manhattan) that Barry Goldwater said in 1964 should be sawed off, floated out to sea, and sunk.

In 1954, a decade before the conservative electoral catastrophe in the North, the Eisenhower administration had a landmark year for efforts to broaden health care insurance coverage. Beyond the sweeping expansion of employer-sponsored insurance, which extended coverage to millions of employed, often unionized workers whose leadership had bargained for the benefit, Eisenhower also sought in that year to find a path toward protection for the elderly. He proposed a "reinsurance" plan that would backstop private insurers' coverage of the elderly. He encountered a wall of opposition from the American Medical Association and from the insurance industry itself, which claimed that the actuarial job of pricing the risk was nearly impossible. Another reason for their opposition was that their industry was regulated by state insurance departments and they feared this would be a first step toward regulation of their industry by the federal government, in their view a less pliant or supportive overseer.

Ike's plan lost by a single vote in the United States Senate. He tried another tack. The new Eisenhower plan carried the name "Medicare Program for the Aged." Senator Jacob Javits of New York introduced the Eisenhower bill, once again finding himself teaming up with Vice President Richard Nixon, who was leading the administration effort. Ike's bill would give federal grants to the states and, matched by them, give money to elderly, lower-income Americans to pay for private health insurance coverage. The name survived, but Ike did not succeed in passing the bill.

A diverse group damned the proposal: The AFL-CIO (organized labor) was opposed to the states' roles and wanted to keep pressure on employers to provide retirement medical coverage. The AMA (organized medicine) opposed it. The emerging conservative icon, Barry Goldwater, of Arizona, who was gathering visibility as the next Robert Taft, but even more of a heartthrob for conservatives, opposed it.

Jack Kennedy, once elected, attempted a Medicare bill—a government-managed program, but adopting Ike's name for it—and failed. Lyndon Johnson, as he did with Kennedy's unsuccessful results on his civil rights bills, took Medicare and Medicaid and saw them through to success. Johnson then gave Harry Truman recognition in the late evening of the former president's life. He went to the aging Truman's home in Independence, Missouri, and there signed into law H.R. 4 and S. 4, the bills creating Medicare and Medicaid.

Once the demand for services induced by Medicare and Medicaid's passage had spurted, costs of care skyrocketed. As Daniel Sledge notes, "Grounded in a retrospective payment system, Medicare invited an almost inevitable inflation of medical costs."[5] Nixon was the first president to be in office when the full effect of these important Great Society initiatives came into play, and the urgency of containing the costs of these "entitlements" was felt. Not only Medicare and Medicaid saw escalating prices. The overall costs of medical care when Nixon took office had been increasing at a rate of 11 percent per year for the prior three years. Cost control was therefore very much on Nixon's mind and a prompt for one of the most significant initiatives he took in the health arena. In fact, it was the element of his 1971 health-care proposals that did first become law and was built upon in later administrations, especially Clinton's and Obama's.

A further prompt for the Nixon administration to look more closely at the financing of health care came from the crafting of his welfare reform proposal of 1969: the Family Assistance Plan (FAP). There was a need to integrate with, displace, or otherwise take account of connection with things like food stamps, low-income-housing assistance, and Medicaid, the new Great Society health insurance plan for the indigent.[6]

Politics and Ted Kennedy Intrude

Apart from the costs and policy requirements of FAP and other economic security proposals, politics was always present. I was in the Cabinet Room on December 18, 1969, along with the president, Moynihan, Finch, Ehrlichman, George Shultz, Don Rumsfeld, Dick Nathan, and Ed Morgan, at a meeting to sort out the relations between OEO and the other domestic departments. Talk turned away from OEO. "The President said, 'Let me digress. Health is going to be the next big push. Teddy Kennedy has a bill and Wilbur Mills has a bill on private insurance. I notice lately there have been full page ads in the papers on research in the area. Rather than a squeaky wheel, let's have a strategy approach. I want all of you to do some real strategy thinking. I would rather do some things very, very poorly and others very, very well, than have all of them done in a mediocre way."[7] This meeting moved health care up in priority. In the same meeting, in late December 1969, Nixon complained to us that we were facing all sorts of mandatory expenditures, and if so, "all our initiatives are gone. As to Family Assistance—they've already spent it. They don't want it."[8]

Over at HEW, there had been a vacuum on health policy. There was no assistant secretary for health, since the candidate favored by Finch and Veneman, John Knowles, the head of the Harvard Medical School, was not acceptable to the White House owing to his support of the Kennedy bill Nixon mentioned. Knowles was involved with the Committee of 100, fighting along with the United Automobile Workers (UAW) to secure passage of the Kennedy bill. That bill, as Lew Butler described it, was "not just a single payer system[;] it was getting close to a British system, where the United States would have clinics and all the rest of it."[9] The AMA opposed Knowles; the California Republican congressman who chaired the House Republican Campaign Committee opposed him. The coup de grace was that finally, deep in 1969, Senator Everett McKinley Dirksen, the Republican leader in the Senate, opposed him. Lew Butler said he had been doing Knowles's job because "we did not have Knowles." They finally arm-twisted an affable, qualified substitute into taking the job. Roger Egeberg was a six-foot-three Norwegian American who happened to be both the dean of the University of Southern California Medical School and a registered Democrat (this was unknown to Veneman and Butler, as they had not asked). He had been General Douglas MacArthur's personal physician all through the war in the Pacific. Egeberg was more interested in things medical about the job, so Lew Butler continued to be in charge of health insurance and delivery. Having fought so hard to keep Knowles from the appointment, the White House acceded to Egeberg.

They were struggling. "We weren't getting anywhere. . . . We were trying to have a health component to our welfare reform, called the Family Health Insurance Plan, but that was getting us into all kinds of trouble because it meant expanding Medicaid—Medi-Cal in California—and we just didn't have a solution." Butler wrote a private paper for Ehrlichman explaining why we needed a national health policy but couldn't get there. Butler and Ehrlichman had a relationship stemming from Stanford Law School, where they were classmates and were partners in moot court finals. This link had proved most helpful in keeping Ehrlichman close as HEW was encouraging the adoption of Family Assistance. It proved equally helpful during the consideration of health care. As Butler noted, Ehrlichman and he were not close[10] friends, but "everything I suggested to him, he took seriously."[11]

HEW pulled in Martin Feldstein, a health economist and later an economic advisor to President Ronald Reagan. Feldstein favored a limited intervention: simply coverage of catastrophic illnesses. Butler says that Finch and Veneman initially almost recommended that. It would be the narrow path down which the powerful Democratic chair of Senate Finance, Louisiana senator Russell Long, would drive.

In California and a few other places, there had emerged, in nonprofit form, organizations whose structures and incentives were to encourage cost-containment. Nixon met with Edgar Kaiser early in 1970, the principal in the Kaiser Permanente prepaid group practice entity. His argument appealed to Nixon: build an incentive structure that emphasizes keeping a patient well, not hospital bound. Preventive attention and care will contain costs.

At about the same time, the hyperkinetic Tom Joe brought to Butler's and Veneman's attention Paul Ellwood, who was doing health research in the

Twin Cities. There was a congruence between what Edgar Kaiser told Nixon in their meeting of early 1970 and what Ellwood was modeling and experimenting with. Butler says they began meeting clandestinely, because even Butler's own staff at HEW was antipathetic. He and Ellwood would meet on Saturdays in a hotel on Dupont Circle. Ellwood was persuasive about organized medical care and prepaid plans, which were to contain costs via their emphasis on preventive care. A fixed prepayment would be the premium that would pay for all care. The incentive then was for the doctors and their practices to focus on early identification and treatment of illness, which, theoretically, would decrease reliance on more costly treatments, such as ever-more-complex diagnostic testing, and then hospitalization.

Ellwood and Butler stayed connected on the health policy front, and later formed the Jackson Hole Group, convening people interested in health policy. They organized it with Alain Enthoven, who had been Robert McNamara's assistant secretary of defense for systems analysis until 1969 and who later returned when Hillary Clinton started her study group in 1993 for her husband on health-care proposals.

Butler and Finch sprang the idea of health maintenance in a speech Finch gave while he was still secretary, so health maintenance, later Health Maintenance Organizations, began as an early, if as yet unconnected, element of a Nixon administration health strategy. Secretary Finch suffered a mild stroke in late spring 1970 while confronting a tumultuous meeting of welfare (NWRO) activists and HEW employees. Fearing for his health, the president brought him to the White House as a counselor and had his own physician, Dr. Walter Tkach, take over Finch's care. Nixon worried that "the pressure was tearing him apart."[12]

While Nixon showed compassion for his friend, John Ehrlichman was a little more tart. A man of considerable wit, Ehrlichman often delivered his witticisms with an edge to them. He and I were talking at the end of an exhausting weekend at Camp David, on June 16–17, 1970, during which the whole Ehrlichman staff was fashioning the relationship the Domestic Council would have with the OMB. Both were to spring into being on July 1, 1970. Of Finch, Ehrlichman said:

> Be tolerant of his inability to be part of a process. Be patient with it. He will call a meeting of truckers and the Mayor of Indianapolis. Just quietly dismantle the meeting and tell everybody to go home. On the campaign, if you were going to the Redwoods, Finch would line up two fundraisers, a speech and an overnight at some prominent Republican's. And not tell you about it. Just as you were landing in Humboldt County, he'd pull it out of his briefcase.[13]

Finch thought he was going to be called "Senior Counsellor" upon arriving at the White House. Counsellor was what he was announced as. Thus, he joined Arthur Burns, Bryce Harlow, and Daniel Patrick Moynihan—and later Donald Rumsfeld—with that title. Maurice Mann, who came with George Shultz to run OMB, had breakfast with me on June 30, 1970. "Maury cracked that the president was turning Camp David into a summer camp, and already had all his Counsellors hired. He wondered only about the Junior Counsellors at this point."[14]

Elliot Richardson was immediately shifted from undersecretary of state to head HEW, to start in late June. He was therefor to be a member of the Council for Urban Affairs, and I would be working closely with him, so, on June 6, 1970:

> I talked to Elliot and he said he was looking forward to being part of my group. I mentioned that I had first heard his praises sung by Rod Perkins years ago about the job he had done at HEW, and that he was coming in also with an interest in health, which I have been pushing, feeling it is the next major political issue. He said he had managed to keep up with it in detail until about 1965, as Lt. Gov. [of Massachusetts].
>
> It occurred to me that one of the interesting interpersonal relations to watch over the next year will be that of Volpe and Elliot, since Volpe is a proud man, and Elliot had been his subordinate before; here, however, Elliot's intellectual capacity will be so much on view that it may cause Volpe some discomfort.[15]

This was exactly the time when Nixon's Domestic Council was to launch on July 1. The Domestic Council was authorized by statute, unlike the Council for Urban Affairs, which had been started eighteen months earlier with strokes of Nixon's pens three days after his inauguration. As one of its first acts, the Domestic Council created a committee on health care. Ehrlichman's Ed Morgan was put in charge of staff work to support the group. Morgan was a high school and college basketball player, collegial, witty, and competent. He enjoyed the full confidence of Ehrlichman, and all of Ehrlichman's campaign road assistants now turned into policymakers and desk men at the White House to oversee the departments. They had high regard for Ed and enjoyed a bonhomie with him.

We held a staff retreat at Camp David in late June. We concluded that the health study was to begin immediately, but the approach was "not a White House working group concept. Elliot [Richardson] intends to make this a model for policy development within the department."[16] This so-called "lead agency" approach was in part to defer to Richardson as he took hold of HEW.

Concurrently, Ed Morgan's group was at work, trying to understand what was going on at HEW. Morgan drew in a gaggle of senior and junior Domestic Council staff. Then it morphed into a "working group," chaired by Dick Nathan of the Office of Management and Budget. As of July 1, as with the Domestic Council, the OMB sprang to life. The ever-cautioning Martin Anderson was put in charge of an Economics Review Group on Health Policy, supported by Ray Waldmann and some economists.

The "lead agency" approach failed, at least in Ehrlichman's and Morgan's eyes. Seven overall approaches were mooted by HEW, ranging in price from $1 billion to $30 billion. They had been winnowed from hundreds down to sixty-odd unrelated specifics. Within the department, Butler says, there was confusion. Among the ideas they considered was a "sort of universal Medicare, which was there as a straw man, because we knew the White House didn't want it, and we didn't want it." They were on the verge of recommending only catastrophic illness coverage, letting "everybody else cover themselves." But then, Butler notes,

> [They] moved in the direction of mandating that employers provide health insurance to their employees. . . . General Electric and all the auto workers were getting that, but we wanted to extend that through the country. And then because it would put a burden on low income—small employers, then we wanted to have a subsidy for small employers. And then as part of it, we knew we had to regulate health insurance, which was state regulated. That was this huge package.[17]

On November 11, Nixon met with Secretary Richardson, Finch, Shultz, Morgan, and Ehrlichman. George Shultz pointed out that we were spending more money as a percent of GNP than other countries and getting worse results in positive medical outcomes. Fifty years later, this is still the case. Richardson was pushing for a more orderly consideration of the moving parts of a health strategy. He eschewed what he called a "plug the gap" strategy and said we needed to see the interrelationships of all the parts, of prevention, education, and delivery, including personnel, facilities, and financing. He focused on coverage for the "poor's care and blue collar and catastrophic costs."

Richardson observed that the call by the Committee of 100 (backing the Kennedy "single payer" approach) for national health insurance would require leveraging a huge federal establishment to change the system. He argued that we needed to design levers for opening up the market by using federal dollars for Kaiser or other revolutionary types of care.

After lengthy discussion, Nixon said he wanted to see a whole presentation and understand the arguments. He said, "We need a Brandeis brief," a reference to Supreme Court Justice Louis Brandeis and the convention of exhaustively examining the facts and arguments. Nixon was a man who united the detailed grip of the attorney with the larger scope of the statesman. The president said, "It can't be a dime-store New Deal program. We have to demolish them on the facts and take a new approach." He said we must not "mis-step" like Medicaid, for which, he reminded us, there were no congressional hearings.

A month later, on December 11, the president, vice president, and an "all hands" group met, including myself, the relevant secretaries, the president's science advisor, his CEA chair, and the outside consultant, Martin Feldstein. The material for the meeting was prepared by the "Health Policy Working Group" based on the HEW work on alternatives for the Family Health Insurance proposal and for improving the supply of medical personnel. Over the next weeks, Ehrlichman took over what he concluded was an ineffective, sprawling effort. He directed HEW to find an alternative to Medicaid that would provide better health coverage for poor families; that would include reforms on the "supply side"; and that could be accomplished via terminating or changing existing programs, as there was no new money.

Through January, frantic efforts and multiple meetings ensued, as the president wanted to outline a pending health strategy in his State of the Union address. The vice president was involved in many of the meetings. From the outside, including from Mary Lasker, came pressures for a focus on cancer. Lasker was the activist wife of Bernard "Bunny" Lasker, the CEO of the New York Stock Exchange.

In the first week of January, Kenneth Cole reported that Martin Anderson had met with the oracle of Chicago, Milton Friedman, about minimum standards for mandatory national health insurance to be set by the federal government. Assistant Secretary for Legislative Affairs Steve Kurzman, at HEW working for Richardson, told me in 2019 that this was one of the most crucial and highly controversial parts of the HEW package. Friedman was in favor of this over any of the existing alternatives. Even the American Conservative Union, which had made a crusade of opposition to Nixon's Family Assistance Plan, told us that they would praise the administration's bill if it proposed "Federally mandated standards."

After that December 11 meeting with the president, watching these many moving parts, I told Ehrlichman I wanted to get involved. Ehrlichman agreed, saying "that I would begin picking up health."[18] Ken Cole, Ehrlichman's principal deputy "and I in the winter, on a crash basis . . . put together another White House working group to pick up the pieces." Cole focused on the insurance features, while I took charge of the novel cost control part of the Nixon initiative. By January 27 of the new year, Cole wrote to Ehrlichman that I would be "moving in," at first on the supply side, such as health maintenance organizations (HMOs), family health centers (FHCs), medical education, and the use of Public Health Service personnel. Then he told Ehrlichman, "I plan to phase Price into a completely in charge position as soon as the supply side is well on track."[19]

I worked hard with the HEW staff to refine the ideas. The final form they took was to roll out and incent a nationwide program of prepaid group practices, in both the private and the nonprofit sectors. Butler had run his meetings with Paul Ellwood on the idea secretively, thinking it highly contentious. It proved to be so in certain high quarters. The vice president became involved. I sent him my February 9, 1971, memorandum, summarizing the options that were to go to the president. Two days later, I got a phone call from Ken Cole. He said that the president told him he had just received a phone call from Vice President Agnew. Agnew was on Air Force Two, winging his way westward to play golf with Frank Sinatra at Palm Springs, California. His airplane reading was my February 9 paper for him on the president's health strategy. Agnew weighed in with Nixon about how I had either not consulted with him properly or, if I had, then had not listened. Regardless, he disagreed with the recommendation to Nixon. Nixon asked Cole to call me and tell me of the phone call and not to worry.

Later that day, Haldeman in his scrupulous notes describes Nixon's points about Agnew's call as he related them to Ziegler (the press secretary), Henry Kissinger, and Ehrlichman.

> He feels that we've got to keep the VP out of substantive policy development, that we cannot have him fighting the White House staff or the Cabinet, that he must not get involved in policy because he tends to zero in on one feature and jump on it rather than looking at the whole picture. He feels we need someone on our staff who has the confidence of the VP who can hold his hand, and he's decided Weinberger is the one who should do this.[20]

Only some days later did Agnew respond to my memo with a couple of useful concerns about the incentive features of the HMO proposal. He also accurately pointed out that the FHIP program only covered those with families, leaving many singles or childless couples no better off than before. This was later rectified in 1974, when Nixon proposed a Comprehensive Health Insurance Program (CHIP), providing full coverage.

Naturally, I was concerned that the vice president had bent the president's ear, complaining of me. John Ehrlichman, when I expressed my anxiousness to him, told me not to worry about Agnew's enmity. In his memoir, *Witness to Power*, Ehrlichman mentions that the early idea from Nixon was for Agnew to be in charge of planning a new health program. Health experts were to be added to Agnew's staff. In his memoir, Ehrlichman is caustic about Agnew in this context, hence his confident reassurance to me when I needed reassurance. He wrote,

> Agnew then chaired a series of interdepartmental meetings on health issues, but he seemed incapable of organizing the work and guiding the staff to a result. I watched the Vice President closely during this health project, trying to discover the cause of his mental constipation. . . . I concluded that the man was exceedingly narrow; new thoughts were un-welcome to him. As a result, his health project did not gather for the President all the practical alternatives for a final choice. Instead it became a narrow reflection of Spiro Agnew's preferences.[21]

In a cabinet meeting on February 16, 1971, which I attended, Nixon introduced Richardson to brief the cabinet on the "health proposal . . . [which] is the result of months and months of study ranging all the way from a completely compulsory program."[22] He then left, and the briefing was constantly interrupted. Mel Laird chimed in on an issue, saying, "I got into that in the HEW Appropriations Committee," and Richardson replied, "I'll see you after class." The postmaster, Winton Blount, "then pointed out that there was an error in some total on one of the charts, and Finch said to Elliot, 'You have to get rid of all those old Finch charts.'" Blount chimed in, "This is a tough crowd to work."[23] The back and forth became more substantive. The vice president was huddling with Ken Cole, "and we then came to the preventive health measures [the HMO section, which I had put together], over which so many arms and legs had been severed during our arbitrary sessions with the working group in the Roosevelt room as we tried to keep within the budget; and on the health insurance sections, which Ken Cole had supervised." More arguing occurred over the impact on small business, over tax issues, over copays, with the secretaries of commerce, labor, and transportation chiming in. As tensions gathered, the postmaster said, "The proposal has some problems of a substantial nature. We're going to run into a buzzsaw when this goes public."[24]

At this point, the Vice President said rather firmly, "Gentlemen, the President has made his decision, and this meeting is meant to be informative." I couldn't help but think at that moment of the day when the briefing group got back to a late lunch in the Mess after having given the story on

Family Assistance to the Cabinet at Camp David, with the Vice President virtually trying to blackmail the President by talking about calling him once more on it if it came to a vote for him due to a tie in the Senate on the ABM system, and I thought that the Vice President had been made to heel at last.[25]

The vice president's tutelage was by now complete, a year or more after the Camp David episode around FAP. "The vice president, trying to bring the discussion to a close, said, 'Having been shot down myself in trying to delay this going up, I have no sympathy with you (to Blount).' Blount replied, 'I may say, there is no general approval of this.' The vice president, with the coup de grace, said, 'General Approval is not required when the president has made his decisions.'"[26]

Around the time of the fractious cabinet meeting, there was, on the plus side, support—or at least a temporary noncombatant posture—from unexpected quarters. On the same day of my memo to the vice president, Secretary Richardson and Bob Patricelli of HEW, Jim Cavanaugh, and I met with the American Medical Association (AMA). In his minutes of the meeting, Jim Cavanaugh noted that, "relatively speaking," their strongest support was of the HMO concept. Cavanaugh came over to the Domestic Council staff in late 1970 from HEW, where he was in the public health area, then assistant secretary for health. He became the Domestic Council's staff person on health as I turned in summer to national growth policy, then began to run for Congress back in New York more aggressively, and then left on December 1, 1971. Cavanaugh was involved in the revival of Nixon's health ideas in 1973 and 1974.

The plan went forward. In a briefing for the congressional leadership, held after the cabinet meeting and before the unveiling of the Family Health Insurance Plan (FHIP) in February 1971, the president was expansive in his description of his pending message: "Some sixty-five percent of employers have insurance now which is up to the minimum [standard]. We'll expand to the balance." He went on to say it would provide diversity, competition, and experimentation. "We have to think of the horse and buggy—if the horse doesn't like it, it won't pull it." We had to have something that was acceptable, at least minimally, to the profession. "This," Nixon said, "will save the best of the private initiative medical care system."[27]

The core parts of the 1971 plan included a National Health Insurance Standards Act, a Family Health Insurance Plan, and Health Maintenance Organizations. It also included the $100 million initiative on cancer and sickle cell anemia, a malady particularly affecting African Americans. Some of the staff referred to the cancer focus as a "moon-shot" effort in the health field.

As he told us in the leadership meeting, Nixon would extend private insurance coverage "to the balance" by having all employers of one or more employees provide a minimum standard coverage for employees and their dependents, including inpatient hospital care, extended care facilities, or home health services, outpatient care, and catastrophic cost protections, all with employers paying 65 percent of the premiums to start and 75 percent after a few years. Private insurance pools were to be established for risk sharing among small employers, the self-employed, and people outside of the labor force, to permit purchase by these health consumers at lower group rates.

The Family Health Insurance Plan (FHIP) would provide insurance to all low-income families with children not covered by employer plans and with uniform national definitions of eligibility. Like FAP, the FHIP removed inequities between male- and female-headed families, the working poor, and the dependent poor. There was also to be a "residual" Medicaid program for the low-income elderly, the disabled, the blind, and the poor. Like Nixon's rationalization for the food stamp program, FHIP eliminated the eligibility inequities between states based on income and made uniform the existing wide variation in benefits.

The president's message was drafted by Lee Huebner, former president of the Ripon Society, who had campaigned with Nixon for the national ticket in 1964 and was to become the deputy head of the speechwriting staff. As seemed true of all of Nixon's main messages, addresses, or ex tempore comments on his consequential social policy initiatives, there was in their language, not alone their substance, the tone of the more liberal and humane side of this complex man. This was true of the February 1971 message on health; true of the May and December 1969 messages on hunger and the expansion of the Food Stamp Program; true of the August 1969 announcement of the Family Assistance Plan. For all his calculation, realism, cynicism, even spleen or bile, his coherent and strategic approach to poverty and need was striking. And passionately felt.

Nixon's Quaker background intrudes from time to time in these welfare and health policies. A suggestive example was his conversion of the former Fort Detrick, Maryland, facility for manufacturing biological warfare agents into the home of the National Cancer Institute, the headquarters for cancer-fighting research and funding. At Thanksgiving 1969, Nixon announced the termination of US offensive biological weapons development and repeated the pledge that there would be no first use of chemical weapons. Richard Nixon would beat swords into plowshares. This did not appear to be just an act of political theater but to speak to something deeper in Nixon's persona.

In his radio speech on health, delivered on November 3, 1972, Nixon spoke of Fort Detrick, for years "perfecting the instruments of death [and now] dedicated to the preservation of life."

I visited Fort Detrick last year—on the day I announced its conversion. I directed that now it should be thrown open to scientists from all over the world. And it was in that spirit that Fort Detrick welcomed the Russian Minister of Health almost one year later. There he stood—in a place which had once been the symbol of a closed world, a world of suspicion and confrontation—a place where some of the best minds of our Nation had prepared for a possible war against his Nation. Our goal is clear. And for me its symbol is Fort Detrick, Maryland welcoming the Soviet Minister of Health.

Reception to the insurance proposals was positive, with the exception of small businesses, who were concerned about the cost effect on them of providing insurance to one or a couple or three employees. On April 22, 1971, Nixon, Gerald Ford, Secretary Richardson, Treasury Secretary John Connolly, Ken Cole, Clark McGregor (Legislative Affairs), and I met with Congressman John Byrnes of Wisconsin, the ranking Republican on Ways and Means. Quite astonishingly for the Republican leader on the key committee for health-care legislation, when soundings had been taken a couple of weeks before Nixon's February 18, 1971 message, Byrnes told White House legislative staff that he was "in favor of the Federal Government taking over the health system in the country," according to a February 2, 1971, memo Cole sent to John Ehrlichman. Cole's opinion was that Byrnes could be brought around and would likely be supportive if there were adequate safeguards for the small businessperson and lower salaried employees. This was an issue Byrnes felt strongly about, and the April 22 meeting was intended to assuage his concerns.

The Oval Office session was after the message went up and after I and the head of the Small Business Administration, Tom Kleppe, met with the lobby for small business. It was agreed that Byrnes would offer an amendment that the "one or more employees" would be eased to ten or more employees. The legislation then went to the Hill, joining other proposals that went in all directions, especially in the Senate. Utah Republican Wallace Bennett introduced S. 1623, the National Health Insurance Partnership Act of 1971, which was the administration bill, and worked for it, as he was trying to do for the Family Assistance Plan.

Senator Kennedy was leading the way with his S. 3, the Health Security Act, that was, as former HEW assistant secretary for policy Lew Butler had described it, a full-blown nationalized and federally run and financed health insurance scheme. Butler observed in his oral history that after HEW priced the Kennedy proposal at around $80 billion and the figure became known, Kennedy's bill's movement slowed down to a crawl. Others, including Sena-

Health strategy discussion, April 22, 1971. *Left to right*: John Roy Price, Kenneth Cole, Clark McGregor, Congressman James Byrnes, Richard Nixon, Gerald Ford, Elliot Richardson. Courtesy Richard Nixon Presidential Library.

tor Caleb Boggs of Delaware, in his National Catastrophic Illness Protection Act, and, crucially, Senator Russell Long, chair of the Finance Committee, with his S. 1376, a catastrophic health insurance proposal, represented the other outliers with the more limited coverage of only unexpected and extraordinary expense.

Nixon's old comrade in arms, Jacob Javits, had moved away from full reliance on the private sector insurers that had been central to Nixon's and Javits's 1949 and 1960 efforts. In his S. 836, the National Health Insurance and Health Improvements Act, Javits proposed a hybrid approach, quite similar to ideas proposed in the 2020 presidential campaign. He would have a gradual expansion of the Medicare program to cover the general population. At the same time, individuals could opt out by securing coverage from private insurers offering comparable or better coverage and thereby exempt themselves from paying payroll taxation for federal health insurance.

No part of the 1971 Nixon plan achieved passage that year. I left government in December, emptyhanded on health. Casper Weinberger succeeded Richardson at HEW in January 1973 and delivered where Richardson had not in securing one part of Nixon's health legacy. On December 29, 1973, Nixon signed into law S. 14, the Health Maintenance Organization Act of 1973, a "demonstration" program to support the creation of HMOs. It included

Nixon's 1971 proposals on managed care and HMOs. It preempted state laws that banned or restricted HMO-type practice. It beefed up and mandated the health services that must be offered by these entities. As Weinberger came into the act, the Watergate drama and its increasing consumption of White House attention gave him more sway over policy than his predecessor had enjoyed. And the president was eager to seize the moment with more ambitious proposals. After a meeting with Nixon, Weinberger called in Deputy Assistant Secretary for Health Stuart Altman. The secretary told Altman that the president was demanding we put together a "very credible" proposal, with "all the options." Altman asked, "Including a government takeover?" Weinberger said, "Absolutely." Intense work began by Altman, his assistant Peter Fox, and Deputy Assistant Secretary for Health Legislation Frank Samuel, all working closely with Paul O'Neill at the OMB, who had succeeded Richard Nathan.

By Pearl Harbor Day, December 7, 1973, the HEW secretary had described to the president the options he hoped that Nixon would embrace. There followed a cabinet meeting that, based on Stuart Altman's description, seemed to me not unlike the Camp David session in August 1969 on Nixon's Family Assistance Plan or the February 1971 cabinet meeting preceding his FHIP proposal, which I had attended. Altman was attending his first cabinet meeting. "Before the president came in, all of the Cabinet members are yelling at Weinberger 'What are you doing? This is too governmental!' Nixon comes in, sits down, turns to Weinberger and says, 'Cap, put together this bill we've been working on so I can discuss it in the State of the Union,' then leaves." Altman concluded this was "his own more liberal social policy."[28]

Instead of FHIP there was CHIP, the Comprehensive Health Insurance Plan. It pushed beyond the 1971 plan and mandated that all employers provide comprehensive coverage for their employees, as had the 1971 proposal but with reduced employee cost sharing and with very generous benefits. Deficiencies or gaps in his 1971 proposals were cured: in 1971, there was no coverage of singles or couples who were childless and certain other individuals. To augment the reach of CHIP, there was now the Assisted Health Insurance Program (AHIP). Nixon's proposal now was for a truly universal national health insurance program. This provided health insurance for anyone who did not get it through their employer or Medicare. The states were involved. As with Nixon's food stamp reform, which became law, and his welfare reform, only part of which became law, the eligibility and benefit standards would be set by federal law and be applied uniformly across the country.

A benefit Nixon proposed that has particular resonance today was that no individual could be denied insurance because of preexisting conditions. That alone made Nixon's health strategy a dramatic advance over other proposals. It would anticipate by decades coverage included in the Affordable Care Act, for particularly vulnerable parts of the public. Premium levels and any copays or deductibles would be related to income, and the poor would not have to pay any premiums at all. The coverage would include prescription drugs—a benefit that would not materialize until thirty years later with President George W. Bush's Medicare reform, and then only with that elderly population cohort to enjoy it, unlike Nixon's prescription drugs proposal, which was universal. Nixon also proposed that the existing Medicare benefits be improved to match those he was proposing under CHIP and the Assisted Health Insurance Program (AHIP).

Beyond coverage for all for preexisting conditions and prescription drugs, the comprehensiveness of the February 1974 proposals was extraordinary. They included hospital care and physicians' care in and out of hospital, ancillary health care, lab tests and X-rays, medical devices, ambulance services, treatment for mental illness, alcoholism, and drug addiction, home health services, and nursing home services, and there was no exclusion of coverage based on the nature of the illness. The health needs of children were in focus, including preventive care up to age six, eye exams, hearing exams, and regular dental care.

Nixon staked out frontier policy in health coverage and care. What's more, Nixon might have been the twentieth-century president who secured a universal plan of coverage for health. The planets almost aligned. Senator Edward Kennedy's government-sponsored version of health insurance and care were an outlier on the liberal side. However, Kennedy inched toward the center and made overtures to Nixon. This may have occurred as early as Nixon's first, February 18, 1971, effort. Of the possibility that, during this first effort by Nixon at a health-care bill, Kennedy and Nixon might move toward some agreement, Dr. Jim Cavanaugh said, "I think there was. Elliot thought they had a chance to do something. Kennedy was on board. Javits was on board."[29]

Steve Kurzman, assistant secretary for legislation under Secretary Richardson at the time, remembers even more clearly hearing from Richardson of a failed deal in 1971, when Richardson was at HEW. Richardson told him there had been Kennedy discussions, but they had aborted, and, "as a result, we will not get health care reform for twenty years."[30] This mystery will have to wait for later sleuths to solve. What is clear is that in 1974, Kennedy saw Nixon and Mills moving toward agreement on CHIP, with its profusion of coverage, and likely did not want to be left out. Unlike 1971, there is clear confirmation of an effort in 1974 for Kennedy, the president, and Wilbur Mills coming together. In late spring that year, Senator Kennedy had his aide, Stan Jones, approach the HEW staff. The administration, Kennedy, and Mills all had concrete bills at this time. Kennedy linked up first with Mills and told

Mills that he liked CHIP (Nixon's Comprehensive Health Insurance Plan) and could improve it. The resulting Kennedy/Mills effort had more liberal subsidies and smaller copays and coinsurance premiums. Kennedy himself then went to Weinberger, who anointed Frank Samuel and Stu Altman to represent the administration in three-way talks with Stan Jones and Mills staff. Will Taft, chief of staff at HEW at the time, recalled the meetings that started in June 1974, in St. Mark's church on Capitol Hill.[31]

Twenty years later, on June 18, 1994, Frank Samuel faxed a four-page memo to Jones. He spoke of the meetings in the "Rathskellar" basement of the church, where he and Altman, Jones, and representatives of Mills met. Samuel noted that "the secret meetings continued for several weeks, in good faith. Kennedy was willing to discuss compromise with the Nixon Administration, even though Watergate had seriously impinged on Legislative-Executive Branch comity and in spite of the different ideologies represented by the Health Security Act and the Administration's bill."[32] Toward the end of the basement huddles, Altman and Jones were together at a New Mexico conference, at the top of a summer gondola ski-lift ride. They thought they had found a solution, but when they descended from the heights and took their idea to their bosses, "Neither would buy it." Kennedy was "beaten up" by labor. As to Weinberger, he told Altman, "We're already getting killed by the conservatives."[33] Samuel wrote to Jones in the 1994 fax that he never fully understood why Kennedy later pulled back, "at the apparent behest, we in the Administration thought, of the labor unions—the chief lobbying force for the single payer proposal."[34]

Samuel recalled for Jones that "Mills and Weinberger persisted and eventually came to general agreement on a compromise. Mills then tried to secure Ways and Means Committee approval for it in a series of public executive sessions during June and July. He failed."[35] Actually, Mills managed to get a combined Nixon/Mills bill out of his Committee, but the Republican opposition on the Committee was so strong, giving Mills only a one-vote victory, that he chose not to take it to the floor for a House rule and vote, as his practice was to have a strong vote out of Committee before seeking a rule.

Frank Samuel reflected, "For this alumnus of St. Mark's cellar, the reasons for the failure in 1974 included a classic mix of personality, interest group politics, program objectives and political ideologies. But the fundamental cause of failure was liberal insistence on giving more benefits and taking more control and conservative disbelief in any official cost estimate for the massive new program."[36]

In 1999, scholar Flint J. Wainess concluded in a paper for the *Journal of Health Politics, Policy and Law* that this had been a ripe moment for agreement:

The momentum for NHI [National Health Insurance] in the [Ninety-Third] Congress was greater than in virtually any other session of Congress in American history. The lineup of players who supported some variation of NHI was broader, more bipartisan, and less ideological than during any other NHI episode . . .

The political environment was similarly ripe for changing the status quo. A moderate Republican in the White House had the potential to give comprehensive health care reform bipartisan backing. . . . The positions of the various factions in Congress were closer together than they had been during other NHI episodes; trust in government was still fairly high . . . and public opinion was strongly in favor of changing the status quo. . . . 1974 remains a time of unparalleled opportunity for health care reform.[37]

That was the high-tide moment for Nixon's dream of a national health-care bill bearing his name becoming law. As Kennedy told Elliot Richardson, "We should have passed that when we had a chance."[38] Kennedy was to confess that to others until his death. It was almost within their grasp. As Wainess wrote,

The Nixon administration had unveiled a centrist reform package. . . . It was not just the specifics of CHIP that mattered. More important was the fact that a Republican president was proposing it . . . Nixon was immunized from the charge that his real goal in proposing health care reform was to hasten the death of private enterprise . . . it would be difficult to make the "socialized medicine" epithet stick.[39]

Now the riptide of Watergate carried Nixon out to California in exile by the sea. Stripper Fanne Fox then took down Wilbur Mills months later, splashing with the chairman in the Tidal Basin at the Jefferson Memorial that same fall. Mills's immense Hill power vaporized after the incident.

Major efforts in health policy waited for three more presidents. Within five days of his inauguration, President Clinton announced that his wife would lead an effort on health care. What followed was a sprawling hydra-headed committee that consulted with hundreds of experts. The endless late-night and weekend sessions teething on the issues of health care and its financing came to be called "Oxford on the Potomac," which was not meant as a compliment.

Only a few weeks following the January 1993 inaugural, First Lady Clinton came to my bank headquarters in Manhattan. Honoring a commitment to speak she had given before the election, Mrs. Clinton was given an office in our building prior to the reception for the nonprofit she was to address. Before the event, she agreed to meet with a few of us senior officers, and I was among the first to arrive. I greeted her by mentioning mutual friends of mine and the Clintons, Donald Stewart and his wife, Isabel. She warmed up immediately. I went on to say that she was embarking on a very difficult task in trying to forge a health-care strategy. She nodded, and I continued saying that I wished her every success, knowing it would be arduous and fraught. She smiled. Graciously. I said I was aware of the difficulties and hoped there would be a positive outcome because I had been one of those who put together Richard Nixon's 1971 health-care proposals, too little of which had, alas, become law.

Her smile became a cold mask. She turned on her heel and walked away.

President Clinton gave a September 1993 speech calling for universal coverage through an employer mandate and managed care—both Nixon ideas—but also federal regulation of premiums. In the State of the Union in January 1994, he again made health a centerpiece, threatening to veto any piece of health legislation sent to him that did not "guarantee every American private health insurance that can never be taken away." His efforts collapsed. Democrats were themselves divided, and Republicans were in lockstep to oppose him.

In 1992, before Clinton's election, the Heritage Foundation, an influential right-wing policy shop from the time of the Reagan presidency, called for private sector–based health insurance, intending to fight another Kennedy push for a government system. It put forward a "Consumer Choice Health Plan," relying on private insurance in which "Americans are allowed to choose the health plan they want." The Heritage plan mandated individuals to buy insurance, requiring "all households to purchase at least a basic package of insurance, unless they are covered by Medicaid, Medicare, or other government health programs." It was proposed as a "market-based" solution. The purpose—and the logical need for a purchase mandate—was to ensure that there would be within the pools of insured the full range of age, health experience, and risk. This would mean that the insurers actuarially could accurately assess the risk of coverage and consequently price it rationally. By not permitting the healthy to opt out of coverage, the premiums could be kept low. If they were to opt out, only more costly cases would be left in the pool and premiums would have to be higher. Mandating would be a natural part of a rational, self-contained system of providing privately financed insurance.

The Heritage Foundation argued forcefully that individuals must purchase health insurance. Heritage argued by analogy that all drivers are mandated to purchase and carry automobile insurance as a way of protecting them, and those they might harm, and of spreading the costs over all, thus keeping cost down, as risk is priced to reflect the risk from all users, combined. This continued to be Heritage's position until a Democratic president, Barack Obama, proposed it and Republicans moved into opposition. Heritage's "Consumer Choice Health Plan" disappeared from the Foundation's website.

Opposition to Clinton's effort was as nothing compared to the lockstep opposition by Republicans to the Patient Protection and Affordable Care Act, better known for its sponsor, Barack Obama, as "Obamacare." President Obama avoided embracing a government-run and general-revenue or Social Security tax–financed health insurance program and chose the private sector route. Having made that crucial choice, his approach did not radically differ from what Nixon had sought almost forty years earlier. He turned to principles Nixon had laid down. He chose the private health insurance industry as the main vehicle, despite lingering antipathy to the industry that had crushed Clinton's care proposals with its brilliant advertising campaign of "Harry and Louise" sitting around a kitchen table ruminating over the problems the Clinton plan would pose.

He was concerned with cost. He proposed "accountable care organizations" that had much the same concept and remit as Nixon's HMOs: to incent prevention and to reduce more costly forms of care. Some other Obama efforts were to use data about quality of care to justify reductions in Medicare reimbursements to institutions whose performance was measurably poor, for example, hospitals that had a higher percentage of readmissions of patients than did peers.[40]

He understood what Nixon had understood, namely, that you needed to mandate the private sector to cover its employees. He understood, as Nixon also had, that to get premiums down to affordable levels, you needed to create pools of risk that were broad enough. They both called for risk sharing through pools: in Nixon's case, for small employers and the unemployed or unemployable to buy into, with premiums subsidized for those unable to afford them; in Obama's case, the state-sponsored exchanges, and some subsidies to insurance companies to bring premiums within reach of those who could not afford them. Republican attacks on the ACA have included those very subsidies, as well as the individual mandate and other features.

In 2020, I talked with Dr. James Cavanaugh and Dr. Stuart Altman, veterans, as am I, of the 1971 proposals by Nixon. None of us recalls any discussion of the individual mandate for that February message and bills. In 1973–1974, to the contrary, there was extensive discussion of it among Nixon and much of the cabinet, with voices and memoranda going in different directions. The decision was made, for administrative, philosophical, and political reasons, not to require it and to rely instead on incentives from affordable premiums to draw people into the program.

Obama faced up to the conundrum about adverse selection. Nixon had always been for as universal a program as possible, but he did not have an individual mandate to compel the elimination of "slippage," which occurs when the young or the healthy, or the insouciant, simply do not sign up. Those left were older, sicker, or more worried about their health and, with reason to be so, more costly to care for.

All the way back to the 1940s, Nixon had been more on the forward-looking frontier of health care than were his Republican colleagues. He and Jack Javits were on the Flanders-Ives bill; Taft and the conservative wing of Republicans were not. Nixon supported Eisenhower ideas such as the reinsurance of private health insurance to enable coverage for the elderly- then a revival of a form of Flanders-Ives in 1960 that would help everyone through support of the private-sector provision of insurance. The recollection of his work on health insurance twenty-two years earlier was very much on his mind as Nixon prepared for the 1971 State of the Union section on health care. In a cabinet meeting on January 19, Nixon asked Secretary Richardson to get the language Nixon had used in 1949, when sponsoring and describing the Javits, Prouty bill. He instructed it to be given to Ray Price, the speechwriter drafting the address.[41]

In his 1971 and 1973–1974 efforts, Nixon forcefully advocated for universal coverage, including support for those who would need help paying premiums. He was the first to propose prescription drug coverage for all and capping out-of-pocket costs, including those from catastrophic illnesses. Nixon understood the tug-of-war between cost and coverage. His HMOs were meant to be major artillery in that battle. He grasped the idea that pooled risk really did mean pooled risk. He felt that the lower premiums available through his plans would appeal to consumers and motivate them to take advantage of the coverage offered by their employer or through group pooling opportunities for the self-employed and others. Nixon wanted universal health coverage, the steady supply of doctors, facilities, research, and good public health campaigns. He believed in finding and moving the levers in the private sector to bring about a public good. But he was having enough trouble mobilizing his own Republican House and Senate members to support his then quite radical ideas.

Where are we today? The critics in the Republican Party have been undermining the Affordable Care Act for a decade. Between the support of court challenges to the ACA, the threatened withholding of essential federal elements and financing for it, and constant criticism, they have tried to cause the collapse of Obamacare. Their proposed replacement does not exist, even after the luxury of that decade and a whole term of a Republican administration for development of an alternative. The miserably messy rollout of Obamacare gave them explosive ammunition against it. It has its faults. It has its court challenges. But time has run out.

In January 2019, the death of Harris Wofford, a one-term US senator from Pennsylvania, was noted. He ran in 1991 against a formidable former

Republican governor, Richard Thornburgh, who enjoyed a forty-four-point lead in initial opinion polls. Wofford's campaign focused on a single-payer health insurance program. He won. It put that issue on the front pages in 1991. The George H. W. Bush White House was in disarray and had not seriously thought through its own health policy, to say nothing of a coherent domestic policy. Bush in his turn was stunned by his defeat by Bill Clinton of Arkansas.

In the 2018 midterm elections, and again in 2020, the campaigns of many candidates for the Congress and the Democratic presidential nomination centered on health care. As Wofford had in 1991, many, not including Joe Biden, called for a single-payer health insurance plan: "Medicare for all." The political landscape for intractable opposition is bleak. In early 2019, a widely respected Gallup poll showed that the percentage of adults without insurance climbed to 13.7 percent in the last quarter of 2018. This is compared to 12.4 percent in 2017 and only 10.9 percent in 2016. This two-year trend was in stark contrast to the increase in actual enrollment from passage of the ACA in the years just prior. The pandemic has underlined the lack of any protection for millions of Americans and patchy protection for millions of others, and its aftermath and lingering problems will only accentuate the urgency of coverage of preexisting conditions.

Today we see a landscape not too dissimilar to what Nixon saw in the early 1970s. There is a patchwork of coverage and a mishmash of states having differing eligibility requirements for such programs as there are. Many states have chosen not to expand Medicaid for the most indigent. Many plans do not really protect against catastrophe or against preexisting conditions. There are legitimate concerns about cost.

The push toward more comprehensive coverage in health care seems to be relentless. The costs will be imposed on someone. At their root is the disproportionate costliness of American health care and the lack of affordability of care, regardless of whether it is a federal program, a municipal program, or one provided through the mediation of a private health insurance industry. Coverage versus cost.

Nixon would likely despair at the continued disparities and lack in coverage today. He would be disappointed that the managed care concept he promoted did not do more in terms of cost containment by incenting prevention. Most of all, he would wish that in 1974 he, Ted Kennedy, and Wilbur Mills could successfully have concluded their three-way negotiations for a comprehensive national health care program and made it law. Passage might have made the American public feel more invested in the institutions of their country, because then those institutions would be truly serving and protecting them.

Conclusion

In the 1972 presidential election, my former boss went on to a historic land-slide victory against his Democratic opponent. My foray into the campaign world ended in failure. I tried to get the nomination for Congress in my swing district on the North Shore of Long Island, New York. The pollster Arthur Finkelstein felt I could win as I matched the nature of the district. As a boy, I had savored dreams of elective office. I read of Teddy Roosevelt overcoming asthma with sheer willpower and was familiar with his nearby Sagamore Hill home. I had seen Winston Churchill driving up Park Avenue once during his second tour as prime minister. Those two were half of my incongruous quartet of heroes of my youth. Besides Winston and Teddy Roosevelt, they were Mahatma Gandhi and Dr. Albert Schweitzer (I had been a church organist in my high school days and was sore amazed that Schweitzer had a medical degree, a doctorate in theology, and a Nobel Peace Prize, and had compiled a complete edition of J. S. Bach's organ works, all the while tending the sick in Lambaréné in West Africa).

Seeking help to get the nomination, I sat with Governor Rockefeller on the back porch of his Foxhall Road estate in Washington. He sipped his Dubonnet, and I spoke of my ambition. He said, "Jesus Christ, John, why Nassau County?" Nassau was a Chicago-style political boss fiefdom—though Republican. I said, weakly, "K through 12 in the public schools there, Governor." Neither his help, nor Richard Nixon's as he sat strategizing with me about the district and getting the attorney general to intervene on my behalf, availed. The boss, Joseph Margiotta, the imperious county leader who controlled thirteen thousand patronage jobs, reacted to me a bit as Henry II had to Beckett. His refusal to shake my hand in front of my wife and his underlings in a reception in my hometown was his version of "Who will rid me of this meddlesome priest?" While I was not slain before the altar at Canterbury, Margiotta's acolytes recognized shunning when they saw it. Margiotta ignored my efforts and entreaties by Governor Rockefeller and Attorney General John Mitchell and gave the nomination to a conservative who promptly lost the moderate district in the election while Nixon carried it. Joe Margiotta later went to federal prison.

Two years later, in 1974, Richard Nixon resigned. The "Mandate of

Heaven" had been withdrawn and Nixon left office. I saw it coming. That January, I was at a meeting at the New York Clearing House, an entity made up of the twelve "Money Center" banks, or the largest and most international. David Rockefeller, chair of the Chase, presided. The guest at the lunch for twelve of us was Senator John Tower of Texas, there because of his role on the Senate Banking Committee. Talk turned to the Watergate inquiry. Tower, with bitterness, told us, "Loyalty only works in one direction with this White House." I knew at that moment on January 15 that it was over for Nixon. This was one of the "bulls" of the Republican leadership in the Senate, and he sounded tired of the devious and darker side of the president. From the party's perspective, he was alert, as Dirksen had been in 1964 regarding the Goldwater candidacy, to what Nixon would cost the Republicans in the 1974 election.

At the end, after he had been served notice of nonsupport in a visitation to him of the Republican Senate leadership, Richard Nixon went with grace. He understood he had spent his moral authority and lost his ability to use his office for building the things to fill his life with large meaning, purpose, and accomplishment. Though recoiling from the idea he would capitulate and be the first president ever to resign from office, he knew his time to leave had come. As he had in 1960 put the country first in not challenging the election results, so in 1974, he went, finally, in quiet acceptance of the virtually complete loss of his party's support, certainly in the Senate, and the nation's. He understood he could not any longer use power for decency, as he had started out to do in 1969. He was spent, and the people would not have more of him.

Even in this exit, otherwise gracious and so unlike his bitter rant in California in 1962, there were faint hints of the hurts, the sadness, that inhabited part of Nixon's soul. He spoke of his mother, Hannah, as a "Saint"—and he truly believed that. He went on to say, "But no one will write a book about her." Some may have understood he was referring to the biography of Rose Kennedy, mother of his rival, Jack Kennedy, released by its publisher only three weeks earlier. The resentments, envies, and never forgotten slights were deep, always there or just below the surface. But here it must have particularly wounded him, making him reflect on his own mother and the values and aspirations that she had raised him to hold. After all the quest for power, all the rawness in his exercise of it, Richard Nixon was leaving office and power. He was now measuring himself, finally, not by attitudes of the liberal press, or the political class, or attention paid to others. Rather, he was measuring himself against his mother's and, if you will, the Quaker Meeting's, hopes and expectations for him.

In late spring of 1974, I received a phone call from and met on June 17 with Vince Albano, chair of the New York County (Manhattan) Republican

Party, and Republican State Senator Roy Goodman. They offered me the party nomination to run for Congress in the Eighteenth, or "Silk Stocking," Congressional District. Dreams die hard. Giddy with excitement, I phoned Arthur Finkelstein for his reaction, since he had been so positive two years earlier about my race. Hardly pausing, Arthur said, "John, if you want to start your elective career with a race where you get 26, maybe 27 percent of the vote . . . this is the race for you!!! Ed Koch [the Democrat incumbent congressman who would later be mayor of New York] will wrap Richard Nixon around your neck like a Boa Constrictor." I let the cup pass from my lip. Chosen instead to run against Koch and into oblivion was a woman who was one half of a sister act of soft shoe hoofers. She could not have won even if she had a back-up line of Ginger Rogers, Fred Astaire, Rita Hayworth, Gregory Hines, Cyd Charisse, Gene Kelly, and Ann Miller performing on her behalf in front of Bloomingdale's, so strong was Koch and so difficult the year. It was 1974, and Republicans all over the country were in voters' sights to pay for the transgressions of Richard Nixon.

In November 1973, I was at a cocktail party in London at the home of George Weidenfeld, a prominent publisher. So was US senator Eugene McCarthy, who was on the Senate Finance Committee before which Family Assistance came because of committee jurisdiction over Social Security and welfare issues. I opened conversation with McCarthy by recalling that Pat Moynihan had told me of going with McCarthy into the back reaches of Rock Creek Park in Washington one sunlit Sunday afternoon, with a thermos of whiskey. McCarthy took over the narrative from me, noting that it was a full gallon of martinis, and that as they stumbled back down to the parking area, they encountered a constable. Moynihan impressed on the policeman that McCarthy was a US senator, and they were let go, though the constable could be under no illusion that they were capable of navigating a car. McCarthy told me that he had a phone call the next morning from the officer, describing his frustration with slow advancement in the Capitol Park Police.

McCarthy and I talked of the Nixon welfare reform. I rebuked him for having voted against the Nixon bill in Senate Finance. McCarthy himself, as he was campaigning against Lyndon Johnson, had offered a version of a guaranteed income. He argued to me that the National Welfare Rights Organization's (NWRO) bill was better than FAP had been because it had a much higher floor of payments. I told him I had watched liberal Democrat Fred Harris of Oklahoma squirm, defending his similar welfare reform bill from strident attacks that its floor was not as high as the NWRO proposal, and I said with a Republican president embracing the principle, liberal and moderate Democrats should be onboard and floors could be negotiated.

McCarthy then shifted his argument and said that no one in the White

House but Moynihan wanted it and that Moynihan had been duped by others into thinking the president was for it. In rebuttal, I told of my conversation with the president on Christmas Eve 1969: Nixon said then to me that we should and would get FAP. He noted, philosophically, that every year there would be a push by the Democrats to raise the floor of income. Every year, he said, the Republicans would vote against doing so. Yet every year, it would be raised. He then said it didn't matter: "The important thing is that we will have established the principle."

I turned to the argument Moynihan had made in the autumn of 1969 to the Leadership Conference on Civil Rights. Moynihan pleaded that this was a liberal proposal coming from a conservative president and that if this chance were not grasped and turned into legislation with the liberal and moderate Democrats and the liberal and moderate Republicans holding together, there would not be welfare reform for another generation.

I repeated that this president had bought into it. He had kept plugging away at it for more than two years. His energy was sapped slowly because of relentless opposition from the conservatives and grave disappointment that the liberals had not supported it, as the president had thought they must. The senator said to me that the president should reintroduce it and that it would not only be good policy, but good for Nixon at this troubled juncture in his political fortunes (resignation over Watergate lay only ten months in the future). At this very time, there was the renewed effort, led by Secretary Casper Weinberger at the Department of Health, Education and Welfare, to persuade the president to reintroduce a more expansive Family Assistance that sought to solve some of the problems that had caused its death a year earlier. This was "Big FAP," as the Right termed it. I had just learned of this a couple of weeks earlier from Frank Carlucci, the deputy secretary of HEW. I mentioned this to Senator McCarthy, and we parted on this note, in hope that something of the principle of Family Assistance might yet be salvaged.

It came to naught. Unlike Nixon's reprise in 1974 of his comprehensive health proposal that came within a hair's breadth of securing passage, a second push for FAP did not ever emerge from the White House. Moynihan and Nixon were in communication until Nixon's death in 1994. Moynihan would send Nixon reading suggestions. They stayed in touch and engaged on the welfare issue. I think they brought out the better angels in one another, and both of them knew this. Moynihan wrote to Nixon about the 1987 efforts at welfare reform, which he termed, "Pathetically small, when compared with your truly titanic legislation nearly two decades ago, but there you are. We are a somewhat diminished polity!"[1] Nixon responded two weeks later, "Our joint labors, which finally produced FAP at our meeting at Camp David, may not have been in vain if your current efforts bear fruit. The critics of welfare reform must face up to the fact that the division between blacks and whites is much worse than it was twenty years ago."[2]

When the bill passed, Nixon wrote Pat,

> After all of the blood that was left on the floor at Camp David and then in our lobbying efforts with the Congress for F.A.P., I was particularly pleased to see the Welfare Reform Bill enacted into law.
>
> As I am sure you will agree, it is only a beginning in dealing with what has been a virtually intractable problem for a quarter of a century. I am convinced, however, that it is without question a step in the right direction.[3]

Moynihan wrote back, "There were a half dozen moments when it looked as if it was lost. Then there were second thoughts. Most of them going back to the blood left on the floor, as you put it, over F.A.P. It took twenty years to get back to the subject. No one wanted to risk this a second time. And so your efforts were not in vain."[4]

Four years later, Moynihan wrote to Nixon about SSI (the adult categories: aid to the aged, the blind, and disabled), that it was the "one feature of the Family Assistance Plan to make it into statute. Only the children were left out. Benefits for children under AFDC are now about 60 percent, in constant dollars, of what they were when you proposed FAP."[5]

Nixon wrote back that Pat was "right on target. It is a national tragedy that an unholy alliance of the far right and left killed FAP."[6]

It was only eighteen months later that President Nixon died. There had been such focus and interest in the problems of poverty and economic security in his administration. For me, that came into bright clarity on the occasion of a visit to us by Albert, then the Crown Prince of Belgium, on June 10, 1970. We took him to a meeting on national growth policy at the office of the National Goals Research Staff (NGRS), which was a unit Nixon had created with prompting from Len Garment and Pat Moynihan to look beyond the day-to-day concerns of running the government and toward trends in demographics, economics, and social science and their implications for policy. After listening for a couple of hours, as the prince departed, he said to me, "Europe seems concerned with traffic. You seem concerned with poverty." It reminded me of Pat Moynihan's oft-repeated remark that our administration seemed obsessed with the poor.

Pat Buchanan, in *Nixon's White House Wars*, finds many ways to lament how receptive Nixon was to ideas and personnel from the liberal wing of the party. He says "Javits [Jacob K., Senator from NY and Nixon's co-sponsor in the 1940s of ambitious health care legislation] . . . had ideological allies not only heading our domestic departments, but high in the Nixon White House. And the President, an ideological eclectic, knew it, and was comfortable with it."[7] In recent years, I pressed Buchanan about whether he agreed with my premise that Nixon's presidency was the "last gasp" or the final extrapolation of Eisenhower "modern," or moderate, "liberal Republicanism." Buchanan told me he agreed with me. Pushing his finger into my lapel, he told me, "We [the Right] were winning all the political battles. YOU were winning all the policy ones!" *Nixon's White House Wars* makes much the same point. Early on, Buchanan observed how the moderates or liberals were winning policy battles. In chapter 2, "Storm Warnings," the epigraph of the chapter is: "*The conservatives get the rhetoric, and we get the action*—Senator Hugh Scott, Republican Minority Leader, 1969."[8] Buchanan spent years with Nixon and has telling insight into his man. With some of those insights Buchanan was almost bemused but respectful. Reaching back to Nixon's start in January 1969, Buchanan concluded

> The Nixon of January 1969 was the Wilsonian idealist and utopian who believed with Quaker and Christian pacifists that one day men will "beat their swords into plowshares, and their spears into pruning hooks" and "nation shall not lift up sword against nation, neither shall they learn war any more." . . . It would be the goal of his presidency . . . to fulfill the wish of the girl who held up the sign at the train station in Deshler on our whistle-stop tour of Ohio that read "Bring us together." Nixon's dream was to bring America and the world together and enter history as the Peacemaker President.
>
> Buchanan added, "The remarkable thing about Richard Nixon is that he truly believed this."[9]

Another anecdote involving Buchanan is revealing—one he told me he cannot recall. It came from my friend, Thomas A. Farmer. Farmer was born in Berlin, Germany, in 1923, and his family moved to Great Neck, Long Island, NY, in 1935. There, his classmate and friend all through school was William Rusher, who later, as publisher of *National Review* and a key strategist for the Goldwater campaign and Reagan's rise, held a secure place in the pantheon of the American Right. Farmer was a liberal Democrat, but they remained the closest of friends all their lives. Farmer had a career that included time in the CIA, where he trained to recall details of conversations. For an important birthday for Rusher in the late 1980s, Rusher invited Farmer to join a celebration with his conservative friends, onboard a yacht on the Potomac. Pat Buchanan was another guest. Farmer recounted to me that Rusher stood up and said, "When Pat told me in 1965 that he had an offer to work with Richard Nixon, I urged him not to. I told him, 'Richard Nixon will break your heart.'"

Buchanan was convinced of Nixon's core determination to be a peacemaker. I hold the same conviction about his purpose in social policy. Nixon was determined to use his presidency to protect and to change the lives of those living in peril at the edge, in frightening uncertainty and great economic risk, facing terrible costs for health care, or with no stable employment and ability to provide for a family. I recalled in my diary entry on April 21, 1970,

> JDE [John D. Ehrlichman] took all of us from the staff meeting (which RN had walked in on at 7:30) into the Office. RN then began a half hour monologue, starting by saying he had just dictated a memo to DPM [Daniel Patrick Moynihan] . . . the gist was that he should not be concerned by the leaking of a few memos, or worried that for the rest of his life he would be known for "benign neglect": since you "have to have a broad perspective, and that comes only from reading a lot of history and to realize that it is not the little 'BB shot' type things . . . that count, but the bigger things." He said, "I told Moynihan that with Family Assistance, and it will pass, that is what he will be remembered for—he's done something with his life.[10]

Nixon was speaking not only of Moynihan but also of himself. Nixon, at some place buried inside him, needed to know that he had used his time on earth well. Nixon continued that early morning, saying,

> It's what you leave behind that counts. Don't expect credit. . . . [Getting our goals] will take dealing with the Congress and the Press—we may have to deal with McGee and Fong, and put a radar installation in Hawaii. As I look around, I see that so many of you are young, and you may be saying, that's awfully cynical. It's not. It's idealistic, because it is realistic. But the key thing is to keep your eye on the main ball. And so, you will have satisfaction in having done something, as you get your dismissal notice, or are asked to take on another job.[11]

Richard Nixon was to get his dismissal notice.

The vaulting ambition of this nervous, brilliant, often angry, and unsettling man was married with endless gestures of kindness to individuals and a desire to become a beloved leader. His empathy was so outside the normal picture of this unstoppably ambitious man. He was going to change the world. He had a Quaker thirst for the ultimate scope of things. He wasn't just going to warm the bench. As a boy, he listened to trains in the night and entertained large thoughts of faraway places. Steven Vincent Benet, author most famously of *John Brown's Body* and popular in Nixon's youth among the reading public, captured young men's dreams with this image of the as yet unclear and distant possibilities their lives held. It evoked what Nixon had in common with millions. He was not a visionary but a dreamer—a little closer to earth. And a liberal in much, closer still to earth.

With Nixon, it had to be not only pride in achievement or zeal for winning. His domestic policies were an absolute kaleidoscope of achievement. So various. So seemingly unrelated. But at the core was a sense of the efficacy of government and its importance. For Richard Nixon, government was not the enemy. Government and its intelligent and focused use are part of the social contract. That social contract must be firmly in place to be proof against hopelessness and strains that can otherwise tear us apart.

Family Assistance, his central, early reform, was imperfect. Many around him had opposed it. They wanted something "incrementalist." They might be satisfied with singles or two-baggers. Richard Nixon was not an incrementalist. He swung for the fences. It was fifty years ago when he proposed and pushed for two increasingly dispiriting years his Universal Basic Income, which we called the Family Assistance Plan.

And it died with Richard Nixon's presidency. The conservatives had won. Will Taft, chief of staff at HEW to Weinberger and then HEW's general counsel, told me, "We tried to sell FAP to Ford, with a little help from Nelson Rockefeller [by now Ford's vice president] and Jim Cannon [domestic affairs advisor], but there was no enthusiasm from Ford."[12] Within months, Rockefeller would be dropped by Ford in an effort to appease the Right and win his own renomination. Reagan and his allies were making sure that Nixon's would be the last liberal Republican administration.

Nixon did get part of Family Assistance; he secured passage of the Supplemental Security Income (SSI). Thomas Dewey in 1938 had called for help for the indigent elderly, the blind, and the otherwise disabled. These were the people helped by Nixon's SSI, which put a federal floor under their income, throughout the country. It would have astonished Dewey, as the liberal leader of the Republican Party, that it would take more than three decades to get this remedy for what he thought was such pressing need. It was the last liberal Republican president, in his lineage from Dewey and Eisenhower, who secured it. Building upon Nixon's proposed help for the working poor, the Earned Income Tax Credit program carried forward part of Nixon's proposals, but it was hedged and cut and threatened by recent Republican Congresses.

Nixon also successfully rationalized and vastly expanded the Food Stamp program that has grown into the Supplemental Nutritional Assistance program, feeding tens of millions of people who would otherwise go hungry. Food Stamps and SNAP have been a key element in protecting the needy, indeed the destitute, but Republicans in the decades since Nixon have tried to cut deeply into this entitlement in the form of a negative income tax that Richard Nixon secured.

He proposed consistently for more than twenty-five years a universal health insurance program,.. In its use of the private sector, with strict federal regulatory oversight, and its reliance on the forces of competition to help control runaway medical costs, it is arguably the most perfect example of Nixon as the last liberal Republican. It was definitely not a government-run program. But it had such generous benefits, along with subsidies for those unable to afford the premiums, that it had higher quality coverage than Medicare, which Nixon proposed should raise its generosity to seniors to the level Nixon's Comprehensive Health Insurance Plan (CHIP) offered to all. CHIP and its accompanying Affordable Health Insurance Plans laid the foundation for Obamacare and were even broader in coverage, including prescription drugs for all.

Republicans fought, strenuously, with not a single Republican vote for it, Obama's attempt to fashion a Nixon-like private sector–based response to the huge holes in health coverage. Since its passage, Republicans for more than a decade have sought to extirpate it—pull it up by the roots. At this very moment, the national COVID-19 crisis is laying bare the conceit that the population is being well enough served by the patchwork of health care that Nixon sought to integrate, enrich, and make available to all.

The Republican Party from whose orthodoxy Nixon strayed—to their astonishment—fought his ideas at the time. And they kept fighting Nixon's social policy progeny, to the extent that today, it is hard to believe that there was a Republican president who himself tried so hard to "place a platform over the pit of despair."

A wide-thinking Nixon felt we were going to out–New Deal the New Deal, although he would never express it that way. He said to Pat Moynihan and me in his office on October 24, 1969, "You know, the reason Hubert Humphrey lost the election—well, one of the main reasons anyway—was that he was the last of the New Deal."[13] The side of Nixon that scorned bureaucracy and felt anger that many in the permanent government were hostile to efforts to curb government excess, hostile to the Republican Party, and—for sure he felt—hostile to Richard Nixon himself was soothed by this thought. Pat Buchanan wrote that Nixon was "no New Dealer." And yet, like Tom Dewey, Nixon was not going to tear up the pea patch. Like Dwight Eisenhower, Nixon was going to make sure that the social contract was solidly in place and that government would do its part to protect the unprotected. Hubert Humphrey may have been the last of the New Deal, as Nixon said to me in the fall of 1969. But Richard Nixon was the last liberal Republican.

The next time I saw Richard Nixon was emotional for me. It was in the summer of 1976, and the former president was on "Elba" at San Clemente, in exile. He was still concerned about risks from the phlebitis that he had suffered. I was spending my vacation in nearby Riverside with my in-laws. I lunched at a Chinese restaurant with Ken Khachigian, who was helping Richard Nixon with his memoirs. I was in shorts and a polo shirt. Ken said, "The Old Man knows you are here and wants to see you." I protested, pointing to my clothes. We went to the office. Once there, we knocked on Nixon's office door. He opened it, reached out, and took my hand in both of his. Still cupping my hand, he walked backward through the office, leading me with my hand in his hands. He sat me down and took his chair, putting his leg up on a hassock.

He smiled broadly at me and his first words were, "So John, you were the 'House Liberal' then, weren't you?" We talked of faith and reason. We talked of Gabriel Hauge, my boss at the New York bank. We talked of the upcoming election. He was in no hurry. He seemed glad that I was there.

Nixon was regathering his strength. He was not finished. This was the Nixon who had been teething on the idea of normalizing relations with Communist China in 1960. The Nixon who seriously thought of talking of China relations in his 1968 campaign, until forceful opposition to that came from Nelson Bunker Hunt in a letter of August 20, 1968, and from Pat Buchanan, who warned him the Right would be up in arms. Twenty years later, the breakup of the Soviet Union caused another ambitious effort by Nixon to influence global events. At a luncheon talk he gave in New York upon return from a Moscow trip in 1991, I understood more profoundly just who Richard Nixon was. At the University Club, he held perhaps 350 people, including me, spellbound. He described his meetings days earlier in Moscow with Mikhail Gorbachev and Boris Yeltsin. Of Yeltsin, he said he was a "gut," visceral politician, instinctual, physically courageous. Of Gorbachev, he said he was "cerebral" and thought things through and with understanding of the broader implications of what he did. He said Gorbachev, having permitted the peaceful unification of Germany, would go down as "a pivotal, hinge figure" in the whole last half of the twentieth century. However, he felt Gorbachev was not the one to take Russia forward, since he was too shackled to the institutions of the Soviet Union and the Communist Party; he carried baggage. He felt Yeltsin was the future of Russia and that American policy should support the reformers. When Yeltsin took over, Nixon attempted to persuade President George H. W. Bush to support massive aid for the transition on the scale of the "Marshall Plan" to ensure that Russia's first democratically elected, free-market, nonexpansionist government would not go down. In March 1992, at a conference at a DC hotel the Nixon Library put on, he referred to Truman's aid to 1940s Greece and Turkey, threatened then by communism, and said, "We responded magnificently to the threat of war then. . . . Can we not respond to the promise of peace now?" His plea to Bush to seize a historic moment to turn Russia firmly westward and encourage peaceful and fruitful transition to democracy did not succeed.

Nixon's political, and not just his strategic, instincts were still acute. Years earlier, Nixon's prescient forecast after Lindsay's first mayoral election had flabbergasted columnist Murray Kempton. This time, it was my turn to be stunned at the accuracy of a Nixon forecast. A weekend guest, Jamie Humes, told me in early August 1991 of a conversation he had in the summer of 1988 with Nixon. Democrat Mike Dukakis led Republican presidential nominee George H. W. Bush by almost 18 percent in the polls. Nixon said to Humes, "Don't worry. Bush will win, as the third Reagan term. But then he will lose in 1992."

Bush had been exceptionally kind to me. In the midst of his 1980 campaign for the presidential nomination, he called me from his mother's place in Florida and spent time counseling me about a possible job opportunity with his former oil patch partner, Hugh Liedtke, at Pennzoil, which they had cofounded. Yet my mother's question to me in autumn 1992 and Bush's loss made Nixon's prediction ring in my ears. My mother had said, "Yes, he is a fine man. But what does he want to DO if he wins again?" She asked the question I then put to Bush's White House staff and said they needed to answer.

At that University Club talk by Nixon on Russia, I grasped what drove Richard Nixon. He wanted—he needed—to change the world, to have a positive impact. For all the bitterness, all the demons with which he struggled, in the end his calling, his imperative, was to use his life for something larger than himself, larger than his ambition.

Evan Thomas, a recent and fine biographer of Nixon, says in the acknowledgments to his *Being Nixon*:

In 1988, Nixon came to *Newsweek* magazine, where I worked, to talk to a group of editors and writers. After his talk, he came up to me and said, "your grandfather was a great man." I was taken aback—I had never met Nixon and I was one of thirty or forty people in the room. Not sure of what to say, I spluttered something about how he had been a good grandfather. My father's father, Norman Thomas, had been the leader of the Socialist Party in America for many years from the 1920s to the 1960s.[14]

Norman Thomas was an ordained Presbyterian minister. He had run six times for president of the United States as the Socialist Party candidate. Perhaps the invisible Quaker could feel the depths of conviction of the invisible Presbyterian, and recognized him as a person of courage and conviction.

The last time I saw President Nixon for a private conversation was in his New York office, suitably enough in the Jacob K. Javits Federal Office Building, down at Federal Plaza in Manhattan. While he had seemed "needy" to me when I saw him in San Clemente, this time he was more businesslike and serious. After talking of many things, we turned to welfare, as he well remembered my connection with his Family Assistance initiative. Unfortunately, it was only years after this meeting with Nixon that I learned of work done at the University of Wisconsin Poverty Research Center, where much of the research and thinking on negative income tax and poverty have occurred for decades. It took partial issue with the conclusions of the most important income maintenance experiments of the 1970s. Those seemed to question a negative income tax, the underpinning for Nixon's plan. When I talked with the former president, I was not aware of the more supportive work in Wisconsin but only of the earlier conclusions widely drawn about the Trenton, Seattle, and Denver experiments, which encouraged FAP's enemies.

Nixon asked me, "John, would FAP have worked?" I paused. I then, reluctantly, told him of the apparent conclusions of the income maintenance experiments and said, "I just am not sure." He paused at length and looked, silently, into the distance.

Nixon, had he been able to overcome the resistance of the Republican Party and the visceral animosity of most liberal Democrats, would have put in place a solid and far-reaching safety net, surpassing that of the New Deal. It would have provided an income guarantee and covered health care. Had he succeeded, the edgy, sometimes paranoid, dark angel on one of Nixon's shoulders could have been firmly, possibly permanently, pushed off the center position in the public's view of him by his better angel. He might have been taken to heart by the American people, as he must often have dreamed of being.

Notes

Abbreviations Used in Notes

SMOF   Staff Member Office Files
WHCF   White House Central Files

Introduction

1. Patrick J. Buchanan, *Nixon's White House Wars: The Battles that Made and Broke a President and Divided America Forever* (New York: Crown Forum, 2017), 25.

Chapter 1. The Path to Eisenhower and Nixon

1. Thomas Mallon, review of *Ike and McCarthy: Eisenhower's Secret Campaign Against Joseph McCarthy*, by David A. Nichols, *Wall Street Journal*, March 18–19, 2017, C7.

2. William Manchester, *American Caesar: Douglas MacArthur, 1880–1964* (Boston: Little, Brown, 1978), 166.

3. Joseph F. Wall, *Grinnell College in the Nineteenth Century: From Salvation to Service* (Ames: Iowa State University Press, 1997), 90.

4. Jean Strouse, *Morgan: American Financier* (New York: Random House, 1999), 436.

5. Strouse, *Morgan*, xv.

6. Albert Gallatin, also a Pennsylvanian, and a senator and House member, was the record holder, serving almost thirteen years under Presidents Jefferson and James Madison.

7. Richard Norton Smith, *Thomas E. Dewey and His Times* (New York: Simon & Schuster, 1982), 278.

8. David Cannadine, *Mellon: An American Life* (New York: Alfred A. Knopf, 2005), 362.

9. These active efforts to combat the collapse included the creation of the Federal Home Loan Bank system in December 1931, which was the first Government Sponsored Enterprise and for which, decades later and in another financial collapse, I served as a CEO.

10. Arthur Larson, *A Republican Looks at His Party* (New York: Harper & Brothers, 1956), 3.

11. Smith, *Thomas E. Dewey and His Times*, 448.

12. Herbert Brownell, *Advising Ike: The Memoirs of Attorney General Herbert Brownell* (Lawrence: University Press of Kansas, 1993), 39.

13. Brownell, *Advising Ike*, 87.

14. Brownell, 40.

15. Smith, *Thomas E. Dewey and His Times*, 99.

16. Brownell, *Advising Ike*, 16.

17. Brownell, *Advising Ike*, 27.

18. Smith, *Thomas E. Dewey and His Times*, 218.

19. Smith, *Thomas E. Dewey and His Times*, 218.

20. Smith, 232–235.

21. Smith, 266.

22. Smith, 266.

23. Smith, 273.

24. Smith, 264.

25. Smith, 304.

26. Smith, 334.

27. Smith, 401.

28. Gabriel Hauge, "Putting Economics to Work," chapter 5 of unpublished memoir, 1.

29. Hauge, unpublished memoir, 3.

30. Hauge, 4.

31. Hauge, 4, 5.

32. Hauge, 6.

33. Hauge, 6.

34. Brownell, *Advising Ike*, 81.

35. Gabriel Hauge, unpublished memoir, 7.

36. Brownell, *Advising Ike*, 117.

37. Brownell, *Advising Ike*, 99.

38. Brownell, 114.

39. Robert M. Pennoyer, *As It Was: A Memoir* (Westport, NY: Prospecta, 2015), 207. Also, Robert M. Pennoyer, telephone conversation with the author and his son, John Mason Milnes Price, on March 21, 2020.

40. Smith, *Thomas E. Dewey and His Times*, 584.

41. Brownell, *Advising Ike*, 121.

42. Brownell, *Advising Ike*, 120.

43. Larson, *A Republican Looks at His Party*, 10, 11.

44. Larson, *A Republican Looks at His Party*, 17.

45. Larson, 18.

46. Brownell, *Advising Ike*, 86.

47. Stephen Hess, Brookings Institution and former Eisenhower speechwriter, conversation with the author, May 8, 2014.

48. David Blumenthal and James A. Marone, *The Heart of Power: Health and Politics in the Oval Office* (Berkeley: University of California Press, 2009), 115.

49. Blumenthal and Morone, *The Heart of Power*, 127, 128.

50. Gabriel Hauge, "Economics of Eisenhower Conservatism" (speech, Commonwealth Club of California, San Francisco, October 14, 1955).

Chapter 2. The Disruptive Decade

1. Joseph Persico, *The Imperial Rockefeller: A Biography of Nelson A. Rockefeller* (New York: Simon and Schuster, 1982), 38.

2. A. James Reichley, *Conservatives in an Age of Change: The Nixon and Ford Administration* (Washington, DC: Brookings Institution, 1981), 51.

3. David L. Stebene, *Modern Republican: Arthur Larson and the Eisenhower Years* (Bloomington: Indiana University Press, 2006), 175.

4. Stebene, *Modern Republican*, 230.

5. Persico, *The Imperial Rockefeller*, 296.

6. John Roy Price, *Diary: Iberia to White House, 1967–1970*, 194.

7. Geoffrey Kabaservice, *Rule and Ruin: The Downfall of Moderation and the Destruction of the Republican Party, from Eisenhower to the Tea Party* (New York: Oxford University Press, 2012).

8. W. Dennis Shaul (former president of the National Student Association), interview with the author, April 5, 2017.

9. Benjamin Disraeli, *Sybil, or the Two Nations* (London: Henry Colburn, 1845).

10. Price, *Diary*, 99.

11. Bruce K. Chapman and George Gilder, *The Party That Lost Its Head: The Republican Collapse and Imperatives for Revival* (New York: Alfred A. Knopf, 1966), 86.

12. William Timmons, lunch conversation with the author, Spring 2014.

13. Barry Goldwater, *The Conscience of a Conservative* (Shepardsville, KY: Victor, 1960).

14. Henry Kissinger, *Nuclear Weapons and Foreign Policy* (New York: Harper, 1957).

15. E. J. Kahn, Jr., *Jock: The Life and Times of John Hay Whitney* (Garden City, NY: Doubleday, 1981), 12.

16. Kahn, *Jock*, 205.

17. William O'Shaughnessy, email message to author, September 24, 2020. Also, William O'Shaughnessy, Facebook post, August 18, 2019.

18. Kahn, *Jock*, 206.

19. Price, *Diary*, 119.

Chapter 3. Partisan Strife, San Francisco's 1964 Convention, and Electoral Calamity

1. Patrick J. Buchanan, *The Greatest Comeback: How Richard Nixon Rose from Defeat to Create the New Majority* (New York: Crown Forum, 2014), 246. Buchanan writes, "In his campaign and White House, Nixon created a radar system that picked up and sent back signals from all points on the political compass, but ideologically, he was himself an eclectic."

2. John Roy Price, *Diary 1960–1965*, 123. This 1907 song, which I have known practically all my life, has lyrics by Thurland Chataway, about an Indian princess. "Oh, the moon shines tonight on pretty Red Wing. The breeze is sighing, the night bird's crying. For afar 'neath his star her brave is sleeping, and Red Wing's weeping her heart away."

3. David L. Stebenne, *Modern Republican, Arthur Larson and the Eisenhower Years* (Bloomington: Indiana University Press, 2006).

4. Geoffrey Kabaservice, email message to author, April 10, 2017.

5. Milton Eisenhower, *The President Is Calling: A Veteran Advisor for the Presidency Suggests Far-Reaching Changes* (Garden City, NY: Doubleday, 1974), 389.

6. Eisenhower, *The President Is Calling*, 390.

7. A. James Reichley, *The Life of the Parties: A History of American Political Parties* (Lanham, MD: Bowman & Littlefield, 1992), 329.

8. Reichley, *The Life of the Parties*, 329.

9. George Gilder and Bruce Chapman, *The Party That Lost Its Head: The Republican Collapse and Imperatives for Renewal* (New York: Alfred A. Knopf, 1966), 87.

10. Handwritten note of phone conversation with General Eisenhower, June 4, 1964. Walter Thayer Papers, Herbert Hoover Presidential Library.

11. Thomas E. Petri, ed., *From Disaster to Distinction: The Rebirth of the Republican Party* (New York: Pocket, 1966), 16.

12. John Ehrlichman, *Witness to Power: The Nixon Years* (New York: Simon and Schuster, 1982), 36.

13. Ehrlichman, *Witness to Power*, 35.

14. Ehrlichman, 35.

15. Patrick J. Buchanan, *The Greatest Comeback: How Richard Nixon Rose from Defeat to Create the New Majority* (New York: Crown Forum, 2014), 16.

16. Buchanan, *The Greatest Comeback*, 17.

17. His witticism was a wordplay on Irving Stone's biographical novel about Michelangelo, *The Agony and the Ecstasy* (New York: Doubleday, 1961).

Chapter 4. 1965–1968

1. Thomas E. Petri, ed., From Disaster to Distinction: The Rebirth of the Republican Party (New York: Pocket, 1966).

2. Patrick J. Buchanan, discussion with the author, November 12, 2015.

3. Governor Daniel J. Evans, interview by the author, Edgewater Hotel, Seattle, April 7, 2017.

4. From "Chapter 2: The Ripon Society during the Presidency of John S. Saloma III (1965–66)," in Geoffrey Kabaservice, *The Ripon Society: A History* (unpublished draft), 13, 14.

5. Lee W. Huebner, email message to the author, August 3, 2017.

6. "The Potential to Govern," *Ripon Forum* 2, no. 8 (November 1966): 5.

7. Mahout, "The View from Here," *Ripon Forum* 2, no. 8 (November 1966): 1.

8. Lee Auspitz, interview by Geoffrey Kabaservice, October 21, 2006.

9. Leonard Garment, *Crazy Rhythm: My Journey from Brooklyn, Jazz, and Wall Street to Nixon's White House, Watergate, and Beyond* (New York: Times, 1997).

10. Bruce K. Chapman, *The Wrong Man in Uniform, Our Unfair and Obsolete Draft—and How We Can Replace It* (New York: Trident, 1967).

11. Kabaservice, *The Ripon Society*, 14.

12. "The Negative Income Tax: A Republican Proposal to Help the Poor," *Ripon Forum* 3, no. 4 (April 1967).

13. Robert D. Behn to Joseph A. Morein, 20 May 1967. Ripon Society Papers (Cornell University) 7: "Behn corr."

14. "Ripon 'Take-Over,'" *Ripon Forum* 3, no. 12 (Dec. 1967): 2.

15. John Roy Price, *Diary: Iberia to White House, 1967–1970*, 83–91.

16. Price, *Diary*, 87.

17. Price, 95.

18. Price, 96.

19. Price, 120. Later still, dim hopes were there for the Lindsay forces, but these were soon extinguished. At the Miami convention, when the vice presidential choice had not yet been made, Deputy Mayor Robert Sweet came to see me and asked, of the chance that Lindsay might be Nixon's choice, "What should we do if this cup comes to our lip?" "Drink of it," I said.

20. Geoffrey Kabaservice, *Rule and Ruin: The Downfall of Moderation and the Destruction of the Republican Party, from Eisenhower to the Tea Party* (New York: Oxford University Press, 2012), 223.

21. John Roy Price, *Diary: Iberia to White House, 1967–1970*, 93.

22. Kabaservice, *The Ripon History*.

23. Walter DeVries, telephone conversation with the author, November 5, 2015.

24. De Vries, telephone conversation with the author, November 5, 2015.

25. DeVries, telephone conversation with the author, November 5, 2015.

26. Lee W. Huebner, "The Fierce Urgency of Now," *Ripon Forum* 4, no. 5 (May 1968): 4.

27. Archibald L. Gillies, former president of the John Hay Whitney Foundation, phone conversation with the author, spring 2017.

28. Patrick J. Buchanan, *Nixon's White House War: The Battles That Made and Broke a President and Divided America Forever* (New York: Crown Forum, 2017), 53.

29. David Owen, "The Best-Kept Secret in American Journalism Is Murray Kempton," *Esquire Magazine*, March 1982, 49.

30. Price, *Diary*, 100.

31. Price, *Diary*, 116.

32. Price, 117.

33. John Roy Price, *Daybook, March 5, 1970–Feb. 17, 1974*, 35.

34. Price, *Diary*, 194.

Chapter 5. The Oval Office Has a New Occupant

1. The other is the artist Charles M. Russell.

2. John A. Farrell, *Richard Nixon: The Life* (New York: Doubleday, 2017), 309.

3. Richard M. Nixon, *RN: The Memoirs of Richard Milhous Nixon* (New York: Simon & Schuster, 1978), 317.

4. Anatoly Dobrynin, *In Confidence: Moscow's Ambassador to America's Six Cold War Presidents 1962–1986* (New York: Times Books, 1995), 176.

5. Dobrynin, *In Confidence*, 176.

6. Nixon, *RN*, 336.

7. John Roy Price, *Diary: Iberia to White House, 1967–1970*, 127.

8. John Topping, conversation with the author, April 7, 2016.

9. Patrick J. Buchanan, conversation with the author, November 12, 2015.

10. Joe McGinniss, *The Selling of the President 1968* (New York: Trident, 1969).

11. I thank Godfrey Hodgson, journalist and historian, for this insight, offered at an April 29, 2016, symposium on the life of Daniel Patrick Moynihan at the Rothermere American Institute at Oxford University. Hodgson wrote one of the early books on Moynihan. Godfrey Hodgson, *The Gentleman from New York: Daniel Patrick Moynihan; A Biography* (Boston: Houghton Mifflin, 2000).

12. Lindsay had been at the Central Intelligence Agency, heading its clandestine services division of all activities in the Soviet Union, Eastern Europe, and China. He once told me that the break by Josef Tito and Milovan Djilas of Yugoslavia from Stalin's Soviet Union was hatched with Yugoslavs in Frank's Georgetown living room in Washington.

13. Ash himself would later become the head of the Office of Management and Budget.

14. This was an entity whose location in the Executive Office of the President (EOP) Nixon sought to emulate first with the creation by executive order of his Council for Urban Affairs, and then by statute with the July 1970 creation of the Domestic Council.

15. It is of interest that Hoover saw Nixon as playing a role as vice president under Eisenhower that Hoover himself had thought desirable for the vice-presidential position when Hoover was president. In a speech honoring Nixon in 1954, Hoover laid out these thoughts. Their shared Quaker background aroused my curiosity as to whether they ever had compared notes on this connection. An archivist at the Hoover Library in West Branch, Iowa, Spencer Howard, said they had occasions to talk often over the years, but there is no record of a conversation on this point. He opined to me that unlike Nixon, Hoover never felt as rooted in his Quaker ancestry, although in a sense his turn in his maturity to public service was a bow in that direction. Spencer Howard, conversation with the author, October 27, 2017.

16. Farrell, *Richard Nixon*, 352.

17. Vincent J and Vee Burke, *Nixon's Good Deed: Welfare Reform* (New York: Columbia University Press, 1974), 41.

Chapter 6. Organizing for Domestic Policymaking

1. Richard M. Nixon, *RN: The Memoirs of Richard Nixon* (New York: Grosset & Dunlop, 1984), 341–342.

2. Conversation of Elizabeth B. Moynihan with the author, March 17, 2017.

3. Elizabeth B. Moynihan, email to the author, March 30, 2016.

4. John A. Farrell, *Richard Nixon: The Life* (New York: Doubleday, 2017), 64.

5. Farrell, *Richard Nixon*, 16.

6. Farrell, 39.

7. Farrell, 15.

8. Kim Philby, *My Silent War: The Autobiography of a Spy* (London: Grafton, 1969).

9. Leonard S. "Story" Zartman later left his job at Eastman Kodak in Rochester, New York, and joined us on the small staff Pat created to support the work of the Council for Urban Affairs, in January 1969. He then became General Counsel of the Small Business Administration before making the trip home to Rochester and Kodak for the rest of his career.

10. John Roy Price, *Daybook*, March 16, 2017.

11. *The Negro Family: The Case for National Action*. 1965. US Government Printing Office.

12. I enlisted as a Republican for Moynihan. Abzug was a polarizing figure. Moynihan's defeat of Abzug likely caused many centrist and conservative Democrats to come home to him as he ran against Conservative James Buckley in the general election.

13. See a series of books, written by two Anglo-Irish cousins, E. Somerville and M. Ross, for vignettes about the English rule of Ireland, set in a somewhat less harsh period a few decades after the famine and peak flight. The stories turn on the "Regional Magistrate," an ex-British army officer, posted to remote counties in Ireland while it was still wholly under British rule. E. Somerville and M. Ross, *Some Experiences of an Irish RM* (London: Longmans Green, 1898).

14. John R. Price, "The 1928 Presidential Campaign and Election" (senior honors thesis, Grinnell College), 1960. Grinnell College Archives. Also archived at the Herbert Hoover Presidential Library, West Branch, Iowa.

15. John Roy Price, *Day Book March 15, 1970–Feb. 17, 1974*, 26.

16. Daniel P. Moynihan, as quoted in Jay P. Dolan, *The Irish Americans* (New York: Bloomsbury, 2008), 278.

17. Joseph Dorman, Tobi Perl Freilich, directors, *Moynihan*, documentary film, 2018, available Amazon Prime.

18. Greg Weiner, *American Burke: The Uncommon Liberalism of Daniel Patrick Moynihan* (Lawrence: University Press of Kansas, 2015).

19. Weiner, *American Burke*, 8.

20. Weiner, 8.

21. Weiner, 17.

22. Daniel P. Moynihan, *Coping: On the Practice of Government* (New York: Random House, 1961).

23. Stephen Hess, *The Professor and the President: Daniel Patrick Moynihan in the*

Nixon White House (Washington, DC: Brookings, 2015). Hess became the deputy to Moynihan on our small staff of seven at the outset, and then a year later departed to chair the White House Conference on Children and Youth, as I took Moynihan's job as executive secretary of the Council for Urban Affairs.

24. Daniel P. Moynihan Memorandum to H. R. Haldeman and John D. Ehrlichman, July 24, 1970. Nixon Library, WHCF, SMOF.

25. Steven R. Weisman, ed., *Daniel Patrick Moynihan: A Portrait in Letters of an American Visionary* (New York: Public Affairs, 2010), 165, 166.

26. The term "Negro" had not yet, in 1968, been supplanted by "Black" or "African American." Where it appears in documents or memoranda, I have kept it.

27. Steven R. Weisman, ed., *Daniel Patrick Moynihan: A Portrait in Letters of an American Visionary*, 148.

28. Weisman, ed., *Daniel Patrick Moynihan*, 206. Theodore White was the chronicler of multiple presidential campaigns.

29. As told to the author by Thomas A. Farmer, a confidant of Weisl's. Farmer worked for John F. Kennedy in 1960. He was named general counsel of the Agency for International Development and helped create the Asian Development Bank. He was counsel to the US Conference of Catholic Bishops. He was appointed by President Jimmy Carter to chair the Intelligence Oversight Board, where the two other members were Senator Albert Gore Sr. and Governor William Scranton.

30. Price, *Daybook*, April 21, 1970.

31. Sam Tanenhaus, former editor of the *New York Times Book Review* and an assistant editor of the *New York Times*, told me this in a conversation. He is the author of a forthcoming biography of William F. Buckley Jr., the founder of *National Review*.

32. John Roy Price, *Diary: Iberia to White House, 1967–1970*, 139.

33. Price, *Diary*, 139.

34. Price, *Daybook*, January 21 and 23, 1969, 2.

Chapter 7. The Council for Urban Affairs

1. John Roy Price, *Daybook*, January 21–23, 1969, 1, 2.

2. At the second CUA meeting, on February 3, 1969, the subcommittee chair, director of the Budget Bureau Robert Mayo, reported that the group had met and decided to transfer its efforts to the aegis of the cabinet council on economic policy. This was part of an effort to rationalize where various subjects were best to be treated. It was not always simply a power struggle but did have a basis in logic.

3. Price, *Daybook*, January 21 and 23, 1969, 3.

4. Nixon Library, WHCF, SMOF. John Roy Price, Memorandum to Attorney General Designate Mitchell, January 16, 1969.

5. John Roy Price, Council for Urban Affairs, Minutes of First Meeting, January 23, 1969, 1.

6. H. R. Haldeman, *The Haldeman Diaries: Inside the Nixon White House* (New York: G. P. Putnam's Sons, 1994), 20.

7. Price, Council for Urban Affairs, Minutes of First Meeting, January 23, 1969, 5, 6.

8. John Roy Price, *Daybook, March 15, 1970–Feb. 17, 1974*, 43.

9. Price, Council for Urban Affairs, Minutes of First Meeting, January 23, 1969, 2.

10. Robert Ferrell, ed., *Inside the Nixon Administration: The Secret Diary of Arthur Burns 1969–1974* (Lawrence: University Press of Kansas, 2010), February 3, 1969.

11. Ferrell, *Inside the Nixon Administration*, February 18, 1969.

Chapter 8. A President in a Hurry

1. John Roy Price, Council for Urban Affairs, Minutes of First Meeting, January 23, 1969, 1.

2. Price, Council for Urban Affairs, Minutes of First Meeting, January 23, 1969, 4.

3. Price, Council for Urban Affairs, Minutes of First Meeting, January 23, 1969, 4.

4. Richard Nixon, *RN: The Memoirs of Richard Nixon* (New York: Grosset & Dunlap, 1978), 424–425.

5. John Roy Price, Council for Urban Affairs, Minutes of Meeting, February 3, 1969, 3, 4.

6. Michael Harrington, *The Other America: Poverty in the United States* (New York: Simon & Schuster, 1962).

7. Price, Minutes of Meeting, February 3, 1969, 4.

8. Price, Minutes of Meeting, February 3, 1969, 4.

9. Price, 11.

10. H. R. Haldeman, *The Haldeman Diaries: Inside the Nixon White House* (New York: G. P. Putnam Sons, 1994), February 14, 1969.

11. Robert Ferrell, ed., *Inside the Nixon Administration: The Secret Diary of Arthur Burns, 1969–1974* (Lawrence: University Press of Kansas, 2010), February 14, 1969.

12. Haldeman, *The Haldeman Diaries*, February 21, 1969.

13. John Roy Price, *Diary: Iberia to White House, 1967–1970*, 150.

14. Price, *Diary*, 142.

15. Ferrell, ed., *Inside the Nixon Administration*, February 14, 1969.

16. Ferrell, *Inside the Nixon Administration*, February 24, 1969.

17. Ferrell, *Inside the Nixon Administration*, 16

18. Ferrell, *Inside the Nixon Administration*, 17.

19. John Roy Price, Council for Urban Affairs, Minutes of Meeting, March 6, 1969, 1.

20. Price, *Diary*, 147.

21. Price, *Diary*, 148.

22. Price, 149.

23. Price, 150.

24. According to William O'Shaughnessy, Thayer's son-in-law, he heard around the Thayer dinner table that Thayer had also been approached about running HUD

and about becoming Nixon's ambassador to France, both of which he also declined. William O'Shaughnessy, email to the author, September 24, 2020.

25. H. R. Haldeman, *Presidential Daily Diaries*, CD Rom, Searchable PDF Finding Aid, Nixon Library, March 6, 1969.

26. H. R. Haldeman, *Presidential Daily Diaries*, CD Rom, Searchable PDF Finding Aid, Nixon Library, March 11, 1969.

27. Price, *Diary*, 152.

28. H. R. Haldeman, *Presidential Daily Diaries*, CD Rom Searchable PDF Finding Aid, Nixon Library, April 11, 1969.

29. Lee W. Huebner, email to the author, May 11, 2015.

30. Donald H. Rumsfeld, *Known and Unknown: A Memoir* (New York: Sentinel Penguin Group, 2011), 121.

31. Rumsfeld, *Known and Unknown*, 120.

32. Rumsfeld, 122.

33. Rumsfeld, 118.

Chapter 9. "Our Monument"

1. Daniel P. Moynihan, "The Crisis in Welfare," *Public Interest* 10 (Winter 1968): 7.

2. Milton Friedman, *Capitalism and Freedom* (Chicago: University of Chicago Press, 1962).

3. As quoted in Gareth Davies, *From Opportunity to Entitlement: The Transformation and Decline of Great Society Liberalism* (Lawrence: University Press of Kansas, 1996), 216.

4. "The Negative Income Tax," *Ripon Forum* 3, no. 4 (April 1967): 3–8.

5. Daniel P. Moynihan, *The Politics of a Guaranteed Income: The Nixon Administration and the Family Assistance Plan* (New York: Random House, 1973), 62.

6. John D. Ehrlichman, Notes of Meeting with the President, with H. R. Haldeman and George Shultz, December 16, 1970. Nixon Library, WHCF, SMOF.

7. James Tobin, Joseph Pechman, and Peter Mieszkowski, "Is a Negative Income Tax Practical?," *Brookings Studies of Government Finance*, 1968; and Joseph Pechman, *Brookings Research Report 94*, 1968, "Improving Social Security Benefits and Financing." Tobin was Sterling Professor of Economics at Yale University. In 1966–1967, Pechman was also at Yale, on leave from his post as director of research at the Brookings Institution. John Topping, coauthor of the Ripon Society's negative income tax proposal, had considerable interchange with him before Ripon released its paper on April 10, 1967, advocating the NIT.

8. Moynihan, *The Politics of a Guaranteed Income*, 11.

9. Moynihan, 39.

10. Moynihan, 30.

11. Moynihan, 31.

12. Davies, *From Opportunity to Entitlement*, 159.

13. Vincent and Vee Burke, *Nixon's Good Deed: Welfare Reform* (New York: Columbia University Press, 1974), 9.

14. Moynihan, *The Politics of a Guaranteed Income*, 41.

15. Moynihan, *The Politics of a Guaranteed Income*, 22.

16. Moynihan, 47.

17. Miller's obituary, at his death age 101 in November 2017, noted his many achievements, including helping to found the Urban Institute, and celebrated his support for income maintenance and notably the negative income tax. This interest likely began with the debates at the Arden House conference. "Mr. Miller was the first major business executive to advocate a negative income tax to alleviate poverty." Obituary by Sam Roberts, *New York Times*, November 8, 2017.

18. John Roy Price, *Daybook, March 15, 1970–Feb. 17, 1974*, 79–80.

19. John D. Ehrlichman, Notes of Meetings with the President, December 3, 1970.

20. Moynihan, *The Politics of a Guaranteed Income*, 65.

21. Merton Peck had earlier worked in the Defense Department for Secretary McNamara as director of systems analysis.

Chapter 10. The Battle for Nixon's Decision

1. Daniel Patrick Moynihan, *The Politics of a Guaranteed Income: The Nixon Administration and the Family Assistance Plan* (New York: Random House, 1973), 131.

2. Richard P. Nathan, interview by the author, Winter Park, Florida, May 16, 2018.

3. Vincent J. Burke and Vee Burke, *Nixon's Good Deed: Welfare Reform* (New York: Columbia University Press, 1974), 41.

4. Burke and Burke, *Nixon's Good Deed*, 43.

5. Burke and Burke, 47.

6. John Roy Price, *Daybook*, March 2, 1974.

7. Burke and Burke, *Nixon's Good Deed*, 53.

8. John Roy Price, Council for Urban Affairs, Minutes of Meeting, February 17, 1969, 6.

9. Richard P. Nathan, interview with the author, May 16, 2018.

10. John Roy Price, Council for Urban Affairs, Minutes of Meeting, February 17, 1969, 6.

11. John Roy Price, Council for Urban Affairs, Minutes of Meeting, February 12, 1969, 2, 3.

12. John Roy Price, *Diary: Iberia to White House, 1967–1970*, 140 (February 23, 1969).

13. John Roy Price, Council for Urban Affairs, Minutes of Meeting, February 12, 1969, 5.

14. John Roy Price, Council for Urban Affairs, Minutes of Meeting, February 1, 1969, 11, 12.

15. Price, *Diary*, 140–141.

16. Burke and Burke, *Nixon's Good Deed*, 52.

17. Burke and Burke, *Nixon's Good Deed*, 55.

18. Burke and Burke, 55.

19. Burke and Burke, 56.

20. Richard P. Nathan, interview with the author, May 16, 2018.

21. Burke and Burke, *Nixon's Good Deed*, 58–59.

22. John Roy Price letter to Vee Burke, 1974, undated, 1.

23. Burke and Burke, *Nixon's Good Deed*, 63.

24. John Roy Price letter to Vee Burke, undated, 2.

25. John R. Price letter to Vee Burke, 1974, 1.

26. Daniel P. Moynihan, Memorandum for the President, March 25, 1969; Nixon Library, WHCF, SMOF.

27. John Roy Price, Draft of "Report of the Committee on Welfare of the Council for Urban Affairs," April 4, 1969, 15.

28. Moynihan, *The Politics of a Guaranteed Income*, 148.

29. Price, *Diary*, 152.

30. Price, *Diary*, 152–153.

31. John Roy Price, Council for Urban Affairs, Minutes of Meeting, April 7, 1969, 3.

32. John R. Price letter to Vee Burke, 1974, 3.

33. Richard P. Nathan, interview with the author, May 16, 2018.

34. Richard P. Nathan, telephone conversation with the author, September 16, 2019.

35. Martin Anderson, *Welfare: The Political Economy of Welfare Reform in the United States* (Palo Alto: Hoover Institution, Stanford University, 1978), 69–70.

36. Anderson, *Welfare*, 69–70.

37. Anderson, 71.

38. John Roy Price, Council for Urban Affairs, Minutes of Meeting, March 6, 1969, 10 a.m., 7, 8.

39. Steven R. Weisman, ed., *Daniel Patrick Moynihan: A Portrait in Letters of an American Visionary* (New York: Public Affairs, 2010), 162–163.

Chapter 11. The Fencing Moves from Épées to Sabers

1. George Drake, *Mentor: Life and Legacy of Joe Rosenfield* (Des Moines: Business Publications, 2019), 160.

2. Drake, *Mentor*, 160.

3. Memorandum to Paul W. McCracken from Technical Subcommittee of Task Force on Family Security System, May 9, 1969, 1; Nixon Library. WHCF, SMOF.

4. Nixon Library, WHCF, SMOF. Memorandum from William Branson and David Ott to Members of the Technical Review Committee: Revised Memorandum on FSS, USS and the Burns Plan, May 9, 1969.

5. John Roy Price, Daily Notes, May 2, 1969, 1.

6. Price, Daily Notes, May 2, 1969, 1.

7. John R. Price letter to Vee Burke, 1974, 2.

8. John Roy Price, *Diary: Iberia to White House, 1967–1970*, 154.

9. John Roy Price, Council for Urban Affairs, Minutes of Twelfth Meeting, May 16, 1969.

10. Price, Council for Urban Affairs, Minutes of Twelfth Meeting, May 26, 1969, 3.

11. John Roy Price, Council for Urban Affairs, Minutes of Meeting, June 13, 1969, 4, 5, 6.

Chapter 12. The Hunger Issue and the Food Stamp Revolution

1. John R. Price, Memorandum for the Staff Secretary, April 14, 1969, 3; Nixon Library, WHCF, SMOF.

2. Nick Kotz, *Let Them Eat Promises: The Politics of Hunger in America* (Englewood, NJ: Prentice Hall, 1969), 56.

3. *New York Times*, February 21, 1969.

4. "Rise of Hunger as Hot Political Issue Reveals Fierce Bureaucratic Struggle," *Washington Post*, February 28, 1969.

5. "Hollings Fight on Hunger is Stirring the South," *New York Times*, March 8, 1969.

6. John Roy Price, Council for Urban Affairs, Minutes of Meeting, March 17, 1969, 8, 9.

7. John Roy Price, *Daybook* and CUA Notes, July 2, 1969.

8. Price, *Daybook*.

9. Vincent J. and Vee Burke, *Nixon's Good Deed: Welfare Reform* (New York: Columbia University Press, 1974), 119.

10. Burke and Burke, *Nixon's Good Deed*, 116.

11. Steven R. Weisman, ed., *Daniel Patrick Moynihan: A Portrait in Letters of an American Visionary* (New York: Public Affairs, 2010), 210.

12. Daniel P. Moynihan, *The Politics of a Guaranteed Income: The Nixon Administration and the Family Assistance Plan* (New York: Random House, 1972), 114.

13. John Roy Price, Council for Urban Affairs, Minutes of Meeting, August 25, 1969, San Clemente, 5.

14. Moynihan, *The Politics of a Guaranteed Income*, 371.

15. Email from Richard P. Nathan to John Roy Price, October 13, 2018.

Chapter 13. "A Gamble on Human Nature"

1. John Roy Price, *Diary: Iberia to White House, 1967–1970*, 167–169.

2. George P. Shultz, interview with the author, November 8, 2017.

3. Price, *Diary*, 155.

4. John D. Ehrlichman, Notes of Meetings with the President, October 10, 1970; Nixon Library. WHCF, SMOF.

5. Price, *Diary*, 159.

6. Daniel P. Moynihan Papers, *Journals*, Library of Congress, Moynihan, Box I 226.

7. Martin Anderson, *Welfare: The Political Economy of Welfare Reform in the United States* (Palo Alto: Hoover Institution Press, Stanford University, 1978), 84.

8. Price, *Diary*, 162.

9. Moynihan, *Journals*, Box I 225, August 5, 1969.

10. Moynihan, *Journals*, Box I 226, August 7, 1969.

11. Moynihan, *Journals*, October 24, 1969.

12. Moynihan, *Journals*, August 7, 1969.

13. Price, *Diary*, 167–170.

14. H. R. Haldeman, *The Haldeman Diaries: Inside the Nixon White House* (New York: G. P. Putnam's Sons, 1994), 79.

15. Moynihan, *Journals*, September 15, 1969.

16. Moynihan, *Journals*, September 22, 1969.

17. Moynihan, *Journals*, September 18, 1969.

18. Steven R. Weisman, ed., *Daniel Patrick Moynihan: A Portrait in Letters of an American Visionary* (New York: Public Affairs, 2010), 202.

19. John Ehrlichman, *Witness to Power: The Nixon Years* (New York: Simon and Shuster, 1982), 246.

20. John Roy Price, *Daybook*, December 19, 1969.

21. Ehrlichman, *Witness to Power*, 246–249.

Chapter 14. Briefing Ronald Reagan

1. Daniel P. Moynihan Papers, Library of Congress, Box I 225, Subject File, Paul Niven, Transcript of NET Interview, November 18, 1969.

2. John R. Price, Memorandum for the File: Meeting of the President with Daniel P. Moynihan and John R. Price on October 24, 1969; Nixon Library, WHCF, SMOF.

3. John Roy Price, *Diary: Iberia to White House, 1967–1970*, 171–172.

4. Daniel P. Moynihan Papers, *Journals*, Library of Congress, Box I 226.

5. Price, *Daybook*, August 13, 1969.

6. John D. Ehrlichman, Notes of Meetings with the President, August 4, 1969 (Nixon Library, WHCF, SMOF), with wide-ranging discussion of day care ("a constructive program that's a long run effort to cure the problem—kids shouldn't sit around—they become non-workers") to tying this into the "First Five Years of Life" initiative of the administration, to "opposing negative income tax—no incentive."

7. Price, *Daybook*, August 13, 1969,

8. Price, *Daybook*, August 13, 1969.

9. Robert B. Carleson, *Government Is the Problem: Memoirs of Ronald Reagan's Welfare Reformer* (Alexandria, VA: American Civil Rights Union, 2009), xix.

10. Carleson, *Government Is the Problem*, 12.

11. Carleson, 11.

12. Richard P. Nathan, email to the author, July 8, 2020.

13. Council for Urban Affairs, John Roy Price Minutes of Meeting, August 25, 1969, 2–4.

14. John D. Ehrlichman, Notes of Meetings with the President, February 12, 1970.

15. Steven R. Weisman, ed., *Daniel Patrick Moynihan: A Portrait in Letters of an American Visionary* (New York: Public Affairs, 2010), 211–214.

16. John Roy Price, *Daybook*, April 25, 1970.

Chapter 15. The Center Does Not Hold

1. John D. Ehrlichman, Notes of Meetings with the President, August 11, 1970; Nixon Library, WHCF, SMOF.

2. John Roy Price, *Daybook*, 1970–1974.

3. David Blumenthal and James A. Morone, *The Heart of Power: Health and Politics in the Oval Office* (Berkeley: University of California Press, 2009), 123.

4. Patrick J. Buchanan, *Nixon's White House Wars: The Battles That Made and Broke a President and Divided America Forever* (New York: Crown Forum, 2017), 52.

5. John Roy Price, *Daybook, March 15, 1970–February 17, 1974*, 32.

6. Price, *Daybook*, April 22, 1970.

7. Ehrlichman, Notes of Meetings with the President, October 12, 1970.

8. Ehrlichman, Notes of Meetings with the President, October 11, 1970.

9. Ehrlichman, Notes of Meetings with the President, October 19, 1970.

10. John Roy Price, *Daybook, March 15, 1970–Feb., 1974*, 22.

11. Price, *Daybook, March 15, 1970–Feb., 1974*, 28.

12. Robert B. Carleson, *Government Is the Problem: Memoirs of Ronald Reagan's Welfare Reformer* (Alexandria, VA: American Civil Rights Union, 2009), 11.

13. Carleson, *Government Is the Problem*, 46–47.

14. Daniel P. Moynihan Papers, *Journals*, Library of Congress, Box I 225, July 31, 1969.

15. John Ehrlichman, *Witness to Power: The Nixon Years* (New York: Simon and Shuster, 1982), 212.

16. Kevin P. Phillips, *The Emerging Republican Majority* (New Rochelle, NY: Arlington House, 1969).

17. Ehrlichman, *Witness to Power*, 212–220.

18. Elizabeth Moynihan, email to the author, April 11, 2020.

19. John Roy Price, *Daybook, March 15, 1970–Feb 17, 1974*, 2.

20. Price, *Daybook*, 46.

21. Price, *Daybook*, 51.

22. Ehrlichman, Notes of Meetings with the President, November 23, 1970.

23. Ehrlichman, Notes of Meetings with the President, December 28, 1970.

24. Ehrlichman, Notes of Meetings with the President, December 6, 1970.

25. Ehrlichman, Notes of Meetings with the President, December 30, 1970.

26. Allan Ryskind, email to the author, November 17, 2019.

27. Carleson, *Government Is the Problem*, 24.

28. John D. Ehrlichman, Notes of Meetings with the President, January 15, 1971.

29. Ehrlichman, Notes of Meetings with the President, June 11, 1971.

30. Allan Ryskind, email to the author, November 17, 2019.

31. Patrick J. Buchanan, Memorandum to the Attorney General; H. R. Haldeman; Nixon Library, WHCF, SMOF, December 3, 1971.

32. Patrick J. Buchanan, email to the author, March 10, 2019.

33. Chuck Colson, Memorandum for Pat Buchanan; Nixon Library, WHCF, SMOF, December 29, 1971.

34. Allan Ryskind, email to the author, November 17, 2019.

35. Ryskind, email to the author.

36. Ryskind, email to the author.

37. Carleson, *Government Is the Problem*, 47–48.

38. Ehrlichman, Notes of Meetings with the President, April 21, 1972.

39. John Roy Price, letter to Vee Burke, 1974, 3.

40. *Human Events*, "Your Weekly Washington Report," August 7, 1971, 1.

41. *Human Events*, February 24, 1973, 1.

42. *Human Events*, February 24, 1973, 2.

43. *Human Events*, February 24, 1973, 1.

44. Patrick J. Buchanan, email to the author, March 10, 2019.

45. William Howard Taft, IV, phone interview with the author, February 26, 2020.

46. John Roy Price, *Daybook, March 15, 1970–Feb. 17, 1974*, 127.

47. Price, *Daybook, March 15, 1970–Feb. 17, 1974*, 127.

48. Price, 128.

49. Price, 128.

50. Price, 129.

51. Price, 129.

Chapter 16. Richard Nixon and a Health Strategy

1. David Blumenthal and James A. Morone, *The Heart of Power: Health and Politics in the Oval Office* (Berkeley: University of California Press, 2009), 224.

2. Dr. James H. Cavanaugh, interview with the author, July 5, 2020.

3. Blumenthal and Morone, *The Heart of Power*, 53–70.

4. Blumenthal and Morone, *The Heart of Power*, 89.

5. Daniel Sledge, *Health Divided: Public Health and Individual Medicine in the Making of the Modern American State* (Lawrence: University Press of Kansas, 2017), 189.

6. Daniel Sledge, Paper on "Policy Escalation: Richard Nixon, Welfare Reform, and the Development of a Comprehensive Approach to Health Insurance." Research in progress.

7. John Roy Price, *Daybook*, December 18, 1969.

8. Price, *Daybook*, December 18, 1969.

9. Lewis H. Butler, *A Life of Public Service: Interviews Conducted by Ann Lage in 2008–2009* (Berkeley: Regional Oral History Office, The Bancroft Library, University of California, 2010), 229.

10. 11. Butler, *A Life of Public Service*, 240.

12. John D. Ehrlichman, Notes of Meetings with the President, May 25, 1970.

13. John Roy Price, *Daybook, March 15, 1970–Feb. 17, 1974*, 18.

14. Price, *Daybook, March 15, 1970–Feb. 17, 1974*, 12.

15. Price, *Daybook*, 3.

16. Price, *Daybook*, 34, 35.

17. Butler, *A Life of Public Service*, 229.

18. Price, *Daybook, March 15,1970–Feb. 17, 1974*, 67.

19. Nixon Library, White House Central Files, Staff Member Office Files, Kenneth Cole to John D. Ehrlichman, January 27, 1971, 1.

20. H. R. Haldeman, *The Haldeman Diaries: Inside the Nixon White House* (New York: G. P. Putnam's Sons, 1994), 247.

21. John Ehrlichman, *Witness to Power: The Nixon Years* (New York: Simon and Schuster, 1982), 147.

22. Price, *Daybook, March 15, 1970–Feb. 17, 1974*, 80.

23. Price, *Daybook, March 15, 1970–Feb. 17, 1974*, 81.

24. Price, 82.

25. Price, 82.

26. Price, 83.

27. Price,74–76.

28. Stuart Altman, telephone conversation with the author, June 5, 2020.

29. Dr. James H. Cavanaugh, interview with the author, July 5, 2020.

30. Steven Kurzman, conversation with the author, December 2, 2019.

31. William Howard Taft, IV, phone interview with the author, February 26, 2020.

32. Frank E. Samuel, Jr., FAX to Stan Jones, June 18, 1994, 2.

33. Stuart Altman, telephone conversation with the author, June 5, 2020.

34. Frank E. Samuel, Jr., FAX to Stan Jones, June 18, 1994, 1.

35. Samuel, FAX to Stan Jones, June 18, 1994, 1.

36. Samuel, 1.

37. Flint J. Wainess, "The Ways and Means of National Health Care Reform, 1974 and Beyond," *Journal of Health Politics, Policy and Law* 24, no. 2 (April 1999): 307, 309.

38. Cavanagh and Kurzman discussions with the author. Both told me that Secretary Richardson had quoted Kennedy's comment to them.

39. Wainess, "The Ways and Means of National Health Care Reform," 316.

40. Daniel Sledge, *Health Divided*, 201–202.

41. Nixon Library, White House Central Files, Staff Member Office Files. Kenneth R. Cole, Minutes of Meetings, January 19, 1971.

Conclusion

1. Daniel P. Moynihan, letter to President Richard Nixon, July 23, 1987.

2. Richard Nixon, letter to The Honorable Daniel P. Moynihan, August 10, 1987.

3. Richard Nixon, letter to The Honorable Patrick Moynihan, October 3, 1988.

4. Daniel Patrick Moynihan, letter to Richard Nixon, December 21, 1988.

5. Daniel Patrick Moynihan, letter to The Honorable Richard Nixon, September 8, 1992.

6. Richard Nixon, letter to The Honorable Daniel Patrick Moynihan, September 17, 1992.

7. Patrick J. Buchanan, *Nixon's White House Wars: The Battles That Made and Broke a President and Divided America Forever* (New York: Crown Forum, 2017), 236.

8. Buchanan, *Nixon's White House Wars*, 21.

9. Buchanan, 23.

10. John Roy Price, *Daybook*, April 21, 1970.

11. Price, *Daybook*, April 21, 1970.

12. William Howard Taft IV, interview with the author, February 26, 2020.

13. John Price, Memorandum for the File, October 29, 1969; Nixon Library, WHCF, SMOF.

14. Evan Thomas, *Being Nixon: A Man Divided* (New York: Random House, 2015), 533.